LANGUAGE PLANNING

from practice to theory

Robert B. Kaplan
Richard B. Baldauf Jr.

MULTILINGUAL MATTERS 108
Series Editor: John Edwards

Shieldon
1997

Language Planning
From Practice to Theory

Robert B. Kaplan
Richard B. Baldauf, Jr

(1997)

MULTILINGUAL MATTERS LTD
Clevedon • Philadelphia • Toronto • Sydney • Johannesburg

Library of Congress Cataloging in Publication Data

Kaplan, Robert B.
Language Planning From Practice to Theory
Robert B. Kaplan and Richard B. Baldauf
Multilingual Matters: 108
Includes bibliographical references and index.
1. Language planning.
I. Baldauf, Richard B. II. Title. III. Series: Multilingual Matters (Series): 108.
P40.5.L35K36   1997
306.44'9–dc21   97-2118

British Library Cataloguing in Publication Data

A CIP catalogue record for this book is available from the British Library.

ISBN 1-85359-372-9 (hbk)
ISBN 1-85359-371-0 (pbk)

Multilingual Matters Ltd

UK: Frankfurt Lodge, Clevedon Hall, Victoria Road, Clevedon BS21 7HH.
USA: 1900 Frost Road, Suite 101, Bristol, PA 19007, USA.
Canada: OISE, 712 Gordon Baker Road, Toronto, Ontario, Canada M2H 3R7.
Australia: P.O. Box 586, Artamon, NSW, Australia.
South Africa: PO Box 1080, Northcliffe 2115, Johannesburg, South Africa.

Typeset by Archetype: http://www.archetype-it.com
Printed and bound in Great Britain by WBC Book Manufacturers Ltd.

Contents

Part 3 Case Studies in Language Planning

Part 4 Towards a Theory of Language Planning

Foreword

In one sense, our knowledge of language planning is probably as old as recorded human history as it is a part of how people use language. In Europe, when the Romans conquered the circum-Mediterranean world, Latin and Greek acted as lingua francas and the authorities of the Empire did a certain amount of language planning as Latin spread throughout the vast conquests of the Empire (Kahane & Kahane, 1988). For example, when Julius Caesar invaded Britain in 55 BC, the legions came to Britain speaking Latin, and there was some attempt to teach the language to the local inhabitants, not so much in formal schooling settings as through the practical realities of everyday life. The Romans drew maps in which they used the rules of Latin nomenclature to designate places and to describe features; they built fortifications and cities using Latin names for architectural features and for completed buildings; they enslaved local residents into Roman households in which those local residents had to learn Latin in order to understand their masters. No doubt there were other examples of 'informal' language planning affecting other segments of Celtic society.

A similar situation occurred some centuries later when Arabic-speaking armies spread across the Mediterranean world and entered Europe bringing with them the Islamic religion and texts in Arabic. The crusades, the Mogul invasions of India, the Confucian system of bureaucratic appointments and later the Mongol invasions of China, the powerful missionary movements of the eighteenth and nineteenth century, European colonialism over the last 500 years, the internationalisation of business since World War II, and most recently the internationalisation of mass media and the advent of large-scale international tourism, provide other instances which have brought about elements of language planning. In sum, every time a territory is captured and occupied (whether physically or metaphorically), the conquerors and the inhabitants of that territory, if they are speakers of languages which are not mutually intelligible, must become involved in some sort of language policy development in order to establish and maintain civil administration, in order to convert souls or to promote trade. When natural disasters, civil disorders and large-scale economic migrations occur which instigate a significant dislocation of some population, the government receiving the displaced population must engage in some sort of language planning in order to maintain civil administration and facilitate commerce. Indeed, whenever two populations speaking mutually unintelligible languages are brought into fairly extended contact for whatever reason, some degree of language planning occurs quite naturally. More recently language planning for mutually intelligible languages, e.g. varieties of English (Delbridge, 1985), has also become more common.

These early examples may or may not have involved a great deal of conscious language decision making. It seems likely that, through most of recorded human history, language planning occurred, but that it did so at a relatively slow and stately pace. It is likely that ordinary individuals were able to live their lives without being much affected by language change, unless they happened to be among the unfortunates whose land was occupied or who were among those displaced to an alien land. Indeed, events of this sort have occurred with such frequency and regularity in human interaction that they have come to be taken for granted. When new populations materialised in a polity, it was simply assumed that they would assimilate to the language of the polity, and when occupiers dealt with a conquered people they simply assumed that their relative power status would cause the conquered people to assimilate to their language.

The twentieth century has, for a complex variety of reasons, telescoped time; things seemed to be happening faster. *Time* magazine, about a decade ago, designated the twentieth century as the 'Century of the Refugee'. In this particular span of years, vast populations have been uprooted and dislocated by man-made and natural disasters and, in addition, the century has also witnessed the repeated collapse of colonial empires and the emergence out of the wreckage of those empires of new nations faced with the need to establish and maintain civil administrations and to promote commerce. This acceleration of language change problems has gradually supported the emergence of a new discipline – *Language Planning.*

Thus, while language planning may not be a new phenomena, it is a new discipline. Indeed, the major interest in this area is no more than 35 years old, and the greatest interest has developed only in the past 20 years. This new discipline is most clearly related to the established field of sociolinguistics (the study of the social forces that influence language change, and the kinds of change motivated by social forces). Whether it can be claimed that language planning is a subordinate or a superordinate relative of sociolinguistics remains an unanswered question, since language planning may involve more or less than sociolinguistics depending upon a number of variables which can only be understood on a case-by-case basis.

The defining literature for this relatively new and complex academic discipline – *language policy* and *language planning* – is scattered across books and journals in many fields. This is so because it has developed relatively recently from several disciplinary sources and because it has tended not to

be theory driven, but rather responsive to real-world interdisciplinary solutions of immediate practical problems. Key documents are often buried in ephemeral governmental publications, and many key papers have appeared in volumes of edited work not always transparently related to language policy and planning. However, academic interest in the discipline has given rise to several specialist journals (i.e. ₍New Language — ?
Planning Newsletter, Language Problems & Language Planning), and language planning is sporadically represented in other sociolinguistic journals (e.g. International Journal of the Sociology of Language, Journal of Multilingual and Multicultural Development) and yearbooks (Annual Review of Applied Linguistics, Sociolinguistica).

Just as the literature is sometimes opaque to easy search, those involved in the discipline of language planning have not always been clear or consistent in their use of terminology (see Chapter 1). In particular, the key terms 'language planning' and 'language policy' are frequently used, both in the technical and in the popular literature, either interchangeably or in tandem. They actually represent two quite distinct aspects of the systemised language change process. 'Language planning' is an activity, most visibly undertaken by government (simply because it involves such massive changes in a society), intended to promote systematic linguistic change in some community of speakers. The reasons for such change lie in a reticulated pattern of structures developed by government and intended to maintain civil order and communication, and to move the entire society in some direction deemed 'good' or 'useful' by the government.

The exercise of language planning leads to, or is directed by, the promulgation of a language policy by government (or other authoritative body or person). A language policy is a body of ideas, laws, regulations, rules and practices intended to achieve the planned language change in the society, group or system. Only when such policy exists can any sort of serious evaluation of planning occur. 'Language policy' may be realised at a number of levels, from very formal language planning documents and pronouncements to informal statements of intent (i.e. the discourse of language, politics and society) which may not at first glance seem like language policies at all. Indeed, as Peddie (1991a) points out, policy statements tend to fall into two types – symbolic and substantive, where the first articulates good feelings toward change (or perhaps ends up being so nebulous that it is difficult to understand what language specific concepts may be involved), and the latter articulates specific steps to be taken.

Language planning as it exists at the present time is primarily an outgrowth of the positivist economic and social science paradigms which dominated the late 1960s and early 1970s. Originally designated 'language engineering', the discipline emerged as an approach to articulating programmes for solving 'language problems', however defined, usually in newly independent 'developing countries'. Nevertheless, by the

mid–1970s, it had become apparent that language problems were not
unique to developing countries, and that some solutions that had become
available were widely applicable, well beyond the constraints of 'social
development' or of the nation-state.

As this latter idea has grown, most applied linguists have been asked in
some context to function as language planners. The spread of language
planning from the macro to the micro level – which, incidentally, is not
widely reflected in the literature (see, e.g. Fishman, 1981) – and the wider
involvement of applied linguists implicates such things as working with:

- local education agencies faced with multilingual populations;
- employers faced by what seems to be increasing illiteracy;
- commercial organisations attempting to devise advertising campaigns to infiltrate minority communities;
- multinational corporations faced with polyglot employee pools;
- engineers attempting to develop automated translation systems;
- manufacturers trying to build intelligent machines; and
- a vast variety of other activities.

In human resources terms, language teachers, materials developers,
curriculum specialists, information scientists, advertising writers, personnel officers, and other human resource development planners at all levels
of the public and private sectors have been asked to engage in micro
language planning activities, although they would often not be aware that
this is what they were doing.

It is precisely because the language planning activities listed here have,
in a more or less conscious sense, permeated society that this book is being
written. It constitutes an attempt to make the field of language planning
more accessible to both the specialist and the non-specialist. This volume
attempts to draw together key aspects of the widely scattered literature, to
clarify the origins and history of language planning over the recent past,
to point to various trends that have emerged, to examine particular issues
in their language planning context, and to explore the possibilities of
moving toward the development of an adequate theory of language
planning. To provide the greatest scope possible for the review, an
overview of materials related to language planning in national situations
is given in the Appendix.

Tauli (1984) has argued that early language planning research and
practice with its emphasis on purism has failed to provide a dynamic basis
for language planning. He argued that for language planning to develop
as an independent discipline, a theoretical basis is needed to complement
its contributions to the descriptive sociology of language. The purpose of
this volume is to move in that direction by synthesising the broad variety
of contributions from many disciplines, together with the orientation of the

field toward practice and the solution of immediate problems, into a coherent disciplinary description, using examples to illustrate key issues. We use this as the basis for moving toward what a theory of language planning would entail. We are not so bold as to attempt to promulgate such a theory of language planning at this stage in the development of the field; such an attempt could well be fruitless given that certain issues (as we note in what follows) have not yet been adequately examined and developed. Rather, we have attempted, by drawing together some of the disparate threads of language policy and language planning, to offer in this volume a prolegomena to such a theory.

To accomplish these goals, the book is divided into four parts. The first part has as its focus initial concepts in language planning and provides an introduction to language planning, introduces the terminology, concepts, processes, frameworks and goals used to describe actual language planning situations. In the second part, key cross-national issues are discussed including methodology for language planning, language in the workplace, language-in-education and literacy planning and the economics of language planning. In the third part, case studies are used to examine 15 selected issues illustrating the importance of language planning in the world in which we live. These issues, which are related to language and power, language and status and language for specific purposes, have been selected for elaboration. The fourth part looks at language planning in theory. It asks, based on what we have looked at in practice in the first three parts, 'What do current approaches and issues tell us about the nature of language planning as a theoretical system?' and what are its key components.

A problem in understanding the nature of the discipline of language planning, and therefore developing theory, is that language planning has developed in a dichotomous manner similar to the two aspects of de Saussure's (1916/1959) linguistics with its equivalents of *langue* and *parole*. Just as linguistics for much of its disciplinary history has concentrated on descriptive form and analysis, *langue*, language planning has concentrated on technical solutions to language problems, *language planning*. In both cases, such an emphasis was undoubtedly necessary to build initial expertise and to develop an empirical basis for the discipline. Linguistics has in the last 10 years begun to explore *parole*, primarily through the study of discourse. Meanwhile, language planning has been increasingly criticised for its technocratic approach to language problems (e.g. Luke *et al.*, 1990). Like linguistics, language planning needs, using de Saussure's terms, to think more about the relationship between *langue* and *parole* by examining the discourse of language politics and society or the more informal but powerful political and social aspects of *language policy*. A theory of language planning must include both these aspects, but the work on the latter has only just begun (Jernudd & Neustupný, 1987).

In practical terms this dichotomy in the literature has tended to mean that only lip service has been given to the notion that political, social and economic decisions can be framed as language planning constructs. Such decisions have often been viewed as being in the hands of people who are outside of the language planning process, and who, as such, have been excluded from serious discussion within the discipline. As a result, language planning as a discipline has become primarily the application of a non-judge-mental, technically based sets of skills for language correction. This book examines these assumptions which have guided conventional approaches to language planning and makes explicit the embedding context and the dilemmas these practices pose for language planners and other sociolinguists.

We believe that this book will be of use to both specialist and non-specialist audiences. Our primary audience, we believe, will be those graduate students – in linguistics departments, in language departments, in schools of education, and in similar academic entities – who want to gain an organised overview of the general field of language planning. However, we also expect that this volume may be of use to:

- individuals in government agencies attempting to implement language choice;
- personnel officers in business organisations attempting to understand the implications of stated and unstated language policies within those structures;
- individuals in local education agencies attempting to plan curricula for multilingual populations; and
- teachers in classrooms everywhere who are faced with multilingual populations whose needs are not well understood.

We are not so naive as to believe that this volume will answer all possible questions for the divergent audiences we have suggested. Rather, we hope that the text will provide for those audiences some better understanding of the terms used, some clearer view of what is and what is not possible, and some notion of how to find guidance in the context of particular real-world problems. For those readers who are already specialists, we hope to provide a dialogue concerning the basis on which anyone dares to undertake language planning.

Robert B. Kaplan
Emeritus Professor of Applied Linguistics
University of Southern California

Richard B. Baldauf, Jr
Research Manager
National Languages and Literacy Institute of Australia and
Associate Professor of Education, James Cook University (on leave)
August 1996

Part 1: Initial Concepts for Language Planning

In Part 1 of this volume the reader is introduced to the field of language planning, including its terminology, some frameworks for understanding the language planning processes and some of the specific goals for which language planning is often undertaken. The purpose of this section is to provide a basic introduction to the discipline as a precursor to an examination of some of the key issues to be found in the practice of that discipline.

In Chapter 1 the field of language planning is introduced in its wider context, the key actors in language planning situations are described and problems associated with the definition of terminology are discussed.

In Chapter 2 several frameworks which provide overviews of the language planning process are introduced. Haugen's (1983) model provides a general perspective on the major tasks which language policy and planning must face. Haarmann's (1990) ideal typology builds on Haugen's work by adding the concept of prestige planning, while Cooper's (1989) accounting scheme provides a more process oriented overview of what it means to do language planning. Whereas the language planning literature has focused mainly on the macro level, it is important to understand that language policy and planning operates at the micro level as well.

In the third chapter, 11 goals for which language planning has been most often undertaken are described and brief examples are provided. Finally, reference is made to some of the critiques of language planning as a discipline. This section provides an overview of the discipline and the bases for the practice of language policy development and planning.

Part 1: Initial Concepts
for Language Planning

1 A Contextual and Terminological Basis for Planning

Introduction

Language issues have some of the characteristics of sex – everyone does it, and consequently everyone is an expert. However, it is not teachers nor even parents who teach most adolescents about sex; rather it is a cadre of other adolescents, mostly characterised by knowing little about the matter. From there on, it is largely a matter of on-the-job training. It is not until one reaches maturity that one even discovers that there are real experts who might teach one something about the subject. So it is with language issues. Every segment of society has language and individuals competently use language for a variety of purposes. However, when users engage in talking about language, which they frequently do, that talk is largely marked by profound ignorance.

A Definition

What is language planning and how is it accomplished? Language planning is a body of ideas, laws and regulations (language policy), change rules, beliefs, and practices intended to achieve a planned change (or to stop change from happening) in the language use in one or more communities. To put it differently, language planning involves *deliberate*, although not always overt, *future oriented* change in systems of language code and/or speaking in a societal context (Rubin & Jernudd, 1971b). The language planning that one hears most about is that undertaken by government and it is intended to solve complex social problems, but there is a great deal of language planning that occurs in other societal contexts at more modest levels for other purposes.[1]

In the simplest sense, language planning is an attempt by someone to modify the linguistic behaviour of some community for some reason. The reasons are complex, ranging from the trivial notion that one doesn't like the way a group talks, to the sophisticated idea that a community can be

3

assisted in preserving its culture by preserving its language. The actors are many, though at the macro level some element of government is usually involved. The language modifications are also complex, ranging from a desire to 'modernise' a language so that it can deal with the vast technological changes that are occurring, to a desire to 'standardise' a language, often with the underlying political motivation – to achieve 'unification', so that it can be understood by various sub-groups within a population who may speak different varieties of that language, or perhaps to provide a way of writing a language which has not previously been written. While micro language policy and planning may focus on quite specific and limited language issues – e.g. should the local library stock foreign language newspapers, what language(s) will be taught at a local school, in what language will the signs be in a local shop window to attract customers, how can I use language effectively to market my product overseas – formal language planning is rarely so modest and uncompli-cated.

The reality is that complex motives and approaches, and large popula-tions, are involved in modern states, and language policy makers and planners have to date most often worked in such macro situations. Increasingly, however, micro language planning is gaining attention, and applied linguists are beginning to be hired to work in these areas.

The Context of Language Planning

In the complex, interdependent and increasingly crowded world in which we live, planning is a critical feature of human existence. Language planning in its larger or macro sense is an aspect of national resource development planning. Such planning normally falls into two broad categories: the development, and increasingly the conservation, of natural resources – mineral resources, water power, fisheries, forest policies and the like – and the development, and increasingly the conservation, of human resources. These areas are not merely different because of the object of development; they are significantly different in terms of planning time and in terms of the type of outcomes that can be expected.

When a government becomes involved in natural resource development planning and decides to develop, for example, water resources, it may undertake to build a dam. The planning and building of such an edifice is, relatively speaking, short in duration. While it may take eight or 10 years to accomplish the project, it can often be completed within the life of a single political administration. At the end of the project, there is a palpable dam, and its output in kilowatt hours, in irrigation flows, in urban water supplies, can be measured in finite numbers and reported. The benefits are verifiable. Everyone can see the actual dam; tourists can visit it and marvel at its huge generators, fishermen can approach it in their boats, naturalists can measure the effect on wildlife. One can take a picture of politicians opening it and print the picture in the newspapers. Any problems are also identifiable – e.g. increased erosion downstream from irregular water flows, lack of access to water supplies downstream, valuable areas being flooded and so forth – although planners have been less ready to identify these types of problems or to find solutions, and politicians don't like to be reminded that projects with major benefits can have their down sides.

On the other hand, human resource development planning and the resultant changes in human behaviour are rather different. It may take several generations to alter behaviour. The life of such a project usually goes well beyond the life of any political administration. At the termination of the project, there is no palpable outcome to see. There is no easy or agreed way to measure the benefits derived from the project; indeed, it may be difficult to see that there are outcomes because there is no way to guess what might have happened if no plan (or some different plan) had been put into operation. It is difficult to assess costs, and it is virtually impossible to correlate benefits to attendant costs.

It is not our purpose to discuss natural resource development planning, nor indeed, other areas of human resources development planning in this volume. The attention here will be on language planning exclusively. However, it is both important and necessary to see language policy, language planning and language planners in their larger sociopolitical context, particularly as resources for language planning must compete with the demands made by other planning areas for funds. Figure 1.1 suggests how language planning fits into the larger scheme of national resource development planning.

Those involved in language planning (the *who* or the *actors*) as noted in Figure 1.1, can be seen as working within four basic areas: (1) governmental agencies involved at the highest level; (2) education agencies, sometimes acting under the impetus of higher level structure or acting in lieu of higher level structure; (3) other quasi-governmental or non-governmental organisations acting according to their own beliefs, and (4) all sorts of other groups or in some cases influential individuals creating language policy as an accidental (or sometimes purposeful) part of their normal activity. Each of these planning areas is now briefly described in turn.

Governmental agencies

In the late twentieth century most governments have became involved in the language planning business, either because they wanted to or because they have stumbled into it. Such governmental planning may be presumed to have the broadest scope, since government generally has the power to legislate and the ability to foster incentive structures (and disincentive structures) to enforce planning decisions.

The governments of most of the newly independent states of Sub-Saharan

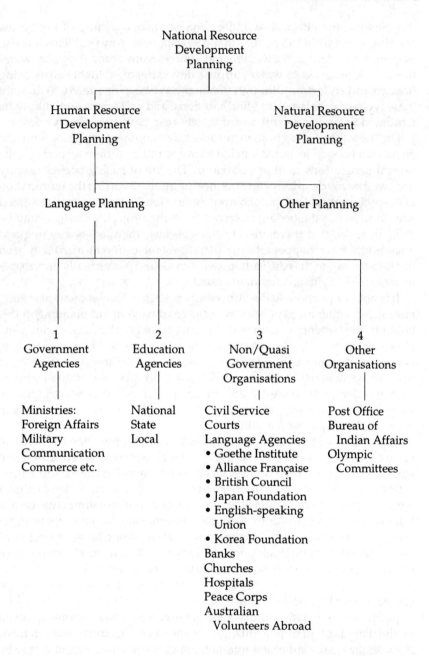

Figure 1.1 Context and elements of the language planning process

Africa, for example, got involved in language planning almost at the moment of independence (post-1960) (e.g. Akinnaso, 1989; Bokamba, 1991; Breton, 1991; Djité, 1991; Greenberg, 1963; A.M. Mazrui, 1996; Tucker & Bryan, 1966). Colonial boundaries and practices had left them with a legacy of a linguistically heterogeneous population, a population with a limited literacy base which was in general also under-educated, and the wide-spread use of a foreign language – the language of the former colonial power – for administrative purposes.

They needed to select a language or languages that could serve the needs of national unification, that could be used to enhance the myth of historical identity, that was spoken by some significant segment of the population and was acceptable to other population segments. Having selected a language, they needed to standardise its orthography, its lexicon, and its syntax, and in many instances they needed to undertake a lexical elaboration and enrichment programme so that the language could be used in a wide variety of sectors characteristic of the modern world. Then they were faced with the dissemination of that language through the population. In virtually every case they had to undertake this enormous range of activities with extremely limited resources and in the face of a plethora of other problems all demanding instant attention.

In every case, a range of governmental agencies became involved. The commerce ministry was, for example, concerned to develop the ability of the state to trade internationally; the military ministry was concerned with the acquisition of sophisticated weaponry and with the necessity of maintaining that weaponry despite the fact that the hardware tended to come with manuals not written in the indigenous languages; the foreign affairs ministry was concerned with the rapid training and posting of foreign service officers to virtually every country in the world; the communications ministry was concerned with accessing the global communications networks; the labour ministry was concerned with developing a multilingual workforce designed to attract foreign business into the state.

Although the tertiary educational academy is in some cases not a government agency, the academy is concerned with achieving access to the world's great scientific and technical information storage and retrieval networks. (The education ministry has, for the moment, been left out because it has an entirely internally driven set of concerns while the majority of the other ministries have externally driven concerns.) Frequently, these various ministries went about their business isolated from all the other ministries and either in the absence of a general plan or in the context of a general plan that was so vaguely written as to be of relatively little use.

This descriptive overview has been drawn from decolonising Sub-Saharan Africa, but similar planning activities have been undertaken elsewhere in the world – indeed, literally in every region of the globe – for example, in Malaysia, in Indonesia, in Singapore, in the Philippines, in Mexico, in Australia, in New Zealand, in Belgium, in Israel, in Canada, and in a whole range of smaller states in the South Pacific (Papua New Guinea, the Polynesian island-states, etc.) and elsewhere even in long-established states in the context of a whole range of 'little' languages – for example, Basque, Catalan, Frisian, Sami, and the indigenous languages of Latin America and of North America. Even in the United States, the legislatures of some individual states have in the past blithely declared the territory under their jurisdiction to be bilingual, without much understanding of the implications of their actions.[2] These language policy and planning decisions have occurred not only at a policy level, but have been taken within the bureaucracy as well (e.g. Cloonan & Strine, 1991; Sommer, 1991).

Education Agencies

In every case in which any sort of official language policy activity has been undertaken, the education sector has been involved to some degree, often extensively. Indeed, in some cases, the entire burden of planning language change has been allocated to the education ministry without reference to the fact that the education ministry does not have the scope, the resources or the authority to influence language use to any extent beyond the education sector.

The education sector has an influence, largely on children, roughly between the ages of 5 or 6 and the ages of 15 or 16. It may also have an influence through such specialised segments of the education structure as technical education, adult education, distance education, and 'special' education for other groups of individuals, including those who are emotionally or psychologically constrained and therefore separated from the mainstream population. It may also have to deal with immigrant populations deriving from different educational systems, having different preparation and different linguistic backgrounds, and varying in age from pre-school children to elderly adults. In this context, it must be kept in mind that not everybody goes to school, that certainly not everybody goes to school for the same length of time, and that not everybody goes to school at the same time – that is, it takes generations to educate an entire population through the education sector.

The education sector has to make a number of language policy and planning decisions. Six of these are introduced here:

First, it has to determine which language(s) will be taught within the curriculum (recognising that the curriculum is not endlessly permeable – that is, that new areas can only be introduced through the reduction of other areas because the curriculum is absolutely constrained to a specified number of hours/day, days/week, and weeks/academic year), to determine when in the curriculum the onset of instruction will occur and what the duration of instruction will be, and to determine what sort of proficiency is deemed to meet the needs of the society by the end of whatever instruction can be provided.

Second, it must define the teacher supply, taking into consideration who will teach the language(s) included in the curriculum, where in the population pool available to the education sector those individuals will be drawn from, the nature of pre-service training that will be required to produce proficient teachers, the nature of in-service training that will be required to maintain proficiency, and the distribution of that segment of teachers through the system as well as equity in the reward structure.

Third, it will need to determine what segment of the student population will be exposed to language(s) education and how that segment will be identified, provided with readiness training, and induced to undertake the available instruction, and it will need to devise strategies to garner parental and community support for any plan put in place.

Fourth, it will need to determine what methodology(ies) will be employed in the system, what materials will be used to support those methodologies, how and by whom those materials will be prepared, and how they will be disseminated through the system.

Fifth, it will need to define assessment processes that can be used for initial placement, for in-course testing, and for output (summative) testing, and at the same time it will need to develop an assessment system that can measure teacher performance and system performance so that language instruction fits with societal need.

Finally, it will need to determine how to support all of this activity fiscally and physically, where the resources will come from, and how the language education system can be maintained across the contexts served by the system and over time.

Quasi/Non-governmental organisations

There are a variety of other, generally quasi- or non-governmental sectors which are also heavily involved in language policy development. Such quasi-governmental organisations as the British Council (Phillipson, 1994), the English-Speaking Union, the Alliance Française (Kleineidam, 1992), the Goethe Institute (Ammon, 1992), the Japan Foundation (Hirataka, 1992) and the Korea Foundation are each, respectively, engaged in the dissemination of English, French, German, Japanese, and Korean beyond their native-speaker communities and with some level of governmental support. There are other such organisations concerned with the dissemination of other languages, e.g. Spanish (Sánchez, 1992), Portuguese (Lopes, 1997, Silva & Gunnewiek, 1992) and Hindi (Dua, 1994).

Still another quasi-governmental sector is represented by national language academies and language planning boards (Joseph, 1987: 110 ff.). Beginning in the seventeenth century, a number of European states put in place national language academies whose function was to preserve the purity of what was intended to become the national language; Italy (Accademia della Crusca 1582), France (Académie Français 1635), Spain (Real Academia Española 1713), Portugal (Instituto de Alta Cultura), for example, all have national language academies of long standing and great prestige. These academies have been instrumental in the preparation of definitive dictionaries and have in some instances pronounced policies regarding the standard grammar of the language in question, as well as policies concerning the sorts of foreign borrowing that would be permitted as well as the rate of inflow of foreign terms. They have been responsible for lexical development as new technologies have demanded new terminologies, and they have helped to define the international participation in lexical standardisation.

In the more recent past, new language academies have come into existence, in Bangladesh, Japan, Israel, Ireland, Indonesia and Malaysia, Mexico, Brazil, Mozambique, Egypt and in a great many other states. The Real Academia Española has engendered offshoot 'affiliate' academies in every country in Latin America (Joseph, 1987). These academies have, to a significant degree, been involved in lexical development for purposes of modernisation. In the quite recent past, disciplinary academies have sprung up – in medicine, for example, but in a variety of scientific fields and endeavours, so that there are attempts, for example, to standardise terminologies in international fisheries (Jernudd & Thuan, 1984). Still other attempts have sprung from the development of international functions like international aviation, high-seas transportation (Strevens & Weeks, 1985) and police communication (E. Johnson, 1994). Professional Associations through their editorial policies are also involved in language planning not only through their dictation of the use of style, but also of what languages are acceptable for publication and for use at conferences and in their journals (Jernudd & Baldauf, 1987).

It is interesting in light of this discussion that Britain did not develop a language academy, though the question was discussed but rejected in the Royal Academy in the seventeenth century. It is also the case that, at the time of its founding, the leaders in the United States consciously rejected the notion of a language academy. Joseph (1987: 112) suggests that 'in the creator-hero tradition . . . the appearance of Samuel Johnson's *Dictionary of English Language* in 1755 made the founding of an Academy unnecessary; the same is said of Noah Webster and the failed attempts at founding an American Academy (see Baron, 1982).' The importance of such individuals on style, standards and usage continues today (e.g. Fowler, 1965; Follet, 1966; Safire, 1984).

However, since the late 1980s, a movement has arisen in the United States to make English the official language of that nation, and a number of the states have enacted local 'English-only' legislation, but as of the writing of this volume, no national language policy has been adopted. In the 1992 Session of Congress, a bill known as the 'Language in Government Bill' was introduced, requiring the use of English in all actions of government, and in the 1995 session of Congress four bills were introduced, but no bill has yet been enacted. These bills, though they seek to designate English as the sole official language of the nation, do not create a national language academy. The most influential organisation spearheading the movement toward an 'English-only' policy, is known as *U.S. English*. The debate has generated a large literature (e.g. Adams & Brink, 1990; Amorose, 1989; Bikales, 1986; Crawford, 1992a, 1992b; Daniels, 1990; Fishman, 1988a; Marshall, 1986; Peña, 1991) both for and against.

Language planning is also important in the religious sector. For example, because Protestant churches take as a matter of faith the belief that personal access to the gospels is an important element in the achievement of personal salvation, they have both facilitated the spread of languages like English through the dissemination of the gospels and accelerated the orthographic development of indigenous languages through the translation of the gospels into a wide variety of languages. The Protestant population of the early settlements in northeast North America were among the most literate communities in history and, on the basis of their Protestant theology, they established schools virtually as their earliest acts after basic survival was assured. Organisations such as the Summer Institute of Linguistics – the Wycliff Bible Translators – or the Language Teaching Mission of the Church of the Latter-Day Saints are heavily engaged both in the dissemination of the English gospels and in the translation of the gospels into other languages.

The Catholic and Orthodox churches have played a somewhat different role, because they did not require literate participation in clergy-managed ritual; they have, however, played a key role in the preservation of various languages (e.g. Church Latin, Church Greek, etc.). Islamic religious bodies have played a central role in the spread of Arabic and in the preservation of Classical Arabic, as they believe the word of God should be read and spoken in the language in which it was given to the prophet. Other examples could be cited. In addition to this important language policy sector, religious bodies, particularly in colonial times, were virtually the sole dispensers of education. Schools were often the exclusive domain of religious groups, and church domination of education has continued well into the twentieth century in Sub-Saharan Africa, Latin America and Asia.

In the latter part of the twentieth century, multinational corporations have taken up some of the roles traditionally held by religious organisations. Multinational corporations establish clear language policies dictating what languages are necessary for success both within the multinational structure and at the local level. They have promoted and rewarded bilingualism, and they often provide in-house language education for their employees (see Holden, 1990 for a discussion of the reasons for such funding in Japan). For example, one of the oldest and most successful language teaching facilities in Japan is operated by the Nippon Electric Corporation, but other examples can be found in such multinationals as IBM, Royal Dutch Petroleum, the Arabian-American Oil Company (ARAMCO), or Union Oil.

Indeed, business in general and government at the local level often also play key roles in language policy formulation. For example, in the greater Los Angeles area, a large hospital recently got itself into serious trouble by prohibiting Tagalog-speaking nurses from speaking Tagalog among themselves during break-time; a large bank has developed a system of encouraging Spanish and Chinese bilinguals in its employ to function bilingually, without compensation, to promote business outreach into those ethnic communities, but it has not encouraged Armenian, Korean, Chamorro, or Samoan bilinguals because it is not concerned with serving those ethnic communities; the City of Pasadena has a programme for promoting and rewarding bilingualism among its civil servants, while the County of Los Angeles does not contemplate such a programme. Although United States Federal Courts require the availability of an interpreter for defendants who are not fluent in English, lower courts leave the determination of whether or not to provide an interpreter to the discretion of the presiding justice. The law requires that arrested persons have their Miranda rights explained to them in whatever language they can understand, but local police jurisdictions are free to conduct prisoner interrogation exclusively in English. This list of examples illustrates the range of levels involved in language policy making. Note that policy may be directed toward multilingual or monolingual objectives. Indeed, virtually every organisation, from the multinational corporation to the local 'mom-and-pop' corner convenience store, engages in some form of language policy formulation.

Other organisations/individuals

The final category of organisations and agencies involved in language policy formulation includes those in which language planning is an accidental outcome of the primary function of the body. For example, the United States Postal Service is a participant in the International Postal Union. The primary activity of the Postal Service is getting the mail delivered, but to simplify mail delivery the International Postal Union and the United States Postal Service are agreed that envelopes must be addressed in Roman script. They will, in general, not accept for delivery envelopes addressed in Japanese or Chinese characters, or Arabic script, or other orthographic systems. The United States Bureau of Indian Affairs does not have a primary concern with language, but over the past 200 years it has used language policy to accomplish its primary objectives – objectives which have witnessed a gradual change from viewing Native

Americans as an enemy to be exterminated, to seeing them as property roughly equivalent in importance to the land in the Federal Park system, and finally – and only quite recently – to the view which recognises that Native Americans are sentient human beings.

The United States Immigration and Naturalization Service, whose primary concern is the management of non-US citizens entering, passing through, or attempting to settle in the United States, has regularly published all of its innumerable and inordinately complex forms exclusively in English and has required basic literacy in English as a condition of entry. The International Olympic Commission, clearly not a language agency, determines the languages that may be used in international athletic competition. These are just a few examples of the bodies which generate language policy despite the fact that their primary missions are not in any sense language-related. Indeed, anyone who posts a sign anywhere for any purpose can be said to make language policy without meaning to.

Implications of language planning contexts

Planning language has to take place in the context of this reticulated structure of language policy formulation activity. In this section we have looked at a number of language planning contexts, i.e. government agencies, education agencies, non/quasi government organisations and other organisations as well as individuals, who in Cooper's (1989) terms are some of the *actors* in policy formulation, or as Haarmann (1990) would define it, are related to 'language prestige', the efficiency in terms of organisational impact on the planning process. In Chapter 2 we will see how these contexts, *actors*, or aspects of 'language prestige' fit into some broader conceptual frameworks for language planning.

However, it is not merely a matter of declaring politically that it is for some reason desirable to preserve or promote or obstruct some language; it is not merely a question of charging the education sector to teach or not to teach some language. As Schiffman (1992) points out, indigenous language planning often fails because the basic structural work is not done. Rather, it is a question of trying to manage the language ecology of a particular language to support it within the vast cultural, educational, historical, demographic, political, social structure in which language policy formulation occurs every day.

It appears to be the case that languages which serve important societal functions for their speakers survive, regardless of the ministrations of government. But it is also the case that, if languages come to serve fewer functions outside the home, as the speakers of those languages are drawn away from their home communities by the siren call of urbanisation, by the need for increased economic mobility, and by other powerful societal forces, as majority languages or languages of wider communication replace smaller languages in important registers, small languages die, larger languages struggle and no amount of educationist intervention is likely to save them. In sum, language policy formulation is everybody's business, and without the help of the communities involved, as well as of the larger community, a stable language ecology will not develop and no amount of planning is likely to bring sustained language change.

In this volume we consider in much greater detail the various issues raised in a preliminary way in the first part of this chapter while trying to understand the interaction among the various forces which have an influence on language change, whether such change is planned or whether it occurs as the result of circumstances beyond the control of governmental and societal structures. We also examine macro and micro instances of language planning. However, in order to do this, we need to be familiar with the language used and the perspectives taken to discuss language, the *meta-language* used to discuss language planning.

Terminological Difficulties

A multiplicity of terms and usage of terms have appeared in language planning studies, perhaps reflecting the impact that a variety of disciplines have had on the language planning literature and the different usage perspectives from which the terminology is borrowed (see e.g. Gupta, 1985 for status planning issues). As we noted in the Foreword, the literature normally employs the terms 'language policy' and/or 'language planning' synonymously, though they refer to different processes. This is typical of the terminological problems that beset the field. The basic problem is that in this area, as in other areas of popular concern, words mean exactly what a given speaker wants them to mean – much like Tweedle Dee and Tweedle Dum in *Alice in Wonderland*. To illustrate this terminological maze, a number of common terms are set out in Table 1.1 under four headings: political definitions; social definitions; educational definitions; popular definitions; and each of these headings is now considered briefly in turn.

Political Definitions

These are terms largely to be found in government documents, and they are characteristically defined by legislation and not by linguists. Because they are defined by governments, usually as part of actual legislation, they are often without reference to the functions they may or may not serve in a community.

A. Thus, English and French are generally recognised in official documents as *languages of wider communication* largely because they are widely used for official purposes across communities which speak primarily some other language(s). Swahili is recognised as a *pan-African language*, though it is not spoken across all of Africa, because it is a language held in common among a number of east African states and because it

Table 1.1 Terminological usage and problems

Political Definitions	Social Definitions	Educational Definitions	Popular Definitions
A. language of wider communication	A. educational languages	A. foreign languages	A. foreign languages
pan-regional languages	(1) majority language	B. second languages	
B. national languages	(2) as a 1st language	C. mother tongue	B. native language
C. official language(s)	(3) as a 2nd language	(1) non-standard varieties	C. foreigner languages
D. literary language	(4) as a creole/ pidgin		D. pidgin
E. regional languages	(5) foreign languages		
	B. vernacular community heritage	D. community languages	
F. religious languages	C. classical/ historical	E. heritage languages	

serves to link communities which otherwise speak mutually unintelligible languages. Melanesian pidgin is another example of a *pan*-regional *language* (Mühlhäusler, 1995).

    B. *National languages* are so recognised in official political constitutions; for example, the 1976 Constitution of the Philippines (perpetuated in the 1987 Constitution) actually established politically a national language that did not exist. The language situation in the Philippines is very complex, and the state is linguistically extremely heterogeneous. In recent years, a substantial effort has been made to promulgate a dialect of Tagalog (called Pilipino) for nation-wide communication, but the writers of the 1976 constitution envisioned a time in the indefinite future when all of the various languages of the Philippines might assimilate into one language which, when it came into existence, would be called *Filipino*. This non-existent language was designated the official national language. Until such time as it came into existence, the state would recognise Pilipino and English as its national languages. The 1987 Constitution actually mandates Filipino in a variety of settings, and Presidential Executive Order 335 of 25 August 1988, replaces English with Filipino as the official mode of government communication, but this post-1987 Filipino is actually Pilipino/Tagalog under a new name.

Many polities have designated national languages (see Appendix). That is true across sub-Saharan Africa and Asia. However, it is important to understand that a national language is not necessarily one spoken by everyone in a nation, although it is sometimes assumed to be spoken by a numerical majority of the population. Rather, it is one granted special political status within the state. It is often argued that a national language is one spoken by a clear numerical majority of the population of a given polity, but in reality it is more likely to be a language associated with a power-group – e.g. the people living in and around the capital city, the tribal groups which traditionally make up the army, the group with the highest level of education, or the group which controls the greatest part of the wealth. In many cases, the national language is the only language authorised to be taught through the educational system. For example, Indonesian/Malay is the national language in Indonesia, Malaysia, Singapore and Brunei, but has quite different roles, relationships and functions for the populations in each of the states.

C. *Official languages* occur in extremely linguistically heterogeneous polities – states which include within their borders speakers of a large number of languages (e.g. Cameroon, India, Indonesia, South Africa, the Philippines, each with something on the order of 250 or more languages). The United Nations and the European Union provide other examples of bodies with official language policies. In such conditions, the designation of a set of official languages is a political response to the reality that no one language will be acceptable to the entire population and no one language can practically be disseminated throughout the population. Official languages are also specified in the constitution and frequently mandated to be taught through the educational system. It is a complex question whether all official documents must be available in the official languages as well as in the national language; producing documents in many languages is very expensive, and some poorer polities forgo the luxury of creating documents in all the official languages. The list of official languages can be substantial. It is important to understand that languages receive official status for political reasons, not for reasons of their usage, viability, or practicality.

D. *Literary languages* are not usually officially designated, but rather tend to be accepted in practice. They occur in situations where several varieties of a given language have wide acceptability; for example, varieties of Arabic are used throughout the Arabian Peninsula and across much of North Africa, but the spoken varieties differ significantly across the region, approaching mutual unintelligibility at the extremes. While Classical Arabic occurs throughout the region, its use is essentially restricted to the religious sector, and its lexicon is not readily adaptable to the needs of 'modern' societies. As a result of this linguistic phenomenon, 'Modern Newspaper Arabic' has come into wide use across the region as a literary language. It is not a language spoken by anyone, but it is a variety that can be read by most educated people across the region without reference to the spoken variety they normally employ. Although it is called 'Modern *Newspaper* Arabic', its actual use now extends into a large variety of written genres in addition to those employed in newspapers. A somewhat similar situation occurs with respect to English; written educated English is not actually spoken by anyone and does not reflect the range of dialect variation across English, but it is generally accepted – indeed, insisted upon – across the entire English-speaking world. The core of standard Chinese is a common character-based written form, along with some facility in one variety or another of the spoken language, of which there are six or seven mutually unintelligable dialect groups (Harrell, 1993).

E. *Regional languages* also occur in extremely linguistically heterogeneous societies; they are often dominant languages in geographic sub-areas of a polity. In India, for example, such languages as Tamil, Bengali, Marathi, etc., have regional status. It is not uncommon for regional languages to be designated as members of the set of official languages, though that is not always the case. Regional languages receive official sanction through the educational system in some polities which employ three- or four-language educational systems; e.g. in countries like India, South Africa and Cameroon, a child may begin education in the village language, may be required to acquire a regional language in late primary school, an official language and/or the national language in secondary school, and a language of wider communication in tertiary education. Thus, an Indian child may be expected to speak a village language, Tamil, Hindi, and English by the time s/he enters tertiary education.

F. *Religious languages* may be given official political status in polities in which there is no viable separation between church and state; e.g. in countries like Brunei and Saudi Arabia, which are 'Islamic Monarchies', the religious language – in both of these cases, Classical Arabic – is officially designated as one of the languages of the State.

Summary. It is important to note that in all of the cases discussed in this category, the designation of a language is politically achieved, constitutes part of the legal structure of a polity, and receives official recognition and sanction through the institutional educational system. These designations may have little reference to linguistic reality – to the basic issues of who speaks the language, for what purpose, under what circumstances, to which interlocutor, or to such other issues as the natural frequency and distribution of the language through the polity. There are cases, particularly in Africa, where, for example, a European language has been designated the 'national' (or an 'official') language, even though that language is actually spoken by only a small proportion of the population, and only a small number of whom may be native speakers (Robinson, 1993; Greenberg, 1963). Such has also been the case in Hong Kong where 95% of the population speaks Cantonese, but where the law and government has largely been conducted in English.

Social Definitions

Social definitions have little relationship to official political designation, but rather tend to reflect the broader value system of the community. Most communities recognise several broad categories of language, but most communities believe that language is primarily a function of the educational system and that the educational system ought to deal with these issues.

A. *Educational languages* are those that are the responsibility of the educational system and somehow ought to be included in the curriculum, though not necessarily for all students.

(1) Obviously, the most important consideration for the educational system should be the *majority language* (which is sometimes designated the *mother tongue*). This is the language that is assumed to be the one spoken by 'everybody who counts'. In the United States at the present time, English is considered the majority language. Because it is so perceived, it is taught throughout the educational system; children learn basic literacy in English and have at least one language course in English from first grade through the first university year, and in addition they study the canonical literature in English throughout the educational system from primary through tertiary education.[3] Thus, being literate in English is perceived as being 'in a state of grace'. English is seen as the language of power; it is through English that one can exercise one's rights as a citizen – thus, literacy in English is a requirement for naturalisation. The notion *majority language* is clearly presumed to be representative of the greatest bulk of the population, and, no doubt, in a statistical sense it is, but there are areas in the United States where it clearly is not.

The notion *mother-tongue* is extremely difficult to define; in its simplest meaning it can be understood literally – 'the language of one's mother', or the language one speaks with one's mother. In reality, one may in fact be a native speaker of a language even though one's mother was not. For example, an individual born to a Tamil-speaking mother in Malaysia will probably learn Straits Malay and/or Straits Chinese on the playground, and Bahasa Melayu and English as a second language in the school system. Such an individual may then go abroad to undertake tertiary study in English. She or he may be a 'native speaker' of various languages depending on the registers in which the languages are used: for example, for matters of the home and of childhood, Tamil; for matters relating to school subjects or general communication in the community, Bahasa Melayu; and for matters of academic specialisation, English. It is impossible to designate that individual's 'mother-tongue' except in the literal sense, and it is not useful to do so (Ferguson, 1992: xiii). It is not a useful term, but it is, nonetheless, one that is widely used.

(2/3) Society recognises some differentiation of the language designated as 'mother-tongue'; that is, one may speak it as a *first language* or as a *second language*. To a large extent, this terminology implies in a societal sense language acquisition order; that is, one learns English first, and then a second language, or one may learn English second if one has had the 'bad fortune' to learn some other language first. There is no implication in this usage that English may be second in importance; on the contrary, it may be deemed primary depending on the societal setting. It should be noted that this terminology has a quite different meaning in the education sector.

(4) Society recognises that some individuals speak a language 'irregularly', and such irregular speech is usually defined as a 'pidgin' (although it may be recognised as a 'creole'). In the United States, the local English variety spoken in Hawaii is called 'Hawaiian Pidgin', while the variety of French spoken in New Orleans is designated 'Creole' and that designation has been extended to the French spoken by refugees entering the United States from Haiti. While these varieties may be very important markers of community identity, they are perceived as 'non-standard' and in need of correction by the wider community, and it is generally deemed to be the role of the education system to fix the inappropriate speech of such individuals. In these cases pidgins and creoles are perfectly appropriate linguistic systems and are not in any absolute sense 'bad', but they are socially proscribed.

(5) Because of the existence of such entities as the United States Peace Corps and because of the compaction permitted by modern global communication systems, speakers of any language recognise that a particular language may be a foreign language for some people. For instance, there is not only a legitimacy but a political desirability in arranging for the teaching of English (or French or Japanese) as a foreign

language in remote places in the world where the residents are sufficiently disadvantaged not to know that language. Again, this is not the designation made among professional members of the education sector, as will be discussed later.

In addition to the majority language, the educational system is expected to deal with foreign languages. In this broad category, many special sub-branches are recognised. Foreign languages are, typically, that set of languages of which most people are aware; the United States educational system has, for decades, taught French, German and Spanish as foreign languages. Up until World War II, German was the most important foreign language in the US; indeed, the initial language debate in colonial times was about German/English bilingualism vs. English monolingualism. In recent years, a small additional number of languages have achieved some popularity; e.g. Chinese, Japanese and Russian among them. In addition to European languages, Australia has demonstrated a political awareness of the need to teach such foreign languages as Indonesian, Japanese, Korean and Chinese (when Chinese is mentioned without modification it is usually intended to imply Mandarin). However, because the economics of education limit the number of languages that can be taught, and because language education is in the popular mind, inextricably tied with the culture of speakers of those languages, the primary purpose of foreign language study typically remains to access the canonical literature of those cultures, although there is a growing recognition that oral language must be taught for tourism and trade.

B. In nations like the United States, Canada or Australia, there is a substantial population of speakers of vernacular (or indigenous or aboriginal) languages – Native American Languages (e.g. Navajo, Hopi, Sioux), Australian Aboriginal languages (e.g. Miriwoong, Yorta Yorta, Guugu Yimithirr). In more recent times, these languages have been recognised as having legitimacy and may be taught in the educational system to individuals who are participants in those cultures, though it would not be common to teach those languages to speakers of the 'majority language'. In New Zealand, on the other hand, there is great interest in the Maori language, and extensive efforts are being made to disseminate Maori to all New Zealanders through the educational system – indeed, under the Maori Language Act of 1987, Maori is the only 'official' language in New Zealand. Sometimes vernacular languages are dealt with as oral languages, partially because some may not have developed written forms, partially because the canonical literature – which is almost always the objective – is oral.

In the United States, Canada and Australia, where, in the relatively recent past, there has been significant immigration from non-English-speaking areas, a number of other languages have been imported. These languages, perceived as a sub-set of vernacular languages, are variously designated as community languages, minority languages, ethnic languages, heritage languages – all euphemisms intended to recognise that they are not the majority language, yet they represent populations of citizens. In Australia, for example, Melbourne now has the largest Greek-speaking population of any city in the world except Athens. These languages are recognised as having a certain legitimacy, and are sometimes taught through the educational system (if the economics of the situation permit), but the teaching of these languages is most often systematically relegated to 'ethnic' or 'Saturday schools', outside the formal educational system and supported largely by the local community rather than by the official educational establishment.

A special sub-set of vernacular languages are the religious languages (e.g. Hebrew, Koranic Arabic, Church Greek, etc.), most commonly treated like community languages – that is, taught in special circumstances outside the official educational system.

C. Finally, the existence of a set of classical/historical languages is recognised and sanctioned for inclusion in the educational system. This set includes languages like Classical Latin and Classical Greek on the one hand, but in English-speaking countries it also includes languages like Anglo Saxon, Middle English and Sanskrit.

Summary. Thus, a number of language categories are recognised as social designations for languages. To a large extent, these languages are sanctioned through the educational system if they are sanctioned at all, the clear emphasis being on the so-called 'majority language(s)'. It is important to notice that these definitions are not politically sanctioned as the first set of definitions is; rather, these are socially sanctioned but have little to do with the kinds of definitions employed within the educational system.

Educational Definitions

Given that the education sector is charged with teaching these various languages, it has developed a set of professional definitions that govern language pedagogy. The education sector sees itself as dealing with basically four categories of language.

A. First, it deals with foreign languages. When language teaching was first introduced into the academic sector in the medieval university, it was concerned exclusively with the teaching of the classical (non-spoken) languages – namely, Latin. Greek, Hebrew and Sanskrit. Given that there were no native speakers of these languages, and given that the vestiges of these languages which were available for teaching were written, largely literary, and limited in scope (since no new texts were being generated), the methodology for teaching which was devised was quite appropriate to the circumstances. The objective of language teaching was to provide access to the thought and art of dead civilisations. Therefore, spoken proficiency was not entirely relevant, and a grammar-translation approach was a perfectly viable teaching method. Since the objective of language learning was to access the thought and art of former civilisations, the activity was highly intellectual, and admittance was reserved only to the brightest students.

Unfortunately, when modern languages (i.e. French, German, Spanish) were introduced into the tertiary curriculum centuries later, this model, which was already well-established, was simply transferred from classical to modern languages. Thus, the teaching of modern languages has remained largely grammar focused, having as its objective access to the canonical literature, and not being much concerned about communicative competence. Foreign language teaching has come to be defined as teaching in an environment in which there is no vital speech community to support learning, in which even written sources are limited, and in which grammatical rather than communicative competence is central. These characteristics define the educational methodologies. In sum, students learning French as a foreign language in the United States are not really expected to be able to speak French for practical purposes but are expected to have an appreciation for French civilisation and to be able to read at least some of the literature in French. In Australia,

> universities considered their role to be that of encouraging the analysis of ideas; studying a language through literature was seen to be as effective a way as any other of increasing students' ability to operate in a language, since literature provided many examples of vocabulary and structures in action, and in a cultural context – if indeed the two can be separated; it was assumed most students would complete their linguistic education overseas. (Mann, 1992: 49)

While primary and secondary schools have had a somewhat greater interest in communicative language work, especially in recent years, they have not been seen as defining the competent foreign language speaker, and are only now beginning to influence teaching methodology at the tertiary level.

B. The educational system has, by virtue of significant immigration in the recent past, been forced to give attention to second language (e.g. English in Australia, Britain, New Zealand and the United States, Japanese in Japan) teaching. The methodology of second-language teaching is of necessity different because its objectives are different. Communicative competence is central to this activity. Although historically the teaching of second languages was also rooted in the grammar-translation methodology, in the recent past there has been a diminution of attention to grammar and an increased emphasis on spoken language. The study of literature is not critical in this approach. While learners are expected to learn to write to some extent, the focus of the writing is practical rather than belletristic. A student learning English as a second language in the United States is expected to be able to converse fluently on any topic within his intellectual ability, to be able to read practical writing (rather than literary writing), and to be able to function in a very large community of speakers. Often the objective of second language learning is assimilation, although increasingly it may be for business or tourism.

C. The primary focus of the educational system remains on mother-tongue education. The system is expected to produce functional literates in the majority language without reference to their actual linguistic backgrounds. This objective has become increasingly difficult to attain for three reasons: (a) the educational base has broadened substantially (education for all for longer): (b) the meaning of literacy has changed (the range of skills has increased); and (c) the system persists in maintaining a disease metaphor with respect to literacy. In the context of this metaphor, it is assumed that *illiteracy* is an evil that must be stamped out (as smallpox was in the last 20 years), and that literacy will automatically politically empower those who have it. All three assumptions are incorrect, serve to obstruct the development of literacy, and ignore the realities of human behaviour – millions of human beings have lived full and happy lives without becoming literate. Illiteracy is the natural human condition, and literacy is the aberrant state (see the section on Literacy planning in language-in-education planning in Chapter 5).

(1) Within mother-tongue language teaching, the educational system recognises the existence of a population of speakers of non-standard varieties. The system recognises, in a rather imprecise way, that possession of only a non-standard variety is somehow limiting; individuals in this category have difficulty in accessing the goods and services provided by the society. The education system, therefore, tries to augment the competence of such individuals by adding to their repertoire an ability to function in a standard variety. In the United States, for example, this population at the present time is assumed to contain speakers of a variety of forms of Black English as well as speakers of a variety of forms of MANSE – Mexican-American non-standard English. This definition is largely dictated by economic considerations; i.e. these two populations are vast, while populations of speakers of other non-standard varieties are relatively small (e.g. speakers of some Native American languages).

D. The educational system also recognises a variety of community languages. In this context (in the United States) are included not only the languages of large recent immigrant populations – Armenians, Chinese, Germans, Greeks, Italians, Japanese, Koreans, etc. – but also the languages of Native Americans and the languages of other linguistic populations somehow politically subsumed within the political structure of the United States – e.g. Chamorros (Guamanians), Samoans, (Spanish-speaking) Puerto Ricans. Also subsumed within community languages are the languages of long-established immigrant groups such as those from eastern and northern Europe speaking languages like Finnish, Norwegian, Polish, Swedish, Yiddish, etc. Religious languages (Hebrew, Church Greek) remain excluded from the list and relegated to subordinate community-supported parochial educational systems.

E. Finally, in this educational set of languages are two groups of languages designated heritage languages in the sense that they constitute part of the heritage of English speakers – languages like Classical Latin and Classical Greek on the one hand, and languages like Anglo-Saxon, Middle English, Welsh, Irish Gaelic, and Scots Gaelic (and possibly Sanskrit, Old Norse, Old High German, Old Church Slavonic, etc.) on the other. These languages, if they are taught at all, are usually offered at the tertiary level, have no great concern with spoken proficiency, and are studied as academic subjects.

Summary. It must be noted that, although the terminology in this category overlaps significantly with the terminology in the social definitions category, the meanings are really quite different. The definitions in this category are educationally based and subsume elements of pedagogical methodology.

Popular Definitions

Quite separate from all of these are the definitions that operate at the level of the popular imagination. In the popular view there are only four fairly simplistic categories.

A. Foreign languages are commonly defined as any language(s) not normally spoken within the polity. In the case of large polities, this normative definition may be regional. For example, in the northern mid-west in the United States, there is a substantial population speaking so-called 'Scandinavian' languages (e.g. Norwegian, Swedish, Finnish). In that region, these languages would not be considered foreign, though Spanish might be so considered. On the other hand, in the south-western United States where Spanish is spoken by a substantial segment of the population, the situation would be reversed; that is, Spanish would not be considered a foreign language, but Swedish would.

B. The native language is, normally, defined as the language of the majority population, often on historical grounds. Thus, in the United States, English is considered the native language of the entire population (though it clearly isn't), partially because the 'founding fathers' are perceived as English-speaking (though they actually weren't; Pennsylvania, for example, originally entered the union as a German-speaking community, and a number of wars were fought between the English-speaking, French-speaking, and Spanish-speaking areas), partially because the core political documents (the Declaration of Independence, the Bill of Rights, the remainder of the Constitution) are written in English, and partially because English has been the functional language of the polity for more than 200 years. English has been the dominant language of education and religion as well as the dominant language of civic activity. Generations of children have learned the English canonical literature and through it an English-based sociology of knowledge and an English-based value system. But native language is not a notion peculiar to the English-speaking world; French is the native language of France, German the native language of Germany, and Japanese is the native language of Japan. The integration of the notion native language with the notion of the nation-state is a 'modern' idea, probably dating no further back than the seventeenth century.

C. Foreigner languages are those languages and varieties spoken by foreigners whom one encounters in the community; in recent years, for example, very large numbers of Japanese tourists have visited Hawaii and the west coast of the United States. Japanese is not widely taught through the United States educational system and not widely recognised as belonging to the formal category of 'foreign languages'. Anything spoken by a Japanese tourist is, by definition, a foreigner language, whether it is standard Japanese (as spoken in Japan), non-standard Japanese (as spoken by second- and third-generation Japanese Americans), non-standard English (English imperfectly learned in school in Japan or elsewhere), or Japanese accented standard English (see Clyne, 1981).

D. The term 'pidgin' is somewhat more complicated in the popular imagination as it designates a non-standard variety of an established language. For example, a variety widely spoken in Papua New Guinea is known as 'Tok Pisin' (the very name being literally, a 'pidgin' phonological representation of the English phrase 'talk pidgin'). The language was long stigmatised as a 'pidgin', and considered unsuitable to express important ideas, though in Vanuatu it has been (not without opposition) elevated to the status of a national language. A similar situation occurs through many of the island-states of the South Pacific region. However, in the popular sense, such a language is thought to be sub-standard, incapable of carrying serious thought, and spoken by individuals perceived to be uneducated – in sum, a stigmatised variety. In the United States, various minority groups – e.g. Blacks, Hispanics, etc. – are perceived to speak 'pidgins'.

Summary. The notions held in the popular imagination are limited, unsophisticated, and tend to overlook important distinctions. They are, largely, conceived in terms of groups of speakers – 'ins' and 'outs' – rather than in terms of broad understanding of linguistic issues. It is not the intent to stigmatise these perceptions, only to enumerate them as distinct from the other three identified categories of terms.

Outcomes

The result of this terminological abundance is, necessarily, a certain amount of confusion. Consider the case of an imaginary individual who resides in, for example, Israel, and who having recently immigrated there from, for example, Russia, is learning Hebrew. That individual is learning a *second* language – both perhaps in a numerical sense and in an educational sense – which is politically both the national language and the majority language and practically the religious language. Because the individual's use of Hebrew would be likely to be imperfect, it would be considered a foreigner language. Educators might recognise his use of Hebrew as an interlanguage – a temporary 'pidgin'. This individual, possibly, speaks Yiddish and Russian. Russian would be considered the individual's mother tongue or first language (but not the first language of the community). Russian would be considered a foreign language in Israel – in the sense that it is taught in the educational system along with other foreign languages – but because there has been a substantial immigration of Russians to Israel, Russian may also be considered a vernacular/community/minority/ethnic/heritage language. Yiddish may also be considered an ethnic language (of the Jewish diaspora), and may be recognised by linguists as a dialect, a non-standard variety or perhaps as a creole (Wexler, 1991).

The point of this lengthy terminological discussion is illustrated through this example; any given language in a particular environment may be described using a wide variety of names, each such designation bearing on a different lexical set – political, social, educational, and/or popular. An individual working in the field of language planning needs to recognise all of these terminologies and understand that the same phenomenon is being variously described. More importantly, the society needs to recognise that this broad range of terminology is being applied to the same linguistic phenomenon – indeed, to this same single representative of the linguistic phenomenon – and the society needs to recognise that the various terms represent different realities, just as a given actual physical field may be differently described by a farmer, a real-estate agent, a military commander, and an irrigation engineer. David Crystal's (1989) *Encyclopedia of Language* and the Oxford *International Encyclopedia of Linguistics* (Bright, 1992) are good sources of basic terminology and concepts.

Summary

In this chapter we have laid out a general framework for language planning. After having defined the general nature of the field we have looked at how language planning is related to other types of planning and have examined government, education, non-government and other agencies' and organisations' roles in language planning. We have then discussed the problem with the usage of terms in the field, emphasising that one needs to examine carefully what is meant, as terms often have several possible meanings depending on their contextual usage. This terminological overview provides us with the basic meta-linguistic tools to look at how the language planning process can be said to work. In Chapter 2 we examine Haugen's (1983) model for language planning as one way of visualising the scope and sequence of the language planning process, Haarmann's (1990) ideal typology of language cultivation and language planning and Cooper's (1989) accounting scheme for the study of language planning as frameworks for understanding the discipline.

Notes

1. In this book we use 'language planning' as the generic term for the discipline and use it to encompass everything from government macro-level national planning to group or individual micro-level planning. While language planning initially referred to government planning for national situations (e.g. Fishman *et al.*, 1968 – *Language Problems of Developing Nations*), the term has been used for many years to reflect a much broader range of issues and approaches to language planning, as we believe this volume demonstrates. However, Jernudd (1993: 133) among others, has argued that as 'language planning . . . takes decision makers', for example governments', specification of language problems as their axiomatic point of departure' and therefore a new term, language management, is needed to describe 'bottom-up' and discourse based planning. Reflecting this argument, language management or *aménagement linguistique* has begun to appear to a limited extent in the literature (Jernudd & Neustupný, 1987; also see Chapter 7, Language Planning and Agency Power).

2. Every session of the US Congress, since the introduction of the first 'English Only' bill (Senate Joint Resolution 72–to amend the US constitution to declare English the official language) by Senator S.I. Hayakawa in 1981, has been faced with a number of similar bills. At the time this book was being written, the Congress (104th Congress, 1995–96) had at least four bills before it intended to make English the sole official language of the nation, *de jure*, or at least to make English the sole official language of government. Some of these proposed bills would end official support for bilingual education. Only fairly late in the discussion did it dawn on some legislators that such legislation would contravene legislation enacted in the very recent past to protect and preserve indigenous (Native American) languages. This left legislators scrambling to discover some means to exempt Native American languages from the effects of the proposed legislation, i.e. to find a compromise between those two essentially contradictory objectives.

3. 'English as a school subject had existed [in Britain] in some form as early as the late sixteenth century but its status was low and even in 1900 largely confined to elementary and girls' schools. It was aimed primarily at providing some basic literacy while the more prestigious boys' public and grammar schools studied classics as a more edifying alternative. The growing pressure that English should occupy a central role in the curriculum culminated in 1921 with the official Board of Education's publication *The teaching of English in England* . . . which declared that for English children, "no form of knowledge can take precedence of a knowledge of English, no form of literature can take precedence of English literature".' (Thompson *et al.*, 1996: 102)

2 A Framework for Planning: Who Does What to Whom?

An Overview of Language Planning as a Process

Having examined the context for language planning and the complex problems of terminology usage in Chapter 1, it is useful to turn our attention to some frameworks for language policy and planning and to look at some of the key defining variables found therein. These frameworks will provide some initial overall perspectives on the discipline which will help to inform our understanding of the specific examples found in subsequent chapters. Three complementary frameworks are initially examined, those proposed by Haugen (1983), Haarmann (1990) and Cooper (1989) along with some other critical variables necessary to provide an overall framework for understanding language policy and planning. For those interested in other approaches, Jernudd (1982) and Neustupný (1978, 1987) have suggested a correction focus as a paradigm for language planning and more recently have argued for a language management approach (see Chapter 7).

First we turn to a structural framework for language planning which looks at the various stages and activities which can be said to occur as part of the planning process. Researchers in language planning have attempted to differentiate two distinct kinds of activities – those that are concerned specifically with attempts to modify language itself, and those that are concerned with attempts to modify the environment in which a language is used. These have come to be designated 'corpus planning' and 'status planning', respectively. Such a separation constitutes something of an oversimplification; it is, in fact, virtually impossible, in practice, to separate the two activities. The fact is that any change in the character of a language is likely to result in a change in the use environment, and any change in the use environment is likely to induce a change in the character of the language.

Over the years there have been a number of attempts to define the activities which make up the language planning process and to provide a descriptive model of those processes. Haugen (1983: 275) has incorporated much of this thinking into an overall model of the language planning process (Table 2.1), to which '4.c. internationalisation' can be added.

The model indicates that the activities which make up the language planning process can be viewed from either a societal or a language focus. The societal focus is called 'status planning' and consists of those decisions a society must make about language selection and the implementation to choose and disseminate the language or languages selected. The language focus is called 'corpus planning' and consists of linguistic decisions which need to be made to codify and elaborate a language or languages. These two foci form the basis for an overview of all the activities which make up the language planning process. The model can also be examined in terms of form or policy planning, with its emphasis on basic language and policy decisions and their implementation, or on function or language cultivation, with its emphasis on language teaching and extended language development and use.

While these activities can be said to describe the overall language planning process, in any particular situation it may be possible or even necessary to omit some of the steps outlined in the process. In part this is so because the activities which are important in a specific language planning situation can be determined by the particular goals for which language plans are being developed (see Chapter 3). In part the model may not be followed because, although such models are conceptually useful in understanding the language planning process, individuals involved in language planning do not necessarily know about or follow this or any other model.

Table 2.1 Haugen's (1983: 275) revised language planning model with additions

	Form (policy planning)	Function (language cultivation)
Society (status planning)	1. Selection (decision procedures) a. problem identification b. allocation of norms	3. Implementation (educational spread) a. correction procedures b. evaluation
Language (corpus planning)	2. Codification (standardisation procedures) a. graphisation b. grammatication c. lexication	4. Elaboration (functional development) a. terminological modernisation b. stylistic development c. internationalisation

According to Haugen's model, the planning process always begins with a status planning decision. In fact, that is not necessarily the case, but for the sake of discussion and because the model provides a good overview of the planning process in an idealised sense, the sequence in the model will be followed, and each cell will be explored in some depth. Assuming, then, that the process is initiated with a status decision, it is possible to examine a typical case. The Sub-Saharan African states might serve as illustrations of this process (see e.g. Tanzania and Uganda in the Appendix).

Status Planning

Status planning can be defined as those aspects of language planning which reflect primarily social issues and concerns and hence are external to the language(s) being planned. The two status issues which make up the model are *language selection* and *language implementation* (see, e.g. Ridge, 1996).

Language selection

Selection of a language(s) focuses on the development of language policy. Selection involves the choice of a language(s) by/for a society through its political leaders. Such decisions are usually made from among competing languages and or dialects. The language or language items selected establish the particular linguistic form which is to be the norm and which is to have status within society.

In the context of our illustration, when a geographic region becomes a polity – an independent state – as many former colonial territories in Sub-Saharan Africa did in the early 1960s, there are some immediately identifiable problems that require political solutions. A state must have a language(s) in which it can communicate with its citizens. As has already been observed earlier in this volume, most of the newly emerging states in Sub-Saharan Africa were polyglot communities containing populations speaking anywhere from two to three or several hundred languages. In political terms, the state must recognise its need for a language (or languages) of communication, and subsequently it must select one or more languages for official purposes.

After the independence of Namibia in 1990, English became the official language of the country, while German, Afrikaans and African languages indigenous to Namibia are recognised on a par for purposes of education and other communication (Haacke, 1994). The post-apartheid situation in South Africa has led to that country reassessing which of its 11 official languages will be used for what purposes (Webb, 1994a; Ridge, 1996). Webb (1994b: 197) has argued that if Africa's autochthonous languages (i.e. non-European African languages) are to contribute to this process, then an environment must be created through 'revalorizing' them where there is an appreciation of the contribution they make to social and cultural life.

Identification of the problem

The choice of a national language(s) is not as simple as it seems on the surface since such selection normally implies a choice among competing languages. Vernacular languages provide the opportunity to establish a common heritage, a common history, and to facilitate unity; on the other hand, exogenous languages often provide access to the external world. The choice of a language(s) ideally should result in the smallest possible disruption to the social structure, yet at the same time the decision should not isolate the polity from the outside world.

Various criteria for selecting a language have been proposed and include such things as political neutrality, dominance, prestige, a great tradition and areal affinity (Kale, 1990: 185–6). However, one must be aware that such criteria are themselves value laden, and cannot all be weighted equally. For example, if a polity is at the point of making a language-choice decision and is also concerned about modernisation, an exogenous language may be a feasible alternative. Language modernisation is a time-consuming and resource-intensive process, as is the translation of key materials into a new language. The fact is that most scientific and technical information available in the major global storage and retrieval networks occurs in one of a very few languages (i.e. English, French, German and Russian). For complex historical reasons, it is currently the case that the vast majority of scientific and technical texts are either published in, or abstracted in, English, and most databases are organised using an English sociology of knowledge. These facts make English and other so-called 'world languages' important competitors for the position as national language, or as a language with some official status.

Polities of necessity then must choose among the available alternatives. The choice is not always an easy one. The former colonial language, spoken by an elite and probably providing access to the larger modern world, may not be a good choice if an objective of the choice is to facilitate national unity, since the colonial language may be regarded as a symbol of oppression by some segments of the population, but also may not be spoken by any significant segment of the population. If not a foreign language, then which of the indigenous languages? The criteria of dominance – that is, a language spoken by a clear numerical majority – may be chosen, provided that the choice is not opposed by other significant segments of the population. It is, however, relatively rare, in genuinely polyglot communities, that any single language is in fact spoken by a clear numerical majority (see the data for South Africa in Table 8.1). Other types of dominance include: the language of the capital city, the language of the wealthiest group, the language of the most powerful group (usually the military, e.g. the linguistic history of Uganda under Idi Amin), or the language of the political elite (namely, the language spoken by or favoured by a charismatic national President – e.g. Malawi's former President favoured Latin). This issue of prestige is examined more specifically in the next framework, Haarmann (1990), which effectively suggests prestige as a third dimension to status and corpus planning (see Table 2.2).

The choice of a national language(s) is normally calculated to create the least possible disruption in the polity. If, for example, French was the former colonial language, French is recognised as a world language, and virtually no one in the polity speaks another world language such as English; if the resources for teaching English do not exist, and if there is among the population no particular emotional attraction to English, then it makes little sense to choose English as a national language because choosing it will create a powerful disturbance in the social structure. On the other hand, if Japanese were a serious contender in a new polity which had formerly been occupied by the Japanese military, and if the population had a strong antipathy toward the Japanese on the basis of that earlier military occupation (e.g. Malaysia, Singapore, Indonesia, Hong Kong, Taiwan, the Philippines), Japanese would probably be a poor choice despite the fact that many older people in the country may know the language and that it is rapidly becoming an important language in other contexts. These illustrations suggest that leaders of a polity should have basic social and linguistic information about the language situation in the polity to make language selection decisions. Such information subsumes an understanding of what segments of the population speak what languages, of the registers in which each language may be used, of the purposes served by the available languages, and of the resources available for each of the competing languages. It also subsumes an understanding of the emotional attitudes of the population with respect to the primary candidate languages.

There are a number of ways which can be used to collect the information (see Language Planning Process, Chapter 4) needed to provide a detailed description of the actual language situation (who speaks what to whom under what circumstances to what end) including sociolinguistic surveys, with their focus on the collection of attitude toward language(s) data. While it is of course possible to change attitudes toward a particular language, such population-wide attitude modification takes a long time and is extremely expensive. For example, Malaysia's national language pro-gramme which was begun in 1967 has put a lot of effort not only into language teaching using a variety of techniques, but also into a media campaign to convince the large numbers of non-Malay speakers in the population of the efficacy of learning 'Bahasa Malaysia'. Language choice cannot be made in a vacuum, but rather needs to be made in light of linguistic information, which in most cases does not readily exist.

To illustrate this point, Tagalog was chosen in the Philippines because it was claimed that it was the language of a numerical majority, because it was the language of the Capital city, and because it was the language of the early political elite; but despite all these excellent reasons, the choice was, and continues to be, resisted by the other numerically significant populations – the Cebuanos, the Ilocanos, etc. Rejection is frequently based on democratic considerations; native speakers of the official/national language have a clear advantage – they don't have to learn that language, they have native facility in the language, and they have easy access to the best jobs. All other groups, then, are, by definition, disadvantaged and will oppose the choice.

By contrast, Bahasa Indonesia, which is a variant of the pan-Malay language used by traders, was selected by nationalists to be the national language of Indonesia in 1928, almost 20 years before independence from the Dutch, because it was more politically and socially neutral than Javanese, the language of the largest and most powerful ethnic group. In a country as culturally diverse as Indonesia, the choice of 'Malay' as the language of resistance against Dutch colonialism and later as the national language was a statement about the need to build unity through diversity. To have chosen Javanese would have been a statement of a new colonialism, and it is unlikely that Indonesia as we know it would have emerged.

Because language is an emotional matter, opposition to a language can become violent. If the language differentiation is echoed in religious, social, or economic differences, the opposition may be all the more instant and violent. For example, Hindi and Urdu are linguistically essentially the same language differentiated primarily by the use of different writing systems, and in their sources for abstract vocabulary — Sanskrit for Hindi, and Arabic for Urdu. But the language differentiation is reflected in a religious difference as well, Urdu being spoken by Moslems and Hindi by Hindus. Some leaders from both groups used these differences for their own political purposes to differentiate the communities (Das Gupta, 1971). Thus linguistic difference was, in part, responsible for the initial violent break-up of imperial India at independence into Pakistan and India. Pakistan in turn had the eastern portion break away and become Bangladesh, although both are Islamic polities, in part over linguistic (Urdu and Bengali) and cultural differences.

While the choice of a language constitutes a difficult problem, polities do, at some point, make a choice. Once a choice has been made, there are a number of other problems to be dealt with. If the choice falls on a foreign language, that language is likely already to have a standard form, and a set of dictionaries, grammars, etc., are likely to exist. But it is often the case that the variety of the colonial language most widely spoken in the new polity is not the same variety that is spoken in the former colonial power. In such cases, there is the problem of which variety to accept. The metropolitan variety has a number of advantages, but it may not be spoken by many people; the local variety may be spoken by many people but may to some extent preclude the wider communication for which it was chosen in the first place. The choice of a local language also raises the question of variety. Modern English and French are the varieties which were dominant around London and Paris about 500 years ago and which have now become accepted as national languages.

Allocation of norms is no less complex than the initial identification of the language to be selected. If one can assume that the choice of a language for a specific purpose (i.e. a national language, a foreign language, a regional variety, etc.) has already been accomplished, the next series of problems deals with the establishment of norms. Let us say that English has been chosen as one of the national languages; the question then becomes 'which English?' Take Hong Kong as an example; there are at least five Englishes spoken in Hong Kong: British English (BE), Australian English (AuE), American English (AmE), Indian English (IE), and Hong Kong Chinese English (CE). BE is probably the most prestigious of the available varieties, but it is spoken by a relative small segment of the population – a segment which is likely to diminish rapidly as integration with China in 1997 approaches. CE (a nativised variety, to use Kachru's term) is the least prestigious of the available varieties but it is spoken by the largest segment of the population. AmE is probably the second most prestigious variety – one which is rapidly growing in number of speakers. As BE is declining with the departure of large segments of the British professional civil service, the number of speakers of AmE is increasing. As early as 1986, the number of speakers of AmE in Hong Kong exceeded the number of speakers of BE. AuE is also of growing importance as a variety not identified with colonialism or imperialism. All three of these varieties (BE, AmE, AuE) provide relatively equal access to an extensive literature and to science and technology. IE is relatively unimportant both in the numerical sense and in terms of access that it provides to the larger world, but it is a variety spoken in a demographically large regional state.

A further consideration has to do with the direction in which China (PRC) will move. At the moment, the PRC seems to be moving in the direction of AmE, but the situation is fluid, and it is difficult to predict what will ultimately happen. The aftermath of the unsuccessful pro-democracy movement and other perceived human rights violations within the PRC could cause a rupture of relations with the United States which might move the PRC in the direction of BE or AuE. A second non-trivial consideration has to do with commerce. Hong Kong has become one of the banking centres of the world, and it is important both to Hong Kong and to the PRC that that situation continue. Whichever variety of English promises the greatest access to the world of commerce is likely to be chosen, if not by government fiat, then by the people's action. While it is possible to devise a variety of English which falls in the centre of a circle of these Englishes, the artificial development of such standard forms has not been very successful (i.e. the attempts in the 1950s and 1960s to develop a 'mid-Atlantic English' between BE and AmE).

The problem of allocation of norms also applies to Chinese in Hong Kong. Hong Kong is traditionally a Cantonese speaking community, but because it has, for a century or more, been the recipient of Chinese migration from all over China, but primarily from South China, a variety of other southern dialects (e.g. Hakka) are also spoken in Hong Kong. The PRC has Mandarin as its official language, and has already urged Hong Kong to disseminate Mandarin in the run-up to 1997. Thus, the allocation of norms among the competing Chinese varieties constitutes an extraordinarily thorny problem. The current tendency is to evolve a high and a low variety in parallel with the situation of English (diglossic situation); that is, BE is the high (H) variety and CE is the low (L) variety, without reference to the proportion of the population which speaks each. It is possible that Mandarin will evolve into a Chinese high (H) variety and Cantonese into a low (L) variety. The planner must decide whether this tendency constitutes an acceptable alternative, and, if not, what strategies can be devised to modify the tendency.

On the other hand, if a local vernacular is chosen, that vernacular may not be standardised. Decisions must be made regarding the variety of the local vernacular that will be 'officialised'. It is further possible that the local vernacular will not have a standardised lexicon and/or a standardised grammar. Indeed, it is possible that the local variety may not have a standardised orthography. It is also possible that the lexicon of the local vernacular may not be particularly well suited to the needs of a modernising society; new lexical items may need to be created to facilitate the language's ability to deal with modern concepts, particularly in education. For example, in the Philippines, Pilipino (since 1987 known as Filipino) – a 'nationalised' form of Tagalog – is mandated throughout the educational system, except in the teaching of science and mathematics where English remains the language of instruction, largely as an outcome of the relative lack of technical terminology in Pilipino.

However, similar problems can arise even with well-established languages. In the United States, in the last decade, there has been a powerful movement to amend the Federal Constitution in order to designate English as the official language of that country. Indeed, a number of states, 22 out of 50 by 1996, have already adopted so-called 'English only' legislation. There are, of course, political issues underlying these actions, but there is also an important linguistic question; if 'English' is designated as the official language of the United States, which 'English' shall it be? In order to instantiate an official language, it is necessary to define which variety of the language will constitute the official standard. The English of the United

States is marked by the existence of a number of regional and socioeconomic varieties. While these varieties are most clearly distinguished by
differences in pronunciation, there are substantial lexical differences
among the several varieties, and there are even syntactic differences.
Logically, if the United States wishes to adopt English as its official
language, it will probably be necessary to create a national language
academy to define the 'standard' variety and to maintain the standards of
that variety over time.

Language implementation

Having taken the decision about what language(s) and what variety(ies)
or norms are to be adopted, these policies need to be put in place. The
implementation of a language plan focuses on the adoption and spread of
the language form that has been selected and codified. This is often done
through the educational system and through other laws or regulations
which encourage and/or require the use of the standard and perhaps
discourage the use of other languages or dialects. While education was the
preserve of the few, it was relatively easy to spread the standard. For
example, 'Oxbridge' English, disseminated through the English 'public
school' system became the 'standard' in the nineteenth century (see G.B.
Shaw's *Pygmalion* and the musical version *My Fair Lady*). However, the
coming of mass education has made language implementation a major
issue. Very few nation-states are linguistically homogeneous, and the
choice of any standard will certainly disadvantage some members of that
heterogeneous community.

'Correction' is the term used by language planners to describe the
specific measures taken to implement the social aspects of a language plan.
Strategies need to be devised to promote language spread and to prevent
the development of a linguistic underclass which has no access to the
language change. While the formal educational system often plays a major
role in the implementation of correction procedures (see Language-in-Education Planning, Chapter 5), it is clear that the education sector alone is not
capable of providing for language correction, partly because dissemination
through the education system requires several generations, and partly
because the education sector lacks the authority to impact on other
segments of society.

Some of the complex range of concerns of the Ministry of Education are
that the education sector has to disseminate and store the teaching
materials prepared – dictionaries, grammar books, etc.; it has to decide
what segment of the school day will be allocated to language education at
what levels of the educational structure. It has to decide what the objectives
of instruction are at each level. It has to decide what other segment of the
population will provide the teachers, what training the teachers shall
receive over what period of time. It has to decide how to induce students

to undertake study seriously and how to convince their parents that language study is a good idea. In the process of making these decisions, it is likely to uncover the fact that the materials prepared in the preceding corpus planning endeavour are not entirely satisfactory, and it has to bring these into line with the classroom reality (see Chapter 5).

Other agencies of government may, for example, need to instigate tax incentives that will promote the use of a particular variety (e.g. the situation of French in Quebec, Canada). In addition, other agencies of government are able to require bilingualism as a condition of employment in the civil service (e.g. Malaysia beginning in the 1960s). Such a strategy can be a powerful incentive to the acquisition of a particular language or variety. Only the government has the resources to mount a major campaign to modify attitudes in the population at large. A number of years ago the Australian government endorsed a media campaign to reduce the tendencies toward alcoholism and sedentary living in the Australian population, the 'Life be in it' campaign. It is obviously possible to devise and implement comparable campaigns in favour of one or another language variety but, more importantly, in favour of language tolerance in the population.

Evaluation

It is not enough to devise and implement strategies to modify a particular language situation; it is equally important to monitor and evaluate the success of the strategies and progress shown toward implementation. Such evaluation should constitute an ongoing process, and must be designed in such a manner as to provide constant feedback for the implementation strategy, so that the implementation strategy can be corrected in the light of the information flowing from the evaluation phase. Such evaluation must occur simultaneously at two levels: i.e. at the level of the plan itself, and as an evaluation of the effect of the plan on various sectors of the population. As we have seen, language plans and their consequences involve complex social change. It is imperative to monitor that change both at the level of the plan and its societal outcomes so that appropriate modifications can be made, where necessary, to the plan itself and/or to the dissemination mechanisms so that implementation leads to appropriate societal goals. Aspects of evaluation are examined in Chapter 4, but it is generally the case that evaluation is a neglected area of language planning.

Status planning summary

Status planning represents the social concerns and social implementation of language planning. Through the process of language selection, the languages to be taught, to be learned, to be made standard are identified. While language planning may play a part in this process, as Luke, *et al.*, (1990) have indicated, language choice is often made on other grounds (race, class, socioeconomic status) and as Sommer (1991) has shown, even that choice may be thwarted by bureaucracy or other conservative forces in the society. Language implementation has as a major component language-in-education planning, but as we will see subsequently, all too often this aspect is allowed to dominate the language plan with problematic consequences, these in general being that formal education represents only one part of language use. Evaluation, when it is carried out, is often done as part of government reports which are not easily accessible to the wider community.

Corpus Planning[1]

Corpus planning can be defined as those aspects of language planning which are primarily linguistic and hence internal to language. Some of these aspects related to language are: (1) orthographic innovation, including design, harmonisation, change of script and spelling reform; (2) pronunciation; (3) changes in language structure; (4) vocabulary expansion; (5) simplification of registers; (6) style; and (7) the preparation of language material (Bamgbose, 1989). Jernudd (1988) provides a more detailed discussion of these linguistic aspects of language planning. Haugen divides these processes into two categories: those related to the establishment of *norms*, and those related to the extension of the linguistic *functions* of language. In his model Haugen labels the former category 'Codification' (or standardisation) procedures, and the latter, 'Elaboration' (or the functional development of language).

Vikør (1988, 1993) has enumerated a set of underlying corpus planning principles which shape the way a corpus is planned. He illustrates these with examples from the Indonesian/Malaysian spelling reforms. The principles show that language planners involved in the corpus planning process are not just applying technical linguistic knowledge, but are involved in choices or alternatives which have a social aspect and which must be resolved for such planning to be successful. These principles can be grouped into four major categories:

- *Internal linguistic principles* (phonemicity, morphophonemicity, simplicity, etymology, invariance and stability);
- *Principles related to attitudes toward other languages* (*rapprochement* or adaptation, reaction [purism]);
- *Principles concerning the relationship between the language and its users* (majority, liberality, prestige, counter-prestige, usage, estheticism, rationalism); and
- *Principles derived from societal ideologies* (nationalism, liberalism, traditionalism, democracy/egalitarianism, modernity, authority).

Corpus planning has generated a lot of interest in the literature. Four collections of papers, edited by Haas (1982), Lüdi (1994), Scaglione (1984) and Woods (1985), have taken case histories of the standardisation of different languages as their primary focus. By contrast, the five volumes edited by Fodor and Hagège (1983–1984, 1989–1990) focus predominantly on current examples of corpus planning for 'major' languages from Europe, Africa, Asia and the Pacific region and endangered languages from around the world. *Sociolinguistica 2* (Ammon, Mattheier & Nelde, 1988) includes eight articles on the theme of standardisation of Romance and Germanic European national languages while *Sociolinguistica 6* (Mattheier & Panzer, 1992) includes 10 articles on the theme of standardisation of languages in Eastern Europe. Taken together these 10 volumes provide a descriptive account of attempts at corpus planning in more than 85 countries.

Codification

Codification of a language focuses on the standardisation procedures needed to develop and formalise a linguistic and usually literate set of language norms. Codification is usually performed by individuals with linguistic training who decide explicitly the linguistic form the language is to take. Joseph (1987) has explored the question of 'what is a standard language', and the Eurocentric nature of this question; he cites as examples French, Greenlandic and Inupiaq. LePage (1988) sees standardisation as stereotypic behaviour by users of a language. Ferguson (1988) offers a contrasting position arguing that standardisation implicates a supradialectical norm that leads to language spread.

For many languages the codification process has become so extensive that language agencies (see Rubin, 1979; Domínguez & López, 1995) have been created to do the necessary corpus planning work. For example, Chaklader (1987) describes the work of the Panshimbanga Bangala Akademy for Bengali in India, while Tovey (1988) discusses the role of the Bord na Gaeilge in the development of the Irish language. Of course, language agencies need not be formal language planning bodies. Pointon (1988) relates how the BBC has dealt with pronunciation standards over the last six decades and Sinclair *et al.* (1992) provides a dictionary basis for that usage.

Yet, there is a growing realisation among those involved in corpus planning that standardisation has its social, cultural and political consequences – for language planners themselves, for individual language users, and for minority language communities (Luke *et al.*, 1990). Corpus planning takes place amidst conflicting interests prevalent in the social context (Jernudd & Neustupný, 1987). As Fishman (1988b) points out, the need to standardise a language at a national level to meet economic and political goals should not be used as an argument to eliminate community languages which serve as the social and interpersonal fabric for many linguistic minorities.

Haugen (1983) suggests that codification consists of three areas: *graphisation, grammatication* and *lexication,* thereby virtually ignoring aspects of spoken language (although see Thomas, 1987). The typical results of codification work are a prescriptive orthography, grammar, and dictionary. There are a few studies (i.e. ÓBaoill, 1988, for Irish) which provide specific details across each of these three areas; most studies, however, relate only to one of them, and thus can be considered separately.

Graphisation has been considered the first step in the standardisation of a language. Writing systems – whether employing an alphabet, a syllabary or a system of ideograms – provide the basis on which literacy materials can be established and have the potential to reduce the linguistic variation in a language community (see e.g. Wurm 1994a). A great deal of graphisation has been accomplished through the work of the Summer Institute of Linguistics [SIL] (Wycliffe Bible Translators); the SIL has provided orthographies for more previously unwritten languages than any other single source. This work, however, has not been without controversy. In some instances, for example, dialect variation has been sacrificed in the interests of 'normative' graphisation (i.e. in Quechua). For a discussion of the role of the SIL with reference to indigenous languages in Mexico, see Patthey-Chavez (1994); for a discussion of the problems of graphisation in the Andean languages, see Hornberger (1992, 1993, 1994, 1995b).

While graphisation activities are often associated with the transformation of oral languages to literate ones, aspects of this type of standardisation apply equally to 'modernised' written languages (e.g. Coulmas, 1989b). Script reform is a matter being considered for a number of languages including Tamil (James, 1985). The choice of alphabetic or character scripts is part of a continuing debate for many East Asian languages (e.g. Chinese [*International Journal of the Sociology of Language*, 1986, 59], Korean [Hannas, 1995]) while issues related to spelling reform – e.g. Kana in Japan (Neustupný, 1986), Tok Pisin and Australian Kriol (Yule, 1988), Dutch (de Rooij & Verhoeven, 1988 and more recently in 1994), German (Augst & Ammon, 1993 and the more recent pluricentric changes in 1996), Portuguese (de Silva & Gunneweik, 1992), and spelling foreign words in English (Abbott, 1988), for example, are continuing issues.[2] However, it can be argued that standardisation of spelling may not be appropriate in all situations, for example, where a language is still developing as a communicative medium as with Australian Kriol (Black, 1990).

In the case of a local vernacular which has not developed a standard orthography or which simply does not have a written history, for literacy to occur graphisation becomes necessary. It is necessary to devise an orthographic system that reflects the phonology of the language. When, for example, Native American (e.g. Navajo), Australian Aboriginal languages (e.g. Guugu Yimithirr) or Asian languages like Vietnamese and Kampuchean acquired orthographies, those orthographies were often devised by missionaries who did not have any very clear concept of the linguistic differences between phonological systems. Hornberger (1992: 192) writes: 'It was the missionary friars and priests who first wrote down many of the indigenous languages, each adopting Spanish or Portuguese orthography according to his own conventions.' Orthographic systems devised for tonal languages by missionaries speaking Spanish or English (in the historical past) often failed to represent the tonal system in any way, and those orthographies have had to be modified over time to reflect the tonal character of the language. In the process of graphisation, local dialect differences must be resolved as well in order to arrive at a standardised representation of the language.

Grammatication involves the extraction and formulation of rules that describe how a language is structured. Most of the grammars developed have been prescriptive and based on the standardised variety of the language, especially those used in schooling or for literacy development. Singh (1987) argues, however, that English grammars used in India during the last 100 years have varied in their sensitivity and appropriateness to Indian conditions thereby creating the feeling that English is either a colonial/imposed language or a national self-expressive one. Soh (1985) illustrates the need to think beyond Eurocentric categories of grammatication. In Korea industrialisation and the resultant social change have altered the use of honorifics and the related pronominal system making the language less polite but more democratic (cf., Masagara, 1991 for similar changes resulting from urbanisation and Christianisation in Kirundi).

In addition, it must be recognised that the grammar of any language is probably too complex to be represented in a simple way – or for that matter captured in a single book. Besides, a living language is protean, constantly changing its shape to meet its communicative needs, so the best grammar book is, at the moment of its publication, a historical document reflective of the past. For pedagogical purposes, additional choices have to be made; what grammar (or really what segment of the grammar) will be taught? How can it be taught most effectively? How can it be taught to speakers of other local vernaculars whose grammars may be readily compatible with, or may vary substantially from, the target language?

While the grammar of a language is, admittedly, too complex to be simply represented, the pragmatics of a language are almost impossible to capture. Youmans (1995) has explored the use of epistemic modals in standard academic American English and in the speech of Mexican American youngsters; she found significant differences in the conditions under which certain modals were invoked. There is ample evidence in research in German (Heidelberg Project, 1975, 1976, 1977, 1979) and in other languages that, while the grammar remains fairly constant, the frequency and distribution of grammatical features changes with the circumstances under which a given speech act occurs, with the interlocutors, and with such sociolinguistic factors as relative power status, socioeconomic class, and relative degree of education. Such changes occur in the linguistic production of a given individual, in the production of identifiable sub-populations, and certainly across populations (e.g. when a native speaker of English interacts with a non-native speaker, and certainly when two non-native speakers interact). Pragmatic issues are virtually never discussed in even the most sophisticated grammars of a given language (but see the Collins CoBuild *English Usage* (1992) London: HarperCollins).

Once pedagogical grammars exist, the polity is faced with three additional non-linguistic problems: (1) how to produce and distribute the grammars to the population; (2) how to train teachers to use the new grammar books; and (3) how to update and republish and redistribute the grammar books on a continuing basis. At least two of these questions have significant economic implications; book production and distribution is expensive, and among the poorer states the capability to produce and distribute books over a vast geographic area may simply be beyond the means of the exchequer. Even if the fiscal resources exist to publish and disseminate books once, it may be quite impossible to continue to do so over time.

Lexication refers to the selection and development of an appropriate lexicon. As Haugen notes 'in principle this also involves the assignment of styles and spheres of usage for the words of the language' (1983: 271). In its initial stages, lexication may involve specifying how words are used in particular domains – e.g. in Telugu native occupations (Krishnamurti, 1985). Baldauf and Eggington (1990), in an examination of Australian Aboriginal languages, demonstrate that lexication is an ongoing procedure both in predominately orate as well as literate cultures. Studies in this area not only examine issues related to lexical development, but also those related to usage. Nichols (1988), for example, shows how many American dictionary definitions and handbooks are anchored in the cultural world of the Eurocentric-American male and urges language planners to treat fully and seriously gender and ethnic language related issues.

While dictionary development has traditionally been the domain of lexicographers who selected lexical items and wrote many of the definitions, with the aid of computers it is now possible to create computer generated dictionaries from large corpuses of a language – e.g. the *Dictionary of American Regional English* (Cassidy, 1987), the *CoBuild Dictionary* (Collins CoBuild, 1987) – or to computerise dictionaries for CD ROM computer access – e.g. *New Oxford English Dictionary* (Weiner, 1987). The *BBC English Dictionary* is another electronic database dictionary developed from a seven million word corpus of broadcast output of news, current affairs and sports broadcasts taken from the BBC in London and National Public Radio in Washington (Sinclair *et al.*, 1992). Specialist dictionaries in electronic form are now becoming available (Heather & Rossiter, 1988).

The lexicon of a local vernacular, now the national language, will inevitably be rich in resources to deal with all the traditional areas of communication, but it may not be sufficiently rich in the kind of technical terms necessary to permit modernisation. New lexicon may need to be devised. A number of different principles may be employed: (1) foreign words may be borrowed directly from other languages and either modified phonologically or not (see for example Heah Lee Hsia (1989) for the influence of English on Bahasa Malaysia); (2) words may be invented from borrowed roots – a process common enough in English naming where Latin and Greek roots have been employed to coin new works like *plastic, solar*, etc.; (3) words no longer in use in the language can be revived (e.g. *broadcast* in English, once restricted to the agricultural sector as descriptive of a way of sowing seed, but now totally taken over by the radio/television industries), or (4) new combinations of existing words can be employed to reflect new concepts (e.g. periphrasal, morpho-syntactic or calquing approaches). Certainly these are processes that have been used in Pilipino and in many other languages with varying degrees of planning.

The processes of graphisation, grammatication and lexification are all corpus planning matters. While the status decisions described above were noted as primarily political matters, the corpus planning issues discussed here are essentially linguistic issues; and whereas status planning is often accomplished by bureaucrats and politicians, corpus planning activity must be undertaken by linguists.

Elaboration

Elaboration of a language focuses on the functional development of that language. That is, once a language has been codified there is a need to continue 'the implementation of the norm to meet the functions of a modern world' (Haugen, 1983: 373). Such a modernised language must meet the wide range of cultural demands put upon it in terms of both terminology and style, from those set by the technological, intellectual, and humanistic disciplines to those associated with the everyday and popular aspects of a culture (Haugen, 1983). Haugen has defined elaboration in terms of *terminological modernisation* and *stylistic development*, but a final and emerging category needs to be added to these established aspects of functional development, that of *internationalisation*.

Elaboration is not merely a matter of increasing the richness of the vocabulary – a matter already touched upon under the topic of lexification; much more is required. For example, literacy in a language is difficult or impossible to maintain if there is nothing to read beyond the literacy materials. Government must actively encourage the publication of newspapers and magazines, of comic books and agricultural pamphlets, in the language that has been chosen. The government must encourage the establishment of radio and television broadcasting in the language. It must encourage the use of the language in the civil service, in the religious sector, indeed in every walk of life. It must encourage literary artists to produce poetry and fiction in the language. It must encourage the publication of books – a flood of books – so that those who are literate have something to read. In a cyclical manner, it must continue the work of terminological modernisation. It must encourage, through the inception of a whole range of published resources, stylistic development of the language, and it must encourage the use of the language in every possible sector so that internalisation of the language occurs throughout the population at a rate much greater than dissemination through the education sector would allow. The national language efforts in Taiwan (Republic of China) from the late 1940s to the late 1980s may serve as an example (Tse, 1986).

Elaboration is a complex and ongoing process. All languages have some mechanism for elaboration. Languages change; they take on new functions as new technologies emerge; they lose functions as older technologies are abandoned; they develop contact with new groups of speakers of other languages through immigration or through the expansion of commercial activities, and any of these changes require further elaboration of the official language. In the world in which we live language change and development is both rapid and continuing. Language communities need, therefore, to have mechanisms to modernise their language so that it continues to meet their needs. This is not, of course, a new problem. Jernudd (1971) has hypothesised that one of the functions of ceremonial meetings in Australian Aboriginal society was to discuss language and its use. The difference now, of course, is that technological change is occurring very rapidly and language must also change to meet these societal demands.

Terminological modernisation, which involves the development of new lexical items or terminology for a language, is undoubtedly one of the areas which has generated the most discussion within corpus planning. In culturally, technologically and economically changing conditions, thousands of new terms must be generated each year in a language if that language is to be fully expressive in every domain. Terminological development is a major preoccupation of language agencies/academies and specialised international organisations. For each language it must be decided how new terms will be developed. Some general strategies include borrowing a term from other contact or international languages (e.g. Cannon, 1990 [Chinese], De Vries, 1988 [Indonesian], Ennaji, 1988 [Arabic], Fisherman, 1990 [Hebrew], Kay, 1986 [Japanese], Malischewski, 1987 [Chinese], Morrow, 1987 [Japanese] and Stanlaw, 1987 [Japanese], Takashi, 1992 [Japanese]), often involving transliteration so that the term suits the host language (see the near universal use of the English term *TV*); translating the borrowed term into the host language; and innovative word building, often involving going back to indigenous root words, or reusing archaic terms which have dropped from use. Some languages, like Khmer (Jacob, 1986), seem to borrow foreign terminology quite readily. However, as Anderson (1987) notes in the case of Indonesian, the basis for the development of new terminology, especially the issue of indigenous roots versus international borrowing, can be an emotive and contentious one (also see Daoust, 1991 for French–English choice in Québec).

Stylistic development implies that a language is more than the sum of its lexical, grammatical and syntactic parts (Gee, 1992). Each language has its own discourses appropriate for each of the domains in which it is used. Stylistic development signals a recognition that, without appropriate development of linguistic style in those domains important to a language, it is not fully able to meet all the demands placed upon it. Arguing for the importance of 'bottom-up' activities in developing style, Nik Saffiah (1987: 68) has proposed that 'the cultivation process of Bahasa Malaysia needs to be accelerated and enhanced within the school environment'. By contrast, Gonzalez's (1990: 330) analysis of Pilipino-English bilingual programmess in the Philippines, shows that 'the utility of a language as a tool for learning depends on the state of its cultivation'. He concludes that educational expansion and the cultivation and expansion of a developing language must occur in tandem. Nelde (1988) argues that even in modernised languages such as Dutch there is a need to maintain and use styles in domains like science where the unnecessary use of English could undermine the vigour of the language. Razinkina (personal communication) reports a similar phenomenon in Russian, e.g. a tendency to use English technical terms even when appropriate Russian terms exist.

An area of stylistic development that is rarely discussed in the literature is the need to develop new genres as a language acquires a written form. Eggington (1992; Table 5.1, this volume), for example, argues how, among Australian Aboriginal people, a lack of awareness of what Martin (1990) has called 'power language' significantly inhibits the ability of Aboriginal people to control their own destiny. Oral language has a different set of characteristics for certain functions – characteristics which change as literacy becomes increasingly important in a given society. It is important to keep in mind that written language is not merely transcribed oral language – written language has functions that oral language does not have. This issue, which is discussed in greater detail in Chapter 5, Literacy Planning in Language-in-Education Planning (p. 146), suggests that some genres (e.g. here, those involved in decision making, negotiation, and contract making) may differ from oral language situations to written language situations. Stylistic development must take into consideration the development of appropriate rhetorical structures to deal with such changes as well as with grammatical and lexical matters.

A critical aspect of stylistic development is the use of the language for media and cultural expression. While such development is often thought of as the end product of the language planning process, Gonzalez (1990: 328) argues that:

> In developing a post-colonial indigenous language as the national language and as the language of scholarly discourse to develop special registers for classroom use, implementation should not start at the bottom, in the primary school, but at the tertiary level, at the university, where a creative minority of scholars who are both linguistically versatile and knowledgeable in their fields can do the necessary pioneering work in translation and production of research in Pilipino so as to be able to create an intellectual variety of the language.

In this context it can be argued that the systematic building up of language skills through a planned programme of language development will not be successful unless there are strong and vigorous models of language use in 'high' status language domains such as politics, technology and culture. Thus, one of the questions that may be asked is, 'In what language is the poetry or the prose fiction of the nation being written: the national or local language or the ex-colonial or world language?' As an example of the issues being raised Cruz (1986) summarises aspects of this debate for the Philippines where there has been considerable discussion about writing in a vernacular language or Tagalog or in English. While many would argue that the choice of language is one of the distinguishing characteristics of the nationalist movement in Philippine literature and is a manifestation of the writer's social consciousness, the use of English can be seen in other contexts, besides one that alienates the writer from the people. Cruz (1986: 167) argues that bilingual Filipino writers of poetry use English 'for two main reasons: to capture certain realities not within the lexical (taken as poetic diction) capabilities of Tagalog, and to exploit the musical qualities of the foreign language'. Tagalog, on the other hand, better expresses the social and political realities of the Filipino world (cf. Tinio, 1990; also see Kaplan, 1993b). However, the struggle to build a continuing literary tradition in 'modernising' languages, where all realities need to be able to be expressed, is an ongoing one.

Internationalisation can be seen as a particular type of language spread which affects the corpus of a language. As a language becomes a medium of international communication, rather than just a national or intranational standard, standardisation problems arise which parallel each of the categories previously discussed. These problems of standardisation are somewhat different in regional or international contexts – e.g. in Scandinavia (Loman, 1988) or for Arabic (Mitchell, 1985). Furthermore, as discourse and pragmatic strategies do not carry over entirely across cultures, despite the use of a shared linguistic medium, communication problems may arise (Smith, 1987). The issue has been summarised by Mauranen in a contractive textlinguistic study of Finnish and English:

. . . [writers] differ in some of their culturally determined rhetorical practices, and these differences manifest themselves in typical textual features. *The writers seem not to be aware of these textual features, or underlying rhetorical practices.* This lack of awareness is in part due to the fact that textlinguistic features have not been the concern of traditional language teaching in schools. Sometimes text strategies are taught for the mother tongue, but rarely if ever for foreign languages separately. Such phenomena have therefore not been brought to the attention of writers struggling with writing . . . Nevertheless, these sometimes subtle differences between writing cultures, often precisely because they are subtle and not commonly observable to the non-linguist, tend to put . . . [various] native language [writers] at a rhetorical disadvantage in the eyes of [other language] readers . . . . This disadvantage is more than a difference in cultural tastes, since it may not only strike readers as lack of rhetorical elegance, but as lack of coherent writing or even thinking, which can seriously affect the credibility of non-native writers. (1993: 1–2; emphasis added)

In this regard the role of English as an international language (Görlich, 1988) and the related development of varieties of Englishes (Kachru, 1988, 1996) has generated a lot of corpus planning interest. Some of the specific issues raised, and related topics previously discussed, include: grammatication (Greenbaum, 1986, 1988), lexication (Lowenberg, 1986; Goke-Pariola, 1987; Pemagbi, 1989), terminology (Stanlaw, 1987; Zhou & Feng, 1987), and stylistic development (Widdowson, 1988).

There is also a growing literature in English which reflects both the internationalisation of English and at the same time its localisation. Indigenous authors in the Pacific, in South Asia and Africa are writing in English, but with the view that:

the English language will be able to carry the weight of my African experience. But it will have to be a new English, still in full communication with its ancestral home but altered to suit its new African surroundings. (Achebe, 1965, cited in Thumboo, 1986: 253)

As Thumboo (1986: 252) says, the question of which language to create in, when there are a number available, has several aspects. However, for most individuals 'languages choose their writers, not writers their languages' as 'a decision to write creatively generally forms after one has acquired an inwardness in a language.' Thus, it is how a language like English, or any other international language, is used and shaped by the author to reflect the native language and culture that is important. As an example, Thumboo (1986: 263), through a detailed analysis of Okara's *The Voice*, 'demonstrates the virtually limitless possibilities offered by English, thus suggesting to writers of new literatures that it can be reshaped and given a local habitation and a name.'

Increasingly, issues of stylistic development and internationalisation are coming together in many polities (i.e. the practical need to learn English, but in a culturally suitable manner). This mixing of issues raises questions of 'What is the relationship of literature to language and culture?' (e.g. Hasan, 1996), and 'What are the implications for what English literature will be taught in schools?' In Malaysia, for example, Zawiah Yahaya (1996) argues that there is a need for a change in methodology and perspectives so as to reinterpret the English canon based on the Malaysian nation building context. Koh Tai Ann suggests that the role of English literature teaching in Singaporian schools needs to be re-evaluated as 'a critical disjunction exists between national language policies and the teaching profession's own stated aims for the teaching of literature' (1996: 27). Thus, while English is being internationalised, there is increasing pressure in schools for it to contribute to local cultural and national development.

Finally, despite (or perhaps because of) this internationalisation of English (and Arabic, French, German, Mandarin, Portuguese, Spanish), there are those who believe the continued development of constructed or planned languages is an important and more culturally neutral way to meet the growing international communication needs that have been discussed (Dasgupta, 1987; also Ashby, 1985; Large, 1988; Harry, 1989; Tonkin, 1987).

Corpus planning summary

A number of trends have emerged from this review of the corpus planning literature. First, the linguistic tension between traditional usage and modernisation of language referenced by Fishman (1983) continues as does the necessity for corpus planners to keep attuned to their public yet provide sound language models. However, there does seem to be a growing awareness that corpus planning does not deal solely with linguistic issues. This is reflected by the fact that in many instances it is difficult to separate corpus from status planning issues in a particular language so as to fit them neatly into Haugen's model. Ultimately, corpus planning operates in real-world contexts in conjunction with social, historical, cultural and political forces. Second, while terminology remains a major focus of interest, the spread of 'Englishes', 'Spanishes' and 'Frenches' is a growing area of concern for corpus planning. Developments in both of these areas are central to information access and dissemination which is necessary to the functioning of modern societies. Third, computers are beginning to make their mark on corpus planning, especially in the development of dictionaries. Each of these trends suggests that a narrow preoccupation with linguistic skills is not, in and of itself, a sufficient basis for corpus planning, and that a critical re-evaluation of the modernist assumptions of language planning is beginning to occur.

What should be clear from this discussion, however, is that corpus and status planning changes cannot be carried out in isolation; the two systems are completely interdependent. It should also be clear that a planning activity does not necessarily start conveniently at the beginning; on the contrary, states at various stages of development – both linguistic and economic – can enter into the planning paradigm at any point. The point at which a state enters into a planning mode will determine which are the first stages.

New Zealand, for example, only recently entered into a planning mode. The country has only two official languages: English and Maori. English is well along in development; Maori less so. Nevertheless, New Zealand had to be concerned about the allocation of norms. Both English and Maori have established orthographic systems, so graphisation has not been a problem, but the languages are uneven in terms of grammatication and lexification. The dissemination of English through the educational structure is well developed, but the dissemination of Maori is still at a relatively primitive stage. English, of course, enjoys broad elaboration across the English-speaking world, but Maori is less elaborated than English; while Maori has a rich oral tradition, the development of a written literature in Maori is still in need of strong support and encouragement. Thus, New Zealand entered into the planning process with its two primary languages at different states of development. But in addition to the two primary languages, there are a number of other languages spoken by segments of the New Zealand population which must be accounted for in the planning process (Kaplan, 1993a, 1993b; Peddie, 1991a, 1991b, 1996; Waite, 1992).

It should be clear from Haugen's model and from the New Zealand example that although for discussion purposes the 2 × 2 matrix suggested by Haugen (Figure 2.1) is conceptually very useful, in reality all the stages suggested in the model may occur simultaneously in a complex reticulated structure. Planning involves both the language itself and the situation in which the language will be/is being used, and the two segments of the planning paradigm in practice cannot be separated; it is inevitably the case that changes in the language affect the sectors/registers in which the language is being/can be used, and these changes in turn define in a new way the language situation. It should also be clear that planning cannot occur in some cleverly isolated segment of the polity; it must occur across all sectors of the state, but this point will be discussed in greater detail in a later section of this volume.

Levels of Language Planning

As indicated in Chapter 1, language planning occurs in a number of contexts and at a number of levels. The impact of any particular language plan depends on the level or context in which the plan is developed and implemented. In the two following sections we examine two ways of looking at this issue as part of an overall framework.

An ideal typology of language planning

Haarmann (1990) has suggested a third range of language planning activities to complement the status planning and corpus planning introduced in Haugen's model. He argues that *prestige planning* represents a separate range of activities. Whereas corpus and status planning are productive activities, prestige planning is a receptive or value function which influences how corpus and status planning activities are acted upon by *actors* and received by *people* (to use Cooper's terms, following section). As Table 2.2 suggests, prestige planning is very much related to the four language planning contexts examined in Chapter 1 (Table 1.1).

Haarmann's typology is useful in that it reinforces the notion that planning occurs at different levels and for a variety of purposes. He argues that these levels (i.e. governmental activities, activities of agencies, group activities and activities of individuals) represent a differential prestige or efficiency of organisational impact levels and that this may affect the success of the language plan. The following examples of ranges of language planning and language cultivation are taken from Haarmann (1990: 120–1, with some added examples) and provide some concrete settings which

Table 2.2 An ideal typology of language cultivation and language planning (Haarmann, 1990: 120–1)[1]

	Ranges of language planning		Ranges of language cultivation	
	Activities of government	Activities of agencies	Activities of groups	Activities of individuals
Status planning	4.1	3.1	2.1	1.1
	↑	↑	↑	↑
Prestige planning	official promotion	institutional promotion	pressure group promotion	individual promotion
	↓	↓	↓	↓
Corpus planning	4.2	3.2	2.2	1.2

Level 4	Level 3	Level 2	Level 1

◄──►

Maximum   Efficiency in terms of the organisational impact   Minimum

1. The table has been reoriented and slightly reworded to be consistent with the terminology used in this book.

illustrate the impact of promotional activity on status and corpus planning:

1.1 the effort made by the Protestant bishop Mikael Agricola in the sixteenth century to promote the Finnish language as a medium of instruction at school (see Haarman, 1974: 40 ff.); the effort by Senator S.I. Hayakawa to make English the official language of the US;

1.2 the efforts made by J.H. Campe, J.G. Fichte, E.M. Arndt and others in connection with language purism (German Sprachreinigung) in Germany (see Kirkness, 1975); the efforts by G.B. Shaw to reform English spelling (see endnote 2);

2.1 the activities of the Gaelic League since 1893 to promote the maintenance of Irish as a mother tongue and colloquial variety (see Ó hAilin 1969: 91 ff.); the activities of the Federation of Aboriginal and Torres Strait Islander Languages to promote language revival, maintenance and survival of aboriginal and Torres Strait Islander Languages in Australia (Baldauf, 1995a; McKay, 1996).

2.2 the attempts to elaborate a written standard for modern Occitan, made by writers and philologists in the movement of the *Félibrige* since its foundation in 1854 (see Kremnitz, 1974: 178 ff.); the efforts of the Maori Language Commission to publish a 'standard' Maori dictionary;

3.1 the activities to stabilise the functions of the two language varieties *nynorsk* and *bokmål* in Norway (see Haugen, 1966); the efforts of the *'loi Toubon'* to purify French (see Chapter 10, Introduction);

3.2 the efforts to provide norms for the terminological modernisation of national languages in Nordic countries (see Språk i Norden, 1986); the creation of new lexical items in Indonesian (Alisjahbana, 1984; Vikør, 1993) and Malay (Omar, 1984);

4.1 governmental legislation concerning the status of French, Dutch, and German in Belgium (see Falch, 1973: 9 ff., 125 ff.); the constitution of Vanuatu stating the national language is Bislama (Thomas, 1990);

4.2 the elaboration of writing systems (alphabets) for new standard languages in the Soviet Union since the 1920s (see Isaev, 1979), or more recently for *minority minzu* in China (Harrell, 1993).

While these examples for each of the eight individual types (status planning by corpus planning by four prestige levels) are useful illustrations, in many language planning situations, the success of the plan and its implementation may depend on multiple impacts, and the boundaries between language prestige levels is often not clear.

Macro vs. micro language planning

Another way of looking at the problem of context or levels is not to examine language problems in terms of the scale of the activity and its intended impact. Both large- and small-scale activities may be prestigious (or not) and may have (or fail to have) the desired impact on their particular language planning situation. However, most general frameworks (i.e. Haugen's corpus vs. status planning model and Cooper's accounting scheme) and much of the exemplary literature cited to support them, suggest that language planning is a large-scale activity, i.e. it occurs mainly at the macro level. However, language planning actually occurs at many different levels, although the micro levels are not well documented in the literature, perhaps because they are not seen to be as prestigious. For large-scale planning to meet popular needs, and indeed for it to succeed at all, it must have effect across all levels of language and society. Williams (1994: 102) illustrates this clearly in his listing of factors which promote the anglicisation of Wales in the modern period (Table 2.3), examining as he does the macro, meso and micro levels of planning impact.

On the other hand, some language policies have much more limited goals and may affect only micro policy and planning, perhaps in a single company or institution. Students of language planning often remark after reading the language planning literature that this is all very interesting, but they can't really see themselves planning for language change in China, Russia, Namibia or Brazil. However, as many people are beginning to realise, although societal language planning is very interesting, micro examples of language planning occur around us every day and for these to be successful many of the same ideas and skills need to be utilised to make them work effectively (see, e.g. Kuo & Jernudd, 1993 for Singapore; Applying the macro to the micro situations on pp. 117–118, and economic examples on pp. 187–189, both this volume).

An Accounting Scheme for Language Planning

Another approach to the development of an overall framework for language planning is that taken by Cooper (1989). He evaluated four frameworks from other disciplines as the basis for developing a process framework for language planning. To develop this framework (Table 2.4), he considered:

> language planning as, in turn: (1) the management of innovation; (2) an instance of marketing; (3) a tool in the acquisition and maintenance of power; and (4) an instance of decision making. (1989: 58)

From this emerges an accounting scheme with eight components:

> (i) What *actors*, (ii) attempt to influence what *behaviors*, (iii) of which

Table 2.3 Factors promoting the anglicisation of Wales in the modern period (Williams, 1994: 102)

Policy	Economy	Culture/society
Macro		
The Edwardian conquest. State integration via theActs of Union 1536 and 1542. Establishment of state church. Parliamentary representation after the Reform Act 1867. Expansion of suffrage. Education Act 1870. Warfare and conscription.	Land transfer. Early urbanisation. Agricultural depression. Promotion of urban bourgeoisie. Urbanisation and industrialisation. Integration into the world economy. Welsh out-migration and regional change. Non-Welsh immigration to selected areas.	Alien nobility. Outlawing Welsh language. Estrangement of the gentry. Translation of Bible, 1588. Educational reform and value reorientation. Inter-generational language loss.
Meso		
Local government reforms. Political radicalism. Chartism, party political electoral representation.	Developing bureaucracy and economic accountability. Trade unionism. Transport and communication. Infrastructural improvements. Print capitalism.	Denominational religious diversity. Popular mass entertainment. Social movements. Adult education.
Micro		
Voter participation. Political party membership. British identification. State support in wartime. Dependency upon state agencies. Educational opportunities through the medium of English.	Entering wage economy. Residential mobility. Socioeconomic and class consciousness. Individual material advances. Benefits of welfare state policies.	Inter-ethnic marriage patterns. Language switching and language loss. Increased bilingualism. Secularisation and reorientation of value system. Passive receptive entertainment.

Figure 2.4 An accounting scheme for the study of language planning (Cooper, 1989: 98)

I   What *actors* (e.g. formal elites, influentials, counterelites, non-elite policy implementers)

II   attempt to influence what *behaviors*

    A. structural (linguistic) properties of planned behavior (e.g. homogeneity, similarity)

    B. purposes/functions for which planned behavior is to be used

    C. desired level of adoption (awareness, evaluation, proficiency, usage)

III   of which *people*

    A. type of target (e.g. individuals v. organisations, primary v. intermediary)

    B. opportunity of target to learn planned behavior

    C. incentives of target to learn/use planned behavior

    D. incentives of target to reject planned behavior

IV   for what *ends*

    A. overt (language related behaviors)

    B. latent (non-language related behaviors, the satisfaction of interests)

V   under what *conditions*

    A. situational (events, transient conditions)

    B. structural

        1. political

        2. economic

        3. social/demographic/ecological

    C. cultural

        1. regime norms

        2. cultural norms

        3. socialisation of authorities

    D. environmental (influences from outside the system)

    E. informational (data required for a good decision)

VI   by what *means* (e.g. authority, force, promotion, persuasion)

VII   through what *decision making process* (decision rules)

    A. formulation of problem/goal

    B. formulation of means

VIII with what *effect*

---

people, (iv) for what *ends*, (v) under what *conditions*, (vi) by what *means*, (vii) through what *decision making process*, (viii) with what *effect*. (1989: 98)

Each of these components of the framework is now briefly examined.

(i) The *actors* or traditional participants in language policy and planning have come from what Kaplan (1989) refers to as 'top-down' language planning situations. These are people with power and authority who make language related decisions for groups, often with little or no consultation with the ultimate language learners and users. Exactly who these planners are is often left in general terms. In their introduction to the classic volume on language planning, Rubin and Jernudd (1971: xvi) put it this way:

> As a discipline, language planning requires the mobilization of a great variety of disciplines because it implies the channeling of problems and values to and through some decision-making administrative structure.

In general language planning has been portrayed as being done (note that the use of the passive here leaves ambiguous who is doing) from within an objective, ideologically neutral and technological perspective in which planners matter little – as long as they have the technical expertise required. Baldauf (1982) was one of the first to point out explicitly that who the planners were was potentially an important variable in the language policy and planning situation.

A number of authors (Luke *et al.*, 1990; Mey, 1989; Watson-Gegeo & Gegeo, 1995) have questioned the role of traditional language planners or *actors* and have argued for the inclusion of a broader participation base, i.e. those *people* for whom language is being planned should have a say in its actual planning and implementation. Kaplan (1989) has described this as 'bottom-up' language planning. The use of sociolinguistic survey techniques (see Chapter 4) or other such methods means that traditional planners have the means to collect information about the impact of potential planned language changes at the macro level. Whether there is the political and social will to do so, is another matter.

(ii) Language policy and planning is meant to influence language *behaviours* in a number of ways including the structural, the purpose or functional and the desired level of adoption. For example, the issue of sexist language usage in English has brought about structural changes in the linguistic nature of English. Over the last 20 years, it has become inappropriate to use gendered pronouns (she, he) or nouns (actress, chairman) and non-gendered substitutes have entered the language instead (i.e. they for he/she; actor regardless of gender; chair or chairperson instead of chairman). Initially, the purpose or function of this usage came from feminist writings which argued English constructed a male gender-biased world and the changed usage first appeared in professional speech and writing. The desired level of adoption was, however, universal and the change is gradually becoming the norm in all written English and increasingly in speech (see Pauwels, in press).

(iii) Which *people* are to be the targets of planned language change and what are their opportunities, incentives or disincentives for making the required language changes? Unfortunately, the incentives for making the required language change are often negative. In Wales, during the late nineteenth and early twentieth centuries (following the Education Act of 1870), Welsh children were not only required to learn English in school, but were prohibited from speaking Welsh at school. Children who, for whatever reason used Welsh, were punished with the 'Welsh Not'. Offending children were required to wear a board suspended on a thong around their necks. The message on the board was 'Welsh Not'. The child wore the board until another offender relieved him/her of the burden. Thus, the objective was not to speak Welsh; the incentive was a rather humiliating punishment. The disincentive might have been Welsh ethnic pride, but it was more likely to be childish unconsciousness, carelessness or even peer pressure. Indeed, the use of Welsh might have been an attempt to circumvent ignorance of the appropriate English structure. Similar practices occurred in the US in the education of Native American children, in Australia in the education of Aboriginal children, and in New Zealand in the education of Maori children.

(iv) The *ends* or goals for which language planning is undertaken can be quite varied. These goals are the focus of the next chapter and include language purification, language regenesis, language reform, language standardisation, language spread, lexical development, terminological unification, stylistic simplification, interlingual communication, language maintenance and auxiliary-code standardisation. Cooper points out that such ends can be overt, to change language related behaviours, or latent, to change non-language related behaviour. The requirement to use 'Bahasa Melayu' in Malaysia, while being about having a common language for communication also has the purpose of building common understandings so as to defuse racial and other tensions within the society.

(v) The *conditions* under which language change is to occur are quite varied. Cooper suggests that situational, structural (political, economic and social/demographic/ecological), cultural, environmental and informational conditions may impact on any particular language plan. The nature and effect of such conditions will become more evident when we look at some case studies in Part 3 of this volume.

(vi) The *means* (e.g. authority, force, promotion, persuasion) by which language planning decisions are introduced vary from situation to situation. As Haarmann's (1990) prestige planning concept suggests, there is always some authority behind any language planning decision, and such authority may be at different levels (also see Chapter 7 of this volume).

(vii) The *decision-making process* refers to the decision rules for the proposed language plan, including both the formulation of the problem/goal and the formulation of the means to reach that goal. As the incentives to achieve target behaviour were often negative, the decision-making processes were often removed from the control of those who were most affected. In New Zealand, for example, decisions regarding which languages would be taught in schools and when and for how long they would be taught, who would teach them to whom, how they would be taught, and how appropriate levels of achievement would be assessed are, at the present time, almost exclusively in the hands of the Minister of Education. Although in some instances the Minister may consult with teachers, teachers are substantially removed from the process. Students are entirely excluded from the decision-making process. The grounds on which decisions are made by the Minister are undoubtedly in part political; additionally, they may be based on theoretical notions of what may be expected to work. The Minister is, in fact, distantly removed from the environment in which the decisions will be implemented.

The New Zealand case is not exceptional. In Mexico, for example, decisions regarding issues pertaining to indigenous language education are made in the capital city. Implementation of the decisions is distantly removed from the decision-making site; instructions for implementation pass through many hands before they arrive in the actual schools in geographically distant provinces, and many layers of bureaucrats interpret those instructions along the way. Any bureaucrat opposed to the decision can delay implementation indefinitely simply by failing to act (Pattey-Chavez, 1989, 1994).

(viii) The *effects* of any particular language planning project as discussed in the previous chapter are not always easy to determine, because it is hard to know what would have happened if language planning had not occurred. In Part 3 of this volume, we look at some specific issues and case studies and in that context the effects of planning.

Summary

In this chapter we have examined Haugen's model for language planning as one way of visualising the scope and sequence of the language planning process. We have done this by examining corpus planning and status planning with their respective focus on language and society. We have then examined the issue of micro and macro planning, noting that much more attention has been paid to the latter than the former. Finally, we have looked at who traditionally is included in and excluded from language planning, although this will become more evident as instances of language planning are examined throughout the book. These first two chapters, then, provide an overview of the field and the major issues facing the discipline. They also provide some terminology and an initial framework with which we can examine language planning in practice.

Notes
1. Some of the material in this section first appeared in Baldauf (1990b).
2. ' . . . English has some impossible characteristics. The *th* is famously difficult for foreigners who find sentences like 'What's this?' hard to pronounce. There are some very rare and difficult vowels: The vowel sound in *bird* and *nurse* occurs in virtually no other language. There are no fewer than 13 spellings for *sh*: *shoe, sugar, issue, mansion, nation, suspicion, ocean, conscious, chaperon, schist, fuchsia* and *pshaw*. An old bit of doggerel for foreign students advises:

   > Beware of *heard*, a dreadful word
   > That looks like *beard* and sounds like *bird*,
   > And *dead*: It's said like *bed*, not *bead* –
   > For goodness sake, don't call it *deed*!

   Various distinguished minds have grappled with this problem. The more spoken English seemed standardised on the air, the greater seemed the need for a simplified spelling system. Such proposals were often heard during the inter-war years. In 1930, a Swedish philologist, R.E. Zachrisson, proposed an international language, essentially English to be called *Anglic*. For all its logic, its drawbacks can be easily demonstrated in the Anglic version of a famous sentence: *Forscor and sevn yeerz agoe our faadherz braut forth on this continent a nuw naeshon, konseeved in liberti* . . . . In 1940 the **British Simplified Spelling Society** mounted a campaign for New Spelling and lobbied hard for government approval. Perhaps the most famous champion of the simplified spelling was **George Bernard Shaw** who bequeathed a part of his large fortune to the cause of a more regular English spelling . . . ' (Emphasis added. McCrum *et al.*, 1986: 46–47)

3 Language Planning Goals

In Chapter 2 three frameworks were examined which provided an overview of the language planning process. Having developed an understanding of the process within which language planners work, it is now appropriate to examine the goals or *ends* to which language planning is put. Language planning can be engaged in for a wide variety of objectives or general goals, and language planners (*actors*) develop plans to work toward those goals. In this chapter we examine some of these macro level goals and briefly provide some examples of each. However, it needs to be recognised that language planning is seldom done with a single goal in mind (e.g. the major goal of language planners in Québec may have been French language maintenance, but purification and language spread were minor goals). It may be based on contradictory goals – e.g. the development and promotion of Bahasa Indonesia as a national language (language spread) while at the same time supporting local language rights (language maintenance). As Haarmann (1990: 123) has pointed out:

> In practical work it is hardly possible to reach a level where all of the relations would be in balance. Most inconsistencies in practical language planning result from conflicts of interest. It is a well-known fact that the objectives of language planning are often incompatible.

Furthermore, many of these goals are carried out to reach rather abstract purposes, which are related to national policy goals in a more general sense. In Chapters 5 and 6 three of these major language planning goals are examined: (1) language-in-education planning; (2) language-in-education literacy planning; and (3) the economics of language. These are general goals with language foci that modern and modernising societies seek to attain and which have a direct impact on individuals within those societies.

Goals of Language Planning

A number of authors (Annamalai & Rubin, 1980; Bentahila & Davies, 1993; Eastman, 1983; Jahr, 1993; Kaplan, 1990a; Karam, 1974; Nahir, 1984; Paulston, Pow & Connerty, 1993) have discussed the types of the goals involved in language planning. While the language planning processes can be characterised by the four cells in Haugen's model (i.e. selection, codification, implementation and elaboration, see Table 2.1), and that framework can be said to define a process for how language planning may be carried out, it doesn't really address the question of 'What goal(s) this process is intended to accomplish?' Haarmann's (1990) typology adds the dimension of prestige planning, but this still does not address the question of 'for what purpose?' Finally, while Cooper's (1989) accounting scheme asks most of the relevant general questions (i.e. what actors, what behaviours, which people, for what ends, under what conditions, by what means and through what decision-making process) needed in a goals oriented approach, most language planning is actually done to meet specific types of goals. Jahr suggests language planning may have as its general goal the reduction of language conflict, but notes that the 'language planning activity may itself ultimately be the cause of serious problems as well as major conflicts' (1993: 1).

Based on published studies of an analysis of language planning agency activity, Nahir (1984) has suggested 11 specific goals or functions, some of which have sub-categories, which can be related to the language planning practice. Table 3.1 lists these and some related goals suggested by other authors. The table provides an overview of some of the types of objectives, goals and functions to be found in language planning. In the following sections, each of those macro level goals is discussed, recognising that in many actual instances planning agencies and planners may be working toward several of these goals simultaneously.

Language purification

Language purification (e.g. Jernudd & Shapiro, 1989) has as its focus maintaining the linguistic consistency and standards of a language, and can be thought of in two senses. First, there is *external* purification where attempts are made to remove and protect the language from foreign influences. Japanese went through this process after World War I, while the French Academy has since its founding been continually engaged in this process (Thody, 1995). The process often centres around the development of prescriptive grammars and dictionaries aimed at reducing the rate of borrowing and the prohibition of certain foreign usages. External purification is often based on the fear that a language may be swamped by a foreign language (currently predominantly English), or that indiscriminant borrowing may undermine spelling and grammatical regularity (Alisjahbana, 1984; Omar, 1984).

Second, *internal purification* is related to the enforcement of standards of correct usage within the language. As the letters to the editor in many newspapers indicate, commenting as they do on language usage, the concern about internal standards is widespread. However, more formal mechanisms also exist. Indirectly, the BBC has served the function of setting internal standards for spoken British English for many years, but

Table 3.1 A summary of language planning goals

Macro level[1]	Alternative formulations	Examples
Language purification		
External purification		
Internal purification		French[5]
Language revival	Language revival[3]	Hebrew[5]
	Restoration	
	Transformation	
	Language regenesis[4]	
	Language revival	
	Revitalisation	
	Reversal	
Language reform		Turkish[5]
Language standardisation	Spelling and script standardisation[2]	Swahili[5]
Language spread		
Lexical modernisation	Term planning[2]	Swedish[5]
Terminological unification	Discourse planning[2]	
Stylistic simplification		
Interlingual communication		
Worldwide IC		
Auxiliary languages		
English LWC		
Regional IC	Regional identity[2]	
Regional LWC	National identity[2]	
Cognate languages IC		
Language maintenance		
Dominant LM		
Ethnic LM		
Auxiliary code standardisation		

Meso level planning for[2]
Administration: Training and certification of officials and professionals
Administration: Legal provisions for use
The legal domain
Education equity: Pedagogical issues
Education equity: Language rights/identity
Education elite formation/control
Mass communication
Educational equity: Language handicap[6]
Social equity: Minority Language access[6]
Interlanguage translation: Training for professions, business, law, etc.[6]

1. Nahir (1984). 2. Annamalai & Rubin (1980). 3. Bentahila & Davies (1993). 4. Paulson *et al.* (1993).
5. Eastman (1983). 6. This volume

style guides, non-sexist language guides and language learning columns in the press (e.g. in Japan, Israel, Sweden, Malaysia and Poland) are also means of internal purification. In the Australian context, the issuing of the *Macquarie Dictionary*, a dictionary of Australian English, serves as a guide to both external and internal purification, defining as it does acceptable Australian English. Although there is no legal enforcement, the dictionary, by setting the standard for, and a reference to, correct Australian English, clearly sets out to exclude specifically British, American, migrant and Aboriginal English usage. The *Oxford English Dictionary* in England and the *Webster's Dictionary* in the United States have a similar purpose.

Language revival

An analysis of the process of language revival as a language planning goal is more complex than it first appears. Paulston *et al.*, (1993) argue the area should be reconceptualised as *language regenesis*, comprising three sub-categories: language revival, language revitalisation and language reversal. Bentahila and Davies (1993), on the other hand, suggest language revival consists of efforts at restoration (backward looking) or transformation (forward looking). As language revival is the term in common usage, we have continued to use it to represent the general phenomenon, but examine it in terms of language restoration, language revitalisation (or transformation) and language reversal.

Language revival occurs, as the name suggests, in a situation where a language has either entirely died off or is on the verge of dying off. The reasons for language death are varied and complex (see Chapter 10), but in simple terms languages die because the number of speakers diminishes to extinction. Although the rate of language death is increasing (Mühlhäusler, 1995b: Chapter 10), the phenomenon is a fairly common one, particularly in reference to so-called 'minority' languages. It may occur when a community of speakers of one language is embedded within a larger community using another language; if both languages can serve all of the same functions and domains, then minority speakers are often drawn to the majority language because it offers greater access to material rewards, employment and economic opportunities. It may also be that there is status to be gained by linguistic and cultural association with the majority group. In addition, in urbanisation situations, where minority individuals are drawn into urban centres – essentially for the same reasons of employment and economic reward – minorities are required to learn and use the majority language. Over time these conditions lead to an environment in which the young have no incentive, and perhaps little opportunity, to learn the minority language. As a consequence, in three or four generations, the minority language may have no native speakers, or those who are able to speak the language may be only able to use it in a restricted set of registers – e.g. registers limited to religious practice or to some other

Lg revival

relatively restricted situation. There may also be official restrictions about how and where a language can be used and these may play a role in reducing language vitality or in language death.

There are many examples of languages which are dying or have died. There is ample evidence, for example, that the number of Native American (Boseker, 1994; Shonerd, 1990) or of Aboriginal Australian (e.g. Baldauf, 1995a; McKay, 1996; Fesl, 1982, 1987) languages is shrinking very rapidly. Dixon (1989: 30) states that 'every Aboriginal language in Australia is currently at risk'. Crocombe (1989: 47) estimates that of the 1200 or more languages of the Pacific, only about 12 will survive. Unless the linguistic ecology can be changed to be more supportive of endangered languages, informed estimates suggest that 90% of all languages worldwide could disappear within a couple of generations (Mühlhäusler, 1995c).

Languages such as Ainu in Japan (see Coulmas, 1989a; DeChicchis, 1995) or the language of the aboriginal people of Taiwan (Kaplan & Tse, 1982), are on the verge of extinction because the linguistic ecology necessary to support these languages no longer exists. Ainu has been replaced across a variety of registers by Japanese, while the language of the aboriginal people of Taiwan is being threatened by Taiwanese (Tai-yü) and Mandarin (Young, 1988; Tse, 1982). There are, however, also illustrations of languages which have been revived through language restoration, language revitalisation (or transformation) and language reversal.

The most dramatic case of *language restoration*, the bringing back to life of a dead language, is undoubtedly that of Hebrew (e.g. Dagut, 1985; Nahir, 1988; Spolsky, 1995; cf. Fellman, 1993), where a language which had been used only as the ritual language of Judaism has become the national language of Israel. This symbolic political act upon independence in 1948 has resulted in an enormous effort to turn Hebrew into a modern language capable of dealing not only with the registers of science and technology, but also with the domains of government and politics, business and economics and even such areas as auto mechanics. The effort has required not only a substantial infusion of funds and extensive linguistic work to modify and extend the lexicon, morphology and grammar, but has implied the willingness of the people living in the state of Israel, a polyglot population, to accept Hebrew as the national language and to use it in the variety of domains in which it is now available (Rabin, 1976; Fisherman, 1990). However, not all of these efforts have been successful. For example, auto mechanics resisted learning the proposed Hebrew lexicon since a perfectly good English and German one was already in wide distribution, and consequently rejected the carefully devised Hebrew terminology (Alloni-Fainberg, 1974).

Language revitalisation refers to the new-found vigour of an endangered language still in use. There are a variety of other illustrations of languages which have been revitalised or in which revitalisation efforts are under way. Interesting illustrations involve such languages as Navajo in the United States (Leap, 1975, 1983; St. Clair & Leap, 1982) or Maori in New Zealand (Benton, 1980; Spolsky, 1995), but there are other examples among the surviving languages of the Aboriginal people of Australia (Eggington, 1992) and the Native American people in the United States (Grenoble & Whaley, 1996). Other illustrative cases can be found in Europe: Finnish in the eighteenth century (Paulston et al., 1993), Breton (Trimm, 1973, 1980, 1982), Catalan (Neugaard, 1995), Welsh (Ball, 1988), Irish (Ó Baoill, 1988; Ó Laoire, 1995) and Scots Gaelic (Dorian, 1981; Withers, 1988). There are also interesting examples in Latin America among the various groups of Indios – for example, in Mexico (cf., Heath, 1972; Patthey, 1989) or for Quechua in the Andes (Hornberger & King, 1996). Not all of these efforts have been successful, but those that have had some success seem to have nationalism as an important feature of the revitalisation effort. However, as Bentahila and Davies (1993: 355) point out, success need not be an all-or-nothing approach. They note that 'while revivalists often dream of restoration, they are far more likely to succeed in achieving a measure of transformation'.

For language revitalisation or transformation to occur, an extraordinary effort is required on the part of the affected language community as well as on the part of the dominant community in which the minority is embedded. The United States Bureau of Indian Affairs has spent large quantities of money on the revival of Navajo, and the New Zealand government has comparably invested in the revival of Maori. But, in addition to the funds required, the members of those communities have had to provide the stimulus to initiate revitalisation and the energy to carry it forward. Without such dedication to a language – and culture – by its speakers and key advocates, language revitalisation is unlikely to succeed.

Language reversal implies the turning around of the existing trends in language usage, with a focus on the circumstances in which one language in a state begins to be used more prominently (Paulston et al., 1993). Language reversal may have a *legal* basis, as with Catalan, which attained official status in 1984, having previously been technically illegal; may be a *reversal of shift*, as with Maori, which has moved from a decline in use to an increase in use; or may be a *rebound of an exoglossic language*, as in Singapore and Malaysia, where the colonial language, English, is once again becoming more important after a period of decline.

Language reform

Language reform occurs in situations where a language has sufficient vitality but is not able to deal adequately with domains and registers that are new to the culture. Generally, this occurs over a brief period and involves changes in or simplification of orthography, spelling, lexicon or grammar with the aim of facilitating language use. While it can be argued that language reform is a process that all languages undergo, rapidly expanding technology has placed the greatest strain on traditional languages for reform. Perhaps the most often quoted example of language reform occurred in Turkey in the 1920s, when Kemal Atatürk successfully changed the writing system to a romanised one, removed many of the Persian influences in the language and borrowed terminology from European languages to make modernisation possible (Doğançay-Aktuna, 1995; Gallagher, 1971; Eastman 1983). The *Pin Yin* writing system for Chinese, the attempt to romanise Hebrew (Rabin, 1971) and the romanisation of Vietnamese (Lo Bianco, forthcoming) are other examples of romanisation for script reform.

The Turkish example suggests that language reform may take many shapes. While Hebrew is normally associated with language revival (restoration), it was also the subject of spelling reform in the 1960s (Rabin, 1971, 1976). Malaysia and Indonesia introduced spelling reforms in 1972 to standardise the spelling – and aspects of grammar and lexis – between these dialects of Indonesian/Malay (Alisjahbana, 1984; Omar, 1975; Vikør, 1993). In its efforts to increase literacy, the People's Republic of China has for most of this century (both before the events of 1948 and subsequently – the current effort being dated roughly from 1911) been engaged in a massive effort to revise the character system for written standard Chinese (Bo & Baldauf, 1990; Tse, 1982). As a result of political events, this reform movement has taken slightly different directions in the People's Republic of China, in the Republic of China (Taiwan), and in Hong Kong (a British Crown Colony until July 1997). Script reform often requires complex decisions, and James (1985) discusses some of these issues for Tamil in Sri Lanka.

Language standardisation

The perceived need for a single language runs parallel to the development of the nation-state. As such, standardisation has been a major goal of language planning and policy. As we saw in the previous chapter, language standardisation was an important aspect of corpus planning, and the language planning frameworks developed to describe the language planning process. In some respects, languages are constantly undergoing standardisation. This may occur formally through the work of language planning agencies such as in France (Joseph, 1987) or Malaysia (Omar, 1984), or more informally through the efforts of individuals, as in the English-speaking world. Thus, every time a new dictionary or grammar is published, that publication may be regarded as an additional attempt at standardisation.

Although standardisation is a continuing process, it occurs in its most dramatic form when a nation is trying to identify a national language (or a regional language for a particular use). Historically, the rise of standardisation in the European context derives from the advent of the printing press and need for the expanding central government bureaucracies to have a common code for communicating with the people. In English, for example, written standardisation around the London standard had substantially occurred by 1450[1] and, as an indication of this, it was impossible, except in distinctly northern texts, to tell with any precision where a text was written. The introduction of printing in 1476, with London being the book publishing centre of England, added to the spread of the London standard. Caxton, the first English printer, used London speech as the basis of many of his translations, and this assured more than anything else the rapid adoption of this standard (Baugh & Cable, 1993: 190). The need for standards to enhance communication and to prevent miscommunication across the population concerned are much the same in modern instances, except that such developments need to be compressed into much shorter periods of time. This is therefore one of the goals of formal language planning.

The major linguistic tools of standardisation are pedagogical grammars and dictionaries. Yet, the production of complete grammars or complete dictionaries of any living language is difficult to do for short-term needs as they take many years to complete.[2] As language is in any case complex, it becomes necessary to select those elements of the grammar and those lexical items that can be considered most essential for school-trained students to know as it is inevitable that these tools are defined in terms of literacy skills. In addition, there is a need to produce special dictionaries: e.g. dictionaries for scientists, for people interested in business and economics, for health related sciences, and so on. Again, such dictionaries pose similar problems of limiting and choosing (cf. Cowie, 1990).

However, as noted previously, standardisation is not restricted to the environment of choosing a national (or regional) language. It is a continuous process. Dictionary publishers provide new editions of their dictionaries about every 10 years, because the language and its usage constantly changes, and it is therefore necessary to attempt to standardise practice at regular intervals. As new dictionaries are produced (cf. e.g. Collins Cobuild, 1987), so new grammars are produced as well (e.g. Quirk *et al.*, 1985). In addition to these types of publications, the literate community is replete with self-appointed critics who write popular books aimed at pointing the way to correct language usage for the ordinary citizen (e.g. Safire, 1984).

National language academies also serve to assure certain kinds of standardisation, as they are often responsible for the production of dictionaries and sometimes of standard grammars. As noted earlier in this chapter, such organisations are almost always concerned with language purity as well as with the standardisation of the language. That is, they seek to keep the standard (authorised) version of the language free of foreign language influences or to integrate such usages appropriately into the language. The French Academy, for example, has long sought to combat

lg spread

the dire influences of English borrowing, and the Mexican Academy has been particularly concerned in recent years with the flood of American English words and with the coinage of mixed origin (e.g. Mexican *groceria* – a combination of the American *grocery* and the homophonous Spanish word meaning to sell wholesale). The role of language academies in standardisation is explored at greater length in Chapter 9, in the section under Academies and Lexical Development.

Whereas standardisation is an important function in maintaining operative communication, if communicants become engrossed in a concern about each others' correctness, it is likely that communication will be severely impaired. Correctness plays an essential role in communication, but communication can (and does frequently) occur with limited correctness. Standardisation, in language planning terms, is not about correctness for its own sake, but about achieving a basis for effective communication. Since language is a dynamic process, correctness is only a momentary (in historical terms) event. Self-appointed critics, language teachers, and sometimes language academics, who carry the concern for standardisation into hyper-correctness, defeat the basic purpose of standardisation and therefore of communication as well.

Language spread

In general terms, language spread is a phenomenon which has been observed throughout human history whenever two populations speaking mutually incomprehensible languages come in contact. One can invoke as illustrations the spread of Latin during the period of the Roman Empire, the spread of Arabic during the period of Islamic expansion, and the spread of French during the seventeenth century. There have been various causes for such language spread; for example, sometimes military conquest (e.g. Rome), sometimes religious missionary activity (e.g. Islam, Christianity, Buddhism), and sometimes economic factors (e.g. English in the twentieth century). Indeed, one can claim that living languages are always changing and there is a pulsing in language history so that at any given time some languages are spreading, others are contracting.

While language spread is a naturally recurring phenomenon, language policy makers and planners have also made it an explicit goal. In language planning terms, language spread is the attempt to increase the number of speakers, often at the expense of another language(s) leading to language shift (e.g. Wardhaugh, 1987). Planned language spread, as Nahir (1984) points out, is often combined with aspects of language standardisation, and examples include Hebrew in Israel (Dagut, 1985), Swahili in Tanzania (Whiteley, 1971), French in Québec (d'Anglejan, 1984), Indonesian/Malay in Indonesia (Alisjahbana, 1984) and Malaysia (Omar, 1984) and *pou-tonghua* in China (Bo & Baldauf, 1990; Tse, 1982).

However, language spread can also be seen as an 'unplanned' language planning (Baldauf, 1994) phenomenon in language contact situations. Populations come into contact in more peaceful and less planned ways as well. For instance, in a contact situation, it is possible that a trade pidgin will spring up between the two communities, consisting of lexical and grammatical elements from each, but substantially reduced in both lexicon and grammar, generally lacking adjectives and using large numbers of nonce words. Over time, it is possible that such a language will gain status and actually become the first language of some segment of the population along the border, and become a creole. If the creole persists, it is likely to decreolise in the direction of the dominant language. Such a form can acquire very high status. An interesting example occurs with Bislama, which is now the national language of Vanuatu. Tok Pisin in Papua New Guinea and Kriol, spoken in northern Australia largely by Australian Aboriginal people, and Torres Strait Broken (see examples in Baldauf & Luke, 1990), are three further examples of stable and expanding creoles. To a certain extent, US Black English is also an example of this phenomenon, where decreolisation in the direction of dominant English has at the extreme of the continuum progressed very far (cf. Dillard, 1977).

The worldwide use of English provides another example of language spread. The causes for the spread of English are discussed elsewhere in this volume (Chapter 9, section under Planning for Science and Technology). Suffice it to say at this point that more people speak English as a first or second language around the world than have ever in the history of the world spoken any single language. Similar though more limited phenomena related to language spread may be observed in connection with Arabic, Chinese, French, German and Spanish, among other languages, though generally for different reasons. This spread of English has given rise to a number of related phenomena; for example, what Kachru (1982, 1992) has called the 'nativization of English' in a variety of former colonial areas. A product of this nativisation process is the development of what has become known as second language literature; that is, a body of literature written in English by individuals who are not native speakers of English and who use English in a non-metropolitan form and in special registers (see also Chapter 2, under sub-head Elaboration). Two examples of this phenomena are the novels *The Palm Wine Drunkard* (New York: Grove Press, 1953) by Amos Tutola, and *Sons for the Return Home* (Auckland: Longman Paul, 1973) by Albert Wendt (see also Cruz, 1986 and Thumboo, 1986 for discussion of the issues).

Lexical modernisation

As already noted in the previous section on language standardisation, there is often a need for a particular language to expand its capacity to deal with new concepts which have come into use in society more quickly than natural development can accommodate. Nahir (1984) argues that the terminological work which results can be categorised as belonging to one of two types: (1) lexical development which is related to the process of language modernisation (i.e. the standardising and enriching a language and expanding its domains of activity); and (2) term creation and adaptation which all standardised languages undergo relates to the process of adding terms for new ideas, concepts or technology for which the lexicon is unprepared. Nahir (1984: 307) notes that lexical development is a *process or activity*, while term creation and adaptation is a *goal or function itself*. Both aspects of lexical modernisation can occur simultaneously in languages which are simultaneously standardising and modernising. Jernudd (1977) discusses some of the sources for terminological innovation.

At this point it may be interesting to examine how lexical modernisation can occur as a language community has a number of means at its disposal for the creation of new words including: (1) words may be created entirely anew; (2) old words may be recycled with new meanings; (3) words may be borrowed from another language; (4) words may be created out of common roots and affixes deriving either from the historical base of the language or from a common external source. Lexical modernisation is also related to terminological unification or term planning, which is being undertaken on an international basis so technological terms will have common agreed upon meanings across several languages.

(1) The creation of entirely new words is actually relatively rare, apart from trade names and acronyms. To the best of our knowledge, only one absolutely unique word has been added to English since the middle of the eighteenth century; it is the word created by Eastman to represent, onomatopoetically, the sound of a camera shutter opening and closing: *Kodak*. While the rate of such additions in English has been very slow, other languages may have differing rates. In languages such as (Mandarin) Chinese, Pilipino, Icelandic and Bahasa Indonesia, for example, the rate of creation is much more rapid, in part because new technologies have been rapidly introduced, but also in part because there has been a concerted movement in the cultures represented by those languages *not* to borrow foreign words.

(2) The recycling in new ways of words whose functions have disappeared is somewhat more common. In English, for example, the word *broadcast* once meant a way of spreading seed by hand; with the advent of machine farming and the development of agribusiness, hand sewing of seed has been replaced. The word was taken over in the 1920s by the radio industry, and has, by the end of the twentieth century, entirely lost its original meaning and acquired a new life as a term to describe the dissemination of information by electronic means through the air. In the early part of this century, the phrase *grid iron* was used to describe a part of a wood-burning stove used for cooking and heating. To a great extent, cooking and heating have been overtaken by electric and gas appliances.

As the technological change was occurring, an imaginative sports writer applied the term as an apt metaphor to describe an American football field. Over the years, the football analogy has become a cliché, and the original meaning has disappeared. Most English-speaking adults under 50 years of age would not know the source of the metaphor.

(3) Words are often borrowed from one language into another. This borrowing occurs quite naturally when a technology is transferred from one culture to another or when a language is re-rooted in a new environment (as in the colonial situation). For example, the English term *TV* has entered virtually every community in which that technology has taken root. In many cases, the word has been adapted to the phonology of the borrowing language, but that is not universally true; the original phonology may be carefully retained as a prestige marker – as the word *prestige*, borrowed into English from French, testifies.

Large numbers of English words have been borrowed into other languages; for example, the entire lexicon of baseball has been borrowed into Japanese, with appropriate phonological adaptation: English *ball* = Japanese *balu; bat* = *batu; base* = *basu;* and even the traditional *hot dog* served in baseball stadia = *hotudogu.* But English has been a borrowing language itself; much of the English vocabulary for music has been borrowed from Italian, and much of the basic military terminology has been borrowed from French and German, with appropriate phonological adaptation (e.g. French *colonel* /kòlònèl/ = English /kë'n'l/), and plant and animal names have been borrowed from Native American languages, again with appropriate phonological adaptation (e.g. Chippewa *shikag* = skunk, Cree *otchek* = *woodchuck*, Delaware *pasimenan* = *persimmon*). A great many words have, of course been borrowed directly from Latin (e.g. *skeletós* = *skeleton*) and from Greek (e.g. *skeptikos* = *skeptic*). Sometimes interesting 'double-plays' occur in the borrowing process; e.g. Spanish *cucaracha* was borrowed into English as *cockroach*, and later was clipped to *roach*, a term which still later was applied metaphorically to the butt of a marijuana cigarette.

Clipping is a common phenomenon; *prof, doc,* and *math* are common English words, derived respectively from *professor, doctor,* and *mathematics,* and English *mob* is a clipping of Latin *mobile vulgus.* In Australian colloquial English many words (including names) are clipped and a vowel added – *garbo* = *garbage collector, smoko* = a *smoking break,* more generally a work break or *Jacko* = *Jackson.* In some cases, a borrowing occurs which later undergoes a change in meaning; e.g. the word *bratt*, meaning a bib, was borrowed from Welsh into English as *brat*, meaning an ill behaved child (i.e. one who soils his/her bib). The French Language Academy has strenuously resisted borrowing from English and has taken legal action to ban such expressions as *le weekend* (see Thody, 1995). Despite the reservations of the French Academy, word borrowing is a pervasive process. In some cases of borrowing, the result is a literal translation –

English *honeymoon* = French *lune de miel* – or a near translation – English *hot dog* = French *saucisse chaude*.

(4) New words for new functions can be created out of a commonly held stock of roots and affixes belonging to another language. English has invented thousands of words based on Greek and Latin borrowings, sometimes creating strange bedfellows in the new words. An enormous number of new technical terms have such an origin – the process importantly augmented by advertising; e.g. *rayon, nylon, microscope, telescope, telephone, sonar* or *solar*. Again, interesting 'double-plays' can occur: the word *solar* was coined as an adjective meaning 'of or pertaining to the sun'; thus, we speak of *solar energy* – energy deriving directly from the sun. Recently, however, scientists have been able to capture the energy of the sun reflected from the surface of the earth; the term *solar* [Latin *Solaris*] cannot be applied to this energy source, since the source is not taken directly from the sun, so a new term had to be coined: *solic*. The process was essentially the same, but a Latin adjectival suffix [-ic] was employed. The stock of roots and affixes need not be Latin and Greek; as has been noted above, in the discussion of new coinages, in languages such as (Mandarin) Chinese, Pilipino, and Bahasa Indonesia, for example, new words have been created from historical roots, in part because there has been a concerted movement in the cultures represented by those languages *not* to borrow foreign words. New words can also be created by the migration of words; for example, in English, the names of people may become general nouns: English *mackintosh* is a raincoat named for Charles *Mackintosh* (1766–1843), the inventor of the garment, while other examples include *macadam* paving and the *gladstone* bag. Additionally, trade names may become generic (e.g. *frigidaire* in US English is a substitute for *refrigerator* and *xerox* for *photocopy*). Once the noun exists, other parts of speech may come into use, so a *xerox* (n.) produces *xerox* (adj.) copies through the process of *xeroxing* (v.).

Additional discussion of these processes and others can be found in Dillard (1992) while a good general source for English etymology is Onions (1966). Lexical modernisation draws on these alternatives ways of generating new lexical items.

An interesting example of lexical modernisation is occurring in the Philippines which has adopted one of its more than 70 languages (cf. Gonzalez, 1990; McFarland, 1981; Sibayan, 1984) to serve as its national language. This language, based largely on the Manila variety of Tagalog, was first called Pilipino, but most recently has been renamed Filipino to signify the intention to borrow more widely from other Philippine languages. This language, which has been in the process of developing as a national language since 1936, has served as a language fully satisfactorily for the discussion of anything of significance for the community of its speakers. However, especially since independence after World War II, there has been an increasing influx of technology into the Philippines and a growing economic need for this new national language to indigenise much of the technology so that technical innovation may become the basis for new economic expansion. Pilipino initially lacked the terminology which would have made possible the indigenisation of technology, and the government has invested in a substantial national effort to expand and 'modernise' the lexicon of Pilipino/Filipino in order to facilitate technology and technological growth (Gonzalez, 1989, 1990).

Several processes have been involved: the large-scale borrowing of terms from other languages, largely English; the adaptation of borrowed words according to the phonological rules of Tagalog; the coinage of new words from classical Tagalog roots, and the adaptation of archaic Tagalog words to new functions. While the process is complex and is basically related to corpus planning concerns, some status planning considerations are involved; for example, while it could make sense in phonological terms (i.e. both languages have a c-v structure) to borrow words into Filipino from Japanese, there is a strong emotional resistance to borrowing Japanese words. It is a curious footnote to linguistic history that, although the Philippines was occupied by Spain for nearly 400 years, the Spanish language has had a very small impact on Philippine languages (except in personal names, e.g. Andrew Gonzalez). Similarly, though the Philippines was occupied by Japan for a time, the Japanese language has had virtually no effect on Philippine languages, but although the Philippines was occupied by the United States as well, for a relatively brief period, English has had a great impact on some of the languages of the Philippines.

Malaysia was formerly an anglophone area; through its language planning agency, the *Dewan Bahasa dan Pustaka*, Malaysia, has mounted a massive campaign to enlarge the lexicon of Bahasa Malaysia so that it will be capable of dealing with technology and language domains previously underdeveloped in that language. That organisation has been charged not only with the creation of new terms for technological and scientific areas, but also with morphological modification, and for mutual intelligibility with the varieties spoken in Singapore and Indonesia. Such an effort is replete with problems; for example, on what basis should a new lexicon be created: foreign word borrowing, borrowing from which languages – English, Arabic, Sanskrit – borrowing and adjusting for the phonological and morphological rules of Bahasa Malaysia, the redefinition of archaic terms, and the creation of new terms from historical roots of the language? Such work must be done for large numbers of words – more than 400,000 since 1972 – quickly, since people need these terms to use immediately (or they will invent their own) and within a modest budget.

Lexical modernisation is today largely an economically driven process, the intent of which is to enrich the word stock of a language which already serves its speakers well in all but the technical registers. As we have seen there are a number of ways in which the word stock may be enriched, but the purpose is to provide the means of dealing with new technologies that are having an important impact on society. Thus, the areas in which the word stock is enriched are specifically limited. Although the case of the Philippines (and Malaysia) has been discussed at some length, examples can be drawn from such languages as Mandarin (as the official language of the People's Republic of China), Japanese, Hebrew (as the official language of Israel), and a large number of sub-Saharan African languages (e.g. Kiswahili). The large-scale nature of the lexical modernisation process is further illustrated by Alisjahbana (1984: 87) who reported 'that the Indonesian language up until now has coined or accepted more than 500,000 modern terms expressing modern international concepts . . . '. This is an enormous undertaking when one considers that a good dictionary one might buy in a book store contains about 100,000 words.

Terminological unification

As technologies have become universal, there has developed in the latter half of the twentieth century a need for terminological standardisation or terminological unification across geographic areas and languages to facilitate discussion of technologies held in common. The need extends over a wide variety of academic and practical areas – from unification of terminologies in Medicine, Chemistry and Pharmacy to unification of terminology in such areas as fisheries (e.g. Baldauf & Jernudd , 1983; Jernudd & Thuan, 1984; Kaplan & Medgyes, 1992), in maritime navigation (Strevens & Weeks, 1985; Weeks *et al.*, 1988), or in Policespeak for the channel tunnel management (E. Johnson, 1994). This process is also called term planning and it is closely related to lexical modernisation.

The focus of terminological unification is on defining the functions and semantic boundaries of terms, particularly for scientific and technological purposes. A number of polities are active in terminological development including Québec (Boulanger, 1986, 1989) and Sweden, where the Swedish Centre for Technical Terminology (TNC) was established in 1941 and 'elaborates terminologies within different technical and scientific fields' which are then published in glossaries (Bucher, 1991: 1). However, term planning is not only of interest nationally, but is being internationally co-ordinated as well (e.g. Stoberski, 1990). It has become an area of interest in scholarship and teaching (Sager, 1975, 1990). As technology becomes more and more important, the development of exactly equivalent terminology across linguistic boundaries had become increasingly important.

Stylistic simplification

The complexity of language may lead to problems in language varieties used in daily situations where the literacy of individuals expected to use the language may fall short of the text being presented. This is particularly the case in situations demanding an understanding of the language of contracts and other agreements (e.g. buying a car, buying a house, buying insurance, etc.) and in situations involving the services of government agencies (e.g. completing one's income tax return, applying for a driver's licence, applying for a passport, etc.); in both instances, texts tend to be written in a variety characterised by legalese and bureaucratese. These terms commonly subsume such features as decontextualisation, writer-centreness, the use of complex conditionals, the use of extensive passivisation, the use of complex noun strings, the use of multiple negatives, the use of jargon, and the use of redundant pairs.

In the practice of the law in the US, the courts have repeatedly held that language must be interpreted as the plain and ordinary understanding among lay people; in other words, words mean what ordinary people believe they mean. For example, in Bank of the West v. Superior Court, the US Supreme Court wrote:

> In summary, a court that is faced with an argument . . . based on assertedly ambiguous contract language must first attempt to determine whether [the language] is consistent with . . . objective reasonable expectations. In so doing, the court must interpret the language in context with regard to its intended function . . . . This is so because language in a contract must be construed in the context of that instrument as a whole, and in the circumstances of that case, and cannot be found to be ambiguous in the abstract (1992, 2C.4th. 1264–65).

In other words, not only must language be interpreted as the ordinary person would understand it, but it must be interpreted in context.

In government documents, the problem is equally complex. During his Administration, President Carter issued an Executive Order in 1978 requiring government agencies to produce their document in 'plain English'. In response to the President's Order, a contract was let by the government to the American Institutes for Research to develop the Document Design Project, the purpose of which was to work with government agency staff ' . . . to help them simplify their regulations, forms, memos, and brochures . . . ' (Charrow, 1982: 173, see also Battison, 1980). The Document Design Project identified four kinds of problems in bureaucratic documents:

- pragmatic issues;
- organisational issues (in written discourse structure);
- syntactic/grammatical issues; and
- semantic issues.

Forensic linguistics has, in the intervening decade, become somewhat more sophisticated (see, e.g. French & Coulthard, 1994–, Shuy, 1993.) It is somewhat more difficult to cite a small number of seminal works dealing with document design.

But it is not only the language of document design and of the law that have been areas of focus in the context of stylistic simplification; work has also been undertaken in relation to the uses of language in health delivery, in advertising, and in employment and public service. A great deal of important work in these contexts has been undertaken in Australia (see, e.g. Clyne, 1994; Clyne *et al.*, 1991; Marriott, 1990; Pauwels, 1991, 1992; Wierzbicka, 1993.)

In general, then, stylistic simplification is an attempt to make text more readable, more clearly addressed to the audience that must deal with it, and less convoluted in lexicon and syntax. Although extensive efforts have been exerted in the US to accomplish these objectives, the results are not stunning. Skyum-Nielson (1978) reports that similar legislation was passed in Denmark, but it is not clear how widely such attempts at language simplification are being made. While stylistic simplification is an admirable goal, there is probably no such style as 'plain language'.[3]

Nor is this a language planning goal free from controversy. There are also those say that plain English (i.e. stylistic simplification) is not the answer if the aim is to improve communication. David Sless, of the Communication Research Institute of Australia, argues that the principles of good communication derive from conversation, so that:

> good communication occurs with collaboration, mutual engagement, exchange and dialogue. [Furthermore,] we must be sceptical of strategies that suggest that by using certain formal stylistic rules we can solve communication problems. We should resist reducing the user of a text to a cipher within the formalism. (1995: 3)

The argument that Sless (1995) makes is basically four-fold:

(1) That there is an absence of evidence that plain English materials are actually easier or clearer for the reader (i.e. in the ability actually to *use* the text correctly).
(2) That language is only one element in good communication (i.e. other factors such as typography, field testing of texts and stakeholder negotiation take more time to develop when creating a comprehensible text).
(3) That plain English principles of simplification are often inadequate for dealing with the complexities of communication problem-solving (i.e. simple words – like *get* or *run* – can often have complex meanings).
(4) That plain English texts may provide a false sense of security about the intelligibility of the document (i.e. people are likely to blame themselves rather than the 'simply written' text if they can't understand the information).

Stylistic simplification is clearly a complex matter and needs to focus on the information to be communicated and the audience as much as the linguistic style.

Interlingual communication

Nahir (1984: 312) suggests that interlingual communication has as its focus 'facilitating linguistic communication between members of *different* speech communities by enhancing the use of either an artificial (or "auxiliary") language or a "language of wider communication" as an additional language'. This may involve attempts to modify certain linguistic features of cognate languages to facilitate better communication. Nahir's failure to mention interpreting and translating in this context may be due to its growth in the last decade as a policy area and to its elite and individualistic nature in much of its early practice. Three types of interlingual communication-related language planning goals have emerged.

Worldwide Interlingual Communication has as its focus Auxiliary Languages and English as a lingua franca. While there has been a lot of scholarly interest in auxiliary/international/artificial languages (e.g. Ashby, 1985; Corsetti & La Torre, 1995; Harry, 1989; Large, 1988; Tonkin, 1987), particularly in Esperanto, these languages seem to be drawing declining interest generally as languages of wider communication like English become more widespread. As do all small languages, they face increased competition. Because they have no cultural and social home – their much acclaimed benefit of being politically neutral – they have no natural base from which to grow. As education is an inadequate basis for sustaining any language, these languages are unlikely to contribute much to worldwide interlingual communication. On the other hand, the growth of English as a lingua franca or as an international auxiliary language has been phenomenal. The reasons for this are examined in Chapter 9, in the section on Planning for Science and Technology (also see Eggington & Wren, 1997).

Regional Interlingual Communication focuses on work on developing regional lingua franca like Spanish in Latin America or Swahili in East Africa, or on improving the mutual intelligibility between speakers of groups of cognate languages. Some examples of the latter include all the Nordic language committees, which try to avoid new and unnecessary differences between their languages (Molde, 1975), co-operation between Malaysia and Indonesia in spelling and other reforms (Omar, 1984; Alisjahbana, 1984) and the spelling and other reforms of Dutch between the Dutch in the Netherlands and Belgium (van de Crean & Willemyns, 1988; van der Plank, 1988). In each of these cases language planners have worked to improve communication between languages/varieties.

Interpreting and translating is a growing area of interlingual communication. This area subsumes a whole range of other considerations but centres on the problem of translation (Roberts, 1992). Some specialists differentiate between *translation* and *interpretation*, where the former is largely concerned with the translation of written, often literary text but also various kinds of business communication (e.g. contracts, legal agreements, treaties, etc.) from one language to another, and the latter deals with the simultaneous rendering of speech from one language to another (as occurs at international meetings in various academic and business areas and in such agencies as those subsumed under the broad aegis of the United Nations). Community interpreting as in legal situations (i.e. the police, in courts), for access to health services and government information and in industrial situations is also a growing area. (See Chapter 9, Section on Government Interpreting in Australia). As global communication has increased in the twentieth century, the need for such interlingual communication has increased at a rapid pace. Although translation and interpretation is certainly a field of specialisation, it has sometimes been criticised for the lack of a theoretical framework. Like language planning itself, this field has been largely concerned with responding to immediate needs. The amount of translating and interpreting has increased substantially in the recent past, having outrun the availability of individuals capable of providing satisfactory service in these areas (cf. Bühler, 1987).

Whereas to a significant extent both translation and interpreting are performed for the most part by human agents, translation at least is open to the intercession of machine capabilities. Since the 1950s, various organisations (e.g. Bell Laboratories, IBM or the CIA) have been working on the perfection of machine translation. Various computer-based technologies have been developed, but to date no translation processing device has been developed which is capable of absolutely accurate translation. Relatively inexpensive personal computer programs (e.g. Globalink Power Translators, Microtac Assistants) are now available for 'translation' of *simple texts* which claim about 80–90% accuracy between major European languages (i.e. English and French, German, Italian and Spanish). Japanese scientists are working on a fifth generation computer which they hope will be capable of translation processing with accuracy to the order of 95% of a given text. In addition to work specifically related to machine translation, a considerable effort under the more general categorisation of artificial intelligence research is also concerned with the intertranslatability of text between languages.

Language maintenance

Language maintenance (LM) is a superordinate category that subsumes within itself such previously discussed areas as *language revival, language reform, language shift, language standardisation,* and *terminological modernisation.* Language maintenance occurs in two contexts: *community LM* and *dominant LM.* On the one hand, when a community language is threatened with extinction, there is an obvious need for language maintenance and, on the other hand, even dominant languages require some effort at maintenance to prevent significant language drift away from the standard model. Language maintenance efforts have been directed at the preservation of a large number of indigenous languages having limited numbers of speakers in North America, South America, Africa, Europe and Australia. Language maintenance in this context is a process that normally precedes language revival. In many situations, before a revival can be undertaken, the extant variety has to be stabilised, and a condition needs to be created in which attrition among speakers is compensated by the addition of new learners. This desirable situation can be weakened, for example, among traditional societies, if there is a shared belief among the group elders that children in the group have fallen so far away from the traditional ways that they *do not deserve* to learn the language. Where such an attitude exists, attrition is not counterweighted by the entry of new learners, and the language cannot be maintained.

In the second context, where every language needs to be maintained so as to prevent it from diverging excessively from some mutually agreed upon standard, English provides an apt example. It is quite clear that, in some countries using English as a national or official language, there is in fact an evident movement of the indigenous varieties away from the norm. This phenomenon may be partially linguistic (e.g. some of the consonant clusters of English may be difficult for speakers of some languages, some structures may not be heavily used in some languages), but it also can be attributed to the educational system which is likely to engender a spiral movement away from the norms; that is, children are taught by non-native speakers whose pronunciation and grammar are likely to be non-standard, and some of those children go on to be teachers whose pronunciation and grammar will be increasingly non-standard, etc. Over time under these conditions, the gap between the local variety and the metropolitan variety widens. In the interim, the metropolitan variety has not remained static but has itself changed, possibly contributing to an even wider gap, and a situation may arise in which the local variety has moved so far away from the norms that the two varieties may be mutually unintelligible. To avoid this situation – this type of language drift – language maintenance is needed to slow the rate of drift and to attempt periodically to narrow the gap. These issues are dealt with in detail in Chapter 8, Bilingualism and Language Status.

Auxiliary code standardisation

Language planning inherent in standardisation occurs at many levels and there is a need to modify:

> the marginal, auxiliary aspects of language such as signs for the deaf, place names, and rules of transliteration and transcription, either to reduce ambiguity and thus to improve communication or to meet changing social, political, or other needs or aspirations. (Nahir, 1984: 318)

The development of manual sign codes for use in the education of the deaf has received relatively little attention in the language planning literature, but it is important to remember that this is a community and a culture just like any other language group. Penn and Reagan (1990) have examined this issue for South Africa, Reagan (1995) has looked at the problems of manual code design in the United States, while Behares and Massone (1996) have examined sign language communities in Argentina and Uruguay.

There is a need to have a standardised way to refer to such things as place names and geographical features. The US Geological Survey has been doing this since 1890 and many other polities have similar processes in place. For example, in some cities there are a number of streets with the same name but a different designation (i.e. street, place, crescent, avenue) which makes things like mail and essential services difficult. With the adoption of spelling reforms in Indonesia in 1972, there was a need to standardise all place names (Djakarta = Jakarta). However individuals were allowed to spell their surnames under the old spelling.

Names are also changed for political or social reasons. Ayres Rock in Central Australia became Uluru when the land was returned to its Aboriginal owners. The capital of Sabah, Jesselton (named after the European founder), became Kota Kinabalu shortly after Sabah (North Borneo when under British rule) joined Malaysia. Cape Canaveral in Florida was renamed Cape Kennedy after the assassination of the president, but had its original name restored some 20 years later. The Richard M. Nixon freeway in Los Angeles was hastily renamed after Nixon's resignation as US President. Many of the cities in central Europe have changed their names several times during the last 80 years (e.g. Danzig = Gdansk), depending on which polity they have found themselves a part of. Nahir (1984) notes that Regina (named after the Queen of England), the capital of Canada's Province of Saskatchewan was called Pile of Bones when it was established. Some of the States in Australia are considering whether geological features like Chinaman's Hat and Black-man's Creek should be given less controversial names. Some place names have survived because of the linguistic ignorance of some sectors of the society. In central California, there is a physical feature called on official maps, 'Putah Creek'. *Putah* is vulgar Mexican Spanish (i.e. *cunt*), and the place name commemorates the location of an early house of prostitution.

The introduction of the 1972 spelling reform in Indonesia has led to the systematic respelling of some place and personal names, i.e. Djakarta became Jakarta and Soekarno became Sukarno. While people were urged to write their names using the new spelling, this is quite different from the banning of 'foreign' language personal and place names by some European countries (e.g. Jernudd, 1994b; Neustupný, 1984).

Meso Level Planning Goals

As Table 3.1 indicates, Annamalai and Rubin (1980) have suggested that there are also a number of meso level language planning goals, which were articulated at a conference on language planning, as issues language planners should be involved in. These goals include:

- Administration: Training and certification of officials and professionals.
- Administration: Legal provisions for use.
- The legal domain.
- Education equity: Pedagogical issues.
- Education equity: Language rights/identity.
- Education elite formation/control.
- Mass communication.

Some other goals that might be added to this list include:

- Educational equity: Language handicap.
- Social equity: Minority Language access.
- Interlanguage translation: Training for professions, business, law, etc.

As these are language planning activities, rather than stemming from an analysis of language planning goals, they are best examined in the particular language planning contexts in which they occur. A number of these are discussed in Chapters 4–9.

Critiques of Classical Language Planning

In the first part of this book, we have examined language planning contexts, frameworks and goals; we need to note that the discipline has not been without its critics (e.g. Luke *et al.*, 1990; Tollefson, 1991). The neo-Marxist and post-structuralist critiques of classical language planning, and by implication of language planners, are, according to Fishman (1994: 91) based around five criticisms:

(1) lp is conducted by elites that are governed by their own self-interest; (2) lp reproduces rather than overcomes sociocultural and econotechnical inequalities; (3) lp inhibits or counteracts multiculturalism; (4) lp espouses world-wide Westernisation and modernisation leading to new sociocultural, econotechnical and conceptual colonialism; (5) only ethnography can save lp research from fostering the above mentioned evils.

However, Fishman argues that such critiques have focused mainly on language planning theory rather than on an analysis of practice, 'even though very little language planning practice has actually been informed by language planning theory' (1994: 97). Where there is such a gap and to the extent that language planners ignore language rights of minorities, they are open to justifiable criticism. At the same time, one needs to be careful not to replace one kind of exploitation of minorities with another kind, or to replace one existing minority with a new minority created by the process intended to redress injustice (see e.g. Eckert, 1983). This is, in fact, what Friere (1979, 1985; Friere & Macedo, 1987) seems to recommend in his approach to the empowerment of minorities; he suggests turning the minority into a majority and creating a new minority out of the present majority so that the new minority may be exploited by the old minority. Language planners need to contribute to the empowerment of the disadvantaged and the education of the advantaged.

> However, language planning theory and theoretically informed lan-guage planning research must have other goals as well. Both of them must be relevant to hegemonic and proto-hegemonic as well as anti-hegemonic efforts. Both of them must strive toward multi-meth-odological skills and train neophytes to be able to choose and implement the research methods that are best suited to particular problems and research circumstances. Language planning specialists must know how to choose between methods rather than being locked into any one all purpose method. Lastly, language planning specialists must realise that although much of the post-structuralist and neo-Marxist criticism directed at them has been and continues to be fully rectified, that most of the issues raised by this criticism cannot be fully rectified, even were society to be entirely overturned and rebuilt. Authorities will continue to be motivated by self-interest. New structural inequalities will inevitably arise to replace the old ones. More powerful segments of society will be less inclined to want to change themselves than to change others. Westernisation and modern-isation will continue to foster both problems and satisfactions for the bulk of humanity. Ultimately language planning will be utilised by both those who favor and those who oppose whatever the socio-politi-cal climate may be. This is a truth that neo-Marxist and post-structuralist critics of language planning never seem to grasp and, therefore, they never seem to go beyond their critique as decisively or as productively as they state their critique. (Fishman, 1994: 98)

There is a growing realisation that companies, groups and individuals can have an impact on the language situation, that there is a place in societies for minority languages and that it is possible to 'reverse language shift' (see Fishman, 1991b). While the latter realisation is growing in macro language planning and has been taken up by some governments and communities, the former micro language planning contexts have not been studied to any great extent, and most participants may not even realise they are involved in language planning. However, their participation in, or resistance to, language related decisions can have an impact on language learning and usage decisions. Thus, while the grand macro national language planning schemes have dominated the language planning literature, the micro situations have been ignored, and much less is known about the participants or how decisions in such situations are made.

Summary

In this chapter we have examined some of the macro goals to which language plans can be oriented. Many of these goals involve aspects of Haugen's model which defines the language planning activities underlying the goals involved in the language planning process. This chapter also looks at why language planning is undertaken at all. Among the purposes examined are:

- language purification;
- language reform;
- language spread;
- language revival;
- language standardisation;
- lexical modernisation;
- stylistic simplification;
- language maintenance;
- terminological unification;
- interlingual communication;
- auxiliary code standardisation.

The chapter suggests that language planning ought not to be casually undertaken, that planning is likely to be time-consuming and expensive, that language planning is not a one-off activity, but must be ongoing, and that implementation requires much more than a set of top-down decisions. Those whose language will be in some way modified must accept the proposed modification as really being in their best interests, and those who are implementing the language change need to perceive that their proposals must be 'sold' not only to the recipients of change but to the entire population. In the next chapter we turn to the methodology issues raised in the preceding section by Fishman. While we focus on the sociolinguistic survey, students of language planning need to have a wide range of skills 'to be able to choose and implement the research methods that are best suited to particular problems and research circumstances' (Fishman, 1994: 98).

Notes

1. Orm's *Ormulum*, a 10,000-line poetic fragment, composed in the first half of the thirteenth century, is an early effort. Orm devised his own spelling system, and

the work throws light on the evolution of English and the desire for standardisation.

2. The *Oxford English Dictionary* for example, was begun in 1880 and only completed in 1935. A 10-volume set of updates and revisions took another 50 years to complete. Although the advent of computers has reduced such time frames greatly, the work involved still means there will be a considerable period of time between their commencement and their completion. Corpus-based dictionary development makes it possible to create dictionaries much more easily – once the corpus is available – such dictionaries are intended to be more descriptive of language than prescriptive.

3. Nevertheless, there are constant reminders in the press that governments are addressing this language problem. For example, in mid-1996 the Ontario/Toronto Ministry of Consumer and Commercial Relations was working on a 'plain language' leasing agreement for automobiles which, once it is in place, will be mandated for all such contracts.

Part 2: Key Issues in Language Planning

In Part 2 of this volume the reader is introduced to a number of key cross-national issues central to the field of language planning. Chapter 4 discusses problems of data collection and methodology, with particular attention to the sociolinguistic survey; this chapter outlines the information needs for language planning and introduces methods for collecting that data.

In Chapter 5 major implementations of language planning through language-in-education planning and literacy-in-education planning are discussed. In Chapter 6 the nature of the data and the economic settings which influence how language is planned are argued. The purpose of this section is to introduce some of the major cross-national issues found in the practice of language planning as a foundation for looking at language planning in specific contexts. Those issues are illustrated by a series of case studies in Part 3.

4 Language Planning Process

If one is going to be involved in language planning, rather than just study it, then it is important to understand the process by which such planning occurs. In Chapter 1 language planning was defined as an attempt to change the language behaviour of a community of speakers in some particular direction for some particular purpose. If language behaviour is to be changed, it is important to know not only what goals are to be achieved (see Chapter 3), but also what the current language situation is in the polity so that processes can be put in place to reach those objectives. Haugen's model in Chapter 2 provided a generalised view of the language planning process, while Cooper's accounting scheme indicated the variables which need to be attended to in that planning process, but neither actually describes how one goes about the process of language planning. Of course, there are many approaches one can take to developing the information on which to decide on language planning goals and the means to achieve those goals, but we have decided to focus on two possible approaches to information collection: (1) the sociolinguistic survey in the macro language planning context, and (2) on the more specific language-in-education planning process, which is so often substituted for language planning. Initially, we also want to explore some tools which can add substance to the information collected as part of a language planning project.

Language planning as a field of study draws on a variety of different disciplines for expertise, and each of these fields in turn contributes its own unique methods and techniques for collecting data as a basis of language planning. While it is not possible in the context of a general overview of language planning to describe in detail all of these unique contributions, particularly as the method or methods to be used are so dependent on the situation to be studied, it is possible to outline some of the major techniques and to point interested readers to published work on these topics. Although the methods discussed in the following section are referred to primarily in the context of developing a language plan, they may be used in the different stages of plan implementation and evaluation.

What this overview of methods indicates is that there are a number of different approaches to understanding the current linguistic situation in a given community. In the following section we briefly examine some of these approaches to data collection. While the most detailed section of the chapter focuses on the sociolinguistic survey process, it is important to understand that other tools are available, and as Fishman (1994) points out, different academic traditions favour different methods. The sociolinguistic survey model proposed here, when conducted at the macro level, is both time-consuming and expensive, but it is proposed despite these drawbacks because it is believed to provide the most complete database from which to undertake planning. It can of course also be scaled back to use fewer resources or to do micro planning studies.

Approaches to Data Collection

As Fishman (1994) has indicated in his rebuttal of the critiques of language planning cited in the previous chapter, there are a number of useful approaches to collecting information for language planning, and language planners need to be multi-skilled so they can use the best method(s) appropriate to the situation. Whereas in large-scale projects language planning teams may be formed to make certain that the necessary skills are available for the project, in micro planning or more modestly funded situations, language planners need to be multi-skilled if they are to be effective in collecting the information needed to investigate language problems. In the sections which follow some of the skills needed and approaches taken to language planning are discussed, references to examples are provided and further readings on the various techniques suggested.

Historical analysis

The roots of many language planning problems lie in the role and historical development of language usage in a particular polity or location. Although historians themselves usually reject the direct application of their work to applied problems, an understanding of the historical circumstances can give planners and decision makers a better understanding of why a particular language problem exists; the past, present and future trends in relation to a language issue (Aksornkool, 1985); a better understanding of the interaction of language and other cultural elements over time (Baker & Mühlhäusler, 1990), and an indication of the basis and nature of some of the assumptions which underlie the problem. It also allows for the re-evaluation of data in relation to specific hypotheses (e.g. Keesing, 1990). A historical reconstruction of the facts paying proper attention to the authenticity of the sources through external (i.e. is the source authentic?) and internal criticism (i.e. is the information contained therein accurate and worthwhile?) can provide such information. Such an analysis can also provide a documentary evaluation of language planning or language change which has occurred over time (e.g. Ozolins, 1991, 1993).

As an example of how historical analysis can be used to shed light on the nature of language problems, Green et al.(1994) do such an analysis of literacy crises in Australia, and based on the historical documentation they argue that:

> literacy crises are not simply about problems with schools and teaching. Since the end of World War II, literacy crises in Australia have occurred with an almost predictable regularity in relation to larger economic and political, social and cultural, demographic and techno-logical movements. Literacy is not a 'stand alone' factor. It never has been. When and how a literacy 'crisis' occurs depends upon these other larger social matters. (Overview Section, p. 1)

They suggest that different models of literacy teaching yield different results, favouring different groups, communities or economic interests, and that if we want to begin to assess those models, 'we need a broader historical picture of educational change'. (Overview Section, p. 1)

> [Their] documentary history does not lay out 'truths' or 'facts' about the literates and illiterates, or about literacy teaching or learning. Rather it is a visible record of the public and political debate over educational access to language and literacy. It follows the debates over the directions and developments of the educational system and about the relationship between education and the broader society . . . . This history shows that whether and how literacy becomes a public issue often depends on forces and interests beyond the control of teachers and students. (Overview Section, p. 2)

Based on the historical documents presented in the text, they then go on to hypothesise four key areas related to literacy crises (i.e. economic change, political and geopolitical change, demographic change and multiculturalism, and technological and mass cultural change) and then proceed to provide a framework that teachers can use to analyse literacy crises in the news (i.e. they provide some criteria for external and internal criticism of documents).

Another example of the usefulness of historical evidence for testing hypotheses about language planning and development is provided by Keesing (1990) who examines why Solomon's Pijin has never been accorded the recognition, legitimacy or a standard orthography present in Tok Pisin (Papua New Guinea) or Bislama (Vanuatu) despite the fact that it has become the primary lingua franca for Solomon's urban culture. He suggests this is because:

[t]he dominant ideology continues to denigrate Pidgin as a bastardized form of English, created by Europeans as a form of domination and to be replaced as soon and as efficiently as possible by a language less demeaning and vulgar with which it is in direct competition for the minds and habits of the young – 'proper' English. (Keesing, 1990: 164)

This ideology still holds sway despite the fact that the historical evidence suggests that from the 1870s onwards it was the Solomon Islanders who were the fluent speakers of Pijin and that most Europeans had a defective command of the language. This situation led Europeans to view Pijin as 'a simple and droll medium for communicating about a superior culture and technology to savages, whose linguistic ineptitude was a mirror of their cultural backwardness and lower mental powers' (Keesing, 1990: 153). Since it is this latter view that became the dominant ideology about Pijin, it 'was never given a standard orthography, committed to writing, or codified with a published dictionary or grammar' (199, 155). Thus, historical analysis can often provide an important basis for understanding the sociolinguistic situation in which a language planner is working.

Language planning evaluation

In her introduction to evaluation and language planning written a quarter of a century ago, Rubin indicated that:

> any approach to evaluation and language planning must remain at this point fairly academic and theoretical because of the dearth of data on the actual processes that characterize language-planning evaluation within a specific setting. (1971: 217)

At the time, both the fields of evaluation and language planning were relatively new, and perhaps such a summary of the situation was only to be expected. She notes, however, that there seemed to be a 'negative attitude in linguistic circles toward all problems of evaluation' (1971: 235). Nevertheless, a decade later, although she was still convinced that good planning implied continued evaluation and revision of a plan during the implementation phase of the language planning process, Rubin (1983: 338) found that in practice 'this is only rarely done'. The situation hasn't changed dramatically since Rubin made that comment. Very little evaluation of language planning activities has been conducted and published (e.g. Eggington & Baldauf, 1990; Doğançay-Aktuna, 1995; Gonzalez, 1990; Noss, 1985; Thomas, 1981) although there are a range of programme evaluations that have been carried out for restricted audiences and have not therefore been published (e.g. Riley-Mundine, 1990; Baldauf, 1995a).

To put language planning evaluation in perspective, it is perhaps useful to look at the more specific case of the evaluation of language education programmes. While the more general notions of programme evaluation and educational evaluation are major fields with professional bodies of their own (e.g. the American Evaluation Association), Beretta, (1992: 5) points out that very few second language education evaluation studies are ever published, despite a seemingly never-ending 'methods' debate relating to research. Beretta (1992) and Brown (1995) have reviewed this second language evaluation research and the latter lists only 60 published studies between 1963 and 1994, barely two a year. Alderson and Beretta (1992) provide perhaps the only text related to second language education evaluation. Although there are a number of books which examine research methods for language education (e.g. Brown, 1988; Hatch & Lazaraton, 1991; Nunan, 1992; Scholfield, 1994; and Seliger & Shohamy, 1989) or language testing (e.g. Bachman, 1990; Bachman & Palmer, 1996; Davies, 1990; Henning, 1987; McNamara, 1996) and these volumes provide good references to specific issues which can arise in language planning evaluation, they do not address the process of language planning evaluation. As indicated previously, the language planning literature is also silent on the matter of evaluation.[1]

While on the issue of evaluating language education programmes, it needs to be noted that the use of (language) educational evaluation to collect language planning data can be fraught with dangers of misinterpretation if there is an attempt to use the results of such studies to answer larger language planning questions with narrower and more focused language-in-education results (e.g. Eggington & Baldauf, 1990). That is to say, normally language programmes are only one aspect of a language plan, and results from an evaluation of such programmes can only contribute to an understanding of the wider sociocultural goals to be achieved by most language plans. Even where language planning is more narrowly focused, as in true bilingual programmes, the educational evaluation will focus on the effectiveness of language learning, whereas the language planning evaluation must look beyond the school at the sociocultural purposes for which the programme was established. Noss (1985) provides some specific examples of evaluations of language in education programmes, while Gonzalez (1990) demonstrates that, under some circumstances, using a national sample, a language plan can be evaluated by what is substantially a language-in-education evaluation.

Turning specifically to the evaluation of language planning and language-in-education planning, as Figures 4.2 and 4.5 indicate, feedback, assessment and evaluation are important both in terms of the initial planning or fact-finding phases, to gather information so that appropriate selection decisions can be made, and in the context of its implementation as well as in execution of the plan. Evaluation should occur at every stage of the language planning process. It should start at the policy development stage, and the various stages of the plan should be monitored and checked against reality. Without formal evaluation, the evidence is hearsay and one cannot be sure whether the goals are being reached. Finally, having implemented a language-planning policy, questions arise such as: How well is the policy being implemented? To what extent? How successful is the implementation? These questions suggest the need for some means of formal evaluation or assessment of the policy.

Brown (1995: 228–34) suggests that there are six types of decisions to be considered by second language evaluators when they are planning their work, and these are also useful for language planners to consider.

(1) *Summative or formative?* In some respects, macro language planning evaluation is almost always formative, as programmes are under development for long periods of time and any evaluation, by definition, seeks to improve the programme. However, summative evaluations can occur at particular points in time and this may lead to a shift in emphasis or a change in some goals. In micro language planning situations formative evaluation may be used to decide whether to continue or discontinue some particular language activity.

(2) *Outside expert or participatory model?* By their very nature, most macro language planning situations involve the use of outside expertise, but the very success of such programmes depends on the co-operation and participation of the stakeholders in negotiating an implementable language plan.

(3) *Field research or laboratory research?* While most language planning evaluation needs to be based on field work, historical data collection or a commission of enquiry, based mainly on a call for submissions and an analysis of reports, means that some language-planning evaluations may have a substantial 'desk' evaluation component.

(4) *Evaluate during or after the programme?* As with many other social programmes, there may be no clear end to a particular language planning process, but rather periods when funding or political decisions need to be made. Evaluations may be mandated to occur at these points in time and the evaluator will have to examine the work in terms of partial outcomes.

(5) *Quantitative or qualitative?* The scale of most language planning activities means that quantitative outcomes of some sort are almost always demanded, but often these can only be understood in terms of their social impact through case studies or other qualitative data.

(6) *Process or product?* Evaluation of language planning is mainly about process. Particular products, goals in terms of numbers of speakers, etc. are difficult to measure and in any case are mainly indicators of the success of the process.

In summary, because of the size and complexity of many (potential) language planning evaluations, evaluators are not really confronted with a choice about how to collect their evaluation data. The requirements of the situation will often dictate what decision needs to be taken and frequently it requires consideration of both of the evaluation alternatives.

As Brown (1995) has noted, there are also a number of problems to be solved as part of an evaluation study. For the language planner, these involve primarily issues of sampling (i.e. At what intervals does one collect information? How is the sample to be collected? Different times of the day, days of the week? How large is the sample?), problems of instrumentation (i.e. the types of data collection instruments to be used – surveys, tests, etc.), problems of reliability, bias and error (i.e. is the sample biased, are the test questions reliable, etc.) and problems of politics (i.e. language choice and use is almost never a neutral political issue). When working in a team, it is important to bring the evaluators together to discuss the evaluation information to attempt to avoid problems.

It may then be appropriate to ask 'What kinds of methods should be used to inform a language planning evaluation?' Given the nature of this section, the response must be brief and indicative, and readers may find information provided in the methods references mentioned earlier useful. Davis (1995) and Lazaraton (1995) provide some further discussion of qualitative methodology. Some useful procedures include conducting surveys of various types about language use and language attitudes. However, a longitudinal survey may take about 10 years to show results. Case studies can provide information about specific types of change related to a language plan. The direct observation and recording of language use in different situations can provide information about language use for different purposes. Language testing of children can help to establish changes in formal language proficiency. There are also a number of non-obtrusive measures that can be used. For example, one might look for indicators of language use such as: sales of books; library use; television, radio, video shop use; cultural activities; advertising; language of graffiti, bumper stickers; or just watching/listening to people on public transport. The methods used and the nature of the evaluation undertaken must be matched to the nature and stage of the evaluation.

Finally, Alderson (1992: 298–9) in his guidelines for the evaluation of language education sums up the purpose and importance of evaluations:

> ... they are intended to serve practical ends, to inform decision makers as to the appropriate courses of action, and, above all to be *useful* and to be *used*. An evaluation not used is in some sense a failure .... The evaluator's main concern must be to obtain results that can be used, and to make recommendations that can be followed .... In order to stand a chance of being used, an evaluation must not only be relevant, but it also needs to be the result of a negotiation process between the stakeholders at the outset; it needs to be adequately resourced and implemented; deadlines and deliverables need to be kept to; the results

and recommendations must be adequately interpreted in terms of educational [i.e. language planning] policy and be adequately reported.

We argue in Chapter 11 that language planning is the ultimate example of applied linguistics. In language planning evaluation this is certainly the case.

Cost analysis

The language skills and behaviour of people can be conceptualised as a national resource. As with any resource, language can be developed and used to achieve certain results and these results can be quantified. As language planning often is about selecting from different possible goals and alternatives for achieving those goals, some form of cost analysis can be used to give decision makers information for comparing the costs and economic benefits of selecting different alternatives (Thorburn, 1971). In cost analysis goals are identified, means are chosen and quantified and results are predicted and evaluated in an explicit and systematic manner. Lundin and Sandery (1993) have suggested that there are five forms of cost analysis that can be undertaken, including:

- *cost-benefit analysis*, the commonly used term for such analyses, which actually refers to a comparison of costs (inputs) and benefits (outcomes) where each is measured in monetary terms;
- *cost-effectiveness analysis* which refers to a consideration of the costs linked to the achievement of a set of objectives;
- *cost utility or outcomes analysis* which refers to a comparison of costs and the assessed utility or value of outcomes;
- *cost-feasibility analysis* which looks at whether or not a project can be implemented within budget in the context in which it is proposed, and
- *partitioning costs analysis* (cost efficiency analysis) which examines specific costs linked to individual programme objectives.

Each of these types of analysis is potentially of interest to language planners, but often the distinctions are not made. For example, Fasold (1984) has noted that there are limitations to the *cost-benefit analysis* approach as it is often difficult to quantify monetarily the outcomes of a planned language activity especially when the impact of that activity may not fully be apparent for a long time (i.e. the cost of producing a book of poetry in a national language can be calculated, but the benefit of doing that on the national psyche is harder to calculate, especially as the impact may be over a long period of time). Most of the literature discusses *cost analysis* in terms of *cost-benefit analysis*, but language planning activities often would be more suitably examined using a *cost-outcomes analysis*.

As Fasold (1984) and Edwards (1985) indicate, very few cost-benefit analyses have been done or are available for scrutiny. Furthermore, what economic analysis seems to have been done to evaluate language planning has often focused on language-in-education planning efforts or on other micro problems. The danger of evaluating a language plan based on a partial analysis (e.g. using language-in-education planning data to evaluate a language plan) has been argued by Eggington and Baldauf (1990) as those partial outcomes may provide a very biased view of the impact of the language plan. Vaillancourt summarises the issue of the impact of economic analysis on language planning when he says:

> The literature indicates that while economists have developed analytic tools useful in understanding the effects of language planning on firms and individuals, they have not done so for society as a whole. (1983: 178)

Cost-benefit analysis is a planning technique widely recognised in a great many sectors of society (see e.g. Department of Finance, 1992) and government frequently engages in it for natural resource development. For example, in the dam building illustration used in Chapter 1, before government enters into the construction of such a project it carefully evaluates the cost of building the dam as opposed to the benefits produced by the existence of the dam. While this is not an easy task, it is a possible task, since the cost of building a dam can be accurately estimated, and the fiscal benefits of increased hydro-electric energy, irrigation, recreation, etc. can be estimated with reasonable precision; the number of jobs created by the project and its various outcomes can be accurately estimated; the increase in real product (as a function of increased boat sales for recreation, new home construction as a result of increased hydro-electric power availability, etc.) can be specified.

For the reasons indicated previously, it is far more difficult to conduct cost-benefit analysis as part of human resource development, in this case a language planning operation, but it is nevertheless desirable to do so. For example, Thorburn (1971: 259) outlines the information that would need to be analysed if a nation were to adopt a 'Language of Wider Communication (LWC) vs .... "one of the National Languages" ' (NL) as the national language (see Figure 4.1). Once the costs of the input were calculated and the potential benefits were worked out for both the LWC and NL, then actual differences in costs and quantification of other potential differences and consequences could be compared. The result would be a cost-outcomes analysis, as it is not possible to quantify the outcomes in specific monetary terms. However, such an analysis could be useful to support decisions by politicians on their choice of language.

To take a specific example, the real costs of a sociolinguistic survey can be calculated quite accurately; this is, in fact, the only segment of the

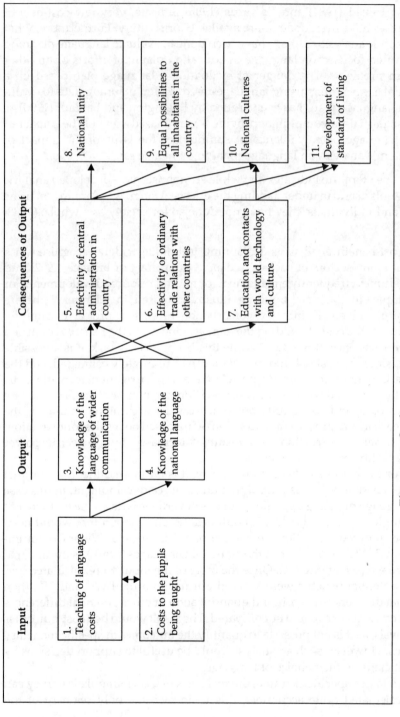

Figure 4.1 Outline of a national cost-benefit analysis

language planning activity in which immediate currency expenditures can be carefully tracked. The real cost of:

- salaries for a survey team;
- salaries for field workers and their supervisors;
- transportation costs associated with the project;
- computer analysis costs (in connect-time, manpower, paper);
- publication and dissemination of a survey report;
- man-hours involved in policy decisions;
- man-hours in implementation plan development;

and so on, can easily be determined. But, unfortunately, the value of an implementation plan is hard to calculate. The costs of implementation in the various sectors can be determined with the same relatively high degree of accuracy, but the value of the benefits accruing from implementation is very difficult to determine.[2]

To the extent possible, then, an important part of the work of any survey team is to initiate a cost outcomes analysis. It is understood that the team cannot assign a dollar-figure to the benefits, but it can at least list them in a cost outcomes report following to some extent the model presented in Table 4.1. Although direct dollar-figures cannot be attributed to the benefit side, listing the anticipated benefits at least shows what can be expected.

Table 4.1 demonstrates the problem more clearly than a great deal of exposition could; on the left are activities that require immediate expenditures of money to accomplish, while on the right are vague statements about improved facilities, resources, and outcomes, to which it is impossible to attach dollar figures because it is hard to isolate proximate cause (that is, there are other factors that might provide the same benefits), because it is unknown what the costs are of maintaining the *status quo*, because it is not known what would happen if a different set of policy decisions were put in place, and because the benefits, whatever they are, are removed in the future while the costs are immediate.

A major problem in all planning is the inability to know what the outcomes would be if the *status quo* were maintained or if a totally different plan were put in place. At the same time, once a plan has been instantiated, a real problem is that there is no going back. If the plan is aborted, it will be impossible to determine what it might have achieved. And because the benefits to be derived are in the distant future, it will not be possible to know in any useful sense whether the plan is viable until it is too late. For example, if greater language access by minorities is intended and achieved, but that greater access does not lead to the predicted stabilisation of the society but rather leads to greater unrest because people come to recognise that they genuinely are disadvantaged, by the time the outcomes become apparent, it is too late to reverse the trends.

Table 4.1 Cost-outcome analysis reporting

Cost	Benefit
Survey costs	Better data for decision making
Salaries	Greater knowledge of in-country
Fringe benefits	language situation
Materials and supplies	Better understanding of needs
Equipment	Better understanding of effect of
Equipment maintenance	existing policies
Transportation	Greater co-ordination among
Publication	government departments
Data processing	
Policy decision costs	More effective policy
Man hours × $	Greater interaction among
Transportation	government departments
Report publication and	Development of wider
dissemination	understanding of language issues
Communication to agencies	Co-ordination among many
	segments
Implementation plan	Greater co-operation between
Man-hours × $	government and private sector
Transportation	
Report production	
Dissemination	
Monitoring	
Language-in-education plan	More children served better
Pre-service teacher training	Better teacher training
In-service teacher training	More efficient teacher pool
Materials production	Better materials
Syllabus development	Improved syllabi
Assessment instrument	Better assessment
production	
Transportation	
Man-hours × $	
Dissemination	
Surplus maintenance and storage	

Finally, it is important to understand that language planning is not a one-off activity. It tends to generate its own needs. Because human societies are always changing, the planning process must change along with changes in the society. Planning, once undertaken, is an ongoing process. As it is difficult to predict what benefits may accrue from a particular planning activity (or to attribute proximate cause to changes), so it is difficult to foresee what additional problems may result as a planning activity unfolds and where the next areas of concern will emerge.

Cost analysis is part of the larger issue of the relationship between language and economics and the role of language in economic performance which is developed more extensively in Chapter 6.

Corpus analyses

Since the early 1960s it has become possible to store large quantities of natural language materials on computers, bring about an increasingly rapid growth in computer corpora, i.e. machine readable collections text (see Johansson, 1995; Leech & Fligelstone, 1992; Meijs, 1966; Murison-Bowie, 1996 for recent reviews of the field). A number of large corpora – some now being developed are to have 50 to 200 million words – have been created (e.g. the Brown Corpus; the Lancaster-Oslo/Bergen Corpus; the London-Lund Corpus; the Birmingham Collection of English Texts; the Longman/Birkbeck Corpus of Learners' English; International Corpus of English). Some are available for academic research purposes through the International Computer Archive of Modern English (ICAME),[3] publishers of the *ICAME Journal*, but research with this resource has been relatively limited. Copyright and commercial considerations have limited access to corpora and there is still some way to go before they become a public resource. As many corpora are based primarily on texts, rather than spoken language, much of the language research with corpora has been on literary topics (e.g. Biber, 1993). Although many of the corpora are based on English, major corpora are being developed in 16 different languages excluding English (Leech & Fligelstone, 1992) Thus, corpus analysis is an area which is becoming increasingly important to language planners interested in corpus planning or language teaching because it can provide accurate information about a language and its use, and materials can be tailored to different groups of users.

Electronic lexicography (Logan, 1991; Meijs, 1992; also the University of Exeter Dictionary Research Centre) has been a major development in parallel with corpora research (i.e. not all electronic dictionaries are developed from corpora or lexicographical databases, but most are now made up using computer tools). The earliest and most comprehensive example of a corpora based work was the *Collins CoBuild English Language Dictionary* (Sinclair *et al.*, 1987) developed using the Birmingham Collection of English Text. In the development of this project, Sinclair (1987) and his colleagues have shown that large linguistic corpus work can be a language planning exercise of major proportions. The dictionary project began as a corpus building exercise in about 1961 with the original main corpus being seven million words in length. By 1987 the general corpus contained around 20 million words and there were about 20 million additional words of text of a more specialised nature. The dictionary was not only corpora based, but entry-selection, entry-construction and entry-arrangement were all computer based. Computerised ways of marking grammatical forms and pronunciation were also developed. This major corpus planning exercise has also generated a whole range of pedagogical materials including *The Lexical Syllabus* (Willis, 1990) and the *Collins CoBuild English Course* (Willis & Willis, 1988). Some of this material is particularly useful to the English-as-a-second language learner because it contains English based on actual usage (e.g. the most common usage of 'well' is as a pause marker). The project demonstrates the contribution that corpora based work can make to language planning. While most people may never become involved in a major corpora project, the concordancing software for examining texts, a key tool in dictionary development, is readily available and can make a useful pedagogical tool in language teaching (see e.g. Tribble & Jones, 1990).

Anthropological linguistics

An important part of any recommendation for implementing a language plan is knowing the degree to which the basic linguistic work, the corpus planning, on the language(s) under consideration has been done. The sub-discipline of *anthropological linguistics* or linguistic anthropology is concerned with the field study of a language (e.g. Healey, 1975) within the framework of sociocultural anthropology. This framework is illustrated by a series of three student oriented case studies by Williams of Dusan society in North Borneo (Sabah) where he sets out *Field Methods in the Study of Culture* (1967), examines *A Borneo Childhood: Enculturation in Dusan Society* (1969) and provides an overview of a village in the society itself in *The Dusan: A North Borneo Society* (1966). This sociocultural background when related to the language being studied shows what aspects of a language(s) are used for which purposes. Historically, anthropological linguistics has dealt with the description of non-Western languages of preliterate societies. Many anthropological linguists are not academics, but work in government departments or are affiliated with missionary organisations such as the Summer Institute of Linguistics. In some cases, such as the development of bilingual programmes in the Northern Territory, Australia (see Russo & Baldauf, 1986; Sommer, 1991), such work may provide the only linguistic material available for the implementation of language programmes. Jernudd (1971) used fieldwork among Australian Aboriginals to develop a hypothesis about how these peoples developed and implemented language change in traditional settings.

The linguistic anthropology strand places more emphasis on the cognitive rather than the social aspects of the field. As such it is interested in culture as rule generated behaviour, and the ethnosemantic tradition suggests that a structural analysis of specifically defined domains of language use can provide evidence for those rules of culture.

> Their concern is what 'ways of speaking', thus observed, can reveal about the representation of cultural knowledge in a wide range of cultural domains: how such representations are organised, how they are deployed and reproduced, and what might be the limits on their diversity. (J.H. Hill 1992: 66)

For language planners, such understandings are useful in the development of terminological equivalence and in understanding the important relationships between language and its more broadly based role within culture. Another important strand within linguistic anthropology is the 'ethnography of speaking' which some would argue is a key methodology for collecting language planning information.

Ethnography of communication

The *ethnography of communication* was originally conceived as the *ethnography of speaking* in a series of papers published in the 1960s by Dell Hymes (see Hymes, 1974 for a comprehensive overview). Hymes called for an analysis of language (and particularly speech) which dealt with those aspects which fell outside the normal concerns of anthropology, linguistics and sociology. He was interested in native-speaker theories about various acts of communication as well as the ways in which native speakers enacted communicative acts in a variety of situations.

He introduced the notion of a *speech event* as being central to ethnographic study; thus, the analysis of such events would require the study of the interrelationships of many factors, including: setting, genres, linguistic varieties employed, manner of delivery, participants, purpose, etc., and such analyses would in turn lead to a description that captures what is unique in terms of culture, language, and communication in each linguistic community. In his view, the ethnographic approach is concerned with at least the following four aspects of language:

(1) What sociolinguistic resources are available in particular speech communities? i.e. these resources go well beyond conventional grammar and include the complex of potentials for social use and meaning – the relationships among words, styles, and terms of reference.

(2) What are the means for exploiting these resources in discourse and

social interactions? e.g. in agreeing, disagreeing, greeting, showing varying degrees of respect, teasing, etc.

(3) Are their consistent patterned interrelationships in various discourses?
(4) What is the interrelationship between such patterns and other aspects of culture in the community? e.g. economics, politics, religion, social organisation, etc. While most extant studies deal with particular single aspects of the set enumerated above, a complete ethnography would deal with all of them.

Collections of papers published through the 1960s and 1970s helped to establish this approach (e.g. Gumperz & Hymes, 1964, 1972; Bauman & Sherzer, 1974). Some of the papers in these collections looked carefully at such areas as 'baby talk', 'code-switching', 'sequencing in conversational openings', etc. In the 1970s, a new group of scholars began to employ ethnographic approaches focusing on particular communities; among the best known of such studies are Scollon and Scollon (1979) – which looked specifically at language practices in an Athabaskan-speaking community – and Heath (1983) – which compared discourse and literacy patterns in two English-speaking communities. These two studies also looked seriously at the differences between oral and written discourse and at the role of language in educational settings. Since then, the literature in the ethnography of communication has grown extensively and has become very rich. (For recent surveys with an educational focus, see Poole, 1991; Hornberger, 1995a.)

One important feature of this approach is that, of necessity, it is discourse-centred, thus escaping the sentence-focus of most linguistic research, especially that of autonomous linguistics. It has called attention not only to *text* itself, but to *context* and *prior text*. It has demonstrated that there are coherent patterns in language practices in societies around the world and that these patterns differ from society to society. And it has given rise to the substantial research in *contrastive rhetoric* and in *genre analysis*, particularly with respect to written text.

Its importance in language policy and planning is apparent; if sociolinguistic surveys (see following section) can be conducted from an ethnographic perspective, the data produced will be vastly more helpful in understanding who speaks what to whom, under what circumstances, and for what purpose.

Sociolinguistic Surveys

The primary focus of this chapter is on the sociolinguistic survey. This can take many forms including: *National or Regional Surveys* (Anderson, 1985 [Singapore]; Bolton & Luke, 1985 [Hong Kong]; Gonzalez, 1985 [Philippines]; Mehrotra, 1985 [South Asia]; Ohannessian & Ansre, 1975 [education – East Africa]; Ó Riagáin, 1988 [Ireland]; Reyburn, 1975

[Honduras, Nicaragua]; Whiteley, 1974 [Kenya]); *Census Data* (Fasold, 1984; Clyne, 1982, 1988b [Australia]); and *Local Surveys* (Ansre, 1975 [Madina, Ghana]; Benton, 1975 [Maori – New Zealand]; Calvet *et al.*, 1992 [markets in Africa]; Krishnamurti, 1985 [Telugu – India]; Ogino *et al.*, 1985 [honorifics – Japan]; Swan & Lewis, 1990 [Tok Pisin – Papua New Guinea]; Veltman & Denis, 1988 [attitudes in Alsace]). In addition, in some places government or parliamentary enquiries are held which can have some of the same characteristics and functions as the sociolinguistic survey (e.g. Lo Bianco, 1987a [Australia]). Let us first look at a small example of how such data can be collected.

As Cooper's (1989) accounting scheme suggests, an understanding of the linguistic situation derives from answering a complex set of questions: who speaks what to whom under what conditions and for what purpose? In a polyglot state, a given individual may use several different languages for several different purposes. When Kaplan was in the Philippines a number of years ago for the government, he was assigned a car and driver by the US Embassy to facilitate his movement about Metro-Manila – a very large, very congested area. Because he and the driver spent a lot of time together in traffic, he took the occasion to conduct a small informal language survey with the driver. The driver had been born in Cebu City and was a native speaker of Cebuano. In adulthood, he had married a woman who was a native speaker of Waray, a language he learned in order to communicate with his in-laws. The family lived in Manila where the children went to school in Tagalog. He worked for the US Embassy where English was the language of the workplace. He testified that he spoke:

- *Cebuano* with his immediate family and in most informal situations with friends;
- *Waray* with his wife's family and her immediate circle of friends;
- *Tagalog* in informal situations in Manila, with new acquaintances in Metro-Manila, when he travelled on business into other parts of the Philippines where neither Cebuano nor Waray was spoken, to shop for necessities, and with his children's school environment;
- *English* with his job supervisor, with his work colleagues (who were native speakers of a wide variety of Philippine languages), to shop for luxury goods, and when he went drinking with his friends because, he said, English was an outstanding language to swear in.

While the study is superficial and cannot be generalised (since it is based on a sample size of one), it is illustrative of one set of answers to the questions 'Who speaks what to whom under what circumstances for what purposes?' This anecdotal survey demonstrates that a given individual can control several languages and can understand when to use each of those languages with clearly identified audiences to achieve quite specific objectives. The subject of the survey was not highly educated and had never had a course in linguistics, yet he was sensitive to the fact that different languages could be used to achieve different objectives with different interlocutors. He seemed to understand the sociolinguistic rules that governed the choice of an appropriate language and of an appropriate register within that language.

A sociolinguistic survey of the type discussed in this chapter is intended to answer such specific questions as the following, with respect to each speech community within the region under study. In what language does one:

(1)   Get married/divorced?
(2)   Vote (in a democratic state)?
(3)   Pray?
(4)   Get one's hair cut?
(5)   Listen to music on radio/TV?
(6)   Read newspapers/magazines/comics, if one is literate?
(7)   Read technical materials, assuming that one is literate?
(8)   Read poetry/stories/novels, assuming that one is literate?
(9)   Hear the news/gossip from whatever source?
(10)   Shop for groceries and other necessities?
(11)   Shop for luxury goods?
(12)   Go to school?
(13)   Address one's parents/peers/siblings/children/dependants/other relatives/marital partner/superiors/workmates?
(14)   Make love?
(15)   Acquire housing?

This list of questions is not exhaustive; it is intended only to suggest the various domains in which most people function (see Ansre, 1975; Nyembwe et al., 1992; Reyburn, 1975; Sreedhar et al., 1984; Swan & Lewis, 1990; Veltman & Denis, 1988 for examples of questionnaires). The answers to these questions, cumulated over a community, begin to form a picture of the language situation within that community. The sociolinguistic survey is intended primarily to supply precisely such a picture of the existing language situation across a state made up of many communities. As the examples in the initial paragraph in this section demonstrate, sociolinguistic surveys can be conducted at a variety of levels for different purposes. We have chosen to discuss a large-scale national survey, because it is the most complex and raises the widest range of issues. While it may be unlikely that most readers will be participating in a survey implemented on this scale, many of the issues raised are also applicable to sociolinguistic surveys completed at a company level by the lone researcher developing a company language policy.

Pre-survey planning

Large-scale sociolinguistic surveys are complex processes which normally require a polity to decide that such an activity is warranted and to invite some person – hopefully a qualified person – to organise and conduct the survey. Before becoming involved in such an undertaking, the person invited to co-ordinate the effort may wish to determine, in so far as possible, that the objectives of government in mounting such a research effort are, for lack of a better term, 'honourable'; that is, one would not, presumably, want to co-ordinate an effort if it was clear that the objective was, for example, linguacide. The person invited to co-ordinate the effort also needs to determine in so far as possible whether government has an understanding of the time and costs involved; that is, one would not, presumably, wish to undertake an effort that was preordained to fail for lack of adequate resources or adequate time.

Being assured of more or less positive answers to these questions, the co-ordinator needs to assemble a team, because such an effort is beyond the capacity of one person. The team should include at least: a historian, an anthropologist, an economist, a professional planner, a data processor, a political scientist, and a linguist, all well acquainted with the target state. To the extent possible, the members of the team should be drawn from the population of the target country, but if no appropriate specialist is locally available, it may be necessary to seek expatriate help. The members of the team will not need to be constantly present throughout the activity; their heaviest workload will occur at the beginning and at the end of the survey process. Although they need not be physically present throughout, they must understand that they are committing themselves to a project that may last as long as three years, depending on the size of the survey to be conducted, the size of the target state, and the available resources.

The members of the team would normally follow the steps outlined in Figure 4.2. Following this model, the survey is perceived as the first step in a more complex process. The *survey* produces a *survey report*, which in turn results in a series of *policy decisions*. The policy decisions lead to an *implementation plan* which finally is realised through *execution* of the plan. The role of the survey team ends with the presentation to government of the survey report, unless some subset of the team is invited to advise in the context of the policy decision phase. At every stage of this model, there is provision for feedback; the survey report may, for example, illuminate some gaps in the survey, or the policy decision phase may turn up a need for information not contained in the original survey report.

The survey is, necessarily, preceded by an elaborate set of pre-survey activities, as illustrated in Figure 4.3. The various steps in this pre-survey phase are concerned with, on the one hand, the assembly of a larger team of field workers who will undertake actual data collection in the various speech communities, and, on the other hand, the assembly of preliminary

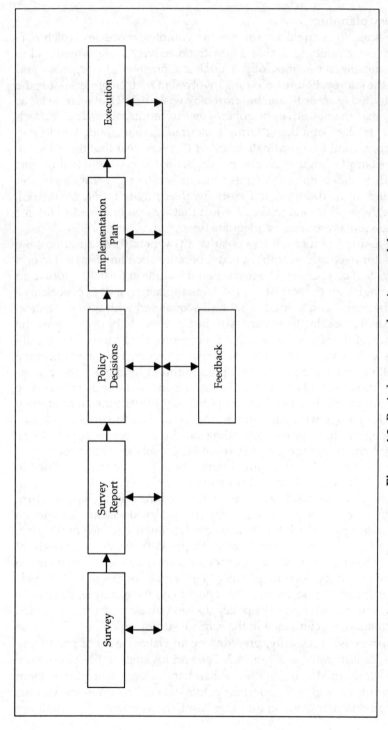

Figure 4.2 Basic language planning model

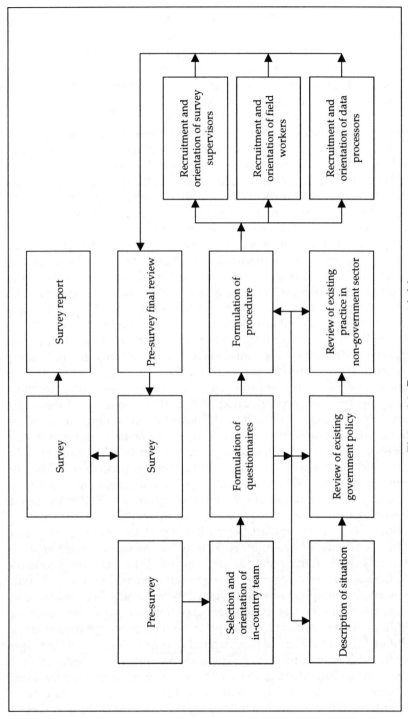

Figure 4.3 Pre-survey activities

data that will inform the design and development of a survey instrument(s). Critical decisions will be made in this phase with respect to the most effective modality of the survey – e.g. direct face-to-face interviews, telephone interviews, mail surveys or a combination of some or all of these. Each of the stages in the pre-survey phase is now briefly discussed.

The selection of the survey team has already been touched upon, but in organising the survey team, great care has to be given to equity; for example, expatriate members of the team cannot be compensated at a rate that is significantly out of line with the compensation of the in-country members of the team, and the in-country members must be compensated at a rate that is consistent with remuneration in the state. Issues of gender and ethnic background must also be considered if the team is to collect and analyse the data accurately. This equity consideration may have an effect on the kinds of individuals who can be recruited to the team.

Once recruited, the members of the team need to be oriented carefully to the project; objectives as specified by the government need to be clearly understood. Lines of responsibility within the team and with respect to various phases of the project must be made clear; and deadlines must be understood by all of the individuals involved. Only after these preliminaries are taken into account can the team begin work on the project.

When the team is assembled and oriented, it needs to undertake two simultaneous activities; the simultaneity of the activity requires some division of labour within the survey team. The historian, the economist, the political scientist and the anthropologist can explore the country situation, developing some conceptualisation of the ethnic make-up of the larger community, the history of the country together with some notion of the political and economic forces at work. At the same time, the linguist, the professional planner and the data processor can begin formulating the survey instrument and working on the survey procedure. The data processor is particularly seminal at this point in designing an instrument from which data extraction and computer entry will be efficient and rapid. Sub-teams can, after preliminary work is completed in each sphere, trade positions, so that the linguist begins looking at the historical linguistic situation while the other group works to refine the survey instrument.

It is important at this point to determine what the team needs to know from the survey, what segments of the population are likely to constitute representative samples from which such data can be acquired, and whether the questionnaire(s) will be monolingual (and in what language) or multilingual (and in what languages). If the data collection instrument is multilingual, the problem of exactly parallel versions in several languages must be dealt with at this point. (There are a number of techniques, such as back-translation, which can be used to ensure maximum comparability.) But there is also the problem that some survey techniques may be so unfamiliar that it is not worthwhile using them; for example, in collecting attitude data, the semantic differential is a particularly useful technique, but it may be quite impossible to build parallel sets of adjectives in several languages or to get village people to respond.

The modalities for the survey need to be determined at this point as well. Will the instrument be written with the expectation that respondents will receive it, complete it and return it, or is the linguistic situation such that literacy is not widely disseminated? If the instrument is literacy-dependent, what segment of the population will not participate? More importantly, what is the most effective means of distributing and collecting questionnaires? Is the post sufficiently dependable or will it be necessary to distribute through some other network – e.g. schools, workplaces, churches, etc.? Will greatest possible return be ensured by personal distribution versus postal distribution? What techniques can be used to maximise the rate of return? If the instrument is literacy-independent, what numbers of field workers will be needed for adequate data collection? In what languages will the field workers operate and what skills will they need to possess in order to collect appropriate data? How long will interviews be? What are the most viable places in which to conduct such interviews – e.g. schools, workplaces, barber shops, churches, village squares, market places, etc.? What is a statistically valid number of interviews of each type? How can one be sure to cover the population along each significant parameter; e.g. gender, urban/rural, etc.? Are there divisions more meaningful in the target society than those used in developed states; e.g. is urban/rural a meaningful distinction, or is there some more meaningful rural/suburban/urban differentiation?

At the same time that these decisions are being taken, the team also needs to accumulate a sense of existing language policies in education, in other governmental sectors, in the communications industry and in the business sector. Such policies are not always explicit and are not necessarily easy to find; often, they are buried in memos or in other obscure ephemeral sources. Every effort has to be made to uncover them, since they implicate the kinds of information to be collected through the survey. For example, there may be a national high-school leaving examination which includes some sort of language assessment; the existence of such an examination may generate practices quite at variance with official education policy and more powerful than official policy.

Finally, the team will need to recruit and orient field worker supervisors (responsible for geographic sectors, or ethnic sectors, depending on what makes sense in the environment), field workers (who will actually distribute the instrument or engage in actual direct collection through some sort of interview process), and data processors (who will enter the data as it is collected, collate the data along pre-set lines, and perform various statistical operations on the data). It is particularly important that data processors understand the nature of the data they will be handling and the nature of the desired output, because inappropriate data handling can easily result in erasure, data loss or inaccurate entry. The same equity problem that arises in the recruitment of the research team arises in this case as well. The various categories of workers have to be remunerated on a scale comparable to scales for other such work in the community. Depending on the target community, loyalty to the project and the dependability of individual workers may be an issue; in societies in which salary scales are very low and workers typically moonlight, for example, the reliability and availability of workers can become an overwhelming problem.

At the end of the scheduled pre-survey time, a final check needs to be undertaken to be certain that no segment of the plan has been left unattended. If the postal services are involved, for example, it is important to be certain that the postal authorities are prepared for the unusually heavy workload that may be involved in processing the instrument; if field workers must travel significant distances within the country, it must be clear that appropriate travel reservations have been booked and confirmed so that individuals do not get stranded. This final check is the primary responsibility of the project co-ordinator, but s/he may need a good deal of local assistance, particularly if the co-ordinator is an expatriate and is not fluent in the language in which logistic details are normally handled. The agency which has contracted the project may be able to offer not only key assistance but key staff familiar with such logistic arrangements.

The survey

At this point, the actual survey process may commence. Field workers may now be dispatched to the various sites in which they will conduct data collection. It is important to be assured that field work supervisors have adequate contact with the groups they will supervise and that supervisors will report in on a fairly regular basis (perhaps weekly) to be certain that the process is actually working. Some field workers may prove unsuitable to the task; it is important that field workers do not offend respondents and that field workers can actually penetrate the societal sectors from which they are to collect data. Supervisors need to be free to make personnel substitutions when problems arise, but the team must be kept constantly apprised of events in the field.

While the field workers are collecting, the members of the team, presumably stationed in the capital city, will be engaged in interviews with leaders in key sectors, as suggested in Figure 4.4. The obvious sectors have been identified in the model – education, foreign affairs, commerce, communications, labour, business – but the identification of key sectors is very much a function of the local situation. The interviews will attempt both to fill in gaps in the team's understanding of the existing situation and will also try to achieve an understanding of the most desired directions of

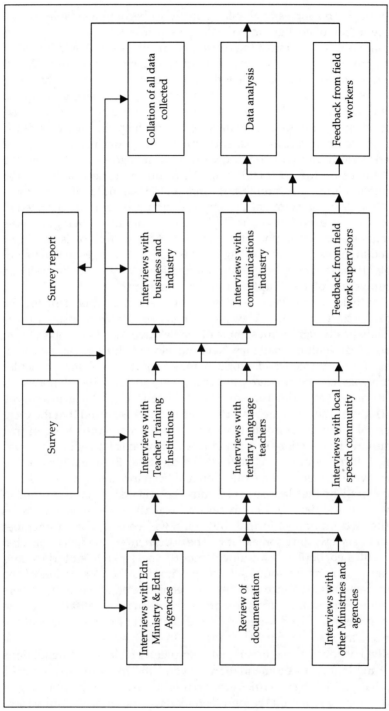

Figure 4.4 The sociolinguistic survey process

change, of the resources available or likely to become available for the implementation of change, and of political sensitivities.

Throughout the course of the collection process, data should be fed to the data processors in a constant stream and entered on a daily basis. Much time can be saved if data are entered on an ongoing basis rather than held until all of the data are available. Regular entry also permits frequent accuracy checks along the way and helps to minimise both data loss and inaccurate entry. Intermediate data analysis can help the members of the team begin to draw conclusions. These preliminary conclusions should be checked periodically with key individuals in the agency contracting the project to ensure the acceptability of the results and the viability of the recommendations that are taking shape; for example, if a national high-school leaving examination is in place and problems are detected in relation to that examination, is it viable to recommend changes in the examination, or elimination of the examination entirely or is the 'face' involved in the examination so high that significant changes really are not possible? If the latter is the case, what alternative strategies can be designed to circumvent problems implicit in the examination?

As the field data collection draws to a close, it is important for the members of the team to interview individually all field worker supervisors and a statistically significant sample of the field workers themselves to get a sense of difficulties that may have developed during the collection process. For example, field workers may report that some particular question was rejected regularly by respondents, or that the orientation of a particular item in the instrument may have been incorrect (e.g. in a survey in which the author was the researcher, he had been assured that the great majority of individuals in the workplace were male; on the basis of that assumption, the question 'What language do you speak to your *wife*?' was designed; in practice, it was actually the case that the great majority of workers were female, and the question had been incorrectly oriented).

Finally, all of the data received must be collated. It is important to observe that the data will be in several formats; some of it will be in computerised numerical format, but some will consist of team-member notes of interviews, and some of it will be documentary evidence collected from published books, government reports, newspaper editorials, and other more ephemeral sources. Collation implies the integration of the various data formats. Once the data has been collated, the team members may begin writing the survey report. The various specialisations of the team members will lend themselves to delegation of various parts of the report to various members of the team. Recommendations need to be carefully developed to be certain that unimplementable recommendations are not made (e.g. recommendations beyond the fiscal resources of the state), that political sensitivities are taken into account in the phrasing of recommendations, and that recommendations do not come as a surprise to officers of government. Any recommendations perceived to be controversial should be discussed with appropriate officers of government in advance. In general, the survey recommendations ought to be conceived of as a supermarket full of good ideas in which various agencies of government may shop. That implies that each problem should be addressed by more than one recommendation and that the implications of each recommendation should be discussed to the extent possible given the team's knowledge of the environment. (It is understood that the team, particularly if it contains any significant number of outsiders, may not be able to foresee all of the implications of its recommendations.)

When the survey report is finished, it is useful to recommend the convening of an international conference of specialists to review the report and comment on it. Such a broad – international – exposure may serve to highlight strengths and weaknesses in the report from a theoretical perspective, independent of the political constraints operating in the target state.[4] It also serves to give the report high visibility and to increase receptivity toward the report. Finally, the report, complete with appendices containing the raw data and the technical data analyses, should be 'published' in an attractive format, in multiple copies, and delivered to the agency contracting for the services. At this point, the working group is disbanded and the team members are expected to return to their normal duties; the survey phase of the activity has been completed. Obviously, the contracting agency may ask for some continuing involvement on the part of the team or some sub-set of the team, but that decision is entirely at the discretion of the agency.

The next logical step in the process is a careful review of the report, the organisation of another group to sift through the report, and from the report recommendations to recommend policy decisions. Those policy decisions, if generally accepted, will create a need for an implementation plan, and that implementation plan will, at some point, become implemented. The team plays no role either in the development of policy (though some team members may advise on policy development) or in the articulation of an implementation plan, and certainly the team members play no role in actual implementation.

Language-in-education planning[5]

Because the education sector rarely has the outreach or the available resources to impact any sector other than the schools, it is unwise (though it is frequently the case) to assign the entire implementation activity to the schools. As illustrated in Figure 4.5, language-in-education planning really cannot be undertaken until the process has reached the policy decision stage. Language-in-education planning, of necessity, has an entirely different set of constraints.

Language-in-education planning has six primary objectives. First, it

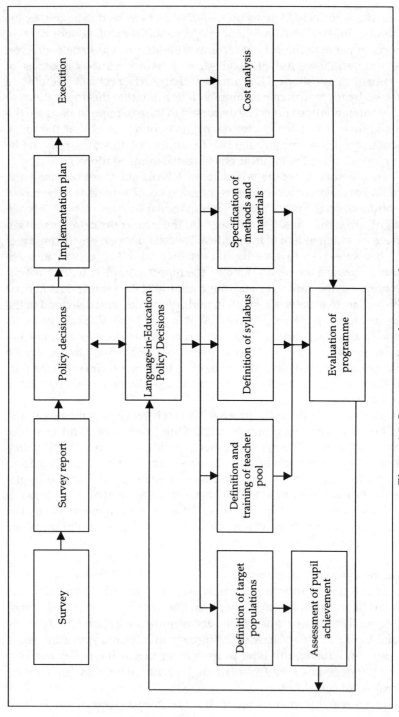

Figure 4.5 Language-in-education planning

must determine who in the school population will receive language education in which language(s). The point here is the need to *identify a target population* of students who will receive language education. Which children? Where are they physically located in the state? Are they concentrated in urban centres, or are they unevenly spread across the entire population? Where are they in terms of readiness? How many will there be? Over what duration? How will the children who participate be selected? Who will make the selection? Will the selection be based on aptitude? On attitude? On motivation? Is there a plan to keep a steady flow of children into the established language curricula over many years, or will new languages be introduced periodically to respond to popular demand as that demand changes in response to real-world political and economic situations? How do parents feel about language education? Will they support or oppose the enrolment of their children in language learning? These are the sorts of questions that must be answered in relation to the identification of a target population.

The second issue for the education sector is the issue of *teacher supply*. From what sector of the total pool of potential teachers will language teachers be drawn? What sort of education will they be provided to prepare them to teach? How is that training different from the training of any other teacher? How long will it take? Who will be the teacher trainers? What is it that the potential teachers need to know? The issue is not merely one of pre-service training but also one of in-service training. Non-native speakers of a language need periodic re-exposure to the language in settings where the language is spoken. It isn't that teachers may forget the grammar or the lexicon (though, indeed, they may); rather it is a question of maintaining a native-like pronunciation, but more importantly of being sensitive to the pragmatic, paralinguistic, proxemic, and sociolinguistic constraints of the language in constantly changing native-speaker environments. Thus, arrangements must be made to provide viable in-service education at sufficiently frequent intervals so that language facility is not lost.

Third, once the student pool and the teacher pool have been identified, it is necessary to be concerned about *the syllabus*. As the school curriculum is not endlessly permeable, so the curriculum is constrained not only by time (there are only so many hours in the school day/school week/school year) but by the values of the system (clearly, science education is perceived to be more important than language education; indeed, language education is, in many cases, pretty far down on the scale of priorities). Thus, when language education is expanded with respect to the number of hours of instruction, or extended in terms of the number of years of instruction, or when a new language is added, something else must be reduced or removed from the curriculum. The problem has been so far described in terms of available time in the curriculum, but the syllabus question also implicates the issue of on-set and duration of training. When should language education begin – at what grade level? If the individual wishes to undertake a second educational language, when should that begin? What is the probable duration of such education? Is the time normally allocated to language study sufficient? Should all pupils be required to achieve the same proficiency? Is there any possibility of variable entry and exit?

Fourth, one cannot in any satisfactory way discuss the question of syllabus without simultaneously dealing with the issue of *methods and materials*. What methodology(ies) will be used to teach language? Will the same methodology be employed throughout the duration of language education, or will various methodologies be introduced depending on the specific syllabus objective and/or the student's initial proficiency level and/or the age at on-set of instruction? How and when will teachers be trained in the recommended methodology? Teachers do not all belong to the same generation; different generations of teachers are likely to be differently trained; how will those natural differences be compensated? What will be the expected degree of fit between the methodology(ies) and the materials chosen? Who will prepare the materials? How long will it take to do so? What density of materials per pupil is necessary to maintain a viable programme? What sorts of audio-visual support will be required? What role, if any, will be played by native-speakers (employed as teacher aids or utilised in periodic language camps) and what degree of familiarity will these teacher aids be expected to have with the selected methodology and materials. What supplementary materials (movies, books, magazines, television) can be drawn from the community?

A fifth major area of concern in language-in-education planning is the *definition (identification) of available resources* to support a language education programme. What will it cost per pupil/per year to provide the necessary classrooms, teachers, and materials (including supplementary materials) to operate a viable programme, and where will these resources come from? As the curriculum is not endlessly permeable, so too the budget is not endlessly permeable. If resources are to be committed to this range of activities, what other activities will have smaller resources? What are the implications on space? Will dedicated classrooms, complete with computer and audio-visual laboratories, be utilised? What is the life expectancy of the necessary equipment? Will it be possible to purchase, maintain, and replace such equipment on some reasonable schedule? It will be necessary to put in place some sort of cost/benefit analysis to determine the answers to this set of questions.

The issue of assessment and evaluation has been left to last, though it is an issue that directly affects all the other areas. A distinction is being made here between *assessment* – the measurement of student success at stipulated programme intervals – and *evaluation* – the measurement of the relative success of the entire programme. Questions to be addressed here are: What level of proficiency is a student expected to achieve at the end of each increment of study? How will it be determined whether the student has in fact achieved that level of proficiency? What will be the degree of fit between the assessment instrument and the sanctioned method(s) and materials? Who will prepare the assessment instruments? How long will it take to prepare such instruments? How will the instrument(s) be administered? How often? What precautions will be necessary to preserve test integrity and security? Who will score the instrument(s)? What will be done with the results? Will the assessment results become criteria for the evaluation of teachers?

At the same time, it is necessary to evaluate the whole system. How effective is the methodology? How useful are the materials? What is contributed by supplementary materials? In short, is the educational programme effective? Is it meeting the societal needs which initiated it in the first place? Are students coming out of the programme able to find employment? Are employers happy with the product?

These are the kinds of issues that can be addressed through language-in-education planning. The schema presented in Figure 4.5 as well as this discussion should demonstrate the fact than an entire language planning activity cannot be delegated to the education sector. The education sector cannot induce business, industry, and the Civil Service to reward bilingual proficiency; the education sector cannot also be responsible for the highly specialised linguistic skills that might be required in the foreign service or in other complex sectors, and the education sector cannot also be held responsible for the language education of the entire population – including those segments beyond normal school age and those segments suffering from various physical and psychological deficiencies. More importantly, the education sector cannot be responsible for policy decisions affecting the entire population and all sectors of society.

Applying the macro to the micro situations

Much of what has been learned about the practice of language policy and language planning in the last two or three decades has applied to the large-scale situation – to the macro-structural environment – at the national and super-national levels. In the last few years, that knowledge has been applied in micro-structural environments – in individual cities, in particular sectors of economic or social activity, etc. There is an increasing interest in the functions and purposes of language planning in limited organisations. Studies have been conducted in the context of business (see, e.g. Klersey, 1989; Touchstone, 1996; Touchstone et al., 1995 and in press; Uljin & Strother, 1995; Wijst & Uljin, 1992), in the uses of particular genre (see, e.g. Bruthiaux, 1996) and in the use of particular syntactic structures in specific speech-communities (see, e.g. Youmans, 1995).

A number of 'problems' have been identified in a range of smaller contexts including:

- the use of native minority-languages by nurses and other employees in majority-language hospitals, the use of minority-languages by hospital patients in majority-language hospitals, doctor-patient communication in situations in which the participants are native-speakers of different varieties or languages, and other applications in the health-delivery fields;
- the use of minority-languages in banking, whether involving basic practices (like establishing a checking account) or more complex practices (like getting a home loan);
- the uses of minority languages with majority-language speaking law enforcement officers, the use of minority languages in the courts, attorney-client communication in situations in which the participants are native-speakers of different varieties or languages;
- the uses of minority languages in the delivery of services in the utility industries (e.g. electricity, natural gas, telephone);
- the uses of minority languages in the communications industries at the local level (e.g. in newspapers, on radio and television, etc.); and
- the sociolinguistic differences between majority and minority language in marginal communities and the resulting communication friction.

The list could be extended much further, but these few examples should illustrate the interest in micro-structural language problems. It has gradually become clear that the problems remain essentially the same in micro-structural and in macro-structural environments, and the data gathering procedures are essentially the same, though the kinds of recommendations that can be made and the implementation strategies are, necessarily, different. In the micro-structural environment, decision makers are much closer to the problem source, can look at the discourse in more detail and are much freer to act. Additionally, in the micro-structural environment, visible change is much easier to perceive.

Importance of Methodology

The importance of methodology and the need to base planning on data is often overlooked or ignored in real-life language planning process situations. Indeed, many politicians (and others who propose 'language plans') go about language planning as if it could and should be done only on the basis of their intuitive feelings, that is, in terms of the language planning model in Figure 4.2, language planning is seen as beginning with the third step, the policy decisions. For example, in Australia, which has a well-deserved reputation for language planning through its *National Policy on Languages* (Lo Bianco, 1987a) and for a number of well-thought-out State and Territory language-in-education policies, there have also been numbers of unsupported (in terms of collecting the basic data) policy based language decisions. The 1971 Aboriginal bilingual education programme in the Northern Territory (see Russo, 1983; Russo & Baldauf, 1986) was apparently proposed and developed over a few days by the Commonwealth government with little or no consultation with the bureaucracy who were actually going to have to run it in the Northern Territory (Sommer, 1991). As a consequence, Aboriginal people and the bureaucracy each had a different view of what the programme promised (a genuine 'two way' bilingual education vs. a bilingual transition to learning English). Inadequate data were also available about what languages should be taught to whom. This failure to plan, or to agree on the intended outcomes meant that, as the programme developed, there were major problems and even difficulties in establishing the extent of its success (Eggington & Baldauf, 1990).

Another more recent Australian example comes from the report of the Council of Australian Governments, the annual meeting of state Premiers with the Commonwealth government, which adopted in its 1994 resolution a statement declaring the national urgency of drastically upgrading language teaching, especially Chinese, Japanese, Indonesian and Korean, basically on economic grounds (Mackerras, 1995). Subsequently, a programme, funded at A$68 million dollars over four years, was set up to increase Asian language teaching and awareness in schools. This sudden push, without any language-in-education planning, to teach Asian languages, when combined with the states expressed intention of increasing the amount of language taught, has meant that the education systems were unprepared for the sudden increase in language teaching being demanded. Without any language-in-education planning, qualified teachers are not available, curriculum materials are in short supply and orderly programmes of language teaching are not in evidence. In fact, there is a danger that the programme could have the opposite effect from that intended, undermining rather than promoting Asian literacy and awareness at a time when Australia is striving to become more closely linked with its Asian neighbours.

The point of these examples is not to belittle the policy initiatives, each of which was laudable in it political purpose and intent. Rather, it is to argue for the importance of methodology, the need to collect proper data on which to base policies so that innovative political ideas will have some possibility of fruition. The examples also show that languages will be planned, whether or not any language planning actually contributes to the policy decision process. This means that any attempts at language planning may only occur during the implementation stage when those faced with implementing the decisions have to tackle the problems as best they can.

Summary

In this chapter the language planning process has been examined from the perspective of someone who might be considering becoming involved in creating a language plan. While methodologically the focus has been on the sociolinguistic survey as the preferred method for collecting the information needed to develop a plan, the roles of historical analysis, educational evaluation, anthropological linguistics, cost analysis, the use of large linguistic corpuses and the ethnography of communication have also been examined. We have noted that the appropriate method needs to be selected for each situation under investigation and that most techniques can be applied to both macro and micro language planning situations. Whether in language planning or language-in-education planning, we have seen that there are many potential questions to be asked, so the selection of questions has the potential to influence significantly the nature of the proposed language plan.

Thus, it is clear that the kind of data needed to reach language policy decisions must be carefully defined, and it is equally clear that the means for data collection must be carefully designed in order to ensure the collection of appropriate and useful information. Not only is it important to have an adequate database for decision making, but it is also important not to force the data to fit desired a priori solutions; rather solutions must genuinely derive from the data. At the same time, solutions must be sensitive to the cultural, social, and historical conditions in the environment in which solutions will be applied. In any language planning exercise, it is important to keep in contact with decision makers to ensure the situational and economic viability of proposed solutions. Decision makers should not be faced with surprises at the end of the exercise. It is further necessary to establish feedback-loops so that, as implementation occurs, corrections may be introduced into the process when difficulties are encountered. Finally, it is important to remember that proposed solutions must be 'sold' to the population; language change will not necessarily be readily accepted by a population, because language issues are most commonly emotion-laden. Data collection and interpretation require time and patience, and implementation requires more.

Notes

1. Except perhaps in the Philippines, where there has been an extensive evaluation on the educational aspects of their language planning (e.g. Gonzalez, 1990), much of the evaluation of language planning has occurred at the sociopolitical level (e.g. Fishman, 1994; Luke et al., 1990; Tollefson, 1991, 1993, 1995) rather than in the context of examining language programme effectiveness (see discussion of these issues in Chapters 7 and 11).
2. Grin (1995: 231) indicates that 'to our knowledge, no satisfactory model of *social benefits* is currently available, whether in the economics of education or in the

economics of language. The problem is of course to identify the *ways* in which foreign language education can be beneficial to society as a whole; . . . .'

3. The address is: ICAME, The Norwegian Computing Centre for the Humanities, PO Box 53, Universitetet, N–5027 Bergen, Norway.

4. The survey may be very constrained, but may still produce useful general information; see, e.g. Kaplan, 1979, 1982; Kaplan and Tse 1982.

5. Cooper (1988) calls language-in-education planning 'acquisition planning', arguing that it is a third category to corpus and status planning, rather than the major activity of 'Implementation (educational spread)' as we have referred to it in Haugen's model (Table 2.1). As the next chapter suggests, this is an important distinction. The notion of 'acquisition planning' suggests an independent process. While that may reflect what often occurs in practice, the failure to embed language-in-education planning with the wider corpus planning/status planning framework is a major cause of the failure of independently implemented 'acquisition plans'. Haugen's description provides, therefore, a better general planning model. Ingram (1990) and Paulston and McLaughlin (1994) have done major reviews of language-in-education planning.

5 Social Purpose Language Planning: Education and Literacy

In Chapter 3 we outlined the major purposes or goals for language planning. However, we also recognised that many of these goals are carried out for rather abstract purposes, which are often related to national policy goals in some general sense. In this chapter we examine language policy and planning in the context of two interrelated social goals, language-in-education and literacy-in-education planning. These two areas represent the public face of language planning as they have a direct impact on individuals within the society.

So far language planning has been discussed primarily from a macro-planning sense. It is now appropriate to go back to the overview of language planning in Chapter 1 (Figure 1.1) and look at the four ways in which language planning can be implemented: governmental, educational, informal and other (i.e. the 'Implementation' aspect of Haugen's (1983) Model in Table 2.1). Of these, language-in-education planning, or what Cooper (1989) has called 'acquisition planning', is often seen as the most potent resource for bringing about language change. As language-in-education represents a key implementation procedure for language policy and planning, it is discussed in some detail here. Kennedy (1984, 1989) has drawn together some articles related to the area, and Ingram (1990) and Paulston and McLaughlin (1994) have reviewed the literature relevant to the topic, but the process itself is not discussed in detail. Literacy planning in language-in-education planning is at once a sub-set and also a broadening of the scope of language-in-education planning.

Language-in-Education Planning

Language-in-education planning is substantially different from language planning. As has already been noted, language planning broadly is a function of government, since it must penetrate many sectors of society. Language-in-education planning, on the contrary, affects only one sector

122

acquisition planning (Cooper, 1989) =
lg-in-ed planning (Kaplan + Baldauf, 1997) but

AP

of the society – the education sector. As it has been undertaken in a number of countries over the past 20 or so years, it has substantially involved only the formal education structure; that is, it has not necessarily penetrated educational activities in other areas (e.g. the military, tourism, banking and economics), nor has it had much impact on informal educational structures (e.g. apprenticeship systems of various sorts, out-of-school teaching in church or community related schools ['Saturday schools', e.g. Janik (1996)], and in some cases pre-school activities).

However, there is an obvious reason why the education sector is frequently selected as the site for language planning activity. Education sectors, of necessity, deal with 'standard' versions of a language – whether the official 'national' language or an official 'foreign' language. A 'standard' language results, generally speaking, from a complex set of historical processes intended precisely to produce standardisation (see e.g. Bartsch, 1987; Joseph, 1987 for French; Milroy & Milroy, 1991 for English). Indeed, a 'standard' language may be defined as a set of discursive, cultural and historical practices – a set of widely accepted communal solutions to discourse problems. Additionally, a standard language is a potent symbol of national unity. If this definition of 'standard' may be assumed to be viable, then the 'standard' language is really no one's 'first' language. On the contrary, the 'standard' language must be acquired through individual participation in the norms of usage, and these norms are commonly inculcated through the education sector (with the powerful assistance of the canonical literatures and the print media).[1]

But the reality of most linguistic communities is marked by the normative use of a wide range of varieties in day-to-day communication – i.e. the use of slang, of jargon, of non-standard forms, of special codes, even of different languages. Consequently a standard language constitutes a purely ideological construct. The existence of such a construct may create an impression that linguistic unity exists, when the reality reflects linguistic diversity. The notion of the existence and dispersion of a 'standard' variety through a community suggests that linguistic unity is the societal norm; it may also suggest a level of socioeconomic and sociopolitical unity which is entirely contrary to the reality of linguistic diversity.

It is, therefore, not surprising that the education sector – the transmitter and perpetuator of culture – is chosen as the site for language planning. In this condition, language planning is seen as implicating only the 'standard'. Why would anyone want to plan for non-standard varieties (cf. Black, 1990)?

A model for language-in-education planning

In the top half of Figure 5.1 a diagram is presented which summarises the various stages that may be invoked in a language planning effort. It shows that, typically, six stages occur: the pre-planning stage, the survey

Language Policy and Planning

1 = PRE-PLANNING Stage: historical research, cost estimation

2 = SURVEY Stage: design, test, disseminate collect data

3 = REPORT Stage: write report, test recommendations

4 = POLICY Stage: design and test policy strategies

5 = IMPLEMENTATION Stage: devise, implement strategies

6 = EVALUATION Stage: Evaluate all phases and feedback into the system

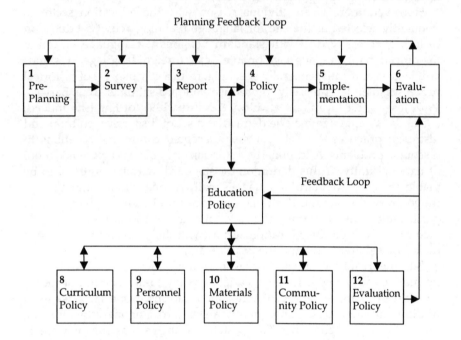

Language-in-Education Policy

7 = EDUCATION Policy: separate from general policy

8 = CURRICULUM Policy: what languages, when

9 = PERSONNEL Policy: in-service/pre-service training

10 = MATERIALS Policy: what, how much, how soon

11 = COMMUNITY Policy: parental attitudes, funding sources, recruiting teachers/students

12 = EVALUATION Policy: evaluation of curriculum, student success, teacher success/interest, cost effectiveness, societal change, basic policy.

Figure 5.1 Schema for language-in-education policy development

(or data collection) stage, the report writing stage, the policy formation stage, the implementation stage, and a recurring evaluation stage which feeds back into the system at various points. Language-in-education planning requires a deviation from that pattern. Often at some point between report writing and policy formation, a branching occurs, leading to language-in-education planning. If a branching is to occur, that is the most logical point at which it may occur, since the data from the data collection stage and the recommendations from the report-writing stage can be of great use to language planners.

However language-in-education planning is initiated, it invokes a series of subsidiary stages as noted in the bottom half of Figure 5.1. As in language planning in general, there is a need for data to provide the basis from which the environment can be interpreted, and there is a need for a series of broad recommendations on the basis of which planning may occur. As in more general language planning activities, there is a need for a policy-formulation stage and an evaluation stage. If language-in-education is being undertaken as part of a national activity, some of the policy formation and the evaluation can occur as part of the general governmental planning process rather than specifically within the education sector (see Figure 4.5). It should be noted, however, that a great deal of language-in-education planning has occurred without any reference to the general stages of language planning (e.g. Baldauf, 1982; 1994, Eggington & Baldauf, 1990; Russo & Baldauf, 1986).

To develop a soundly based language policy, it is necessary to discover what languages are spoken in a society, what purposes those languages serve, who speaks them, where, in the geography of that community, those speakers are physically located, and what motivation there is for preserving those languages. Such information can most conveniently be collected through a sociolinguistic survey – a kind of instrument discussed in Chapter 4 of this volume. It is also necessary to determine what popular attitudes are in relation to these languages. If the languages are stigmatised (e.g. marking speakers as belonging to lower socioeconomic levels, or lower educational levels, or to low status castes), planning may implicate a good deal of attitude change in conjunction with language instruction in schools. If, on the other hand, the languages are perceived as holding high prestige or economic value, it may be necessary to normalise those impressions to prevent a heavy imbalance in the population who wish to study a language, and to preclude anger or bitterness on the part of parents whose offspring are not selected. In short, extreme attitudes in either positive or negative directions can be counterproductive.[2]

Language-in-education policy

Language planning, generally, has been defined as part of human resource development planning, and human resource development planning in turn has been defined as being invoked in the interests of modernisation and community development. Language-in-education, being a sub-set of national language planning, is also part of human resource development planning. Thus, the education sector needs to understand what languages are desirable in the repertoire of speakers in the community and for what purposes those languages will be used. It may be possible, for example, that a nation intends to expand its commercial ties with a particular country or region and, over the long term, the nation may decide that it has need of a substantial pool of individuals who are competent in the language(s) of the new commercial partner(s). The nation may look to the education sector to produce that pool of individuals. Not only does the education sector need to know what languages are becoming desirable, but it is also necessary to know how soon the demand for speakers is likely to occur and over how long a period of time that demand is likely to continue. Such information can most conveniently be collected through in-depth interviews with leaders in the commercial sector and in those agencies of government charged with the development of commercial relationships (in the United States, for example, the Department of Commerce, but in other settings conceivably a ministry of tourism, a ministry of the military – since the military may be a large purchaser of equipment – a ministry of agriculture – since such an agency is responsible not only for the sale of surplus products but for an understanding of the areas of shortage, etc.).

In its National Policy on Languages, for example, Australia has determined that its major trading partners, and source of tourism visits will most likely include the People's Republic of China, Taiwan, the Republic of Korea, Japan, Indonesia and Singapore (Lo Bianco, 1987a, 1987b). These decisions indicate a potential need for speakers of Chinese (Mandarin), Korean, Japanese, and Indonesian. The perceived trading situation is envisioned as continuing into the indefinite future, and the need is immediate. Under these circumstances, the education sector has considered the introduction of those languages at the junior secondary, senior secondary and tertiary levels, with the notion that the upper levels can produce speakers over the short term while the introduction of instruction in those languages will serve to build a pool of speakers in the community over the long term.

It is possible that this is the point at which there needs to be a major articulation between language-in-education planning and more general language planning. Government is in a position to provide motivational structures that the education sector simply cannot provide; for example if a nation wishes to enlarge the pool of speakers of a particular language, it may provide a range of instrumental incentives to encourage young people to study those languages. Such motivation enhancing devices may include tax incentives to commercial organisations which hire speakers of those languages, position designations in the civil service and/or foreign service requiring proficiency in those languages, allocation of funding to the education sector to improve instruction in those languages including special salary incentives for qualified teachers, modification of immigration regulations to encourage the in-migration of teachers and native speakers of those languages, the granting of overseas language study scholarships, etc., as well as the development of one or more media campaigns to enhance popular attitudes relating to the value of those languages.

Language-in-education implementation

Once education policy has been determined, there are a number of issues which then need to be examined as part of any language-in-education implementation programme. Each of these areas of policy development for language policy implementation may develop differently in a particular nation depending on how that nation's education system operates. However, each policy area will be raised and dealt with in its own context.

Curriculum policy

Once the education sector has determined which languages need to be taught (and also which languages do not need to be taught because other mechanisms already exist for the spread of those languages [e.g. private sector 'Saturday schools'], or because the languages do not have value to the community, or because there is simply no student interest in them, or because it is not feasible to develop teaching strength in them within a reasonable time), then the education sector has to turn its attention to a whole range of curricular issues.

A primary issue concerns the space in the curriculum allocated to language instruction. Because the school year (and the school day) is limited, the curriculum is not endlessly permeable; that is, in general, whenever something is added to the curriculum, it is at the expense of something that is already in the curriculum. What subject areas need to be reduced or eliminated in order to make space for language instruction? This is a highly politicised question; most subjects are in the curriculum because there is societal pressure for them to be there. In fact there are groups in most subject areas who feel their subject is already under-represented in the curriculum. In modern science-oriented states, mathematics and basic science are sacrosanct and cannot be tampered with to any significant degree. By the same token, societies demand that the national/official language and the literature of that language should be significantly represented in the curriculum. Practical subjects which enable the graduate to find jobs also have to be included. When one looks at the amount of material in the curriculum which is inviolable, the addition of language instruction constitutes a formidable problem. While bilingual content language programmes can make the curriculum serve two functions, effectively increasing the time available for language instruction, such programmes initially demand additional resources and curriculum development and have not been widely implemented.

A second, no less critical curricular, issue lies in the question when to start language instruction, over what duration is it to be provided, and with what intensity ought it to be administered. On the one hand, the earlier language education is introduced in the curriculum, the greater the probability there is that instruction will be successful.[3] At the same time, the earlier language instruction is introduced, the larger the space it will require in the curriculum over a greater duration. Research in the 1960s suggested that something in the order of 750 to 2800 contact hours[4] of instruction is required to achieve any significant change in linguistic behaviour and that the instruction needs to be administered over a duration which is not so long that the rate of forgetting exceeds the rate of learning, nor so short that the learner is subjected to severe psychological stress. Most foreign language education around the world at the present time is structured to be delivered in classes of 50 to 75 at the rate of three 50-minute periods each week.

With these figures in mind, and remembering that some languages are more difficult to learn to read and write, a little simple arithmetic may help to clarify the value of such instruction. The school year around the world averages approximately 38 teaching weeks; the school week averages five days, and the school day averages six functional 50-minute contact hours (discounting time for the meals and recess). That means that the total instructional time available each school year amounts to 57,000 minutes, or 950 total hours (38 weeks × 5 days × 6 meetings × 50 minutes = 57,000 minutes/60 minutes = 950 hours). Because language instruction is recognised as involving communicative use, lecture classes are only of limited use, especially if the lecture is delivered in the indigenous language rather than the target language. Let us assume that the 50-minute hour for a class of 25 students, provides each student with approximately two minutes of individual communicative instructional exposure to the target language. There are three such periods each week of the 38-week academic year; thus each student would receive 228 minutes of communicative language instruction each academic year, which constitutes 0.004% of the available instructional time per student. While face-to-face contact time in language classes amounts to 95 hours a year, few students have the opportunity to study the same language continuously for their 12 years of schooling. If one takes an estimate of 800–1000 hours seriously for English speakers to learn another European language, a student is unlikely, even in the best of circumstances, to get adequate general exposure to a second language over the course of his/her schooling. Given the limited communicative contact inherent in such study, it would be even more difficult to achieve real language facility on that basis. While the discontinualities in this particular example related to American and Australian patterns of schooling, they highlight the need for successful language study to be more intensive and for there to be external opportunities to practise the language (e.g. as in many schools in Europe). For most students, the rate and duration over which the language is learned means schooling alone is unable to deliver satisfactory learning outcomes.

These calculations suggest that for most students traditional foreign language instruction is for all practical purposes useless, that the activity cannot be defined as cost-effective, and that student motivation is likely to be destroyed since significant achievement is very difficult. While these figures may overstate the problem, one need only look at the drop-out rates in second-language learning programmes in many parts of the world (e.g. Baldauf & Lawrence, 1991) to see the enormous resources that have been allocated to train a relatively few second-language speakers. One aspect of the planning problem is to find space in the curriculum to permit more effective instruction and to set realistic limits on the point of on-set and the total duration of instruction. If it is true that communicative activity is essential to language learning, then it is necessary to devise models which will permit communication to some extent greater than six minutes a week: class size must be reduced, and learner opportunities for real communication need to be increased.

A number of alternatives exist to the traditional mass lecture method of language teaching. With smaller classes, it is possible to create more communicative situations through group and pair work and through the use of the target language for most communication in the classroom. Another approach which is being tried is the use of immersion programmes where one or more subjects other than the target language are taught in that language. Although this requires specialised teachers and teaching materials, it can expose the student to communicative language which the student has a real need to use to pass the subject. This use of curricular time for two purposes effectively lengthens the time available for language study.[5]

However, if planners are serious about language learning, they may need to think laterally about programmes which use out-of-class time. For example, vacation school camps have been shown to provide excellent opportunities for intensive communicative exposure. Perhaps three intensive vacation sessions (delivering approximately 300 hours of instruction [6 weeks × 7 days × 7 hours a day = 294 hours] each Summer) augmented by non-intensive maintenance programmes during the intervening academic years (delivering approximately 30 hours of instruction [50 minutes a day × 1 day per week × 38 weeks = 31.67 hours] each year) might be far more cost-effective than the present pattern (providing 882 hours of instruction over three years as opposed to the current 95 general or 3.8

communicative hours per academic year).[6] If such a pattern were introduced in the junior high/junior secondary level (Grades 7, 8 and 9),
learners would be fairly proficient communicators by the time they
reached 10th/11th grade and might spend the final two or three years of
high school perfecting their reading and writing abilities in the target
language. The results are likely to be better, the costs in the long term
lower, and the pressure on the total curriculum might be substantially
reduced.

Personnel policy

No matter what the duration of instruction, a planning issue that needs
to be addressed is the teacher cadre which will deliver the instruction.
There is a need for a group of teachers trained in language pedagogy and
reasonably fluent in the target language. There are essentially three
problems in this context: the source of teachers, the training of teachers,
and the reward for teachers.

It is clear that a polity undertaking to introduce a new language into the
curriculum will be faced with a shortage of competent teachers, and there
may be pressure to use untrained and limited competence teachers as a
stop-gap measure. There are several different strategies which can be
developed to augment the pool of qualified teachers – some short term,
some long term. For example, market forces may pressure language
teachers trained in one language to retrain in the new 'more popular'
language to retain their teaching positions. This occurred in the People's
Republic of China in the 1960s with the switch from Russian to English and
is occurring in Australia in the 1990s as teachers of French and German are
retraining to teach Japanese or Indonesian. Unfortunately, neither the
specific language skills nor the teaching methods used may generalise
easily and the competent teachers of one language may be turned into
incompetent ones in the new language (Bo & Baldauf, 1990).

Another strategy is to import teachers from a country where the target
language is spoken natively. Japan regularly hires both qualified teachers
and native speakers of English to meet language teaching needs. Australia
is looking at using native speakers of Asian languages as paid teaching
assistants in schools; it has used unpaid speakers of community languages
in schools for many years to provide some language work particularly in
primary schools. Teachers are sometimes imported from a country where
the target language is spoken natively; this is certainly the case with the US
Peace Corps, Australian Volunteers Abroad, etc. which have placed native
English speakers in a variety of countries at little or no cost to the recipient
country. However, because this group of teachers is largely voluntary and
paid only a survival stipend, individuals who participate tend to be mostly
untrained. Overseas teachers may be excellent language speakers, but they
may not have the language teaching or classroom skills which make them

suitable for employment in another country, and in-service programmes may be needed to upgrade their skills and to acclimatise them to their new surroundings.

The other side of the problem is that a large number of such teachers introduced into a relatively small country can serve to destabilise the population. This was a major concern when instructional television was introduced into American Samoa in the mid-1960s (Baldauf, 1982, 1990) and is of concern in the People's Republic of China, where relatively large numbers of native speakers of English have been recruited, but they have not been allowed to stay for extended periods.

Still another problem relates to the attitudes of the trade unions and certifying employing authorities. Neither group may wish to have teachers in classes who are unqualified to 'teach' by local standards, arguing that subject matter is only one component of teacher competence. Even when teachers meet certification requirements unions may not be pleased to see large numbers of teachers imported when there are unemployed teachers in the community, without reference to the fact that subject distribution may be an element; that is, the unemployed teachers may not be qualified to teach the target language. The basis of the importation of teachers may mean that those teachers are not eligible to remain in the country indefinitely and this may create immigration problems. These balancing features are not often perceived in what may be an extremely emotional environment. Nevertheless, importation of teachers may constitute a major viable short-term strategy.

Such a strategy will only work if, simultaneously, the nation is engaged in training indigenous teachers to replace the imported teachers. There are two issues underlying teacher training: one has to do with achieving and maintaining competence in the target language; the other has to do with the incentives to get teachers to place themselves in the pool.

The first problem is complex; since the language is new to the country, there is not likely to be a substantial number of individuals who are competent in the language. In the pattern suggested above, it will take approximately three years to achieve minimal competence in the language (see end note 4). When that time is added to the time required in most countries to train certified teachers, it constitutes a significant investment of time by the individual. It is unlikely that the required number of individuals will choose to enter the teacher pool unless government is prepared to offer incentives to the individuals involved.

Incentives may be of two sorts: initial incentives designed to defray the costs of getting trained both in the language and in general pedagogy; and long-term incentives designed both to provide satisfying careers to language teachers and to encourage the maintenance of language profi-ciency. The nature of initial incentives is clear enough and does not require further discussion, though there is no question that the provision of scholarships to defray the cost of instruction and living stipends may amount to a substantial financial investment on the part of the government. In addition, of course, the use of scholarships and other financial incentives implies the development of some sort of screening mechanism designed to permit selection of those most likely to succeed and most likely to commit themselves to a career in the field.

Long-term incentives are also needed to keep people in the field. In general, language teachers do not hold high status in the teaching profession. This may be a function of the history of language teaching. Language instruction was first introduced into the western academy in the Middle Ages. Latin, Greek, Hebrew and Sanskrit were taught to students. These classical languages were not taught in order to achieve communicative competence (except as 'in' languages among scholars), but rather were taught as a means to achieve access to the thought and art of dead civilisations. The materials studied were classical texts, and the students approached these texts as intellectual exercises. When modern languages were introduced into the academy in the late eighteenth and early nineteenth centuries, they were following the same model; that is, the purpose of study was to gain access to the best literature and not necessarily to achieve communicative competence. Thus, grammar and vocabulary constituted the main emphasis of language teaching; in the classical languages there was little else to learn. Only the best students were encouraged to pursue language education, since it was a complex intellectual exercise. A pattern developed in the academy in which apprentice teachers taught beginning language courses, but they and their more senior colleagues aspired to get past that apprenticeship and be admitted to the ranks of 'real' scholars – those who taught literature. As a consequence of these historical phenomena, teachers engaged in language instruction continue to be viewed as apprentices, and status is reserved for those who teach literature. This practice needs to be overcome, and language teachers need to be recognised as serious scholars teaching serious subject matter.

While it is true that language teachers need to be granted serious status, that in and of itself is not sufficient; language teachers need to discover career paths that do not lead only to the opportunity to teach literature, and language teachers should be rewarded to a greater extent than they normally are. Particularly in instances in which the language being taught has value in society, language teachers need to be rewarded not on a par with their colleagues but beyond the usual limits of their colleagues, since proficiency in another language should be recognised as a valued ability.

Educational systems will need to provide, in addition to subsidised pre-service training and adequate reward, high quality in-service training to permit teachers to maintain their level of proficiency. There is evidence that language skills atrophy over time when language is not used for communicative purposes, or when teachers have little opportunity to use the language beyond teaching introductory language classes. Thus, in-service opportunities must include travel to areas where the target language is natively spoken to permit teachers to retool their skills. While teachers can study grammar and vocabulary anywhere, it is native-like pronunciation and pragmatics that need to be 'retooled'. This sort of in-service training must also be subsidised by the government. Thus, identifying, training and maintaining a cadre of skilled language teachers is a major objective in language-in-education planning.

Materials policy

Language teaching must have some sort of content; the language itself may be the objective of instruction, but instruction must be taught over some content. This problem really consists of two related issues: on the one hand, what content will be used for language teaching; on the other hand, by what methodology will language instruction be delivered. The development of special purposes language teaching offers one approach to the content question, but is in a sense an extremely narrow answer. The objective of language instruction is not to limit the learner to a small set of registers in which to function in the target language, but rather to provide the learner with as wide a base of registers as possible. Just as 'language across the curriculum' has become a fashionable approach in teaching the mother-tongue, so it may be an appropriate device for teaching second languages, perhaps through partial immersion models. As to methodology of instruction for delivering content in an immersion setting, effective instruction must be interactive, i.e. get students using the language. Cummins (1989: 25) points out:

> [t]he experience of traditional second language teaching programmes in countries such as Canada, Ireland and Wales demonstrates the disappointing results typically obtained when principles of interactive pedagogy are ignored. Most traditional L2 teaching programmes tend to be teacher-centred and allow for little real interaction or active use of the target language by students in the classroom. They conform to a 'transmission' model of pedagogy rather than to an interactive model. The results in many countries are similar to this description of the Welsh experience:

> To state the matter bluntly, this policy until quite recently, has been a disasterous failure. Even the Welsh speaking elements in these second language schools . . . frequently failed to retain their natural bilingualism and lapsed into becoming monoglot English speakers. (Evans, 1976: 54–5).

There has been a long-standing debate in the field over the question of the relative 'reality' of the content. Some have argued that language has to be simplified to be accessible to the learner; others have argued that the language presented to the learner has to be authentic. If the objective is indeed to permit the learner the greatest access to the largest number of different registers, authenticity has to be the objective. Simplified materials run the risk of losing the interest of the student because, although simplified language may be more accessible, simplified content may be less interesting.

But materials also have to coincide with the methodology being employed to deliver the language instruction, and the methodologies used to train teachers need to match both of these. In the 1960s, a number of governments spent substantial sums trying to determine whether one methodology was clearly more effective than another; the answer seems to be that a methodology is successful in relation to objectives. If a curriculum is expected to produce competent speakers and listeners, the communicative approach may be an appropriate approach, but it is not equally successful in accomplishing learning of reading and writing skills. A great deal is understood now about the sociolinguistic and psycholinguistic processes involved in second-language acquisition. Methodologies need to be chosen in terms of what is known about language learning and in terms of the objectives of the curriculum.

At the same time, methodologies need to be chosen with some awareness of the skills of the teacher corps available for the delivery of language instruction. The history of language education is replete with experiments in which new methodologies were introduced and failed – frequently because the new methodologies were rejected by teachers without reference to the quality of the methodologies. Teachers may be uncomfortable with a new methodology because they do not understand the theoretical assumptions upon which it is founded, or because the assumptions underlying it contradict the ways in which they were trained, or because the method differs from the way they learned the target language, which they know by definition works, or simply because the exemplary materials for the new methodology are poorly constructed. Language-in-education planning must select an appropriate methodology, must guarantee that the materials to be used are consonant with the methodology, provide authentic language, and are also consonant with the expectations of teachers.

Community policy

Language education does not occur in a vacuum. Students and teachers live in the community beyond the classroom, and students have parents who are concerned about the education their students are exposed to. Funding for the support of educational systems comes from the larger community, whether it is derived from tax revenues, or voted by legislatures, or directed by a bureaucratised civil service. There are two primary issues here: on the one hand, the attitudes of the community toward language teaching in general, towards language teachers as a group, toward the particular target language, and toward the trade off discussed previously that has made room for language instruction in the curriculum at the expense of some other discipline. On the other hand, there are the effects of those attitudes on those who control the curriculum through the purse strings and through the potential sources of students and teachers. It is evident that, if attitudes are negative, there will be few candidates for language education. 'If I don't like you, I won't learn your language' is a truism of language education. Thus, an important aspect of language-in-education planning is the development of a variety of approaches to community attitude. Sociolinguistic surveys, discussed in detail in Chapter 4, can provide some evidence about attitudes in the community, but it may be necessary to try to modify attitudes in order to remove the stigma from some language or variety, in order to convince parents that language education is at least as valuable as football (in an American context) and deserves at least equal funding, to convince learners that language study is not 'effeminate', to convince other academics that language teaching is not a trivial activity, or to convince the entire population that multilingualism is not a threat to national unity. Language-in-education planning, like all human resource development planning, has as its objective the generation of effective and efficient plans to achieve some particular change in behaviour, but it must also have as its objective the mediation of the obstacles to the proposed change.

Not least among the obstacles to successful planning is the availability of adequate resources. It should be clear from the preceding discussion that the implementation of any language-in-education plan, like that of any human resource development plan, is going to be moderately expensive. Thus, language education is not only competing with other subjects for time in the curriculum, but often for a share of relatively fixed resources. One of the intractable problems in language education historically has been the willingness of education agencies to articulate complex and effective plans, but to fail at the level of implementation by withholding the resources necessary for the achievement of the plan.

Evaluation policy

In order to justify the necessary expenditure, as compared to expenditure for all other segments of the education sector, there is need for evidence that the proposed plan and its implementation is cost-effective. That notion immediately raises the question of whether any educational plan directed at the total population has much chance of success. In the past, language education was made available only to the brightest students; that has been demonstrated to be an ineffective criterion of admission into language education programmes. However, the corollary is not necessarily that the entire population ought to have access to language education. There must be a conscious determination of the needs of the society; if a society projects that it will need 100,000 speakers of a particular language, it is inefficient to train one million students in order to ensure the availability of 100,000 competent speakers.

Before moving on with this discussion, it is necessary to attempt some sort of definition of bilingualism (see also Chapter 8). An obvious objective of language teaching in the schools is the attainment of some degree of bilingualism in the target language among the target population by the end of the period of study. A key question which is rarely addressed in policy formulation is: 'What degree of bilingualism in what registers of the target language is attainable?' There are certain unstated interrelated assumptions underlying the notion of educated bilingualism; namely: (1) that the two languages in the bilingual environment are equal in status, in power, and in attraction; and (2) that educated bilingualism implies near-native proficiency in both languages in all registers (Kaplan, 1991). Both assumption are vacuous in a school environment: (1) The two languages cannot be of equal status, power, and attraction precisely because the learners are novices who come into the environment with their first language 'fully' developed. Initially, the L1 will always have greater status, power, and attraction precisely because the pupils can do everything they need to do linguistically in the L1, and they cannot do all those things in the L2[7]; (2) Near-native proficiency cannot be achieved because the duration of instruction is insufficient to accomplish such proficiency and because the school syllabus simply does not permit the inclusion of all possible registers. Since schooling generally ignores the pragmatic features of the L2, proficiency in any actual register is unlikely. (It is also the case that near-native proficiency is unattainable because it is rarely the real objective, since often what is taught is L2 grammar and minimal access to the L2 canonical literature.)

Syllabi are designed to teach what schools can teach, but assessment instruments are designed to measure something quite different. As a consequence, assessment instruments always demonstrate that syllabi are inadequate. In reality, of course, the attainment of bilingualism is a cline ranging from full monolingual proficiency in the L1 to full monolingual proficiency in the L2. Given individuals, regardless of the amount and quality of instruction provided, will of necessity fall at different points on the continuum because they will be differently motivated, will have differing attitudes toward the L2, and will enter the environment with differing readiness (aptitude). The situation may be represented crudely as in Figure 5.2. The representation is crude because it cannot account for all

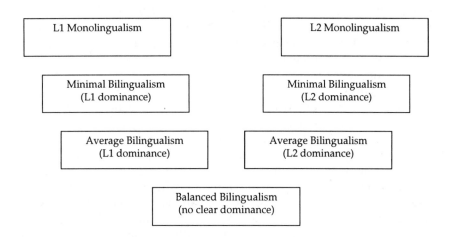

Note: This figure is shown as composed of mirror images on the assumption that one may enter the learning environment from either direction, in which case what is labelled L2 is actually L1.

Figure 5.2 Degrees of bilingual competence

the variables for thousands of individuals and must therefore settle for gross misrepresentations of some segments of the learner population.

Balanced bilingualism, if it can ever be attained, requires years of exposure. Even 'average bilingualism' is much rarer than the name would suggest; the 'average' is calculated among bilinguals, not among the whole student population. In general, given the time of exposure and the nature of teaching, the best schools can hope for is minimal bilingualism – a bilingualism that certainly does not include most registers of the L2. Realistically, however, even minimal bilingualism will only be achieved by part of any given population; the remainder will achieve a certain awareness of the L2 but little if any ability to use it in any register.

Furthermore, there is no theoretical evidence that bilingualism of any sort is a desired objective. Given that schooled bilingualism can hope to achieve only very minimal proficiency, within a limited number of registers, the outcome will always create a diglossic situation, with one language (the L1) always dominant, always offering the greatest range, always marked by the greatest power, always showing the greatest attraction. Thus, an individual who has achieved minimal bilingualism is always susceptible of retrogression in the direction of the L1.

Evaluation must take into consideration what degree of bilingual proficiency is attainable in the schooled environment. A serious problem in many education policy attempts lies in the fact that the expectations set

are entirely unrealistic (e.g. Genesee, 1994; Thomas, 1981). As a consequence, evaluations frequently show that the objectives have not been
achieved, and the outcome of such failure is that those who determine the
allocations of funds and teacher-resources view the activity as not worthy
of continuing support.

In one sense, it must be healthy for a society to have as many
multilinguals (or, more realistically, bilinguals) available as possible,
simply on the grounds that bilingualism seems to provide individuals with
more ways of looking at the world. Over the long term, a society with a
significant level of individual bilingualism will have less difficulty in
continuing language education, but any attempt to generalised high-level
bilingual competence through an entire population is likely to engender
hostility among those who have little motivation to achieve high level skills
and among those who have achieved such proficiency, but have no
opportunity to employ it because they constitute a surplus commodity in
the community. Furthermore, if we look at examples of bi- or multilingualism in naturally occurring situations, competence is found to vary with the
individual needs and the use to which the languages are put. In Australia,
not everyone needs to be trained to negotiate high level coal deals with
Japan, but many people will find Japanese useful to interact with Japanese
tourists.

In sum, the number of bilinguals produced with respect to any particular
language must be estimated in terms of societal needs, paying due regard
to the level of bilingualism necessary. Such estimation implies that the
entire system needs constant evaluation, and that the results of the
evaluation need to be fed back through the system to adjust it at the
appropriate points so that it will become more effective. Specifically,
students must be evaluated to determine whether they are achieving the
objectives set by the system; teachers must be evaluated to determine
whether they have the language skills necessary to deliver quality
instruction at the level demanded by the system, and the entire system
must be evaluated to determine whether the objectives set are commensu-
rate with the needs, abilities, and desires of the population.

Part of this complex evaluation system must gauge the cost-effectiveness of the plan. A plan may in and of itself be excellent, but if the resources
required to implement it cause bankruptcy of the system, that can hardly
be considered cost-effective. In education, as in any other subsidised area,
there must be some reasonable return on investment. In the same way that
plans have failed at the level of implementation because the system starved
them, it may also be the case that plans are so generously funded that
everything else in the system is starved to accomplish the single objective.
Evaluation must be designed to achieve some sort of equilibrium among
competing demands without assuring the failure of any segment through
inadequate resource allocation.

Evaluation of students implies that the objectives set by the system can be defined in measurable terms, that instruments exist or can be developed to measure achievement in terms that are compatible with the instructional system, and that the use of evaluation instruments is itself feasible, e.g. it is unproductive to have great quantities of teacher time committed to exam correction at the cost of instruction. By the same token, evaluation of teachers also requires the articulation of measurable objectives, the development of appropriate instruments, and the implementation of procedures that are not in themselves destructive of the system.

Perhaps most importantly, evaluation mechanisms need to be developed to determine whether societal changes predicted in policy development are occurring and to determine whether they are occurring to the extent needed within the time permitted. Of course, evaluation needs to be designed in such a manner that the results can be fed back into the system in order to produce modifications to the system. This latter objective is difficult because systems quickly become impervious to change and because the time between implementation and perceptible change is likely to be long.

Cost analysis and definition of resources

Returning to the four stages of Haugen's model which were discussed in Chapter 2, the development of a language plan which accurately reflects the needs of the situation depends on funding for some sort of survey work (e.g. Kaplan et al., Taiwan language survey) to make recommendations on what should be done. As suggested in the section on cost-benefit analysis in Chapter 4, at least a rough cost-benefit analysis should be undertaken at this stage to establish probable costs and likely benefits. At the next stage, vast amounts of materials, dictionaries, readers, etc. need to be prepared and teachers need to be trained in order to be able to carry out the plan. In the implementation phase the mass production of materials and the equipment necessary to develop literacy skills needs to be supplied. Finally, language change in one direction can easily revert to the other if adequate resources are not available to sustain and promote linguistic development.

The real problem that language planners face is that most costs occur in real time. Future costs are also relatively easy to predict in purely economic terms. However, benefits are slow to develop and hard to measure. Their worth often seems to be more to the individual than to society, at least in the first instance. There is a need to keep evaluating and reporting on progress of language planning projects to keep information about progress before decision makers. Politicians are used to thinking of planning in terms of physical effects – the Great Snowy Mountains Project in Australia, the Aswan Dam in Egypt, or the Hoover Dam in the United States. These are monuments that politicians and the public can see and appreciate and the economic benefits (and sometimes unintended problems) are there for all to see. What can language planners produce to sell their product (to use the underlying theme of the Chapter 6)?

A few indicators which could be suggested include:

- teaching the language, how many benefited, at what levels?;
- large scale projects, Cameroon;
- under/unemployment related to arrests/prison time; where upgraded language leads to employment;
- upgraded linguistic skills of minorities may lead to reduced health and welfare costs;
- military enlistments may show improvements where language skills provide an entry path for particular groups;
- increased production; as population literacy and language skills grow, productivity should increase;
- missionary activity; church participation, SIL looks at cost-benefit analysis;
- dissemination of scientific information; is it effective?

Language-in-education standards: A case study

As the development of language-in-education policy may seem very complex, it may be instructive to look at the recent development of 'standards statements' by three professional associations in the United States. There, in the absence of a national policy on languages (or even clear guidelines), these elements of the education sector have taken policy development in their own hands. The impetus for this policy development originated during the Bush administration (1988–92), when the nation's Governors met together (as they do annually) and developed a statement subsequently entitled 'The America 2000 Education Initiative' (because Mr Bush wanted to be known as 'The Education President'). The existence of this 'initiative' encouraged the US Department of Education to underwrite some of the activity, and a number of other public and private agencies provided the funding for the development of national standards. The standards for the teaching of history, for example, when released, caused a storm of protest, particularly from conservative politicians.

Partially under the auspices of the 'Education Initiative' and the available funding, partially as a defensive strategy to prevent some other body from imposing standards, three different groups of professional associations went to work on the development of national standards in the language areas:

(1) The National Council of Teachers of English (NCTE) and the International Reading Association (IRA) produced a National English Language Arts Standards document.

(2) The American Council on the Teaching of Foreign Languages (ACTFL), together with the American Association of Teachers of French (AATF), the American Association of the Teachers of German (AATG), and the American Association of Teachers of Spanish and Portuguese (AATSP), produced the National Foreign Language Standards.

(3) The association known as Teachers of English to Speakers of Other Languages (TESOL, Inc.) produced a set of National Standards for ESL.

All these documents were publicly released during 1996 and all are intended for pre-Kindergarten through grade 12 (pre-K-12) application.

None of these groups consulted with any of the others in any formal sense, although drafts of the disparate productions were widely available. All three groups were careful to point out that the standards document ' . . . will not be a curriculum framework, professional development handbook, or assessment instrument. Instead it will establish learning goals . . . , the areas for growth and mastery. The guidelines are intended to help educators prepare students to succeed in US schools and to be productive members of society' (Short & Gómez, 1996: 5).

This activity represents a new and very specific kind of language planning and policy development. These professional groups, in the absence of strong leadership at the national level, have undertaken an unusual kind of language planning activity. Certainly it is useful for the polity to have such standards available, though the process is potentially fraught with problems.

First, it is necessary to differentiate between the existence of *standards* and a movement towards *standardisation*. Second, by undertaking to produce Standards, each of the groups has had to make certain basic assumptions: namely the NCTE/IRA have decided that English is, in fact, the first language of the United States; ACTFL and its co-operating bodies have in fact decided which languages shall be the official foreign languages (NB – the organisations of teachers of Japanese, Chinese, Russian, etc. did not participate, nor is it clear whether they were consulted), and TESOL has decided that ESL is for assimilation. There is no National Standard on Bilingual Education, nor is one planned.

Third, each group has carefully stated that the proposed Standards are voluntary; that is, no one is obliged to participate, and individual teachers have the ultimate freedom to accept or reject the Standards. One may be certain that the Standards will evoke rather different political responses in the several states.

Fourth, because the Standards were conceived in the way they were, they are necessarily extremely general – they speak to the lowest common denominator.

Fifth, and finally, the Standards tend to a significant degree to perpetuate the *status quo*; they do not address the reality that the amount of time available in the curriculum for foreign language teaching, for example, is totally inadequate. They do not speak to the identification of a pool of persons who may become language teachers, and teacher training goals are left to be enunciated some time in the future.

But the exercise in the US exemplifies the difficulties inherent in popular language planning and policy development undertaken in the absence of any experience in language planning. While the exercise is certainly designed to operate in a bottom-up fashion (that is, the exercise was not top-down because the government was conspicuously not involved), it is not clear whether students, parents, and employers were consulted to any significant degree (and in that sense, it is not really bottom-up either). It is also unclear:

- how, within economically constrained local education agencies, any of the recommendations – without reference to their relative importance – will be implemented, and who will determine the priorities for implementation;
- what the implications will be, over the long term, for pre-service and in-service teacher training or for teacher selection;
- how the implications will, over the long term, be interpreted by trade unions, parents, consumers of students such as employers, and students themselves; and
- how, over the long term, assessment and evaluation will be employed to determine student success and system effectiveness.

Summary
The five steps outlined in this section (i.e. curriculum, personnel, materials, community, evaluation) form the major considerations that must be taken into account in language-in-education policy and planning. They are not categorically different from the considerations of more general language planning efforts, but they are separate in the sense that the anticipated changes occur within the education sector, and can be determined to be cost-effective within education. The impact of these changes should spill over into the larger society, and to the extent that they do the plan may be considered part of the implementation of the more general language planning activity. The problem often is that governments have expected the education sector to achieve an entire language plan independently of the rest of society, and that is unlikely (cf. Hornberger & King, 1996).

Literacy Planning in Language-in-Education Planning
In the late twentieth century, the issue of literacy has acquired special significance. For most of human history, literacy has not been an issue. There have been three post-biological evolutionary events which have had

the most profound effect on human societies. All human beings can talk; speech is a defining characteristic of the species, and the normative ranges are defined by the ability to speak. Anyone who cannot speak is, by definition, outside the normative range. The most brutal punishment that any society can impose on an individual is the cutting out of the tongue since that act removes the individual from the normative range.[8] All human children are born with a natural, genetically conditioned predisposition to acquire spoken language, and the early acquisition of spoken language seems to be self-appetitive and self-rewarding, requiring only the presence of a language in the environment to trigger that predisposition; it may even be impervious to teaching. But written language is a very different matter. Literacy (if by *literacy* one means the ability to deal with written text – both to encode it and to decode it) is not part of the human genetic baggage; on the contrary, it must be learned in each generation and by each individual. Millions of human beings have lived full and happy lives without becoming literate.

The development of writing

About 10,000 years ago, the first of the three post-biological events occurred – some communities of human beings stumbled onto the notion that speech could be visually represented – they invented writing. It is interesting that the earliest preserved uses of writing occurred in the fields of accounting and religion; the earliest records were ledgers of things (e.g. how many of something a wealthy person owned) and recorded blessings and curses. It is clear from these records that the ability to use literacy was not widely distributed through the population; on the contrary, it was the preserve of special groups – accountants and priests. Ordinary individuals had no use for literacy; rather, they were somewhat leery of it because it seemed to give some people power over others. People tried to prevent their names from being written, even going so far in some societies as to have two names – a private name that could not be written and a public name that was sufficiently neutral that its representation in writing was not in any way threatening. Even in these earliest manifestations of writing, it was apparent that writing was a technology, but as monumental a technology as the invention of the wheel or the control of fire (Havelock, 1976).

The appearance of writing made possible certain things that had not been possible without it. Given writing, it became possible to *transmit a message any number of times in precisely the same way over time and space.* Readers of this text, given the necessary linguistic skills, can read the works of Plato exactly as they were written more than 2000 years ago in a quite different geographical setting. It made possible the development of archives – the preservation of large bodies of information. But the technology was somewhat primitive; duplication of text was a long, laborious process. A scribe might spend many years transcribing *one* copy of one book. And because there was a very limited supply of copies of any given book, books could be owned only by the very rich and even so by relatively few of them.

The existence of this technology, however, dramatically changed the societies which were in possession of it. Before writing, information was held in living memory; it was retrieved somewhat differently each time depending on the audience and the physical condition of the owner of the memory. That owner of the memory occupied an important position in the society. Once writing became available, the function of the owner of memory diminished. Information could be retrieved in precisely the same way any number of times. Facts could be checked by reference to the written record. All those human activities which depend upon large quantities of unchanging information became possible (e.g. science as it has been understood for the past 300 years). The human mind did not change; there was no 'great psychological divide' between literate and non-literate people; but societies changed.

The development of printing

A major improvement in the technology became possible when some societies, about 1000 years ago, invented printing. Printing speeded up the process of book production and made multiple copies available at a somewhat more modest price. Still, access to written material was limited, only some segments of the population had such access. The total number of books printed in England in any given year in the early seventeenth century was far smaller than the print run of even the most modest single book at the present time. In Tudor England, literacy was defined as the ability to sign one's name, was restricted almost entirely to the male population, and extended only to a fraction of the total population (Cressy, 1980). The existence of royal seals strongly suggests that even kings and queens were not literate – that is, they made their mark; they did not sign their names.

The coincidence between the improvement of the technology implicit in printing and the rise of Protestantism in western Europe constituted an important element in the spread of literacy. Most Protestant denominations believe that personal salvation can be accomplished through direct access to the gospels. The English settlers who colonised the shores of North America in the latter half of the seventeenth century constituted one of the most literate populations in history, and among their first acts after survival was assured was the erection of schools to teach literacy. The definition of literacy changed. It was no longer enough merely to sign one's name; rather, literacy was defined as the ability to read the gospels aloud. The definition had nothing to do with understanding, only with the ability to decipher the orthography and encode it as sound. This notion of ritual literacy persists, for example, in Koranic schools where children learn to read and recite the Koran without any implication for understanding the text that has been read; children in non-Arabic speaking countries, with no knowledge of Arabic, can 'read' the Koran. The technology of printing served to put books in the hands of a much larger segment of the population. The greater availability of written text gradually changed the definition and distribution of literacy.

The development of text processing

Over the next several centuries, the printing technology gradually improved, but the third post-biological change has occurred in the lifetime of most readers of this text – the invention of automated word-processing. This new technology vastly increases the speed with which text can be produced, dramatically reduces the cost of text, and consequently serves to increase the segment of the population having access to literacy. It also reduces the role of 'middlemen' in the literacy-dissemination process – of publishers, printers, book sellers, libraries – because participants in the new electronic technology can transmit large quantities of text directly to each other. The meaning of the term *literacy* has changed as well. It is now gradually recognised that literacy consists of that set of skills required, by any given society, of individuals who wish to function above the subsistence level. And the teaching of literacy has passed unequivocally to the professional education sector; indeed, the primary function of the education sector is to ensure the dissemination of an appropriate literacy through the population. Literacy now implicates not merely the ability to read aloud but also the ability to understand what has been read and to act on that understanding.

Modern literacy planning

Because the population base entering school has increased dramatically in the twentieth century, and because schooling lasts longer for much of the population, because the economic structure demands certain literacy skills, there has been an increasing perception that the system has somehow failed to provide adequate literacy to an ample segment of the population (see e.g. Green *et al.*, 1994). In the late twentieth century, a metaphor has developed which treats illiteracy as a disease which must be 'stamped out' and perceives the achievement of literacy as the achievement of a state of grace. Literacy education, then, becomes like medical treatment, administering an inoculation which will eradicate the disease.

This perception is accompanied by a number of problems. First, as suggested above, literacy is not a single point but rather constitutes a continuum along which an individual may slide or along which an individual may get stalled. The quantity of literacy requisite in any society is defined by the society; it is not a definite quantity. As societies move away from subsistence economies and begin to be heavily involved in the marketing of services, literacy demands increase. Illiteracy is not an evil condition; it is the natural condition of human beings. Individuals cannot be inoculated with a vaccination against illiteracy. And the possession of literacy is not a panacea to all the problems of society. Research has demonstrated that the distribution of literacy is unrelated to many of the problems with which it is associated in the popular imagination.

A second issue relates to the fact that literacy is often defined in the context of only one language. The US 'National Literacy Act of 1992', for example, defines literacy as occurring exclusively in English. Studies of minority populations in the US show that individuals literate in languages other than English are deemed illiterate if they are not also literate in English. Literacy – the ability to encode and decode written text – is, of course, not limited to a single language. The assumption that it is limited to a single language is particularly pernicious, since, as we note in Chapter 7, it has political implications, social implications, and educational implications.

Literacy as a secret code

Language-in-education planning frequently includes a major component dealing with literacy. To the extent that literacy remains ill-defined, to the extent that literacy is defined in terms of a single language, these plans are not likely to succeed. But the issue of literacy in a language has yet another set of implications, ones for oracy. In their interesting article on the problems of oracy and literacy among the Toba of Chaco Province, Argentina, Messineo and Wright (1989) make several very important points: namely that Spanish literacy does not accord well with Toba oracy and that the richness in social, cultural, and political aspects of Toba phenomenology may not be expressible in Spanish while the richness of Spanish literacy may have little meaning for the Toba people. In making these points, the authors have focused on a problem that lies at the heart of language planning and at the centre of the formulation of language policy and literacy policy. The introduction of an irrelevant literacy to a population does nothing to solve the social problems of that population. It has been argued that literacy is empowering; under certain circumstances it may be, but if the literacy is unrelated to the phenomenology of the learner it has little effect on the relative power of the community or can even be disempowering for that community and culture. In an article discussing language policy and planning in Latin America, Kaplan (1990b) has claimed that the Spanish necessary to achieve political equity is not available to the Toba; that is, formal written Spanish is a 'secret' language to which the Toba do not have access.

But the 'secret' language of literacy is not just a cross-cultural problem. In the collection of short stories entitled *The Ebony Tower* (1974), John

Fowles (who also wrote *The French Lieutenant's Woman*) includes a story with the intriguing title 'Poor Koko'. The story concerns an unnamed narrator who is a 'scholar' working on ' . . . a definitive biography and critical account of Thomas Love Peacock . . . ' (139), a less well-known British novelist who lived from 1785 to 1866. The narrator has rented a remote cottage in North Dorset (in the south of England) from friends with the intent of spending time alone working intensively on his manuscript. On the second night of his stay in Holly Cottage, he is awakened in the night by a burglar. The burglar, astonished to find the cottage occupied, is very civil to the scholar, assuring him that he has no wish to harm him. At the same time, having come far to commit his burglary, the burglar is not to be deterred. The burglar convinces the scholar that he must tie him up in order to make his escape, and the scholar – not inclined to physical violence – agrees. Once the scholar is tied up, the burglar proceeds to take what he wishes and, while he collects his booty, the two chat amiably. However, before he leaves, the burglar deliberately burns the scholar's manuscript – four-years' work – page by page, right before his eyes. After the burglar leaves, the scholar spends some unpleasant hours, but he is rescued from his plight the following morning. The remainder of the story traces the stages of the scholar's psychological state from hatred for the burglar and a strong desire for revenge to a more accepting condition and a need to understand *why* the burglar felt compelled to burn the manuscript. The scholar says:

> I must have appeared to the boy as one who deprived him of a secret – and one he secretly wanted to possess. That rather angry declaration of at least some respect for books; that distinctly wistful desire to write a book himself (to 'tell it how it really is' – as if the poverty of that phrase did not *ab initio* castrate the wish it implied!); that striking word-deed paradox in the situation, the civil chat while he went around the room robbing; that surely not quite unconscious incoherence in his views; that refusal to hear, seemingly even to understand, my mildly raised objections; that jumping from one thing to another . . . all these made the burning of my book only too justly symbolic in his eyes. What was really being burned was my generation's 'refusal' to hand down a kind of magic (174).

In an important paper, Martin (1990), the Australian linguist, makes the point that the Aboriginal people of Australia perceive formal written varieties of English as what he calls a 'secret' code – a magic language which empowers those who have it and isolates those who do not. Eggington (1992) carries the point even further, supplying a chart (Table 5.1 as modified by Kaplan 1990b) comparing the functions of formal written language in a literate culture and any oral language in an orate culture. The Toba example, and Eggington's illustration, show that although human

Table 5.1 Variability in oral culture and literate culture power values

Oral culture	*Literate culture*
Decision making	
One only knows what one can recall.	One has access to all information, once it has been recorded.
Power discourse is spoken only by those who have the right to speak and the right to decide.	Power discourse is written by those representing power institutions. Institutions make decisions, not individuals.
Negotiation	
The spoken word in negotiations is considered carefully. It constitutes the only message. It must have a high perceived truth value. Masagara (1991) has shown that some cultures use 'traditional oath forms' to validate the truth value of a spoken message, each individual in a community having an 'ultimate oath form' which must be accepted on penalty of death.	The spoken word is not as carefully articulated as the written word. It is not the final message. It does not need to have a high perceived truth value. The truth value of an utterance only exists when the message is written and the written version is subjected to scrutiny. [English speakers say 'Get it in writing!' and 'Show it to me in writing!'] The only verifiable truth lies in the written text.
Issues are resolved quickly through personal, face-to-face negotiation with practical limitations on the size of the negotiating network.	Issues are resolved slowly through depersonalised committees and legal structures with little practical limit on the size of the negotiating network.
Contract making	
Once agreed upon, a spoken contract between those who have the right to speak is locked in memory.	Once agreed upon, a spoken contract is only validatable through the renegotiation of a written contract. That contract, or demand, becomes more powerful when it is 'published' by institutions and locked in institutional archival memory.
Power discourse must be stored in memory. Consequently, it is structured in such a way that it is easy to retain it in memory and to recall it. Thus, additive relationships and repetition are favoured in such discourse.	Power discourse is packed with complex sub-ordinated and nominalised language, in which processes, qualities, quantities, logical relationships, and assessments are expressed as nouns or adjectives (Martin, 1990).
There is a general *past or present* orientation in the discourse.	There is a major focus (a promissory focus) on the *future* in the discourse.

minds remain unaffected by the presence or absence of literacy, human societies are modified by its availability. Such societies behave in quite different ways from orate societies, evolve quite different social structures, entrust power to quite different groups within the society. Literacy is an extremely powerful technology which reshapes the way human beings deal with each other and which also reformulates the mechanisms that permit access to power within the society.

Literacy summary

In formulating literacy policy, it is important for planners to recognise what literacy is – a technology – to recognise the way in which literacy is defined, to understand that the definition changes as the society changes (yesterday's literacy definition is of no use in today's society), and to recognise the role of the education sector in the dissemination of an appropriate literacy through the society.

It is important to understand that only appropriate literacy counts; e.g. urban gang members may be extremely literate in the graffito-code with which the walls of the ghetto are decorated, but that literacy doesn't count in the larger society. It is also important to recognise that literacy can be lost; for example, in situations where there is nothing to read beyond the literacy-teaching materials, newly acquired literacy is quickly lost. In languages like Chinese, in which the act of literacy demands control of a very large number of 'characters', literacy may be lost through lack of practice; John De Francis (personal communication) argues that staying literate in Chinese is like training for a fight. Additionally, it is important to recognise that literacy learning is not exclusively the prerogative of the young; individuals can acquire literacy at any age and will do so if proper motivation exists, but proper motivation is always intrinsic – it cannot be imposed from the outside. As Halliday has observed:

> What is learning to read and write? Fundamentally, it is an extension of the functional potential of language. Those children who don't learn to read and write, by and large, are children to whom it doesn't make sense, to whom the functional extension that these media provide has not been made clear or does not match up with their own expectations of what language is for . . . . Fundamentally, as in the history of the human race, reading and writing are an extension of the functions of language . . . . This is what they must be for the child equally . . .
> (Halliday, 1978: 57)

Literacy, while certainly an important element in language-in-education planning, may be somewhat overrated in importance. First, linguistic diversity is certainly possible without literacy. Second, it is debatable whether literacy, in and of itself, strengthens languages. Third, literacy does not, in and of itself, solve social problems; disenfranchised populations, when they are provided with literacy, are likely to remain disenfranchised. Literacy alone is not the road to power. Fourth, literacy in the dominant language may not accord well with the phenomenology of an orate minority population, so that the richness in social, cultural and political aspects of a minority phenomenology may not be captured in the literate form of the dominant language, and the richness of the literate form of the dominant language may be relatively meaningless to the minority population. Fifth, literacy is not a fixed quantity or an absolute point; rather, literacy is fluid, changing with the changing circumstances of a society. Finally, illiteracy is not an abnormal condition – a disease to be 'stamped out' as smallpox was just recently; rather, the absence of literacy is the natural human condition. Literacy can be substituted for non-literacy in a population only if literacy matches up with the population's expectations of what language is for. It is a fallacy to see orate languages as 'deficient' – as lacking literacy, among other things – and to see literacy programs as 'salvaging' such languages by providing them with an orthography and, thus, with literacy.

Summary

This chapter has looked at two major reasons why language planning is undertaken at all. Since much language planning is allocated to the education sector, the chapter examines language-in-education planning, and looks specifically at:

- policy formulation and implementation in education settings;
- cost analysis and definition of resources; and
- literacy planning.

In the education context, curriculum policy, personnel policy, methodological specification, materials policy, community policy, and evaluation policy are examined in some detail. In every instance, the chapter undertakes to demonstrate that these several areas of policy development are much more complex than they initially appear, and that comprehensive policy invariably outdistances the capabilities of the education sector to deal with them because the implications of policy and the realities of implementation extend into every sector of a society.

The chapter suggests that language planning ought not to be casually undertaken, that planning is likely to be time-consuming and expensive, and that implementation requires much more than a set of top-down decisions. Those whose language will be in some way modified must accept the proposed modification as really being in their best interests, and those who are implementing the language change need to perceive that their proposals must be 'sold' not only to the recipients of change but to the entire population.

Notes

1. An argument can be made that television may also be a major participant in the process, since the oral language delivered through television is largely scripted on the basis of a 'standard' language, and since television also provides a substantial amount of written text on the screen, in advertisements, titles and other texts – texts which are expected to be in the standard variety. Of course, the standard may vary from the local norm (i.e. American English on Australian television). Deviation in spelling or grammar from the standard often evokes loud and repeated public protest; the now ubiquitously quoted opening lines of the 'Star Trek' programmes and films ' . . . to *boldly go* where no *man* has gone before . . . ,' contains both a sexist allusion and a split infinitive, and on both counts has been widely criticised, but the owners of the text have persisted in maintaining the deviations.

2. The book *Language and Development* (Crooks & Crewes, 1995) provides a negative instance of the consideration of these factors and of how to do language-in-education planning. Contrary to the title, the papers in this volume do not consider the role of language in development, but rather focus on the role of English Language Teaching (ELT) in ostensibly allowing developing countries to enter the modern sector. The authors seem to operate on the assumption that ELT projects are 'good' for the communities in which they are installed while ignoring the impact of English on minority languages, indigenous culture and in causing language death. While several of the papers are about the need to involve 'insiders' and actual 'stakeholders' in the language development process, the 21 authors are outsiders (except for two indigenous co-authors) representing to a large degree the views of outside development agencies such as the British Overseas Development Administration, the British Council, the US Agency for International Development, the Australian Agency for International Development and the Canadian International Development Agency. The papers decry the lack of literature on the topic, while ignoring 30 years of language planning work which has discussed these issues. (See also Kenny & Savage, 1997.)

3. A confounding issue is that the earlier a language programme begins, the more developmental it must be. That is, the programme cannot assume and build on first language school based language and literacy skills, but must help develop those skills as part of the overall programme. Therefore, a developmental programme requires different teacher training and materials than one which builds on pre-existing language and literacy skills. Clyne *et al.* (1994) estimate that students who begin a language in Year 3 develop as good second language skills by the end of primary school as those who begin earlier.

4. Proficiency studies show that languages such as French, German, Italian take between 700 and 800 hours to attain a Level 3 in the four macro skills (i.e. listening, speaking, reading and writing) on the US Foreign Service Institute or Australian Second Language Proficiency Rating Scales, while languages like Arabic, Chinese, Japanese and Korean require 2700–2900 hours to acquire the same level of skills. Level 3 is defined to reflect general social proficiency (e.g. 'I can discuss my own and other people's attitudes and activities. I can adjust my language as required though sometimes I have to search for words.') To acquire near native proficiency would take an estimated 1800 or 4800 hours respectively for those two groups of languages (ALLC, 1994: 6, 130–1). Level 3 is also the standard of proficiency that the Australian Federation of Modern Language Associations recommends that teachers have attained to be properly qualified to teach at pre-tertiary levels.

5. The discussion in this section is meant to raise language planning issues relevant to curriculum policy. Possible solutions are beyond the scope of this book as the topic of immersion has generated a substantial literature based particularly on Canadian (e.g. Genesee, 1995) and European (e.g. Baetens Beardsmore, 1993a, 1993b) experience, but increasingly including material from other countries (e.g. Berthold, 1995; Clyne *et al.*, 1994 – Australia).
6. Gibbons (1994) suggests another possibility which would involve delaying the introduction of a language in primary/elementary school until Grade 5 and then using the accumulated time of perhaps six hours a week to do intensive language study. He also points out that there is often very little continuity between primary and secondary schools in what languages children can study, and where there is, curriculum is not articulated. Thus, even the figures for overall contact with a language are optimistic as the opportunity for students to study a language continuously in an articulated manner in schools is very rare.
7. For most students, this will remain the case, i.e. the L1 will have greater power and status than the L2. However, for some students an international L2 like English or a powerful national/religious language like Hindi may alter that balance. Further examples of language and power are given in Chapter 7.
8. This was especially true historically when literacy was not well distributed throughout the population.

6 The Economics of Language Planning

Early Economic Perspectives

Many of the early roots of language planning can be found in the positivist beliefs so strongly held in the 1950s and 1960s that through rational planning, often based on economic planning models and using economic terminology, governments could overcome many of the problems (i.e. the great depression, World War II, etc.) that had beset them in earlier decades. Language planning emerged in part from this tradition and in part from the complementary structuralist tradition in linguistics where audio-lingualism, based on teaching inherent linguistic structure was seen as a breakthrough to language learning. This belief in the confident ability to create ordered linguistic change was well suited to the planning environment and to the problems of the times, the need for newly independent nations to make language choices suited to their newly won independent status.

Thus, much of the motivation for language planning, during its early development as a discipline in the 1960s and 1970s, was sociopolitical and focused on nation building, primarily using the nineteenth century European model of one state, one language, one culture, regardless of how inappropriate such a model might have been for the new emerging multilingual polities. Although the first language planners came to the emerging discipline from a wide range of backgrounds, much of the initial terminology and concepts, as in general planning, were borrowed from basic economic concepts (e.g. language as a consumer good, supply and demand for language, cost-benefit analysis and the efficient allocation of resources). Jernudd and Jo (1985) extended these economic arguments to make the case for language planning by government agencies. Using the concept of marginal analysis they argue that:

> the private marginal value and marginal costs (i.e. what the private individual takes into account in making a decision to learn or maintain skills in a language) will not be equal to the social marginal value and cost. Such a divergence between the private and the social value and

cost establishes a bona fide case for public (government) involvement . . . (1985: 12)

Language has also been viewed as a special commodity, one necessary
for national and international development and communication. For
example, as an outcome of the four broad social goals (Equality, Economic,
Enrichment and External) of Australia's *National Policy on Languages* (Lo
Bianco, 1987a, 1990) it is argued that an increase in both the amount and
quality of languages studied in schools is necessary so that the country can
benefit economically from the developments occurring in the region and
so it can become more involved in tourism and other human interaction.
As Jernudd and Jo argue:

> In an increasingly interdependent world with such a multitude of
> native languages that receive increased (although localised) attention
> and such an impressive array of increasingly important lingua franca
> (Spanish, Swahili, Arabic, Hindi, Russian, Chinese and others) and
> increasingly important literature in many languages (Jernudd, 1981;
> Baldauf & Jernudd, 1983; Swales, 1985b), decisions on language
> learning for international communication take on increasing impor-
> tance. (1985: 14)

While the issue of access to information is discussed more extensively
in relation to science and technological development in Chapter 9, the
economic implications of not having adequate language resources to access
the world of science, as opposed to the individual scientist's desire to do
the best possible science, need also to be stressed. As most countries in the
world are realising, they cannot be competitive or aspire to a reasonable
standard of living without adequate access to a high level of scientific and
technological information. As much of the necessary literature is now in
English, proficiency in this language is a valuable commodity, both to
individuals and to national economies.

However, it can be argued that the relationship between language
planning and economics is at a critical turning point, if decision makers are
prepared to re-examine the role of language. In the past, the sociopolitical
imperative has generally been to stress the national language and national
economic development (cf. India and the three languages formula, e.g.
Aggarwal, 1988), whether at home or as part of colonial expansion. This
has put pressure on minority languages in national 'colonial' settings.
Furthermore, the growth of international languages, in particular English,
for information access and international trade has put additional pressure
on minority languages as they are pushed one layer further down in
priority. The damage that imperial and colonial policies, nation-state
building and the international political economy have done to small

languages worldwide is substantial and has been described elsewhere (e.g. Mühlhäusler, 1994a, 1995; Wurm, 1994b).

But as Grin (1993) points out in the European context, this clash of economic language forces may prove to be the saviour of at least some endangered languages. If minority language goods and activities become cheaper under European economic integration, then activities in those languages are likely to increase, whereas if such activity becomes relatively more expensive then there will be pressure to abandon those minority language goods and activities in favour of majority language alternatives. Grin postulates that languages like Breton, Irish, Occitan, Scottish Gaelic and Welsh are likely to feel more pressure from European integration and increasing incomes, while other languages like Basque, Catalan, Frisian and Sardinian are likely to benefit. In Australia Lo Bianco (1996, personal communication) has argued that the economic imperatives around the need to create jobs so that Australians can meet the demands of an increasingly globalised economy have the potential to revalorise the language and cultural skills of migrant groups from being viewed by many conservatives as a national problem to being an important national asset. If this were to occur, it would provide a powerful support for the notion of a multicultural and multilingual Australia which has developed over the last 20 years.

Thus, it is not just the rhetoric which links economics and language planning. During the last two decades, a different focus for language planning has emerged. In a world which is continually shrinking in perceptual size (at least in its more affluent parts), where individuals and nations are increasingly closely economically interrelated, where access to information is critical to economic development and where business is increasingly international, language planning is often inspired by economic considerations. The simple fact is that, in the context of language activity in the community, it is very expensive to do it wrong. There are a great number of real and social costs that accrue to a society from inadequately managed language resources, both internationally and nationally, and this makes it an area which is gaining increased attention in the literature (e.g. ALLC, 1994; Bruthiaux, 1993; Chaudenson & Robillard, 1989/1991; Coulmas, 1991b, 1991c; Grin, 1994c, 1995, 1996; Grin & Vaillancourt, 1997; *Language Problems and Language Planning*, 7, 1983).

An Economic Frame of Reference

Before examining a number of roles that language can play in international and national economic and social development and in some national case studies, it is appropriate to examine language from the economist's point of view. While the relationship between language and trade goes beyond strictly economic considerations, initially perhaps there may be a tendency for business and industry to look at language primarily in terms of its economic value. In economic terms the value of language is not a property of language itself, but an index of its appreciation by a relevant community. Thus, language or any other product is not valuable in economic terms in and of itself, but holds a value determined by the community, in this case business and industry. That language is more highly valued in some communities (e.g. Germany, Saudi Arabia and Japan) than in others (Australia and the United States) can be seen by the fact that higher pay is provided for those people with language skills in those societies (see, e.g. Hagen, 1992) or that individuals are willing to put in the time, effort and money to acquire them.

To try to describe this relationship, Vaillancourt (1991) has produced an overall framework for the economics of language which lists 18 factors related to the use of languages for consumption and work and their interactions (see Figure 6.1). It is argued that as these factors change under a supply and demand model, so do the language acquisition patterns of individuals and groups. That is, if languages are perceived as being useful and of value in the economic activities of consumption and work, and considering the cost of acquiring a language, then the language is more likely to be learned by members of society. Thus, second language competence will increase in a community if community leaders (political, social, business) place a premium on language skills and foster ways for those skills to be developed. Vaillancourt suggests that the following factors are related to: (1) language acquisition, including (2) number of workers; (3) number of owners/managers; (4) number of buyers; (5) ownership; (6) management; (7) technology; (8) internal market; (9) external market; (10) labour income; (11) investment income; (12) total income; (13) market power; (14) preferences of buyers; (15) language of consumption; (16) language of work; (17) language use/value; and (18) cost of language acquisition.

Vaillancourt (1991) has discussed these factors in detail and so it is not necessary to describe them again here. Rather, the purpose for presenting the model is three-fold. First, it is important to understand that how language acquisition, business and trade are related is a complex matter, and that different factors may be more or less important in various businesses and various sectors of the economy at different times. From this follows the second point: there are unlikely to be any simple solutions to a polity's language needs for business and trade. These needs are integral parts of the wider perceptions of the need for and value of languages held by the community and the nature of the businesses they are engaged in. Given that the interrelationships are complex, the model suggests that what is needed is long-term policies based on a multifaceted plan for improving all aspects of second language learning, while taking account of those aspects particularly important for business. Only such an approach

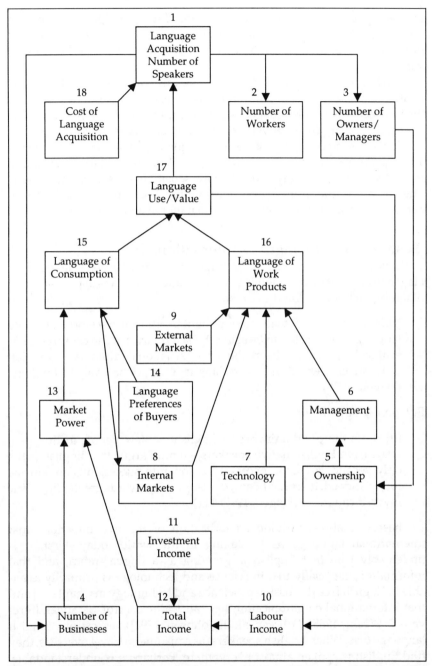

Figure 6.1 Analytic framework of the economics of language: relationships between language acquisition, language use and socioeconomic factors (Vallancourt, 1991: 32)

will secure a country's long-term economic future. Simple solutions like the introduction of more language teaching in schools, are unlikely to have much impact as they do not by themselves address most of the relevant variables.

Third, this model tends to focus on the complexity of the direct relationships between industry and language, but it takes less account of the indirect effects of language. In most competitive world markets, there is a choice of products. Buyers increasingly are accustomed to selecting products based on variety of design, of quality, of service and of price. Thus, products not only need to be good, but also to be designed and marketed[1] in linguistically and culturally sensitive ways if they are to sell.[2] Therefore, it is important to examine both the direct and indirect relations between language and business, at both national and international levels.

Economics and Language Internationally

Economic developments in the international marketplace have led, as Hagen points out in the following two quotations, to a language policy and planning dichotomy. On the one hand

> [t]he rise of English to its predominant position as the world's leading language has accelerated during the last quarter of the century. It has eclipsed French in the realm of international diplomacy and left German far behind as a first language of science and technology. (Hagen, 1988)

But, on the other hand:

> [d]espite the pre-dominance of English . . . few people in Europe – apart from English native speakers – would argue that English is the only second language necessary to operate successfully in Europe today. Indeed, there has been a development towards greater linguistic diversification . . . (Hagen, 1992: 111)

These quotations provide an indication of the two directions that international language use is taking in the world today. First, it is undeniably true that English is growing as a lingua franca, and that information, especially that in science and technology is primarily available in English [see discussion of science and technology in Chapter 9] and that international communication (e.g. air traffic control, Seaspeak [Strevens & Weeks, 1985], Policespeak [E. Johnson, 1994]) has a strong English language bias. When English speakers (as consumers) travel overseas, they find English is spoken almost everywhere. Perhaps it is understandable, therefore, that many English speakers believe there is little point in learning another language (ALLC, 1994).

However, at the same time that this growth in English has been occurring, there has been growth and an assertiveness in the use of other languages (see Kaplan, 1987), in a variety of spheres, perhaps in part as a reaction to the growth of English as a lingua franca. For example, Spanish, Arabic, Hindi and Portuguese are growing at a faster rate than English as a first language and it is estimated that Spanish will overtake the total of English mother-tongue speakers in the world by the year 2000. Furthermore, while we consider French, Portuguese and Spanish European languages, the language base of each of these languages is far greater outside Europe than it is in Europe, and much of this growth in numbers is occurring in the non-European spheres. If the phenomenal growth of Indonesian/Malay and the vast size of Chinese are considered, it is hard to understand how the remarkable strength of English as a lingua franca can be seen as a deterrent to the study of other languages.

With the relative decline in the dominance of the English speaking economies, there has been an increasing confidence in and insistence on the use of languages other than English in appropriate circumstances, such as when English speakers want to sell goods and services to non-English speakers (see the Hydro-Québec example, Chapter 9) or between two non-English speakers. In this context German and Japanese have become relatively more powerful, and are becoming lingua franca in their own right in regions like Western and Eastern Europe and Asia. As these are areas which are growing rapidly and which have strong trade potential, there is a need to accommodate to these developing linguistic norms. Such economic growth factors provide an external justification for language study.

If one takes the case of Australia as an example of the impact of these two seemingly paradoxical developments in language needs, the potential of rapidly developing overseas markets has meant an increasing need for the use of languages other than English, but this awareness of the need to use the customers' language has been slow in coming to Australian business.[3] Perhaps this is because the role that English has played as a powerful lingua franca has overshadowed the essential role foreign languages can play in business success, especially in the traditionally non-English speaking 'tiger' markets in south and east Asia (i.e. Vietnam, Thailand, Korea). This is evident in the lack of facilities for second language tuition, failure to deploy adequately Australia's multicultural resources, and a failure of Australian industry to recognise and reward language proficiency.

Given its relatively small economy and its traditional dependency on primary products for exports, the revival and survival of business in Australia depends on its ability to see itself in an international context where exports, especially those for the rapidly growing non-English speaking markets, are part of a total business strategy. Such a view would also cater for the enormous potential that tourism provides. However, Australia needs to continue to improve its national language skills and use those the country already possesses better, or Australian business will not be in a position to take advantage of developments occurring in the world economy to improve the country's balance of trade or ultimately to maintain the nation's standard of living.

There are also the indirect language and cultural contributions to industry to consider which are harder to quantify, but are equally important because these are activities that ensure that the 'products' available for international trade are suitable for particular markets. This flexibility and ability to think creatively across cultures, and to see products from multiple perspectives helps to develop better products not only for overseas markets, but for Australia as well. These skills are particularly important because on the whole, Australian companies do not have the economic power to dominate markets on cost alone. There is a need therefore to develop niche markets and trade based on personal contacts and long-term relationships, and this usually needs a more creative approach and one in which language and cultural skills can play an important role. There is a need therefore to develop more outwardly oriented personnel who are more aware of international trade and markets, and who have the language and cultural skills to take advantage of them. Many of these people need to be involved at the design stage for products or in the general promotion of products (e.g. the live sheep trade).

Marketing requires not only direct language skills, but being attuned to the more indirect cultural consequences of working in a different linguistic market. For instance, Hagen (1992: 120) cites the example of one Western soap manufacturer, who ran a 'before and after' pictorial sequence (i.e. dirty to clean) in the Middle East, found the ad was having the opposite effect intended on sales. It was finally suggested that this was because in Arabic text is read from right to left and this meant the pictorial sequence was interpreted as making clean clothes dirty. Grin (1994b: 288) cites the example of poor sales for the General Motors Chevrolet Nova (*no va* means 'doesn't go' in Spanish) which picked up immediately after the model was renamed the 'Caribe'. Because such language and cultural skills are less immediate and less directly observable, it is easy to overlook or underestimate the indirect needs for language skills.

While this example has taken an Australian perspective, most governments recognise that business, trade and tourism are important factors in economic prosperity and that success in these areas implicates language and cultural issues. Thus economic motivation has stimulated efforts in language policy planning for international economic purposes.

Economics and National Language Planning

However, economics not only affects international relations and trade, but national policies in multilingual societies, which increasingly involve most polities in the world. Societies measure social cost in terms of phenomena in the society which result in a heavy expenditure of financial and human resources. A number of examples may be looked at, though it is important not to oversimplify the problem or to assume that language treatment is the only factor involved in solving all of these problems. In multicultural and multilingual societies, minority populations often have the following profiles relating to employment, health, criminality and education:

(1) Minorities tend to have unequal access to employment:
   (a) as a result, minorities tend to consume a disproportionate share of welfare resources;
   (b) as a result, minorities tend to live in substandard housing.
(2) Minorities tend to have unequal access to health care:
   (a) as a result, minorities tend to have a higher infant mortality rate;
   (b) as a result, minority populations tend to have disproportionately high birth rates;
   (c) as a consequence, minorities tend to suffer to a greater degree from malnutritian, particularly among children and mothers;
   (d) as a result, minorities tend to have a higher incidence of communicable diseases;
   (e) as a result, minorities tend to have disproportionately high rates of substance abuse;
   (f) as a result, minorities tend to experience disproportionately high incidence of accidents;
   (g) as a result, minorities tend to have disproportionately high use of public medical facilities;
   (h) as a result, minorities tend to have shorter life spans.
(3) Minorities tend to have disproportionately high rates of criminality:
   (a) as a consequence, minorities tend to have disproportionately high incidence of contact with the criminal justice system;
   (b) as a consequence, more minority individuals are arrested;
   (c) as a consequence, more minority individuals tend to be brought to trial;
   (d) as a consequence, more minority individuals tend to be imprisoned.
(4) Minorities tend to do poorly in the educational system:
   (a) as a result, minority individuals tend to be less employable;
   (b) as a result, minorities tend to require subsistence assistance;
   (c) as a result, minority children tend to draw disproportionately on educational support services, tend to be disciplinary problems, and tend to drop out of school earlier.

This brief, but by no means exhaustive list, enumerates four social sectors impacted by minority populations and 17 possible direct consequences which may be influenced by the nature of language contact. All of these consequences are extremely costly to a society. The list has been presented in terms of minority populations, and it is easily demonstrable across a great number of political states that the consequences enumerated are real enough. Although it is not invariably the case, in the great majority of cases minorities are minorities because they are speakers of a language that does not have wide acceptability in the community (see the Australian interpreting and translating example in Chapter 9). With great caution, it may be suggested that some segment of the problems enumerated might be overcome with improved language instruction to linguistic minorities and/or by language instruction to majority speakers so that society is able to address language issues. The caution stems in part from (1) the fact that economic problems are rarely attributable to a single cause and in part from (2) the fact that language treatment must be approached cautiously. Each of these points is discussed further below.

(1) Economic problems are not attributable to single causes. Indeed, there is a substantial amount of evidence (Bruthiaux, 1992) that the connection between language treatment and development is rather tenuous. On the contrary, it appears that development in most cases precedes successful language treatment (Cooper, 1989: 171). That is, for example, women who learn that water must be boiled before it is used to reconstitute milk to feed their children may continue to infect their children through the use of polluted water because there is no source of clean water, because the vessels in which water is boiled are not clean, because the powdered milk is not clean, because the situation is essentially hopeless and no amount of minor correction will provide any significant long-term solution. Problems of social and economic disadvantage need to be attacked in their own right; as the conditions which cause social and economic deprivation begin to be corrected, then – and only then – language treatment may serve as an important factor.

As has been observed in Chapter 1, there is a significant difference between *natural resource development* and *human resource development*. In the context of national resource development, we have argued that:

> When a government . . . decides to develop, for example, water resources, it may undertake to build a dam. The planning and building of such an edifice is, relatively, short in duration. While it may take eight or ten years to accomplish the project, it can often be accomplished within the life of a single political administration. At the end of the project, there is a palpable dam, and its output in kilowatt hours, in irrigation flows, in urban water supplies, can be measured in finite numbers and reported. The benefits are verifiable. Everyone can see the actual dam; tourists can visit it and marvel at its huge generators, fishermen can approach it in their boats, naturalists can measure the effect on wildlife. One can take a picture of politicians opening it and print the picture in the newspapers (p. 4).

But even if one could prove unequivocally – and one never can – that language treatment had a salutary effect on the long list of problems with which this section begins, it would be hard to calculate in any satisfactory sense the relative cost accrued for the benefits received.

(2) Language treatment has to be approached with a certain amount of caution. The objective is not to produce a linguistically homogeneous population, but to produce a population aware of and sensitive to language and cultural difference. *Bilingual education* means, unequivocally, education in two (or more) languages for all members of the population, for everyone; it does not mean education in the dominant language for minorities who do not speak it. Most of what passes for bilingual education in the world at the present time is really no better than transitional bilingualism; that is, minorities speaking some non-centrist language are permitted to use that language for educational purposes until such time as they are able to function in the dominant language. Even maintenance bilingual education is rare – the sort of bilingual education that permits retention and maintenance of the minority language beyond the point at which the minority population can function in the dominant language. Current views of the nature of the nation state mean that the notion that it is useful for all members of a community to speak more than one language is not widely accepted; on the contrary, bilingualism tends not to be highly valued.

When the Olympic Games were held in Los Angeles in 1984, it was proposed that the linguistic resources of what is perhaps the most multilingual city in the world could be mustered to enhance access to the games by the worldwide population that attends. The proposal was rejected by the local organising committee on the grounds that the world Olympic Committee recognises only certain official languages and on the grounds that it was not necessary to provide multilingual resources to the public both because the games were being held in an English-speaking city and because guests would be able to find other language resources for themselves if they wished to do so. This anecdote illustrates the lack of value attached to multilingualism as well as the somewhat xenophobic view often demonstrated by political bodies.

These same arguments for multilingual facilities are now being advanced for the 2000 Sydney Olympic games (Lo Bianco, 1995), which commentators suggest Sydney won in part because of its multicultural nature. As of mid-1996, the Australian Olympic organisers had taken no interest in language issues and had taken no steps toward the development of multilingual facilities, facilities which would be invaluable to cater for the international tourism which is generated before and after Olympic games. In 1997 a language committee was formed, but it will be interesting to see if language eventually plays a more important role in the 2000 games, or if once again language issues are ignored.

In sum, while it is important to permit minority populations to have ready access to language instruction in the dominant language(s), it is also important not to impose linguistic conformity. Bilingual opportunities should be made available for everyone. There is ample historical evidence that legislated linguistic behaviour rarely works, and can be a cause of conflict. While some would suggest that national linguistic diversity brings competition (Cobarrubias, 1983a; Wardhaugh, 1988), if not conflict, it is conveniently forgotten that some of the bloodiest wars have been between same language speakers (e.g. United States Civil War, Cambodia under the Khmer Rouge). However, as Dua (1996: 1) points out, 'Language planning and political theory have not developed far enough for us to understand the nature and scope of language conflicts, nor are we good at anticipating such conflicts.' Thus, while language may be misused as an ideological weapon for power and dominance (also see Das Gupta, 1971), it may also be a force for generating employment, development and ethnic harmony.

Employment and Training Practices

As Vaillancourt's model suggests, employment practices play an important role in learning a foreign language. If it has been established that there is a need for speaking trading partners' languages, the question arises whether it is personally 'worth it' for, say, the mechanically oriented employee to go through the 'painful' process of learning languages. This can be a long and quite tedious process, especially if the learner's interests lie primarily in other areas and/or if the learner already has difficulties coping with his/her native language. According to Vaillancourt's model, this will only happen if language skills have utility and exchange value in the community.

In Germany, for example, language skills are valued and employers advertise quite openly their willingness to offer higher than average salaries and employment packages to such people. A secretary who does not need languages will on average earn a few thousand Deutschmarks less than a secretary who has at least one foreign language to do the same job. Employers recognise the fact that without such language skills they may lose out on business opportunities. Large companies sometimes take on such skilled personnel even when they are not needed just to 'have them when such need arises'. Often they offer travel opportunities and/or career options such as management positions in foreign countries. However, businesses have to recognise that it is in their best interests to have staff with language skills, and should offer incentives to encourage languages as well as providing the opportunity for training.

In Japan, Coulmas (1991c: 19) indicates that:

> [w]henever the Japanese penetrate a market, they see to it that they have enough competent personnel in the local language. For example, an executive in the Bank of Tokyo pointed out that in order to avoid

misunderstandings detrimental to business the Japanese staff of the 650 subsidiaries of Japanese companies in Germany must be fluent in German (Watanabe, 1989). By contrast, it is not uncommon that British and American businessmen rely on English, the supposedly universal language of business, only to find that such reliance is not warranted in Japan and that their inability to speak Japanese and read Japanese newspapers and trade journals is a damaging handicap.

However, in a survey of Japanese companies, Holden (1990) found that they were investing massive sums of money in English and other foreign language training, not necessarily so that they could speak the language of their overseas customers, but rather to enhance the efficiency of their worldwide marketing intelligence effort. Thus, foreign language training and knowledge may have strategic as well as tactical importance.

From surveys conducted in a number of British industries, respondents placed great emphasis on being able to converse in social contexts and on the ability to follow informal conversations at conferences. When dealing in foreign countries, British companies rely heavily on local interpreters and agencies, but largely agreed with the assumption that English is used worldwide for all important transactions and contract documentation. However, the engineering and the manufacturing sectors appeared to need more language training than others, depending on product and company strategies (Hagen, 1988).

A number of large British companies such as ICI have implemented language training and are encouraging their staff to participate in such programmes. In summary, the main objectives of these companies are:

- to compete and expand in foreign markets;
- to discover new products in foreign countries and to extend their own range;
- to communicate better with subsidiaries/headquarters in foreign countries.

Although the British companies are offering a variety of language training programmes, the most common opinion is that long-term training in a work-related context is far more efficient and cost-effective than intensive short-term training. Since this is a 'luxury' which can usually only be offered by large companies, the small to medium-sized company does best if employing skilled people who do not need training or they try to 'get by' on English alone. Large companies realise the necessity of languages when penetrating markets and are more likely to invest in their staff development by offering language training. By comparison:

[i]t is instructive to see what our partners [of the UK] have been doing. Major European industrial groups such as Thomson, Hoechst, Bayer,

Siemens, all have well-developed in house language training centres. Siemens, for example, spend almost £1.5m a year – around half their total training budget – on foreign language training, 40% on languages other than English. In France, the network of the Chambers of Commerce operates one hundred and fifty 'Centres d'étude des langues' across the country. Ten thousand firms use the service each year, training some sixty thousand employees in twenty-two different languages. (Wales, 1990: 1)

Nature of Skills Required

Naturally, opportunities for personnel with language proficiency at any level are largely dependent on other skills. For example, a bilingual secretary, technician or engineer will require additional professional skills. Since language skills are not usually part of professional studies in areas such as law, engineering or architecture – although more joint language and professional degrees are now being offered – professionals are in most cases forced to acquire them as necessary at a later age, with great inconvenience and not always with the desired results. Wabenhorst (1989) cites an example where a talented manager who was about to be posted on an assignment with the parent company in Germany, resigned abruptly and left the company before his departure as he felt he and his family might not be able to cope with living in a foreign language environment. The lack of language and cultural skills can not only lose a company business, but it can make employees less productive.

Setting aside the fact that the more one is fluent in a language the better, just *who* has to be *how* proficient and what type of training do they require? Business language, of course, varies greatly from that spoken in an educational or literary context. To be able to converse with a number of different customs officers at a dozen border posts throughout Europe is more important to a Danish truck driver than to be able to read Molière in French. For the truck driver it is therefore far more important to have acquired proficiency in languages within functional contexts rather than merely to be able to read sophisticated foreign literature.

Since each company is different in size, structure and production, different language skills are required in a variety of jobs, and levels of proficiency requirements vary greatly from company to company and from job to job. A telephonist does not necessarily need to be as proficient as the sales manager but it may help if he/she is able to take a simple message or answer questions regarding the whereabouts of his/her boss (see Ulijn & Strother, 1995).

A sales manager, however, may need to be as fluent as possible in his/her client's language. Although linguistic abilities will not compensate for lack of competitiveness the seller fluent in a customer's language will most definitely have an advantage over the seller with no linguistic abilities. It goes without saying that the more sophisticated the product becomes the greater the language proficiency will have to be.

In summary, proficiency levels depend on the job that has to be done. Any business person trying to market a product has to be able to sell it well. This point is made only too clearly by the rather famous and all too ubiquitous quotation by a German Minister for Economy in a letter to the editor of the *Melbourne Age*: 'If you wish to buy from us, there is no need to speak German, but if you wish to sell to us . . . .'

Cost-Analysis Evaluation

The discussion of national and international needs for language, the model, employment practices and the sorts of skills required, returns us to the wider question of 'Can the supposed benefits of second language learning be demonstrated?' Natural resource development planning has tangible benefits, but what of human resource development? If policies are to be put in place to spend funds on language planning and language learning for economic and economic related social purposes, will measurable gains occur?

In a sense, the issue of funding language planning activities can be seen in terms of the dichotomy which exists between planning agencies, the civil servants, academics, consultants who are responsible for determining the linguistic needs of a community on an even handed and equitable basis, and the politicians or business people who must supply the funds to meet those needs in light of what they believe are the political and economic realities of the situation. While language planners may be able to operate somewhat in an economic vacuum, politicians, business leaders and other decision makers cannot. Language plans and language and cultural training are only one of a series of planned developments competing for governmental or business and industry's scarce resources. In such circumstances it is important that language planners understand something about the economic realities which affect language planning. No language plan no matter how sound is likely to proceed unless the decision makers are convinced of its economic and political value. Any serious study of language planning must therefore look not only at linguistic and social matters underlying language issues, but must consider the political and economic factors on which a language plan will ultimately depend for its survival.

As we saw in Chapter 4 when cost analysis was examined as a language planning method, it is a planning technique recognised in a great many sectors of society; governments frequently engage in cost-benefit analyses for national resource development. However, that is rarely the case with social change as it is very difficult to calculate that portion of cost savings for large-scale activities such as welfare, health care, criminal justice and educational systems that could be attributed to language behaviour modification. It would be even more difficult to calculate with any accuracy the increased gross national product that might result from greater participation of language minority populations in the production of the GNP. However, there are some language related examples of cost-analysis and these are summarised in the next sub-section.

Cost benefits of early literacy

In a recent study by the Australian Language and Literacy Council on *Teacher Education in English Language and Literacy*, a number of cost-benefit analysis studies were cited 'which demonstrated the economic (in addition to the educational) advantages to be gained from investment in prior-to-school educational programs' (1995: 35). In a follow-up to a carefully designed US study, the Perry Pre-School Project, on pre-school children's educational experiences:

> ... 123 disadvantaged children were followed up at the age of 19 years (Burueta-Clement, 1984). An associated cost-benefit analysis showed that for every dollar invested in the pre-school program, at least $4.13 (after adjustment for inflation) had been returned to society. These calculations were based on financial cost to society of indices such as juvenile delinquency, remedial education and joblessness – set against the running costs of an excellent pre-school program. Further analyses of these data when the same sample of young people were 27 years of age confirmed this finding, increasing the cost-benefit analysis to $7.16 returned to society for every dollar invested in the pre-school program (Schweinhart & Weikart, 1993). This economic analysis also estimated the return to society of taxes from the higher paid jobs which these young people were securing as a result of their higher than expected educational achievements.

There have been other cost-benefit analyses carried out on pre-school intervention studies, also in America. One study (Barnett & Escobar, 1990) presents data from a pre-school intervention curriculum (Wiess, 1980) and another from a comprehensive daycare program for disadvantaged families (Seitz, Rosenbaum and Apfel, 1985). Both studies showed that the costs of the program were more than offset by savings later on in the children's schooling and medical care. Research conducted in Australia (Anstie *et al.*, 1988) focused on the loss of skills and subsequent earnings, with consequent decrease in tax payments, of mothers who take long periods of absence from the work force. In this event they become progressively less effective contributors to the family, community and society at large. This Australian research also pointed out that in any one year, for every dollar spent on child care, there was a net addition to the budget of $1.56. Cumulations over several years of the pre-school period would increase this benefit proportionately. (Raban-Bisby, 1995: 4–6, cited in ALLC, 1995: 35–36)

The cost-benefit data cited in the ALLC (1995) review demonstrates the educational, social and economic benefits of good pre-school programmes. The report points out that while children are very resilient and some survive early negative life experiences if circumstances later improve, the research shows that most children from low income families, where mothers had no available form of child care, often start off school a long way behind other children in terms of their abilities in a wide range of areas.

Cost analysis of French in Quebec

Canada is a bilingual country and English and French are maintained for official purposes at considerable expense through translation, language training for public servants, the extension of French language broadcasting and through a bilingualism bonus to public servants. However, these supply side measures were not effective enough and in Québec, both the Gendron Commission and the Montreal Catholic School Commission had highlighted the economic superiority of English as the key reason for the choice of English language schooling rather than French. The Gendron Commission also reported that although French was a common language in the workplace in Québec, a sound knowledge of English was considered necessary for career promotion.

> Thus while French was shown by the report to be alive and well and not in any immediate danger of extinction, the economic supremacy of English in the work place was clear . . . . Clearly the status of English resulting from the control of the Québec economy by English speaking North American business interests, and the predominance of anglo-phones in management presented an obstacle to the upward mobility of Quebec francophones. (d'Anglejan, 1984: 35)

In such circumstances, without some kind of language planning intervention the power of English would continue to increase and the number of francophones would continue to decline. Bill 101 passed in 1977 sought to enhance the role of French and the status and income of francophones by increasing both the supply and demand for French by declaring French the working language of Québec. At the same time expenditure on French education and cultural activities was increased while access to English language education was restricted. Ridler and Pons-Ridler (1986: 54) indicate that these policies have reversed the decline of francophones in Quebec and have led to a decline in the number of anglophones. There have also been an increase in the number of unilingual francophones (100,000 between 1971 and 1981) and an increase in the number of bilingual anglophones (500,000 between 1971 and 1981). This contrasts to the rest of Canada where the number of francophones fell by 9.5% between 1971 and 1981. Much of the francophone population is concentrated in Québec and New Brunswick, and since 1977 this territorial linguistic division has increased.

Against the benefits of French cultural maintenance and Canadian unity, the costs of the implementation of these language policies have been very high. In Québec in the first five years, the switch to the use of French as the usual and normal working language, has cut as much as 0.5% of provincial output and 2% of employment was lost. Furthermore, there were added business costs, an exodus of head-offices and the loss of business confidence. For Canada as a whole, hundreds of millions of dollars a year have been spent on translation, training and the public service bilingualism bonus to maintain Canadian unity (Ridler & Pons-Ridler, 1986). It is one thing to make policy and another to implement it fully. Dion and Lamy (1990) note that the francisation process has been more difficult and slower than expected because of resistance from various quarters, highlighting the need for a successful language policy to find a path of compromise between strict rules and too flexible implementation.

Some other cost analysis related studies

Zhu and Chen (1991: 91) provided a 'cost benefit analysis . . . of English language education in China' which consists of a general description of some of the expenditure on and costs of English language instruction and some of the benefits to be gained by those who know English (e.g. access to overseas study, better paying jobs). While the data are suggestive of individual benefit from language study, it provides no real cost-benefit information. Taking a more general perspective on cost-analysis, Commins (1988) examines the dilemmas of state economic and language manage-ment in the Gaeltacht in Ireland. Here, economic development was intended to strengthen local declining Irish-speaking communities by providing employment growth to locals, thus keeping them in the region and supporting language maintenance. While the number of Irish speakers has increased, the results of this economic intervention as a language planning attempt have been disappointing as the out-migration has continued and the proportion of people using the language has declined. However, the economic modernisation process itself has disrupted the established social networks and introduced English into the community in non-traditional contexts. Unfortunately, the one agency dealing with economic development was also charged with the language maintenance policy, when such policy needed to be developed in the broader context of social reproduction.

This brief survey indicates that cost-analysis studies in language and language planning related areas are hard to do and therefore are not common and as a result do not as yet provide much in the way of hard evidence that can be used to support language planning efforts.

Australia: Languages for Economic Purposes

Australia has changed dramatically in the last 50 years in its economic and social structure. Prior to World War II it was primarily a pastoral country, with very limited industry and an Anglo-Celtic monocultural and monolingual view of itself. World War II forced Australia to re-examine itself and the post-war migration, mainly from Europe, was intended to develop Australia's industrial base. In the past 25 years Asian migration has added to the country's multilingual and multicultural diversity and to the range of skills available.

Economically, Australia's recent export record is one of having had a persistent deficit in manufactures and in services provided overseas, but having recorded surpluses in agricultural produce and mining. However, due to fluctuating world prices and an increasing number of suppliers, there has not been a sufficient surplus in the latter area in the last few years to balance worsening overall trade and balance of payments figures. As a result, current account deficits are running on average at a billion and a half dollars a month, which gives Australia one of the largest per capita current account deficits in the world. Thus, although Australia has become a well-developed country in terms of technology and lifestyle, it has a very significant level of net foreign debt to overcome.

To get a better balance between imports and exports, Australia needs to move more forcefully into the manufacturing and services sectors and/or export more to a wider range of markets. However, marketing of products from the secondary and tertiary sectors of the economy requires more interpersonal encounters with potential customers because individualised products are being marketed to individuals or small groups of customers and not, as with primary produce, in bulk quantities to government agents. These strategies require much more talking to customers and a knowledge of their tastes and preferences. As many of these new customers will be non-English speakers, these changes have obvious policy implications. They will create a demand for second language and culture education and for the proficient and confident use of language skills since secondary and tertiary economic activities necessarily involve the need for diverse language and cultural competencies.

To meet these national economic and social needs, Australia has developed a series of language policy statements directed at meeting them (Kipp *et al.*, 1995; Lo Bianco, 1990; Ozolins, 1993). At the Commonwealth level, the *National Policy on Languages* (Lo Bianco, 1987a) was developed to help achieve four broad social goals: *equality* within a multicultural society; *economic* development and trade; *enrichment* of social and cultural life; and *external* relationships. In 1991 this was followed by the *Australian Language and Literacy Policy*, and in 1996 the government took the first steps to develop a national schools literacy policy. Each of these language and literacy policy documents has had as an underlying theme employment and economic development. State governments (e.g. Queensland) in framing their school language policies have also suggested economic motivations for their actions (Baldauf, 1993; Djité, 1994) and school systems and universities have been keen to export their educational expertise to countries in the region. Perceived economic benefit has been a major driving force behind these government language policies. Business and industry interest in language, to the extent that it exists, has also been based on economic considerations although Australian companies have generally been inward-looking 'passive exporters' (e.g. Stanley *et al.*, 1990: 46).[4] The challenge has been to change the culture of Australian industry to make it active and world-oriented with an understanding of the role that language and culture play in export markets.

Language and internal needs

Kipp *et al.* (1995) have examined the relationship between language and economic status using the 1991 Australian census data. That data indicates that 14.8% of the population uses a language other than English (LOTE) at home. This figure is possibly an underestimate of this potential language resource but reflects an increase from 12.3% in 1976 and 13.6% in 1986. However, many immigrants who have had professional training in their native country are unable to use those skills in Australia because either their English is not up to standard or the Australian authorities are unable to recognise their professional qualifications because they were obtained in another country and are not deemed to be equivalent. This means that the language and cultural resources these people bring to Australia are not able to be used to their fullest extent.

The census data examined by Kipp *et al.* (1995) includes age, proficiency in English, qualifications, occupational status and income. A combination of some of the data they present provides some interesting insights into possible relationships between language and economics. In Table 6.1 unemployment figures, English proficiency and educational qualifications are juxtaposed for a number of language groups and people born overseas. Although the birthplace figures and language figures represent different populations (e.g. those born in Viet Nam would also include speakers of Chinese), they suggest a relationship between unemployment and English proficiency and educational qualifications, with the underlying variable probably being recency of arrival. The Italian, Dutch, Maltese and German arrivals all belong to the post-war period of Australia's immigration history and tend to have higher self-assessed levels of English, whereas the Polish and Asian migrants have arrived more recently and generally have

Table 6.1 Language and economic data from the 1991 Australian Census*

Birthplace	Per cent unemployed[1]	English proficiency[2]	Education qualifications[3]	Language
Italy	8.9	82	8.8 (V)	Italian
Netherlands	9.6	96	14.5 (V)	Dutch
Malta	9.7	88	8.7 (V)	Maltese
Australia	10.5	–	–	–
Germany	11.2	95	21.1 (V)	German
Greece	12.1	78	7.2 (V)	Greek
Hong Kong	13.4	67	11.4 (B)	Chinese
China	15.8	67	11.4 (B)	Chinese
Philippines	16.2	93	26.9 (B)	Filipino
Poland	18.1	81	10.7 (V)	Polish
Lebanon	31.8	78	5.7 (V)	Arabic
Viet Nam	38.7	52	4.2 (B)	Vietnamese

*The data in this table juxtaposes country and language figures (i.e. the employment figures are by country of birth whereas the other figures are by language group). While not all Dutch speakers come from the Netherlands (some come from Belgium) and so on, these comparisons do provide an indication of the relationship between language and economic indicators.
1. Kipp et al. (1995: 90, Table 4.8).
2. Proportion of language groups speaking English 'very well' or 'well' (self rating) (Kipp et al., 1995: 82, Table 4.1).
3. Proportion of language groups with Bachelor degrees (B) or 'skilled vocational' qualifications (V) (Kipp et al. 1995: 84–5, Tables 4.4 and 4.5).

fewer English language skills – excepting only Philippine migrants because they originated in a polity in which English is a language of education. The high levels of qualifications of some of the recently arrived groups can be traced to an emphasis on economic migration criteria. However, despite relative high levels of qualifications, Kipp et al. (1995: 87) note that recent arrivals do not appear to be proportionally represented in the professional workforce, and many were working as labourers in 1991, an occupational area which does not fully utilise their language skills. They conclude that 'while there is a considerable language resource present in the country, this resource appears to be underutilised, and in many cases not utilised at all' (1995: 91).

Migrants from various ethnic groups also make up major proportions of customers in some Australian urban situations, and they have significant buying power. Their needs are often catered for by small shops run by other migrants from their own ethnic communities. Traditional advertising is not effective in reaching these consumers and small shopkeepers, either culturally or linguistically, and so many large Australian companies are effectively shut out of parts of the internal Australian market. In one western Melbourne suburb, a Franklins' store – a no frills supermarket chain – had a higher than average custom, whereas several of the other larger chains of supermarkets found their sales were lower than average. One explanation for these higher than average sales results was that Franklins had put up ads and signs in Chinese to attract customers in this high Chinese migrant neighbourhood. The importance of selling to customers in their own language and cultural context should not be underestimated. Several further examples of the value of being able to present a multicultural message are the 'Lucky Monkeys' New South Wales Lotteries (coming out around Chinese New Year) and the specifically targeted anti-smoking messages which effectively use the cultural norms of particular ethnic groups. While both examples are from government bodies, the success of their efforts gives business something to consider (see, e.g. Koslow et al., 1994; Touchstone, 1996; Touchstone et al., 1995, 1996).

Not only does Australian business lose custom through the failure to compete in internal markets based around specific language and culture based needs, but this failure contributes to imports. Many migrant small businesses source goods from their traditional countries of origin where they may have good business connections. Thus, there are many thousands of examples of the importance of language and cultural ties in business dealings, but unfortunately for Australia's balance of payments, these skills are most frequently being used to increase imports rather than generate exports. Some jobs are generated by this process, and that is beneficial. However, it illustrates Australia's failure to tackle some of its internal markets, and indicates that, even when the language and cultural skills do exist, Australia may not be harnessing them for export.

Language, multiculturalism and economic outcomes

Using primarily economic sources, Stanton et al. (1992) summarised the literature which has examined the economics of a multicultural Australia. They suggest that trade and commerce, tourism and small business are the three ways in which multiculturalism could contribute to economic objectives of the polity. However, they conclude that there is little direct evidence from the literature in any of these areas about the contribution that multiculturalism actually makes to economic performance. Stanton and Lee (1996: 510) go on to point out that Australian access and equity programmes have long been part of multicultural policy and that such programmes may provide economic outcomes. However, they seriously question any attempt to use 'the contribution of cultural diversity to Australian export performance [as] one element of an attempt to establish an economic agenda as a part of Australia's multicultural policy'. Despite the view by these economists that language and ethnic multicultural policy should not be linked, the studies which have been done indicate that there is a need for language and multicultural skills to meet Australia's external needs. While these skills need not all come from the ethnic communities, Australia should not ignore these potential resources either. This leaves open the question of how these language and cultural skills are to be met.

The tourism industry provides an example of the need for such language and cultural skills. It is estimated in *Tourism 2000: Key Directions For Human Resource Development* (Kinnaird, 1992) that the need for highly skilled Japanese speakers in Australia will quadruple by the year 2000, and that there will need to be five times the number of fluent speakers of Asian languages and twice the number of fluent speakers of European languages as there are today to service tourist industry needs. In 1992

> at least 29 per cent of fluent Japanese speakers employed in tourism last year were temporary residents compared to only 5 per cent for Asian staff and 1 per cent for European language staff. (Kinnaird, 1992: 13)

The study further estimates that demand for management and staff in the tourism industry with high language proficiency levels will rise from 9500 in 1992 to 16,200 in 1995 and 33,300 by the year 2000. This means that future requirements for skilled speakers in this industry are substantial and opportunities will arise in a variety of industries directly related to tourism such as transport and hospitality and, quite importantly, too, direct selling of consumer goods.

Language and developing external trade

In terms of external trade opportunities, a number of government reports have been published which examine the directions Australian trade might take over the next few years, and which make recommendations which would be appropriate for language planners to consider. Each report points to the growing business and trade opportunities in the region, and the need to develop appropriate language and cultural skills if Australia is to take advantage of these developments. For example, in a report entitled *Australia's Business Challenge: South-east Asia in the 90s*, it is estimated that if Australia's market share is maintained, trade with South-East Asia will increase from A$6.6 billion today to A$17 billion by the turn of the century, or A$27 billion if market share were to grow by only 1%. The size of the market, its close proximity to Australia, its complementarity and shared commercial and diplomatic objectives, make it an important market for Australia. The report points out that these trade links would be facilitated by building long-term relationships of mutual benefit in a variety of areas through initiatives such as: developing a familiarity with business practices, languages and cultures of Asian markets; focusing on regional languages, particularly Bahasa Indonesian/Malay, at both secondary and tertiary levels; an expansion of postgraduate scholarships; better links with regional think-tanks; establishing enhanced awareness programmes for officials and business people; linking with prominent researchers and publications in the region; and the linking for training with Australian science and technology (East Asia Analytical Unit, 1992).

The North-East Asia market represented more than 40% of Australia's trade in the late 1980s. The complementarity of Australia's economy with those in this region, combined with the higher than average growth of their economies, means that export growth into this area is likely to continue. In particular, the tourism sector should expand substantially with an estimated million Japanese tourists a year by the end of the decade. Tourism from Taiwan and the Republic of Korea should also grow rapidly as their per capita incomes rise (Raby *et al.*, 1992). Australian firms have often avoided expanding into North-East Asia because of the difficulty of establishing business contacts there and the costs that this adds to doing business.

> Business dealings in Asia are commonly based on long-term relationships in which trust is crucial. Companies with whom business is to be done need to know that the person they are dealing with represents the real values of the product and the company. All of this can only be achieved by way of lengthy and intense exposure of the companies' executives to the customers. For such contacts to be productive, corporate representatives must be familiar with the customers' cultural values and characteristics, including language. (Raby *et al.*, 1992: 87)

With the growing policy emphasis on Asian languages and studies in Australian education and training systems, there are now more people in Australia with backgrounds appropriate to such work. However, '[m]uch remains to be done in reinforcing these initiatives, particularly in disseminating the benefits to Australian business' (Raby *et al.*, 1992: 86).

Nor is Asia the only region of focus in the economic review documents. While Latin America is not a large export market for Australia, it was still worth about A$475m in 1990/91 and generated a trade deficit of about A$100m in the same year (Senate Standing Committee on Foreign Affairs, Defence and Trade [SSCFADT] 1992). Although there is variation from year to year, the trend for Australian exports is essentially flat while the underlying trend for imports lies in an upward direction. Austrade expressed the view to the committee that:

> It is difficult for Australian companies, particularly those which are fairly new to the export business, to get into a market like that. Their

attitude is why go through all this hassle with . . . different languages
. . . when they can go to closer markets such as South-East Asia, New
Zealand or whatever . . . . [W]e would certainly underline the importance of language capacity, whether it be Spanish or Portuguese.
(SSCFADT, 1992: 278–9)

Unfortunately, the languages and cultures in Latin America are not well
represented in the Australian educational system, so Australia is only just
beginning to educate people with the language and cultural skills to work
in this area. The Committee therefore recommended that:

> . . . in the implementation of the Government's Language Policy, the
> Federal and State Education Departments ensure that they themselves
> are fully aware, and ensure that potential students of foreign languages
> are made fully aware of the importance and value of Spanish as an
> international language. (SSCFADT, 1992: 284)

Commissioned government reports like these, which focus on the
economic priorities, clearly recognise the need for business to develop
language and cultural skills appropriate to potential clientele and markets.
During this same period, Commonwealth, State and Territory language
policy has emphasised the importance of languages in the schools sector
and the numbers of graduates with a language, particularly Japanese and
to some extent other Asian languages, has increased. While the increase in
school based language students does not provide the language and cultural
facility that business needs, it is still important to examine the response of
business to these initiatives.

Business response to language

It is often suggested that if governments would just get out of the way
and leave it to business, everything would work much better. However, a
number of surveys of business and industry in Australia looking at the
need for language and cultural skills suggest that that mentality needs to
be questioned. For example, in 1991 Monash University's Faculty of Arts
and Engineering (Holgate, 1991) conducted a survey of demand for
engineers with foreign language skills among a sample of Consulting
Engineers in Victoria and from a selection of firms from the *Australian
Business Who's Who* listed as having international business connections. The
majority of companies had some business links overseas, and most of those
carry out work in countries where people speak languages other than
English (see the example of Hydro Québec in Chapter 9). Some of the
findings to come out of the survey include:

(1) English is still a 'lingua franca' in most countries, especially for contract
documentation, so fluency in another language is a bonus, not an
absolute necessity.

(2) However, it is important to understand the customer's culture, and to be able to converse with an understanding of local customs and manners in which business matters are dealt with in a social context.

(3) 'Some' knowledge (i.e. incomplete knowledge) of the foreign language is dangerous in any technical context since it can prove fatal when translating important technical instructions.

(4) The inclusion of language studies – those nominated as most useful were Indonesian, Japanese and Chinese followed distantly by French and German – in all engineering degrees, for survival rather than for technical reasons, was seen as highly commendable.

(5) A distinction was made between setting up an operation in another country and selling goods or market expertise, where companies which are merely selling or buying found English to be the most important language, whereas companies which were entering joint venture agreements found other languages became essential.

In another study by Stanley *et al.* (1990), 2000 companies nominated by Austrade were surveyed by questionnaire, with a 25% response rate, to try to establish what the relationship was between languages other than English (LOTE) skills and export success. The survey found that there was generally a low level of awareness of the relationship between LOTE skills and export success, as evidenced by the fact that, while knowledge of LOTE skills ranked as least important in the survey, obstacles related to the lack of LOTE skills (knowledge of foreign markets) were rated as the most serious. Even when companies did recognise that LOTEs were important, they were not sure which might be important for their own purposes. Exporters viewed the following nine languages as being in demand: Mandarin, Japanese, Arabic, Indonesian, Korean, Thai, Spanish, German and French, roughly in that order.

The study also reports on a survey done of newspaper advertisements for positions requiring foreign languages. This survey, which was updated in the ALLC (1994) report on languages and business (see Table 6.2), indicates a substantial growth in demand for LOTEs from employers from a wide variety of areas, although the volume of advertisements hardly amounts to an understanding of the need for LOTE skills from the business community.

In another study, interviews with 60 of the biggest export companies in New South Wales found that Japan, the United States, New Zealand, Papua New Guinea, the United Kingdom and Ireland were the companies' most important clients in 1988 in terms of income earned. By 1998, they expected Hong Kong, China and Thailand to join that list. This suggests that Australian exporters have a limited vision of what markets there might be for their products (Valverde, 1992).

Although these companies represented the 'exporters' and therefore

Table 6.2 Survey of newspaper advertisements for positions with a LOTE requirement (ALLC, 1994: 113)

	1980		1985		1989		1992	
	Aug	Sept	Aug	Sept	Aug	Sept	Aug	Sept
The Australian	0	3	18	9	28	43	79	79
Sydney Morning Herald	4	5	14	7	29	15	182	163
Monthly total	4	8	32	16	57	58	261	242
Total	12		48		115		503	

were supposedly ones with some expertise in this area, most companies were represented by monolingual/monocultural individuals with very limited notions of geographical and cultural differences (i.e. couldn't necessarily differentiate between countries in South-East Asia and those in Oceania). Only two export managers said they had heard anything about the National Association of Australian Translators and Interpreters (NAATI), and interpreters and translators were seldom used. Although there was a lot of interest shown in many of the issues presented in the survey, there was very little evidence of an awareness for the need for language and cultural skills.

Exporters suggested that Japanese, Chinese, French, Korean, Spanish, Indonesian and German were the main languages of the future. The survey also showed that these companies actually had multilingual employees fluent in many of these languages, except Japanese where the upper management was directly hired from Japan. Thus, attitude, rather than resources seemed to be a prime problem for these exporters: the belief that English is enough. Even when language skills were used, in only one case were these skills recognised by better pay.

Tackling the economic and language problems

The data in the preceding sections indicate that Australia has both a balance of trade and a services problem that is quite severe, and that current exports are based largely on unimproved commodities, at a time when major trading partners are moving increasingly toward labour and capital intensive business and services in terms of their exports. For Australia to deal effectively with these problems, language and cultural issues are clearly implicated. While the discussion has concerned Australia, the issues raised are pertinent to language planning generally and, while the circumstances will obviously vary from place to place, the matter of business' response to language issues constitutes a virtually universal problem.

Language related planning is needed to gather information from a number of sources. First it would be important to identify the data needed to infer how language and cultural skills can aid in business and trade, particularly in terms of which languages and what levels of skills in those languages are necessary to do the various jobs properly. Such data may come from trade figures, from case studies of businesses, and from language audits of particular export companies. Surveys and case studies of any type can only provide limited information. Problems could arise because it is too costly and time consuming to survey all possible users and because it is not always easy to get representative respondents to surveys when they are completed on a voluntary basis. Second, needs are constantly changing and so survey information must be collected on an ongoing basis if it is accurately to reflect current trends. Third, language and cultural training requires time to produce quality staff who have the skills to do their jobs well. Such people cannot be produced overnight, and poorly trained personnel may in fact be worse than none at all, as they could produce a false sense of security that the skills are available when they are not (Tse, 1982, 1986). Finally, future prediction is a risky game at best, as there can be no certainty as to what the language and culture needs will be in five or 10 years' time. When this fact is combined with the relatively long periods of time needed to train people to high levels of language skills, only strategies which produce people with general language skills, which can be built upon in specialised ways, are likely to be successful.

New Zealand: The Economically Driven Plan

As has been suggested at several earlier points, governments rarely act out of pure altruism; rather, they act in accord with some paradigm which they believe is consistent with the philosophy adopted by some particular political administration. While some outcomes of government policy may indeed be consistent with notions of social justice, government policy is not often driven exclusively by motivations based in social justice. Rather, governments tend to act out of economic necessity. Two examples of this phenomenon can be found in New Zealand.

Language for the workplace

In countries such as Australia, Britain, New Zealand and the United States, however, large influxes of immigrant population have had a substantial impact on the make-up of the market and of the workforce, and the commercial sector has begun to be concerned about the significant segment of the workforce which is not fluent in English. As early as 1979, a study was undertaken in New Zealand (Kaplan, 1980) to examine the language needs of migrant workers. New Zealand had an unusual situation. First of all, there is resident in New Zealand as original owners of the land, the Maori people of New Zealand. The limited access of Maori people to employment and to socioeconomic mobility has been a concern of the Maori leadership for many years.[5] But, in addition, because New Zealand had exercised a protectorate over some of the Polynesian states of the South Pacific region (namely, the Cook Islands, Niue, Samoa, Tonga and the Tokelau group) and because these territories have been both overpopulated and relatively poor, New Zealand has admitted large numbers of people from these areas into the country. Furthermore, New Zealand has been very generous in admitting and resettling Indo-Chinese refugees (after the fall of Saigon in April 1976). Somewhat earlier, in the period following World War II, New Zealand had admitted a substantial European migration consisting of Greek, Italian, Dutch, and eastern European people, as well as some smaller numbers of East Indian and Chinese people. The earlier groups had largely assimilated by the time of the 1979 study, but the Polynesian and Indo-Chinese groups constituted a linguistically marked brown proletariat. In the name of greater industrial productivity and in the name of industrial safety, certain steps were undertaken to provide language training in the workplace.

Language for international trade

In more recent years, a number of governments have adopted minimalist policies, withdrawing government from a variety of sectors and functions in which it previously and traditionally operated. In Britain, this economic philosophy was named *Thatcherism* after Prime Minister Margaret Thatcher who implemented it. In the United States, it has been called *Reaganism*, after President Ronald Reagan, during whose administration attempts were made to achieve similar ends. It has occurred in a number of other places as well. Nowhere, however, has it been more rigorously applied than in New Zealand.

In the mid–1980s, New Zealand found itself in a situation in which its foreign debt was so large and its annual debt-service so great that it was unable to borrow further in the international monetary community. It had to get its financial house in order. (In all fairness, the economic problem is attributable to other causes as well – e.g. the loss of export markets after Britain's entry into the EEC.) Given the state of its economy, it was not surprising that the New Zealand government became formally conservative in the late 1980s.

In the late 1980s, then, New Zealand disassembled its long-standing Department of Education (and other national departments as well) in favour of a ministerial structure. It did so on the theory that cabinet officers ought to have greater power, ought not to be constrained by the intransigence of entrenched civil service officers, and ought to be able to implement their individual visions for the sector with which they were charged. The ministerial structure was seen:

- as leaner (and indeed staffing has been significantly reduced in a number of sectors);
- as more egalitarian (that is, it has been assumed that 'policy analysts' [middle-level bureaucrats] are interchangeable, so that personnel can be shifted across government agencies [ministries] as needs change); and
- as more productive (on the grounds that a Minister could 'buy' only those functions s/he wished to have performed [i.e. those perceived by the Minister as having high priority and/or 'payoff']).

In general, this was a cost-cutting measure, both to reduce direct expenditure by government and at the same time to reduce indirect expenditure by reducing government intervention/regulation, but it also constituted a major shift in direction, because New Zealand had previously been universally perceived as a well-developed socialist state, providing extensive social benefits to its citizenry. In the education sector, this policy has led to devolution of schools and to the application of the concept 'user pays'; thus, parents pay directly for services they want for their children and they pay their fees not to government in the form of taxes, but rather to independent schools which are earning their own way in a competitive market. (It is perceived that, in the normal order, government is merely a broker, collecting taxes and disbursing funds to actual providers; this newer philosophy gets rid of the government's function as the middle man and, consequently, reduces costs since the cost of staffing and maintaining the middle man are removed.) Thus, schools compete; better schools attract more students, better teachers, and more funds, and become excellent, while weaker schools eventually either go out of business or of necessity become better – though there is an obvious ceiling to the number of 'better' schools. In sum, the notion is deregulatory, removing governmental control, and subsidy from education (and other social services) and causing providers to compete in the open market.

In 1992, when Kaplan was working in the New Zealand Ministry of Education, the government was still struggling with what precisely to devolve and what to keep. The Ministry of Education was, for example, involved with a range of more-or-less competing activities touching on language education:

(1) It had published requests for proposals to develop syllabi in Samoan and in a few other languages.
(2) It was investing in the creation of a new English syllabus, presumably responsive to current needs.

(3) It was engaged in a major activity to develop a new national curriculum.

(4) It had permitted the development of a 'green paper' for a national languages policy (Waite, 1992).

While all of these activities were centred in the Ministry of Education, they were, to all intents and purposes, separate and distinct efforts with little or no cross-talk among them. Furthermore, the New Zealand Qualifications Authority – a national body charged with assessment and the maintenance of appropriate standards in education and elsewhere in society as well – was independently engaged in the development of assessment instruments in English and in other languages. It remained unclear at the time (mid-1992) which of these activities government ought to be undertaking, this discussion being somewhat clouded by an underlying attempt to differentiate between policy and philosophy on the one hand and implementation and operation on the other. But, it was already fairly clear that languages policy development was not a high priority in the Ministry of Education and was certainly not a priority at all in other government agencies.

Under a supply and demand competitive model, the pool of available language teachers is necessarily always smaller than the language needs of the society, and the pool is unevenly distributed across languages. Nevertheless, both teachers and students have rights which must be protected if language is likely to be delivered and received in a quality environment. However, because language is a universal phenomenon, everybody is an expert, and the seriousness of language teaching and learning is commonly misperceived and under-estimated. Thus, 'popular' languages have access to larger sectors of the market, while 'unpopular' languages – even though they may be socially or historically important – have access to smaller segments of the market.

For example, because languages such as Japanese tend to be perceived by parents as having great prestige at the moment and as holding out the promise of employment for their offspring, while languages such as Samoan are perceived to be the primary concern of the Samoan community and not of the total population, Japanese is likely to attract a far larger share of the market than Samoan, while the teacher-pool for both languages will probably remain well below the needs-level (though for different reasons) and is unlikely to be brought to minimum satisfactory levels (because teachers, like students and parents, seek their individual long-term economic good). It can be said that the government has abrogated its social responsibility to a minority community (the Samoan community in this illustration, but probably all of the Polynesian-language speaking communities in New Zealand and a number of other stigmatised communities – e.g. Vietnamese, Cambodian). It can also be said that, since it is not the case that New Zealanders across the spectrum of the society want to learn Samoan (or other non-prestige languages), the maintenance of Samoan (or other 'community' languages) indeed becomes the responsibility of the respective minority communities and should not be supported with national government (tax based) funding – as a playing out of the minimalist principle 'user pays'. But the Samoan community has (and most of the other minority communities have), for a variety of complex reasons, less internal resources at its (their) disposal than does the middle-class community which is interested in having its offspring learn Japanese. It can be claimed that this is a perfect working out of the capitalist paradigm; at the same time, it can be shown that government is failing to meet the social requirements of the most needy sectors of the community.[6]

In this environment, the 'cargo cult' mentality (mentioned in the Introduction to Chapter 9) comes powerfully into play. Parents want for their children those skills that guarantee employability, a better standard of living, and a greater share of available goods and services. It becomes a matter of faith that proficiency in some 'popular' language such as Japanese will deliver this cargo; equally, it becomes a matter of faith that 'unpopular' languages are not able to deliver the cargo. The obvious circularity of the argument seems to have escaped popular awareness. There is no evidence that supports the 'cargo cult' notion; 'success' in the socioeconomic market is a construct depending on far more variables than knowledge of a language other than the 'national' language. Furthermore, the 'cargo cult' notion overlooks the fact that, for English speakers, languages such as Japanese will require more learning time than languages like, say, Spanish. Finally, the 'cargo cult' notion overlooks the reality that precious little language can be learned in the traditional school environment.

On the contrary, the 'cargo cult' notion is superficially based on the long-term economic outlook; recognising that trade with the EEC has become more problematic, New Zealand has also recognised that it must trade in its so-called 'natural' market in Asia, and the public has assumed that knowledge of Asian languages will enhance New Zealand's economy generally and will allow individuals who 'know' those languages to participate in the benefits deriving from greater trade with Asia – all this in the total absence of any research to support the view. It is a fact that the hundred or so New Zealanders trained to reasonable fluency in Japanese by the end of 1992 were almost entirely employed in sectors in which their knowledge of Japanese served no useful purpose; New Zealand employers are more inclined to hire English-speaking Japanese than Japanese-speaking New Zealanders, in part at least on the assumption that Japanese-speaking New Zealanders simply do not know enough Japanese. In actuality, what Japanese-speaking New Zealanders lack is a sense of the pragmatic rules of Japanese, but then English-speaking Japanese often lack this level of language proficiency as well.

Economics and Language Planning in the United States

In the second half of the twentieth century, two significant sets of events have motivated business and industry to become much more concerned about language issues. It is fair to say that, up to the quite recent past, the commercial sector was largely disinterested. It was recognised that multilingual proficiency was to some extent desirable in international commerce, but certainly in the English-speaking world it was taken very much for granted that English was sufficient for most commercial purposes.

In the United States, which has always welcomed immigration, the inflow of migrants has changed from a European focus in the nineteenth century to a Latin American and Asian focus in the twentieth. It is estimated that immigration will accelerate during the decade of the 1990s,[7] that the influx will come largely from Mexico, the Philippines, Vietnam, Korea, India, China, the Dominican Republic, Jamaica, El Salvador, Iran, Laos, Taiwan and Colombia, and that 75% of these new migrants will settle in California, New York, Texas, Florida, Illinois and New Jersey. Some businesses and public-service agencies have already begun to respond to the changing market. Some examples include organisations that hire bilingual Asian salespeople and produce house organs in several languages; businesses that offer special assistance to non-native speakers to help them establish credit; groups that provide 'welcome packages' to newly arriving immigrants in a variety of languages; supermarket chains that have opened stores catering specifically to Hispanic and Asian customers, many of which produce non-English advertising targeted at ethnic communities; a large cosmetic company that has begun to market cosmetics for darker-skinned women; and a large city government that has developed a policy to provide extra compensation to bilinguals who use their bilingual skills in the service area.

More importantly, it is estimated that the workforce will change in the same direction and at the same rate as the market, becoming less male-dominated, and clearly containing much greater representation from the minorities.[8] Not only has there been a general recognition that the market is changing, but there has been a comparable recognition that something like 30% of job entrants in the next decade will be minorities, that many of these individuals will be poorly educated and in need of training, particularly in language. Comparable changes seem to be occurring in Britain, in Australia, and in many other parts of the traditional English-speaking world. The emergence of the European Community suggests much greater cross-border fluidity in the European population as well.

At the same time, in the face of worldwide recession and economic distress, a number of countries in the early 1990s were motivated to look at controlled changes in the language situation as a means to improving international trade. Australia, for example, which has historically been Euro-centred in its attitudes and in a number of societal functions, has taken steps to change its direction. For most of the last century, the foreign languages most widely taught in Australia were French and German; in the period following World War II, other languages – migrant languages (namely, Greek, Italian, Dutch, etc.) have begun to compete in the language education area. But in the most recent period, as Australia has moved to implement its National Languages Policy (Lo Bianco, 1990), languages such as Indonesian, Chinese, Japanese and Korean have begun to receive serious attention. By 1994 twice as many university students were studying Japanese as French, and the next four most popular languages were Chinese, Italian, German and Indonesian/Malay (Baldauf, 1995b). The obvious motivation for this change lies in the notion of expanded regional tourism and international trade.

Implicit in this movement is the recognition that the chances for selling products improves if the seller understands the culture of the buyer and if the seller can speak to the buyer in his/her language rather than requiring the buyer to speak to the seller in English.

There are some problems with this notion; principally that it is somewhat naive. It will take some time to install the teaching of new languages in the education system; some of the problems related to doing that are discussed in the section on language-in-education planning (pp. 122ff.). Furthermore, there is not a sufficient supply of qualified teachers to provide instruction in these new languages.[9] There is a need to induce students to undertake these languages; clearly, the motivation for studying these difficult (for English speakers) languages is too subtle to have much direct effect on students, but it is not only students who need to be seduced; parents also need to become involved. Most important, perhaps, is the reality that the amount of instruction (both in terms of semester hours and in terms of duration in years) is not sufficient to the achievement of any significant level of proficiency. The approach typical of foreign language instruction around the world (something like a total exposure of 250 contact hours of instruction over the entire primary and secondary career, generally in very large classes, or 450 hours at the tertiary level (Mann, 1992), which is likely to be perpetuated in the new group of languages, is far short of the time needed to achieve even minimal communicative competence.[10] The probable outcome, then, is a large population of individuals having a smattering of a language but quite unable to meet the societal expectations. It is likely that perpetuation of such an approach will produce a negative backlash among parents and more generally among potential employers.

Further, there is a long history of failure to regard bilingualism as a useful skill. In most countries, a bilingual individual who is asked to apply his/her bilingual skills in the workplace is not rewarded for doing so. Except in a few specialised instances (e.g. professional bilingual translation or interpretation, as in international conferences or in courts of law, complex translation), bilingual skills are rarely recognised as having special worth. In some special cases, the compensation of bilingual individuals tends to be below average for professional occupations. Any government which genuinely wishes to promote bilingual ability must provide real incentives to individuals who achieve it. There are a number of means available to government in this context; for example, government may provide tax incentives to businesses which employ and reward bilinguals, or through its civil service government can set the standards for bilingual compensation.

Quite beyond these obvious incentives, government also needs to undertake massive advertising campaigns to change public attitudes toward language learning and towards bilingual ability. Governments have, in the past, undertaken such campaigns through the media. For example, the US government has approached the illicit drug trade and the danger of AIDS through such campaigns, while the Australian government has successfully promoted physical exercise and skin cancer awareness.

But even in circumstances where programmes to teach foreign languages are modestly successful, it is probably a mistake to assume that the sole existence of bilinguals in the sales force will increase sales (and, consequently, profits). Such issues as the quality of products, the pricing of products relative to the international market, the ability to deliver in quality and quantity and on time remain significant elements in the equation, and these issues are independent of the linguistic ability of the sales force.

Nevertheless, the commercial sector has, probably for the first time in recent human history, become aware of the relative significance of language issues in business and industry, and this is all to the good. It is now up to the language planners to capitalise on the new awareness of language issues by encouraging the inclusion in language plans of more realistic approaches to the dissemination of languages through a community, more realistic approaches to the modification of popular attitudes toward language, and more realistic recognition that, at least at the present time, bilingual ability is a unique skill that should be seen as having a high market value. This argument provides yet another rationale for not vesting the entire language planning effort in the education sector, since it is not likely that the education sector can affect the areas where key change must occur if such programmes are to succeed. Language planning is a function that must pervade the entire society if it is to enjoy any hope of success.

The question is not merely one of increasing the market share in international trade; domestic markets are implicated as well. Los Angeles, for example, is perhaps the most polyglot city on earth. Businesses operating in this multicultural, multilingual community should, one would think, wish to take cognisance of this linguistic and cultural diversity in order to increase their respective market share. Banking services may be taken as an example. Such services have been available to residents of Los Angeles almost since the city was founded. The name of the first bank to open in the area and the exact date of its origin are lost, but the presence of banks is attested certainly to the date of the Treaty of Guadalupe Hidalgo (1848). During the twentieth century, banking services have been available almost exclusively in English. In the 1980s, a number of Asian banks opened branch offices in Southern California, and at present, Chinese, Japanese and Korean banks are well established. Without reference to the presence of branches of foreign banks, the banking community has been virtually exclusively English speaking. Even the foreign banks tend to offer services largely or exclusively in English. While federal law (especially, the Community Reinvestment Act [CRA] of 1977)[11] prohibits discrimination on the basis of age, gender, race, religion, or income, and while these banking regulations encourage diversity in banking services, the California banking community has remained essentially impervious to the existence of large non-English speaking populations (Touchstone et al., 1996).

Indeed, some federal banking regulations require that certain types of transactions be conducted in, and recorded in, English. Non-English speaking bank customers are encouraged to bring their own interpreters to such banking negotiations, since the transactions must be conducted in English, and banks are inhibited from providing interpreting services in these contexts. The purpose of requiring customers to provide their own interpreters lies in the desire of banking establishments to avoid future difficulties based on the misunderstanding of terms by non-English-speakers. Banks may – and some do – provide bilingual tellers, but even this service is less well distributed than it would appear on the surface; some of the alleged 'bilingual' tellers are not fully bilingual and, as far as can be determined at this time, there is no standardised practice for establishing the qualifications of a bilingual bank employee. Bilingual ability is not rewarded; on the contrary, known bilinguals are arbitrarily called upon to provide customer assistance over and above their regular duties (without testing or training, without compensation, and frequently to the detriment of their regular duties). Some banks have placed managers who have the appearance of bilinguality in branches in non-English speaking communities, but it appears that the practice is engendered by image-making rather than by recognition of real need; indeed, interviews with some of these branch managers suggest that they are more inclined to limit services exclusively to English than are monolingual English-speaking managers (Touchstone, 1996). (This may constitute an illustration of the 'convert' mentality attributed to some banks.)

The indifference to a significant segment of the population, and the unwillingness of the lending industry as a whole to adopt to the changing demographics of the nation, is unprofitable. Unlikely as it may seem on the surface, banks are driving away these customers, and as a consequence they are voluntarily surrendering the potential profits deriving from this segment of the population. Language is a central issue in this situation (Koslow *et al.*, 1994). Banks have demonstrated a willingness to prepare brochures in Spanish advertising and explaining the services available to consumers, but these brochures are often inaccurate and are sometimes perceived by Spanish speakers as patronising. It is simply foolish for banks to continue to offend this segment of the population by ignoring issues of language use and by refusing to employ readily available translation capabilities. In the larger sense, of course, banks simply reflect the language insensitivity that is characteristic of many segments of U. S. society and of monolingual speakers of English. Should the banking industry recognise the language aspects of the problems, it could increase its role in society, enhance its profits, and spearhead a broadening recognition of the multilinguality of the U.S. and of the importance of language in the economy (Touchstone *et al.*, 1996).

Summary

In this chapter we have examined some issues and examples related to the economics of language planning. We have seen that economic theories played a part in language planning's early development as a field and that cost analysis is still considered a useful, if underused, tool for language planners. The data also suggest that language planning may be related to economic outcomes both within a polity, in terms of reducing social costs and improving employment and business prospects, and externally in terms of enhanced trade and business prospects. Three examples of the relationship between language issues and the economy were described for Australia, New Zealand and the United States. While the link between economics and language planning seems compelling at a macro social perspective, the issues are very complex and the evidence is not at all clear. However, at the micro level, there are many examples which demonstrate that planned language activity can yield profitable results.

Notes
1. Grin (1994a) discusses how language modifies traditional (one language) marketing decisions and the possible effects for minority languages.
2. The business literature is replete with examples of advertising gone awry; for example, in the Philippines, Gerber Baby Foods lost market share because – unlike cans of peas and beans – their label carries a picture of a baby. In Taiwan, the translation of the Pepsi slogan 'Come alive with the Pepsi generation' was translated as 'Pepsi will bring your ancestors back from the dead'. When the the Ford Pinto failed to sell well in Brazil, it was realised that this might be

because 'pinto' means 'tiny male genitals' in Brazilian slang so the name was changed to 'Corcel' which means 'horse'. Parker ballpoint pen ads in Mexico were supposed to say 'It won't leak in your pocket and embarrass you', but 'embarrass' was translated as 'embarazar' and the ads said 'It won't leak in your pocket and make you pregnant'. The American slogan for Salem cigarettes, 'Salem – Feeling Free', when translated into Japanese came out as 'When smoking Salem, you feel so refreshed that your mind seems to be free and empty'. Additional examples are cited elsewhere in this chapter.

3. Gregg Dodds, Executive General Manager of the Japan/Korea region for Austrade says:

> There has always been a corps of believers within Australian business (believers of necessity) that the Japanese speak English, English is the business language of Japan, language skills are of no importance compared with business skills and so on. The outcome has been a very low number of Australian business people dealing with Japan who have any real skills in the language, a fact all the more remarkable considering the very large numbers of people we have had studying Japanese for two decades or so. (ALLC, 1994: 68)

4. A collation and critique of this literature (20 studies) can be found in ALLC, (1994: 33–50).

5. The 'Finding of the Waitangi Tribunal Relating to Te Reo Maori [The Maori language] and a Claim Lodged', prepared by the Wellington Board of Maori Languages in April 1986, demanded formal recognition of the Maori Language as an official language of New Zealand and further demanded that the Maori language should be fostered, that it should be taught in the school system, that there should be Maori language radio and television in the country, and that the State Services Act of 1962 and the State Services Conditions of Employment Act of 1977 [essentially the civil-service enabling legislation] be amended to provide for bilingualism in English and Maori.

6. For a more thorough discussion of language policy development in New Zealand in the early 1990s, see Kaplan (1993a). Mühlhäusler (1995a, 1995b) provides a detailed argument for the necessity of maintaining language diversity and as to why low candidature languages should be taught.

7. Estimates indicate that during the decade of the 1980s seven million people entered the US, a figure rising to 10 million in the decade of the 1990s, and that by 2010 there will be something of the order of 35 million individuals resident in the US who were not born there.

8. By 2005, 11.6% of the workforce will be Black, 11.1% Hispanic and 4.3% Asian, and that of these some 47.5% will be women (as opposed to about 42.5% of the total workforce at present).

9. This fact raises a number of interesting trade union questions. Obviously, one possible solution is to import trained teachers from countries where the languages in question are spoken. Such importation in a tight labour market has the potential of jeopardising positions for domestic teachers. There are complex questions of certification and flexibility in the expatriate teacher groups to take on other functions within the school system. There are complex questions of comparability of compensation, and there is the additional question of what will become of these teachers when it is possible to replace them with domestic teachers. In the United States, there are a number of small programmes operating by inter-governmental agreement under which some relatively small number of teachers from California go to Spain to teach English

while a comparable group of Spanish teachers come to California to teach Spanish; a comparable programme exists in Louisiana with respect to teachers from France. But such programmes are too small to have any significant impact on teacher supply in the long term.

10. Lo Bianco and Monteil (1990) cite figures which estimate that something in the order of 1000 contact hours of instruction are required to produce minimal communicative competence for English speakers in languages like Italian or Spanish, while languages like Japanese and Chinese may take two to three times as long, These contact hours must be provided over a duration not so great that the rate of forgetting exceeds the rate of learning, nor so brief and intense that the instruction is likely to produce anomie in the learner. The ideal duration may be something like a calendar year. Clearly, the 20 hours per week estimated as ideal by this formula is a far cry from the three to four hours per week of the typical foreign language programme. The implications for syllabus are obvious. (See also Chapter 5, Curriculum policy, p.127ff.)

11. This lengthy note is included on the assumption that many readers may not be familiar with US (and California) banking regulations. CRA is a federal law which ' . . . stipulates that banks have an affirmative obligation to make loans to all of the communities in their service area – including low income and communities of color – and may not redline . . . ' (Communities for Accountable Reinvestment, 1993: 1). This law is intended to ensure that all US residents have equal access to banking services and capital. The CRA was based on two commonly held assumptions: (1) Government, through tax revenues and public debt, cannot and should not provide more than a limited part of the capital required for local housing and economic development needs; (2) Financial institutions in the US free economic system must play the leading role: public charters provide banks and savings institutions numerous benefits, and it is fair for the public to ask something in return (Kane, 1991: 15 [citing Senator Proxmire, 1977: 1]). In 1989, the federal government increased the scope of the CRA. With the Financial Institutions Reform, Recovery, and Enforcement Act of 1989 (FIRREA), the federal government can deny a bank's merger application based on poor CRA evaluations (Kane, 1991: 4). While the CRA never specifies minority language services as a right, these services have been cited in several federal regulators' CRA reports for individual banks. It appears, however, that the inclusion of the provision of language services as a criterion of compliance is left to the discretion of the individual regulator. For instance, in Bank of America's (self-published) CRA evaluation, the Comptroller of the Currency gives the bank an outstanding rating, citing its minority language services:

> In 1989, a major Spanish-language marketing campaign was initiated using Spanish-language television, radio and outdoor advertising, and bilingual staff in nearly one-third of the Bank's branches. In April 1991, Bank of America became the first major California bank to introduce a Spanish-language option at all ATM's [Automatic Teller Machines] statewide. Community and ethnic newspaper advertising is used for special products reaching Hispanic, African American, and Asian communities . . . .(1990: 8)

CRA investigators from the Federal Reserve also mentioned language policies in their report on California Center Bank, a Korean-American owned bank with headquarters in Koreatown:

> The bank [California Center Bank] recognized that there are opportunities for the bank to assist aspiring Hispanic businesses. In that regard, the primary obstacle is the language barrier. However, the bank feels this barrier is surmountable and the bank is constantly working on methods of reaching out to that Hispanic business community. (Federal Reserve Bank of San Francisco, 1991: 2)

The regulators continue with their evaluation of the bank's language policies:

> Most of its [California Center Bank's] advertising is in the Korean language which could discourage non-Koreans from seeking application for credit. However, the bank is aware of this possibility and have [sic] begun to address the matter through its Hispanic advertisements. (Federal Reserve Bank of San Francisco, 1991: 5)

Several banks have also mentioned their minority language services in their CRA public disclosure documents as evidence of CRA compliance. In Bank of America's self-published CRA public disclosure statement, the bank explains its 'outstanding' rating, citing the multilingual advertisements and the hiring of '... bilingual personnel who can explain credit services to customers in their native language ...'. (1990: 6)

Part 3: Case Studies in Language Planning

In this third section the reader is introduced to 15 issues in the field of language planning grouped into three chapters. In each of these chapters, the general problem is first discussed and then specific issues, illustrated in terms of case studies, are presented. These case studies examine some aspects of the issues raised in the three frameworks presented in Chapter 2 – Haugen's (1983) language planning model, Haarmann's (1990) ideal typology, and in Cooper's (1989) accounting scheme.

Chapter 7, the first chapter in this section, raises questions related to language and power in the global sense. It addresses issues of class, state and agency power as they relate to the context of policy development, both from the external (sociopolitical, economic) and internal aspects of policy development. The issue of language rights is also examined. This chapter indicates the importance of prestige in planning (Haarmann, 1990) and examines WHO is planning and HOW they are going about that planning. In the terms used in Haugen's model, this chapter relates primarily to status planning selection issues.

Chapter 8 examines questions of bilingualism and language status as they relate to national identity and development. This chapter emphasises FOR WHOM language is being planned and for what purposes, and has as a general focus status planning implementation issues.

Chapter 9, the final chapter in this section, deals with planning language for specific purposes. Here we examine WHAT is to be taught and learned. In Haugen's terms corpus planning elaboration is examined.

7 Language Planning and Power

Luke *et al.* (1990) have suggested that there is a certain irony in many language planning situations, in

> that while language planning sets out to study and control various sociological factors which influence language change, its very character as a form of 'interest-bound' modern social planning has led, in many cases, to a failure to tackle the hidden agendas – political, social, educational and otherwise – of particular forms of government, economic relations, politics and social organization . . . . That is, as a discourse of government policy, language planning has tended to avoid directly addressing larger social and political matters within which language change, use and development, and indeed language planning itself, are embedded. (1990: 27)

The authors argue that there are three critical issues which go largely unaddressed in language policy and planning situations and yet these are issues which are often actually central to the language planning which is occurring. These issues are ones of class, state and power which are often ignored by language planners because they see themselves as 'neutral' purveyors of linguistic information (see Chapter 11 for a fuller discussion of this phenomenon [also see Bruthiaux, 1992]).

(1) *Class* is related to the common-sense version of social power, that is those in social control 'are able to decide what language(s) uses can be deemed to be politically correct, which should be encouraged and furthered, respectively demoted and discouraged . . .' (Luke *et al.*, 1990: 28).[1] The classic examples of class relations are high and low prestige languages, or pidgin versus standard languages.
(2) *State* relates to the rhetoric used by the state to frame language selection, to generate mass loyalty based on language, and to use language to serve internal and external political ends. Much of modern language planning has been bound up with the notion of one language, one nation, and by implication the suppression of minority languages.

(3) *Power* is about the agency use of language planning for social, economic
and political ends as opposed to the social aspects of discourse, the
condition of language in actual use. To put it another way, while
language can and will be planned, language planning is most effective
when it is adopted as part of the discursive strategies of language users.

For each of these issues, social elites are in positions of political, social
and economic power and hence may be able to control language planning
processes for their own advantage (i.e. to engage in linguicism [Phillipson,
1988]. The question may then be asked: in whose interests is language
planned – individuals, the state, or agencies and organisations? Finally, this
raises the question of language rights. What language rights do/should
people have?

By Whom: Top-Down vs. Bottom-Up Planning

The issues raised by Luke *et al.* (1990) engender questions not only of the
role of language planners, but those of language planning by whom? Most
of the traditional participants in language policy and planning have come
from what Kaplan (1989) refers to as 'top-down' language planning
situations. These are people with power and authority who make language
related decisions for groups, often with little or no consultation with the
ultimate language learners and users. Exactly who these planners are is
often put in general terms in the literature as the individuals themselves
may not be important, but rather representative of social (i.e. class) and
political (i.e. state) processes within the polity. In their introduction to the
classic volume on language planning, Rubin and Jernudd (1971b: xvi) note,
in the more technical planning sense, that:

> [as] a discipline, language planning requires the mobilization of a great
> variety of disciplines because it implies the channeling of problems and
> values to and through some decision-making administrative structure.

In general, language planning has been portrayed as being done (note
that the use of the passive here leaves ambiguous who is doing) from within
an objective, ideologically neutral and technological perspective in which
planners matter little – as long as they have the technical expertise required.
Baldauf (1982) was one of the first to point out explicitly that who the
planners were was potentially an important variable in the language policy
and planning situation.

To examine this problem of who does language planning, let us now
look at a national language planning situation to see who the traditional
language planners were/are. If we take the example of Malaya, later
Malaysia,[2] Gaudart (1992) provides an overview of language-in-education
planning in Malaysia while Omar (1982, 1995) and Ożóg (1990, 1993) give
more general overviews in the context of national development. For much

of Malaysian history, language was unplanned. Malays spoke different dialects in different geographical regions while Koranic Arabic was used for religious purposes. Fifteenth-century Chinese (Baba) and Indian (Melaka Chittiar) settlers assimilated with the Malay communities and to this day speak a Malay or a creolised version of Malay. In the eighteenth century Chinese migrants representing many dialect groups came as tin miners, plantation workers and entrepreneurs while Tamil-speaking South Indians came as labourers to clear land and tap rubber. The British colonial system and missionaries brought English. Bilingualism developed as a necessity of life and a non-interventionist colonial policy meant that schooling was left to local communities and missions. Separate development with no general thought of future based national planning characterised early language development in Malaysia.

Language planners were mainly individuals and communities making their own language related decisions, although the British colonial government endorsed the three sets of vernacular schools (Malay, Chinese and Tamil), and English was introduced in schools in the larger towns. The introduction of English created two classes of people based on education – those educated in English with the connotation of high education, high office and socioeconomic power, and those educated only in the vernacular languages with the connotation of peasantry, cheap labour and petty trading (Omar, 1995: 159).

In the post-World War II period, the 11 states making up Malaya were increasingly seen as a whole, and economic, social and political progress was dependent on reducing ethnic tensions. Malay in its various lectal *malay* forms was the informal lingua franca in the region and was widely used *was* for intergroup communication. Formal language planning assumed greater *lingua* prominence with six education reports between 1945 and 1955 all *franca* recommending some form of bilingual education. Given British colonial power, English-knowing bilingualism was the formal norm until Malayan Independence in 1957, when the national language became Malay, with Malay-knowing bilingualism increasingly being promoted. English remained an official language and continued to be used in official ceremonies, the law and in government departments until 1967 in Malaya, 1973 in Sabah and 1985 in Sarawak. These policies did not lead to the expected national unity, and after racial riots in 1969 (Comber, 1983), there was a strict and rapid implementation of a national language policy, based on the belief that, if the status of the Malay language was not upgraded, the political and economic status of Malays would never improve and national cohesion would not be achieved. This policy on the face of it was a much more monolingual one, although continuing space was left for the development of other languages, especially English (Gaudart, 1992; Omar, 1995; Ożóg, 1993). Planners during this phase included bureaucrats, consultants, community leaders and politicians.

The National Language Act was accompanied by the New Economic Policy which aimed to increase economic growth, so even with increased Malay participation in the economy, everyone would be better off. A massive programme in language modernisation and Malay language instruction was undertaken and the school system was expanded to provide more education for all. While there were some initial questions about whether such a massive undertaking could succeed, the Sedition Act of 1970 forbade any discussion of the subject. Once the hard political decisions were made, language planning became mainly the responsibility of the linguists and bureaucrats in the national language planning agency, *Dewan Bahasa dan Pustaka,* and the planners and administrators in the educational system.

Given the importance of the national language, Malay, and the time spent on it as a language of instruction in schools, English standards declined. However, there is much support for English for economic development reasons and many individuals have continued the bilingual tradition (see, e.g. Stedman, 1986). Demands by business for bilingual speakers have also been high. More recently the government, through *Wawasan 2020* [Vision 2020] has put forward a number of ideas about language with Malay given pride of place in education while English is seen as critical for economic development (Ożóg, 1993). This pragmatic approach led in late 1993, despite protests from Malay literary and cultural organisations, to the Malaysian government announcing that university courses in scientific and technical disciplines would be free to be taught in English instead of Malay. One reason cited 'for the change is that many employers prefer graduates with degrees from Universities outside Malaya, or to private higher education institutes, which can offer courses taught in English leading to a foreign degree' (Anonymous, 1994a). Thus, the role of individual parents and business can also be seen to have an impact on language planning.

Given this pragmatic approach, Malaysia has emerged as a nation with a Malay-knowing bilingualism. Pupils' own languages ([POLs], Chinese and Tamil) are taught in schools and the four major languages are represented in the print and electronic media. In Sabah and Sarawak major ethnic languages (e.g. Kadazan, Bajau Darat and Iban) are also given media space. There is much code switching between languages, even in official situations like parliamentary debates and in legal, financial and professional situations. Omar (1995) argues that Malaysia has taken an instrumental view of language where the allocation of language for nationalism is upheld but where this does not sacrifice social and economic language needs.

Thus, language planning participants have included politicians, powerful community leaders, bureaucrats, consultants and language experts and education planners and administrators. Jernudd and Baldauf (1987 :180–1) have listed a number of types of such individuals who could contribute to a language planning for science communication system. As language policy development and planning implementation is complex, it is often the case that a large number of people are involved. In this illustration we can see examples of class (i.e. the British colonial policy), state (i.e. the National Language Act), and agency power (i.e. *Dewan Bahasa dan Pustaka*) in the development of language planning, and issues related to migrant language rights (i.e. Chinese and Tamil) and indigenous language rights (i.e. Iban and Kadazan) are raised. In each of the sections which follow, more explicit examples of these four issues are discussed.

Language Planning and Class

Luke *et al.* (1990: 28) have argued that *class* is related to the common-sense version of social power, that is, those who are in social control 'are able to decide what language(s) uses can be deemed to be politically correct, which should be encouraged and furthered, respectively demoted and discouraged . . . ' In the worst cases of linguistic oppression, languages may be forbidden to be used in schools as with the 'Welsh Not' (see Chapter 8, footnote 7), the 'Basque stick', which pupils were required to carry on outstretched arms as punishment for using a Basque word or expression (Mey, 1985) or the dunce board worn in Taiwan for speaking Tai-yü (Tse, 1982, Hsiau, 1997).[3] Low varieties of languages may be systematically discriminated against, as in the case of the widespread use of pidgin languages such as Torres Strait Broken in Australia (Kale, 1990a), Tok Pisin in Papua New Guinea (Kale, 1990b) or Solomons Pijin (Keesing, 1990; Jourdan, 1989, 1990), where colonial regimes may denigrate or local elites may completely ignore these linguae francae in preference to English. However, Schiffman (1993) has reviewed a number of diglossic situations and examined the power relationships that make them stable or make for language shift. He points out that language shift is not always from the Low variety to the High variety, but may lead to the strengthening of the Low variety (e.g. Alemannic German strengthening at the expense of *Hochdeutsch* in Switzerland through local television usage or *Lëtzebuergesch* strengthening at the expense of French and German as the national 'language of the people' in Luxembourg).

It is well known that community members may have different varieties or languages in their linguistic repertoire, and that some varieties are associated with variables such as education, socioeconomic status, sex[4] or age. Scotton (1993) points out that elites in particular countries may use language as a social mobilisation strategy to establish or maintain their power and privileges. This *elite closure* sets elites off from others in terms of prestige and/or identity and often has utilitarian value. Elite closure exists in most polities, at least in a weak form, but in many cases potential access to the elite language may be available through extensive formal education (e.g. most Western societies). Strong elite closure occurs more frequently in multilingual polities where the official language may not be part of the repertoire of many members of society and where access to the elite language through schooling is limited. In such circumstances, the language used in the educational institutions may have greater power than either the community or official policy (Robinson, 1993: 59). Thus, in countries like Cameroon the language of the educational system may play a powerful role in determining the identity individuals adopt and in the rejection of community languages. Apartheid South Africa was the classic example of the heavy use by the elite of official languages – English and Afrikaans – which were not made available to most Africans because they were taught later in schooling once most Africans had left. However, most former colonial polities in Africa, the Indian subcontinent, the former Soviet Union and the Pacific exhibit strong elite closure. Many have adopted a former colonial language as a 'neutral' official language, but this provides substantial advantages to those already possessing those language skills, who by definition are mainly from the elites. The elites often master the language(s) of the masses – just as their colonial masters did before them (see e.g. Keesing, 1990) – because they know the importance of good communication, but use the elite language among themselves to reinforce their identity (see Omar, 1992 for high level English use in the professions).

The importance of the ruling elites using an indigenous national language in language planning situations has been highlighted by Gonzalez for Filipino in the Philippines. He argues that until a language has been intellectualised or cultivated, which is best done at the tertiary level in universities, school based programmes can only ever reach a limited plateau.

> Nationalism alone can not make up for the intellectual immaturity of a language in the process of development. [What is needed is a] well planned and systematically funded program of language cultivation for the entire society, involving all ministries, government and non-government organizations, learned societies and the universities and their scholars [i.e. the Philippine elites]. (Gonzalez, 1990: 332–3)

Nik Safiah (1987: 61–2) makes much the same point for Malaysia, pointing out that 'the use of Bahasa Malaysia was intensified, slowly taking over the role of English, except in the business world, the judiciary and the non-formal elite circles'. While concentrating on the need for the cultivated variety to be nurtured in schools she argues that it is of the utmost importance that as 'models regarding the variety to be used must come from the upper echelon of the educational hierarchy, Malaysia's current slogan for effective administration "Leadership by example", is most apt' (1987: 66).

These examples illustrate the importance of class, i.e. social elites, in language planning. They can significantly contribute to language oppression and linguacide through repressive practices against speakers of minority languages; they can set up barriers to the use of elite languages thereby retaining elite power and status, or they can hinder the development of indigenous national language programmes by not fully participating in the language across all its domains, leaving the high status domains for exogamous languages. They can also promote the use of newly declared indigenous national languages, as advocated by Alisjahbana (1976, 1984).

Language Planning and the State

State relates to the rhetoric used by the state to frame language selection, to generate mass loyalty based on language, and to use language to serve internal and external political ends. The modern notion of 'state' and the association between language, state and identity was most clearly initially symbolised during the French Revolution by the development of the ideas of French-for-all-citizens, spread through a national educational system, and which 'has regularly been called on, internally and externally, as the main means of national self-definition' (McDonald, 1989: 93; also see Grillo, 1989). Much of modern language planning has been bound up with this notion of 'one people, one language, one nation', and by implication the suppression of minority languages, and this has become the predominant model for nation building in polities around the world. In this context, Bourdieu has argued that the

> official language is bound up with the state, both in its genesis and in its social uses. It is in the process of state formation that the conditions are created for the constitution of a unified linguistic market, dominated by the official language. (1991: 45)

There is a perceived tension between language as a vehicle for national unity and any multilingual cultural and personal needs of groups and individuals, which are viewed as divisive and therefore needing to be controlled. In multicultural societies, the 'person in the street's' view often is that the dominant language is under threat, despite the fact that census and other data shows that it is the minority languages that are finding it difficult to hold their own. LaPonce (1987, 1993) has argued that languages, like animals, need and defend their territories. It is in this context that the nation-state model of language policy and planning development has led, in almost all cases, to either the overt or covert suppression of minority (i.e. not in the numerical sense, but non-national, non-official) languages, even where there are multilingual policies in place.

In some cases the 'suppression' of languages could be argued to be benign or to varying degrees unintentional and can be understood in terms of a lack of funding, ignorance about the nature of the minority language problems or neglect. This is particularly applicable to polities with low gross-national products combined with a large number of languages which makes language planning difficult. However, far more common is an overt and often aggressive attempt to suppress if not eradicate minority languages in an act of linguacide. Specific examples of state suppression of languages have been available in the literature for some time (e.g. McDonald, 1989 – Brittany; Tollefson, 1980, 1991, 1993 – Yugoslavia; Day, 1985 – Hawaiian & Chamorro; Norberg, 1994 – Sorbian)[5] but it is only more recently that such practices have been brought together in the context of linguistic human rights (e.g. Hernández-Chávez, 1988; Karetu, 1994; Varennes, 1996). In the three sub-sections which follow, an example of the suppression of a majority-minority language (also see Tickoo, 1994 for Kashmiri) is examined for Taiwan, the suppression of a long-standing Hungarian minority language in Slovakia (also see Skutnabb-Kangas & Bucak, 1994 for Kurdish, Hamel, (1994) for Ameridian peoples in Latin America and Skutnabb-Kangas, 1996 for Finnish in Sweden) is described and the reassertion of majority-minority languages in Pakistan is discussed.

Majority-minority language suppression in Taiwan

The major languages spoken in Taiwan include Mandarin, the national language, Taiwanese or Tai-yü and Hakka. In addition, there are speakers of all the other Han languages and Taiwan's aboriginal people speak Austronesian languages.[6] English is the major foreign language especially in the areas of science and technology (see Chapter 9 Planning for Science and Technology, p. 241ff.).

Taiwan was a Japanese colony from 1895 to 1945 and Japanese was promoted as the language of education and as a lingua franca among language groups (Tai-yü, Hakka, aborigines and Japanese). It has been estimated that 50% of Taiwanese could understand Japanese by the end of the colonial period and as a result many older people can still converse in Japanese. In the period after 1945, the new Chinese government had the task of eradicating Japanese as the language of education and government and replacing it with Mandarin, a task which was accelerated from 1949 when a large number of mainlanders (about 15% of the population) from all parts of China came to Taiwan (Young, 1988). Tse (1982) has argued that this national language programme was a success as 94% of the population could speak Mandarin. However, it was also estimated that native speakers of Tai-yü made up about five-sixths of the population, meaning that most people were bilingual.

Mandarin is the sole official language of Taiwan and all 'other languages are uniformly referred to as "dialects" and the public use of them is deliberately discouraged. In some domains, such as the school, students may even be symbolically punished for using dialects' (Tse, 1982: 36). Since 1965 Mandarin has been the language of the civil service and the courts and non-Mandarin radio and television programmes have been severely limited. These restrictions on the use of Tai-yü have led to its dying out among the younger educated generation and to the language being associated with backwardness, crudeness, illiteracy, low socioeconomic status, rurality, etc. (Hsiau, 1997). This 'Chinaizing' of Taiwan has been used by the ruling Chinese elite from the mainland to legitimise their rule and to justify the claim that Taiwan is an integral part of China. Thus, language policy and the suppression of dialects has been linked to the political aim of regaining the mainland. It was only in 1994 that the president of Taiwan, Lee Teng-hui, felt able for the first time to talk about the suppression of Tai-yü (Hsiau, 1997).

Those supporting Tai-yü also tend to support Taiwan's opposition parties because it is the political situation (i.e. the dominant mainlander elite) which holds current language policies in place. They reject the official definition of Tai-yü as a dialect, promoting it as not only different from, but better than Mandarin Chinese. They argue for bilingual education as an effective way to revive Tai-yü and support the development of a writing system for the language, preferably without the use of Chinese characters. Hsiau (1997) points out that the Tai-yü movement has some of the same inherent problems that confront the adherents of the Chinese Mandarin standard. Both take as given the need for the nation-state model of language planning, one exalting traditional Chinese culture while the other idealises local Taiwanese culture. Other minority languages are now becoming wary of the Tai-yü movement as the movement to save a minority language may turn out to be a form of oppression for other minority languages (see e.g. Eckert, 1983). The Taiwanese example leaves the question unanswered of how to balance national identity (cohesion) with ethnic equality (multilingualism and multiculturalism).

Minority language suppression in Slovakia[7]

Hungarians and Slovaks have lived together in southern Slovakia for a millennium. However, with the break-up of the Austro-Hungarian Empire at the end of World War I, about half of all Hungarian speakers found themselves living outside of Hungary in successor states including Czechoslovakia. Indigenous Hungarians now living in Slovakia number about 600,000 and constitute 10.8% of the population, living in a compact area of 400 towns and villages. Since 1920 Hungarians have been a recognised national minority and the rights of this community were guaranteed at the Paris Peace Treaty on 10 February 1947. These rights were quite limited and should not have been seen as a threat to the state. However, since 1989 Hungarians and other minorities have been under increasing linguistic and cultural pressure, although the 1990 law 428/1990 on the official language of the Slovak Republic, in localities with at least 20% minority population, allowed the use of minority languages in oral official contacts. From 1 January 1996 a new law defining the State Language of the Slovak Republic has been in effect which makes Slovak the legislatively required language in all official contacts, in education, in the mass media, at cultural events and at public meetings, in the armed forces, in the courts and in legal proceedings, and in the economy, in services and in health care. The law is to be strictly monitored and severe fines can be levied for breaches of usage; these penalities are to be enforced from 1997.

While the law does not outlaw the use of minority languages and does not regulate the use of languages of national minorities, there is no provision for the use of such languages in any of the previously mentioned public domains which are reserved for Slovak. The law is at best contradictory and unclear and 'is widely interpreted as outlawing the use of minority languages in a number of domains' (Istvan Lanstyak, 1996, e-mail document). This interpretation is supported by acts such as the requirement that only Slovak can be used in the consultative body to the mayor of Komarno, whose population is predominantly Hungarian (Slovak and Hungarian have been used up until now) and the removal of bilingual road signs (Kontra, 1996), because 'the language law does not allow for any other inscriptions than those written in Slovak' (Istvan Lanstyak, 1996, e-mail document). This law provides a clear case where the state is using its power to suppress the language of its citizens in the name of language standardisation and nation-state building. The law severely disadvantages its Hungarian and other minority citizens and makes it difficult for them to participate in the affairs of the state.

It has been said that the Slovak language law was strongly influenced by Québec's Bill 101: Charter of the French Language of 1977 (see Bourhis, 1984; Cost analysis in French Québec, pp. 169–170, this volume) and by the US English debate (see p. 230ff.). All of these measures make compulsion rather than attraction the basis of linguistic and cultural development. These are but instances of state involvement in using language as a powerful weapon to suppress its fringe citizens' language rights in the name of nation development and language standardisation.

Majority-minority language reassertion in Pakistan

Although Urdu formed a major symbolic rallying point for the nationalism of pre-partition Muslims in the Indian subcontinent, the majority of them did not speak Urdu, even as a preferred second language. The partition of the subcontinent left the major Urdu-speaking area out of Pakistan and the 1961 census indicated that less than 4% of the population were mother-tongue Urdu speakers – 52% being speakers of Bengali (Das Gupta, 1971). Even after the breakaway of East Pakistan from West

Pakistan to form Bangladesh in 1971, in which the status of Bengali was a major underlying issue (Musa, 1996), Urdu remained a minority national language in Pakistan.

Hussain (1990) documents how the creation of a separate Muslim state has undermined the original rationale for an Urdu linguistic unity to reinforce Muslim religious solidarity. Since independence, regional forces within Pakistan have been working counter to the national Urdu language policy and have stretched the already scarce economic resources for language development. For example, in the North-West Frontier Region of Pakistan the teaching of Pushto and the use of Pushto as a medium of instruction was introduced in competition with Urdu, because of regional demands. In the Sind province, the introduction of the Sindi language for use in education was planned in 1973 as a consequence of regional political disturbances focused mainly against Punjabis. The Sindis felt that Punjabis were too dominant in most aspects of daily life. In order to bring about political calm in the province, the authorities decided to introduce Sindi as an educational language while not doing the same in the Punjab where Urdu is still the language of education. Rahman (1995) indicates that these regional language and cultural forces are still at work, as witnessed by the agitation for a Siraiki province in the south-west of the Punjab based on language and cultural factors.

Thus, while Urdu may be the national language, internal regional interests have limited its spread. On the other hand, international factors such as trade, employment and immigration have also been potent influences on language planning. As English, which is an official language in Pakistan, is the major international language of business, certain tertiary level institutions in Pakistan use English alongside of Urdu as a medium of instruction (Baumgardner, 1993; Huizinga, 1994). Furthermore, in some regions of Pakistan colloquial Arabic has been introduced, mainly for employment reasons. As jobs are scarce at home, many are looking to find employment in Arabic-speaking countries (Hussain, 1990). Classical Arabic is also learnt as the language of the Koran. Pakistan is one of the few polities where state power to enforce the national language has been limited by the internal regional political and external economic and religious aspects of the linguistic situation. While the ideology of Urdu as a unifying force for all Muslims still has some currency, the diminution of the already scarce resources available for languages through regional and exogamous language development can hardly be seen as fostering the development of Urdu as the national language.

Language Planning and Agency Power

Language planning and agency power centres around the neo-Marxist and post-structuralist critiques of language and linguistics – as opposed to discourse – which they characterise as providing a sterile, positivist view of the world. For instance, Luke *et al.* argue that:

> [i]f traditional linguistics construed language in terms of the triple division of phonology/syntax/semantics and has now added 'social' topics to these, it has *necessarily* ignored discourse, in the sense that we use it here. For discourse, in the seminal works of Foucault (1972) and also of such theorists as Bakhtin (1986) and Bourdieu (1984), is not identical with 'talk' or 'conversation' or even 'text'. It is not the utilitarian end of language (with language construed linguistically). Rather discourse is that central, yet also diverse, analytic field in which language, power and discipline(s) come together. (1990: 37)

Discourse analysis in this sense is seen as a new 'cross-discipline' to which established disciplines like linguistics, education, sociology, anthropology and other social sciences have contributed. For example, Fairclough (1989: 14) suggests that systemic linguistics, continental pragmatics and other cross-disciplinary trends in discourse analysis 'harmonize to a degree with CLS' (critical language study) which he suggests as an analytic technique for understanding the discourse used to shape social, economic and political institutions. He provides examples of the effects of language and power in areas such as advertising and political rhetoric. This discoursal approach to language is increasingly widely reflected in the language and literacy literature (e.g. Gee, 1990, 1992; Collins, 1996).

This issue of the centrality of discourse, in relation to language planning and agency power, was raised obliquely in this volume in conjunction with critiques of language planning (see p. 80ff.). We saw there that while from a language planning point of view such post-structuralist critiques can be powerful tools for understanding language planning problems or how language planning itself may go wrong, Fishman (1994: 98) argued that 'they never seem to go beyond their critique'. Therefore, such critiques were not very helpful for those who actually have to do language planning, other than to provide armchair comments on it (also see Chapter 11, p. 310ff., Description vs. Prescription).

However, several language planning writers have tried to work within a discoursal approach to the discipline. For example, Chaudensen (1989: 25) makes the following distinctions[8] among three ways in which language planning can be described and understood.

(1) *Language policy* (politique linguistique) specifies the overall national choice in some matter of language or of language cultivation (without predetermining, of course, decision making processes which would be considered elsewhere). Language policy defines general long-term objectives (i.e. educational levels, formations, uses, functions, and

language statutes) and which are based on as precise and complete an analysis of the initial problem as possible.

(2) *Language planning* (planification linguistique) applies to any operation which is based in language programme work (in the short, middle and long term) and which has some definite functional policy objectives and some means and considered procedures for their realisation.

(3) *Language management* (aménagement linguistique) applies to the totality of some operation (of a very diverse nature) which allows for *the specific realisation* of some defined operation in a particular setting. (In Canada and Québec, this perspective became the essence of the operation of language management – at the point of contact between them – because previous political choices had rendered this unavoidable; in another political context, 'the terminological definitions' of the language could be – and this often is the case – of relatively secondary importance.) Therefore, linguistic management must not be confused with corpus planning. To illustrate the language management process, Chaudensen (1989: 38) provides a diagram which describes the analysis of a minor decision making process (i.e. the choice of elements of graphic code for an oral language – a creole in the Seychelles). The aim of the diagram is to illustrate the complexity of that process – which is as complex as it would be for a much more important choice – and the necessity to integrate all relevant factors into the decision making process (see Figure 7.1).

Jernudd (1993: 133; also see Jernudd & Neustupný, 1987) indicates a language management model differs from a language planning model in that it:

> . . . seeks to explain how language problems arise in the course of people's use of language, that is, in discourse, in contrast with approaches under Fishman's definition of language planning [i.e. 'the authoritative allocation of resources to the attainment of language status and corpus goals, . . . ' (1987: 409)] which takes decision-makers', for example governments', specification of language problems as their axiomatic point of departure.

In this context, Jernudd (1983: 134) suggests that language planning can be taken to be an aspect of language management in:

> . . . which particular people are given the authority to find and suggest rigorous solutions to problems of language potentially or actually encountered by members of their community . . . . The language management approach to language planning represents a shift of focus from the concern of language planning concerned with finding optimal strategies for government-initiated action, to an interest in explaining

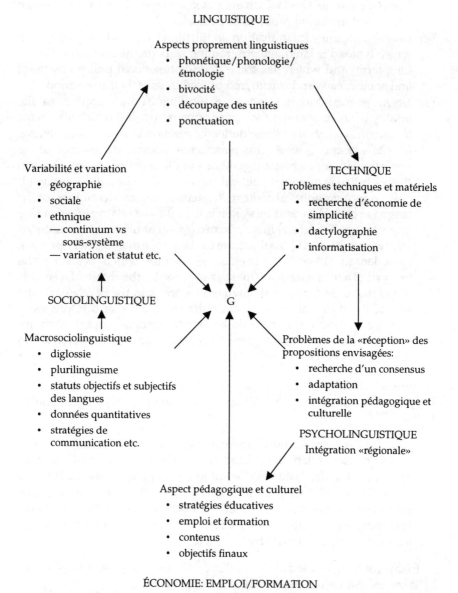

LINGUISTIQUE

Aspects proprement linguistiques
- phonétique/phonologie/ étmologie
- bivocité
- découpage des unités
- ponctuation

Variabilité et variation
- géographie
- sociale
- ethnique
  — continuum vs sous-système
  — variation et statut etc.

SOCIOLINGUISTIQUE

Macrosociolinguistique
- diglossie
- plurilinguisme
- statuts objectifs et subjectifs des langues
- données quantitatives
- stratégies de communication etc.

TECHNIQUE
Problèmes techniques et matériels
- recherche d'économie de simplicité
- dactylographie
- informatisation

G

Problèmes de la «réception» des propositions envisagées:
- recherche d'un consensus
- adaptation
- intégration pédagogique et culturelle

PSYCHOLINGUISTIQUE
Intégration «régionale»

Aspect pédagogique et culturel
- stratégies éducatives
- emploi et formation
- contenus
- objectifs finaux

ÉCONOMIE: EMPLOI/FORMATION

Figure 7.1 Language management and development: a model for the resolution of a management 'operation' (in this case the choice of the graphics for a writing system (G) but the principles of analysis could be used for any type of language management) (Chaudensen, 1989: 38).

how individuals manage language in communication, and uses this as the starting point for community-wide management.

However, while problem identification arises from the community out of discourse, Jernudd also indicates this does not presuppose a democratic authorisation process, and leaves open how this authorisation will occur. While a language management approach with its focus on discourse represents a focus on a 'bottom-up' (i.e. the language community) authorisation to language planning, in contrast to a 'top-down' (i.e. government initiated) action, it does not represent the only way a 'bottom-up' approach can be developed (e.g. Kaplan, 1989) nor does it necessarily resolve the problem of the use (and misuse) of agency power.

The language situation in Québec, from which the term language management arises, provides examples of both 'top-down' and 'bottom-up' language planning and management. The 1979 Québec language law (Bill 101) provides one of the better known examples of 'top-down' status planning (see Bourhis, 1984) where French was mandated to be acquired and used in certain domains to overturn the dominance in the economy of English. Although the law in the mid-1990s was declared invalid as a violation of human rights, Jernudd (1993) has pointed out that it has had a number of consequences on discourse in Québec which could be seen leading to a more 'bottom-up' or discourse based language planning perspective, including:

- the acceptance of individual and institutional bilingualism in Canada;
- the systematic evaluation of variation in French (metropolitan vs Québec French usage); and
- the expansion of French language domains and the need for the availability of correct terminological usage.

However, while a discourse perspective gives language planners another way to validate language problems and needs, as we have indicated in Chapter 4, there are a number of ways of collecting data about language use so that the solutions developed by language planners reflect 'bottom-up' language planning. The lack of many 'bottom-up' issues to language problems is not just a problem related to the lack of a 'bottom-up' theory, but rather is related to widely held 'top-down' notions of management and of political decision making which are not exclusively confined to language planning.[9] While one can argue as Jernudd does that taking a discourse-based language management perspective means that language planning is

no longer silent on potential violation of people's interests and rights, [because it must] find out what the language problem is, whose

> problem it is, and how language problems arise out of discourse and
> how they affect discourse (1993: 140),

agency power is still vested in individuals and those individuals may still
abuse that power.

Most consultants who have done a significant amount of work on
government funded policy development or project/programme evaluation would have experienced the abuse of agency. 'Unfavourable' reports
are often suppressed, as in many instances agencies do not actually want
independent advice based on a careful analysis of the situation/data,
unless the outcomes of those analyses confirm their preconceived notions
about a language situation. This is not to suggest that politicians or to a
lesser extent agencies should not be free to consider, and then to accept or
reject, advice they have been given. Rather, the abuse of agency power,
which is often 'legitimised' by some vague and unsubstantiated need for
confidentiality, results from the cover up and suppression of information
and debate, the implementation of, or failure to implement, policy or
programmes based solely on agency bias and the resultant lack of agency
accountability. While such behaviour *may* be acceptable in totalitarian
regimes or in small business or in personal companies, it is not good
management practice and should not be tolerated in open societies or in
public organisations or companies.[10] In this context, those interested in
working in language planning may find themselves under significant
pressure to produce policies and programs, grounded not on the best
available theoretical and practical knowledge about the issues, but based
solely on agency preconceptions of what is politically or economically
feasible.

Language Rights

As the examples related to class, state and agency in the preceding
sections of this chapter have made abundantly clear, language is a powerful
marker of identity and as such forms an important element in the
nation-state model for language teaching and learning. Since that model is
predicated on having a common language to act as a facilitator of
communication and to act as a powerful factor for national unity, many
polities, most of which are multilingual and multicultural, have set out to
create a single national language accessible by all citizens. This has been
attempted in a variety of ways, including through the use of language
planning (e.g. Tollefson, 1989), and as the examples of class, state and
agency show may involve the suppression of language and cultural
groups. This raises the question of what rights do individuals or groups in
a society have to language? Is '. . . it reasonable to assume that [language]
falls into the category of things that may be essential to a decent human
existence and hence may give rise to rights' (i.e. where 'language plays a

central role in defining identity') (Coulombe, 1993: 141; also Breton, 1996)?

While the answer to that question may seem obvious, the notion of linguistic human rights is rather a recent one. Gomes de Matos (1985: 1–2) noted that he had

> not come across explicit references to the individual's individual human rights, although inferences to the latter certainly can be made . . . . Although ours has been said to be 'the age of rights' . . . there has not yet been a thorough, well-documented, carefully thought out discussion of the crucial problem of the human being's linguistic rights. (1985: 1–2)

Annamalai (1986) and more recently Coulombe (1993) have argued that language rights may be both individual and communal. Individual rights against undue interference or discrimination can be justified, regardless of community status, as matters of a right to privacy and fairness – the right to personal autonomy (Kaplan, 1995a). They are confirmed under the United Nations Charter in Sections 26 and 27 which respectively guarantee the civil and political rights without discrimination based on language and affirm the right of linguistic minorities to use their own language among themselves. As language is a shared communal good and as language cannot exist without communication and a community, it can also be argued that language is an essential component of community identity.

In the age of the internationalised modernised cultures and nation-states, the question must be asked: Are such negative *laissez-faire* rights – rights against the state – sufficient? Such rights might include:

> . . . the right to speak our language at home and on the streets and to use it in private correspondence; to keep our native names and surnames [Neustupný, 1984; Jernudd, 1994b]; to use it within our cultural and religious institutions, including newspapers, radio stations and community centres, etc. [Coulombe, 1993: 143].

Can minority languages survive if they are just allowed to exist or is some stronger version of communal human rights necessary or even desirable if these languages and cultures are to survive? Skutnabb-Kangas and Phillipson (1994: 89) argue;

> . . . [n]ot even overt maintenance-oriented permission is enough for minority (or powerless majority) mother tongues to be maintained, developed and handed down from parents to children over several generations . . . . What they require is overt maintenance-oriented promotion (which necessarily includes the allocation of the economic means for supporting mother tongue medium schools . . . .

What this suggests is that the *laissez-faire* attitude does not offer much in the way of protection or support to minority languages and can lead to the assimilation of such groups who are unable to compete with the benefits that the majority language can offer. If *some* intervention appears to be necessary if minority languages are to be protected and sustained, whose responsibility is it to promote the language: minority individuals, minority communities, outsiders, the state? Coulombe (1993) argues that leaving language preservation as an individual responsibility has proved unsuccessful as language is a communicative medium and needs to be a vehicle for expressive power, recognition and self-respect. Minority individuals may choose to assimilate if these aspects of identity cannot be catered for in the minority language setting. The state cannot support these needs for minority identity simply through linguistic tolerance and pluralism – anti-discrimination policies – because unlike other individual characteristics like sex, race, social class or religion, language is a community based attribute and respect for an individual's language rights alone will not sustain a language. This community basis of language means there is a role for language planning not only to allow individuals to *sustain* their language, but also space in which to *live* it (Coulombe, 1993). If we accept that such language rights exist, the question then becomes how can the right to *live* in language A be reconciled with the right to live in language B or C or D within the same community? Is a territorial approach necessary to the survival of minority languages (see e.g. Grin 1994a; LaPonce 1993)? There are certainly those in Québec, among other places, who think it is. As this section suggests, the discussion of language rights has become a major issue for language planning and an increasing amount of material has been published on the subject (e.g. Phillipson *et al.*, 1994; Skutnabb-Kangas, 1996; Varennes, 1996; Vilfan *et al.* 1993).

Australia provides an interesting example of the language rights issues related to *sustaining* or *living* in a language. In the post-World War II years, Australia has moved from being an Anglocentric polity with a 'White Australia' policy, which did not give its own indigenous people citizenship until 1967, to a nation which by and large accepts that it is a multicultural and to a degree a multilingual nation. In the past 10 years in particular through a series of national and state language policies, Australia has developed a reputation for being a country where a broad range of language issues (i.e. English, languages other than English, Aboriginal and Torres Strait Islander languages and language services) are considered as part of the language planning process. This has resulted in a series of Commonwealth and state policies that are supportive of language study, both in English and in languages other than English. Thus, since the acceptance of the *National Policy on Languages* (Lo Bianco, 1987a), not only has there developed a *laissez-faire* official – and increasingly a community – tolerance of and support for languages other than English, but a considerable degree of language *sustenance* has occurred (see Djité, 1994; Eggington, 1994; Herriman, 1996; Lo Bianco, 1996; Smolicz, 1994 for examples).

However, there are an increasing number of people with an interest in language who are uncomfortable with the results of these policies. At the political and social level, there is the question of how far the monolingual English majority is willing to go in its acceptance of multilingualism and multiculturalism. There seems to be a growing fixation with the narrow 'problem' of English literacy and the alleged failure of Australian schools to produce literate graduates (see Green *et al.*, 1994 for previous incarnations of this debate), rather than on the more positive multilingual concept of multiliteracies (The New London Group, 1996). From the more multilingual perspective, while there is some evidence of a small rise in the number of Australians using a language other than English at home (Kipp *et al.*, 1995), there is also a realisation that recent language policy efforts are not providing the real gains that might have been expected (see, e.g. Moore, 1991, 1996). Furthermore, to date much second language study in schools has been little more than an exercise in language awareness as language tuition is of insufficient quality and duration (see Language-in-education implementation, Chapter 5, p. 127ff.) for a general discussion of these problems.). Thus, a *laissez-faire* and *sustaining* language policy does not seem to have generated much, if any, serious interest or widespread efforts in the area of bilingualism (i.e. the ability for people to *live* in a language). Increasingly, this is leading to serious concerns among applied linguists that despite the apparent gains from a broadly based national policy on languages, those gains will be insufficient even to maintain Australia's multicultural character in the long term.

There is a growing literature related to language rights, and a realisation that such rights need to be considered as part of any language planning exercise. For example, the Fédération Internationale des Professeurs de Langues Vivantes (1992) has issued a statement calling for human language rights, and Gomes de Matos (1994) has urged language-in-education planning to further humanise linguistic education policies. Increasingly this is an area that language planners will need to consider in their work.

Summary
In this chapter we have examined a number of ways in which language planning and power are related, with a particular emphasis on those who can wield power as part of the language planning process. Initially, who was involved in the language planning process was examined because those individuals can have a major impact on how language is planned. Three foci – state, class and agency power – were then presented as ways in which language planning and power are related. In the final section the issue of language rights was examined. Issues related to language and power, while relatively new are beginning to have a major impact on the

way language planning is conceptualised and thus how language planning will be done.

Notes

1. For example, in 1998 all schools and government offices in Germany will be required to introduce spelling changes approved in mid-1996 which systematically dismantle anomalies, but which will affect only 185 core words. Gone will be the 'ß' to be replaced by 'ss' and spelling of words like 'Thunfisch' (Tunfisch) and 'Spaghetti' (Spagetti) will be regularised.

2. Malaysia consists of 11 states in Malaya, which gained their independence from Britain in 1957, and Sabah (formerly North Borneo) and Sarawak, which joined with Malaya in September 1963 to form Malaysia. Singapore initially gained its independence as part of the newly formed Malaysia but withdrew in August 1965 to become an independent country.

3. See Corson (1993) for a more general discussion of the role of power in minority education.

4. The issue of feminist language reform has not been widely discussed in the language planning literature, being limited primarily to media related issues (e.g. Fasold, 1988; Hawes & Thomas, 1995). However, Pauwels (in press) examines what can be done through language planning to make language less sexist. Taking the perspective of feminist language reform as a form of corpus planning, she details feminist language planning efforts for a wide range of languages including many European and some Asian and African languages. A. A. Mazrui (1996) argues that language planning can contribute to gender reform in Africa. From a more language-in-education perspective, Corson (1993) looks at the issue of language, gender and power in education.

5. 'I can only imagine the world with my ethnicity in place. Its disappearence signifies loss. Slowly but surely the impoverishment would be perceptible across the country's breadth. Perhaps even continentally and planetarily. One color less. Increase of greyness. One sound less, one language less. Increase of silence.' (Koch, 1992: 42, cited in Norberg, 1994: 156).

6. Taiwanese is variously referred to as Southern Min, Hokkien or Amoy (Young, 1988), Southern Fukienese (Tse, 1982) or Tai-yü (#767, 1996). We have used the latter term as it represents current usage. The language ethos of the Chinese government (Harrell, 1993) and the government in Taiwan is that there is the Han (Chinese) language which has a standard writing system and a standard variety, variously called Mandarin, *Guoyu* (National Language – Taiwan) or *Putonghua* (Ordinary Speech – China). However, dialectologists would divide Han into six or seven mutually unintelligible dialect (or regionalect) groups each of which has a number of varieties which vary internally to the point of being mutually unintelligible. The unity of the Chinese language system is based on the standard writing system which extends across dialects and across Han identity. Harrell (1993) points out that none of the Chinese leaders since 1916 has spoken standard Chinese well. However, this ideology means that the everyday languages of the majority of Taiwanese people (e.g. Tai-yü and Hakka) are relegated to dialect status.

7. This section draws extensively from a 15-item e-mail document posted on the 'Linguist list: Vol–7–167. Friday Feb 2 1996. ISSN: 1068–4875. Lines 185.' Where it has been possible to identify specific authors of documents, we have done so in the text.

8. As summarised and translated by the authors from the French.

9. There is very little discussion of the relationship between language policy and planning and political issues in the literature and where it does occur (e.g. Ozolins, 1993, 1996) the discussion focuses on macro level issues. The 'top-down' political management of language related information in the language policy situation to fit with political interests is seldom discussed, despite being a characteristic of most political systems. In democracies, political parties are anxious to claim a mandate from the people for their programmes, but once in office they feel free to interpret broadly that mandate to fit their interests and feel only limited obligations to act on the information available or to fulfil pre-election promises, especially if 'circumstances have changed'. Thus, it is not only important to have good language planning information, popular support, etc. on which to make and support decisions, but to convince politicians to look beyond their immediate and short-term interests, i.e. actually to act on the information available in a just and unbiased manner. While good information is important to language planning decision making, and in the past lack of the critical information needed or the control of information has made it easier for those in power to make 'informed' decisions without reference to popular interests, ultimately language and power is about the attitudes, values and standards that politicians or language planners take as their guiding principles.

10. Some examples which illustrate the abuse of agency power related to language planning may be helpful. President Carter created a major Task Force on language and education in the United States. The task force completed its report just as Carter was leaving office and President Reagan was coming in. The report was suppressed and only made available in an unofficial – without government imprimatur – form. In New Zealand in the early 1990s, Jeffrey Waite wrote a language policy document for the New Zealand Ministry of Education and Robert Kaplan contributed several supplements to the document. When the document was published, it was without the supplements and without any comment from the Ministry of Education.

8 Bilingualism and Language Status

Introduction

This chapter examines bilingualism and language status from several different perspectives. There is a key question that must be answered: Is it a matter of 'languages in competition' (Wardhaugh, 1988) or languages requiring territories (Laponce, 1987, 1993: chap. 7) or can and do languages co-exist depending on their use, function, and status?

Before moving into this discussion, it is necessary to attempt some sort of definition of the terms *bilingualism* and *multilingualism*. *Bilingualism*, then, is an *individual* phenomenon; that is, it represents the achievement of a single person immersed simultaneously in two or more language communities. Ordinarily, it means unequal command of two languages – *unequal* because one's 'first' language (not necessarily 'first' in the order learned) remains one's dominant language throughout life.[1] The degree to which an individual commands a second language is highly variable, ranging from the skill attained in studying a foreign language at school for a year or two, to the skill attained from being immersed for many years in a community using another language as its primary language. An individual is, furthermore, capable of commanding several bilingualisms, depending on the conditions in which one lives; that is, one may have an unequal command of more than two languages. The degree of command of the other (third, *n*th) languages will also be variable; that is, one may have relatively high proficiency in many registers of one additional language and minimal proficiency in a few registers in another. The situation may be represented as in Figure 8.1 – line length suggests differing degrees of proficiency.

The United States Information Agency (USIA), for a period of five years, sponsored a summer short programme for a group of approximately 25 educators from West African countries at Northern Arizona University. Kaplan had the opportunity to teach language policy and planning to these groups in each of those succeeding five summer periods. In each of the sessions, he conducted informal sociolinguistic surveys among the participants; among the 125 individuals thus surveyed, the average number of

216

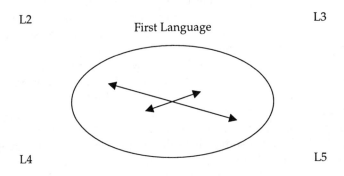

Figure 8.1 A graphic representation of multilingual fluency

languages spoken by each individual was five. All spoke English, and most spoke at least one other European language (i.e. French, Spanish, Portuguese, Russian, German – because these were important languages of wider communication in the polities from which they came). In addition, each spoke at least two, and in many cases three, African languages. This is demonstrative of a group of individuals who were bilingual, having unequal command of a relatively large number of languages. By contrast, some people (e.g. many North Americans, New Zealanders, Australians, Japanese, and Koreans) unfortunately have only their first languages; that is, they are *monolingual*, not bilingual. Bilingualism is not a requisite for survival in many places, but – despite the evidence of these few communities – bilingualism constitutes the normal human condition.

Multilingualism, by contrast, is a *societal* – not an individual – phenomenon; that is, a society made up of many individuals some substantial number of whom command two or more languages to some degree of proficiency is a multilingual society. Under the best of circumstances, some substantial number of these individuals will have one language in common. That common language is likely to enjoy some sort of 'official' status (see the section on terminology in Chapter 1, p. 16). It is, of course, the normal case that the bilingual individuals will have in common several languages, but that those languages will be used for different purposes in the society.

For example, an individual living in New Mexico, in the south-west of the United States, may speak English for exogenous communication (e.g. to vote, to get a driver's licence, to access health delivery services, to shop for luxury goods, etc.), Spanish for some endogenous communication (e.g. to talk to one's peers and some more distant relatives, to shop for necessities, to communicate on the street, etc.) and a Native-American language (e.g. Navajo) for other endogenous communication (e.g. to talk to one's immediate family and for purposes of communal ritual). English, which is a majority language in the United States, will be shared with a large segment of the total national population; Spanish will be shared with an important minority group, and Navajo will be shared with a still smaller community. If the individual is of Navajo ethnicity, Navajo may be the strongest language for the individual and even for the Navajo community in general, but English will be the strongest language for the matrix multilingual community. These three languages will be variably held by each individual; that is, some will be dominant in English, some in Spanish, some in Navajo (see Figure 8.2). It is even possible that the individual may have a special kind of language as part of his/her bilingualism – a language like *American Sign Language* (ASL), used in the deaf community, or like *Braille*, used in the blind community.

Thus, to summarise, *bilingual* individuals (sometimes able to use more than two languages – that is, possessing several bilingualisms of varying degree) may co-exist in a *multilingual* society in which at least one language in the set of bilingualisms is widely shared.

Inevitably, it will be the case that all of the languages in a bilingual's repertoire will be shared with some community. Since a language is a communicative system, an individual who has no one to speak to in a given language has that language only in an academic sense. Let us assume, for example, that a native-speaker of Lao migrates into the community just described; there may be no other speakers of Lao with whom that individual can communicate. In the absence of use, that language may atrophy to some greater or lesser extent.[2] Post-graduate students in some academic disciplines may 'know' classical languages such as Latin, Classical Greek, Sanskrit, Anglo-Saxon, Old Church Slavonic, Old High German – these are 'dead' languages which are not spoken for practical purposes. They are academic languages, learned usually for such purposes as having access to the thought and art of dead civilisations, not for the purpose of daily, routine communication.[3] It is a real question whether, in

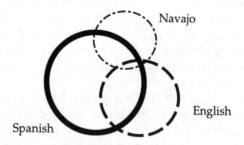

Figure 8.2 Schematic view of language usage overlap for an individual

the contemporary world, a person who speaks, e.g. English and Latin, except in some areas of the Catholic church and in Romanish speaking areas of Switzerland, may be said to be bilingual. Such an example suggests that bilingualism implicates not merely 'knowing' two languages but 'having' communicative competence in two or more living languages.

This definition further implies that the relative degree of knowledge of another language in a bilingual environment is extremely variable. In Chapter 5, the problem of defining the amount of proficiency in an alternative language was discussed, and the point was made that the expectations in schooled bilingualism are frequently entirely unreasonable. There are two unstated interrelated assumptions underlying the notion of schooled bilingualism; namely: (1) that the two languages in the bilingual environment are equal in status, in power, and in attraction; and (2) that the end-product of schooled bilingualism will constitute near-native proficiency in both languages in all registers. Both assumption are vacuous in a school environment: (1) The two languages cannot be of equal status, power, and attraction precisely because the learners are novices who come into the environment with their first language 'fully' developed. The L1 will always have greater status, power, and attraction precisely because the learners can do everything they need to do linguistically in the L1, and they cannot do all those things in the L2. (2) Near-native proficiency cannot be achieved in the school environment because the duration of instruction is insufficient to accomplish such proficiency and because the academic syllabus simply does not permit the inclusion of all possible registers. Since schooling generally ignores the pragmatic features of the L2, proficiency in any actual register is unlikely. (It is also the case that near-native proficiency is unattainable because it is rarely the real objective, since what it commonly taught in school language curricula is L2 grammar together with some minimal access to the L2 canonical literature.)

While we have claimed that bilingualism is the natural human condition and monolingualism[4] is the aberrant condition, it is important to point out that there is no linguistic evidence that schooled bilingualism is necessarily a desirable objective. It can, however, be argued that schooled bilingualism promotes language and cultural sensitivity, metalinguistic awareness and the development of thinking skills (Hakuta et al., 1987). There is also sociolinguistic evidence that bilingualism is a desirable objective. But given that schooled bilingualism can hope to achieve only very minimal proficiency, within a limited number of registers, the outcome will always create a diglossic situation, with one language (the L1) always dominant (High [H]), always offering the greatest range of registers, always marked by the greatest power, always demonstrating the greatest attraction. Thus, an individual who has achieved minimal bilingualism is always susceptible to retrogression in the direction of the L1. 'The message to the educational planner, then, is not to expect bilingual education to produce native-like competence in two languages if the contextual variables do not allow for this to develop' (Baetens Beardsmore, 1993b: 117). But, these constraints apply to schooled bilingualism and not necessarily to naturally acquired bilingualism.

It should be apparent from the preceding discussion that the terms *bilingualism* and *multilingualism* are difficult to disambiguate, except in the sense that *bilingualism* may arbitrarily be defined as being an individual attainment while *multilingualism* may be defined as a societal function. The difficulty arises from the fact that linguistics (at least as it has been practised in the West for the last century) assumes certain views of language. Western linguistics assumes that a language is:

- a system of autonomous rules for the generation of language structures;
- a system separate and distinct from culture, behaviour, and belief systems;
- a system intended to express information by means of speech signals; and
- a system that is clearly bounded so that it is absolutely distinct from all other languages. (Mühlhäusler, 1995c: 1)

The difficulty we have experienced in trying to disambiguate the terms *bilingualism* and *multilingualism* suggests that the traditional linguistic view is artificial and not at all helpful in understanding such phenomena as bilingualism. Indeed, for the bilingual individual, the boundary between languages may be fairly fluid. Furthermore, especially in the sense of trying to define the term *multilingualism*, there has long been a popular mythic identification of a language with a polity. English, the myth holds, is the language of Britain and the US, French is the language of France, German the language of Germany, and Russian the language of Russia. Fishman (1972) long ago questioned the validity of such a complementarity.

- First, it is not the case that only Frenchmen speak French or that only Germans speak German.
- Second, it is the case that not only Frenchmen speak French and not only Germans speak German.
- Third, it is not the case that all French-speakers speak the same French, that all German-speakers speak the same German or that all Chinese-speakers speak the same Chinese.
- Fourth, it is not the case that all French-speakers live in France, all German-speakers in Germany, or all Chinese-speakers in China.

Since we have used French, German, and Chinese as examples, it may be noted: (1) that French speakers also live in Algeria and Morocco, in Zaire,

Côte d'Ivoire and Québec, in Tahiti and New Caledonia, and that they do not all speak Parisian French; (2) that German speakers also live in Switzerland and Austria, in Australia and New Zealand, and that the Swiss and Austrian German speakers speak recognisable varieties of German (as indeed do Bavarians within Germany) (Cillia, 1996; Takahashi, 1995); and (3) that the Chinese Diaspora is global in its distribution, and all Chinese speakers do not in fact speak Mandarin (Sun, 1988/1989; Harrell, 1993).

Furthermore, one must deal with the additional mythology of the 'metropolitan model' of a language; that is, with the notion that there is a 'most correct' variety as opposed to all other varieties. Sometimes the metropolitan model may be defined as the speech of the capital city of a polity, as in the case of Parisian French; sometimes the metropolitan model may be a widely disseminated variety, as in the case of BBC English; sometimes it may be the speech of a particularly charismatic individual (in our youth, Franklin Roosevelt set the style for many US English speakers and Winston Churchill for many British English speakers). The fact is, there is no 'most correct' variety. A 'language' is a 'variety' that has an army, a navy, and a police force. Every language, every variety, is the ideal mechanism for a community of speakers to deal with the phenomenological world in which they live and with each other. Undeniably, certain varieties gain in social prestige for various reasons, but that social prestige is a passing notion; the prestige of some language (or some variety) will, in time, be replaced by another language (or variety).

Thus, it can be said that, for the bilingual, everything in his/her repertoire co-exists peacefully, though each code is likely to be used for a different purpose.[5] On the other hand, in multilingual communities, languages compete with each other in social status. As the old saying goes, 'where you stand depends on where you sit'. Even in the case of the individual, languages are complementary only when they are not used for the same functions in the same linguistic community – that is, one does not order a beer in a bar either in English or in Spanish.

The Ethnic Model

In some communities, an 'ethnic model' has been employed; that is, in circumstances where two relatively equal communities marked by different codes co-exist in the same geographic (usually political) space, efforts have been made to allow the two languages to co-exist with more-or-less equal status. For example, in Canada, English and French ostensibly co-exist as equal national languages. While English and French are legally mandated as equal partners, that is not the circumstance for Native American languages. As Dorais (1990) points out, Inuit in Canada has suffered the same fate as indigenous languages have suffered elsewhere when assimilationist policies have been put in place, when essentially nomadic people have been resettled into permanent communities, and when there has been rapid change in material culture.

> The fact that the Inuits were numerically strong and culturally homogenous did little to arrest the decline of their language. The story is one of increasing dependency on white institutions, white knowledge and white economic practices. Even where bilingualism in a traditional language and English is maintained, it is of the diglossic type. Recent attempts to get some official recognition of indigenous languages has done little to redress the imbalance created by previous history . . . . (Mühlhäusler, 1995c: 9)

But even English and French are not actually equal. In Québec Province and the Maritimes, French is the High (H) language, and English is the Low (L) language; that is, a classically diglossic situation exists.

> This is a state of linguistic relations where two or more unequal languages co-exist: Inuktitut and English in the Northwest Territories and Labrador; Inuktitut, English and French in Arctic Québec; Inuktitut, English and another native language in some areas of the Mackenzie Delta, Arctic Québec and Labrador. Each of these languages has its specific functions and value. The 'higher' functions (higher education, government, well-paying work, literature) are performed in the dominant language: English or French. They are the most valued. Inuktitut and other native languages are used only for 'lower' tasks: private conversations, non-specialised jobs, and, sometimes, to help young children during their first years at school. Inuktitut may have some official status, but it is generally more symbolic than real. (Dorais, 1990: 306)

While English and French are most valued, they do not peacefully co-exist. French is the High language in parts of eastern Canada, and English is the High language in much of the rest of Canada – certainly in the Provinces of British Colombia, Alberta, Saskatchewan and Manitoba. *Francophonie* in eastern Canada is not merely a matter of language, though certainly language is a key identifying characteristic; also implicated is Roman Catholicism, and *Québecois* cultural identity. Even though various acts of the Canadian government have enshrined French as a co-equal official language, in much of Canada that status is reflected in bilingual signage, in the bilingual civil service, and in a number of other visible bilingual functions, but has made little significant difference in the behaviour of the public. On the contrary, it has aroused a certain amount of resentment among English speakers and a great deal of interprovincial squabbling.[6]

In the Benelux countries, a number of languages do in fact co-exist officially, though it is not always clear whether they co-exist as equal partners. In Luxembourg:

> The entire population of the Grand Duchy . . . becomes trilingual (in Luxemburger, German, and French) through school and the environment. Luxemburger, the national language, belonging to the Germanic family, is partially standardised, lacks technical vocabulary, has limited register variants, uses many loan words from French and German, has few books, and is spoken by everyone from the head of state to the humblest citizen. Officially it is used in only 125 hours of the whole school curriculum yet 77 per cent of citizens use it most frequently in private life. The order of preference for oral communication is Luxemburger, French, German; the order of preference for written communication is German, French, and Luxemburger. (Baetens Beardsmore, 1994: 101)

In Belgium, French (Walloon) and Dutch (Flemish) officially co-exist, though there are clearly marked geographic areas delegated to each. The Foyer Project may serve as an example of how this works educationally:

> This project supports a trilingual + bicultural program offered to immigrants in 10 Dutch-medium primary schools in Brussels. Brussels is a French-Dutch bilingual city, though predominantly French. Three schools cater for Italians, three for Turks, two for Moroccans, one for Spaniards, and one for Armenians. The aims are to integrate minority immigrants in Dutch-language minority schools into the French-dominant bilingual city and to give them comparable chances to succeed in secondary schools with Flemish Belgians. (Baetens Beardsmore, 1994: 101–2)

The language legislation is extensive and quite explicit. In officially designated bilingual areas, the law even specifies which language will occur first in official signage.

The Netherlands presents a much more complex picture. The dominant language is Dutch, but most people speak Dutch, English, French, and/or German. Also present in the environment are Frisian and a number of the languages of Indonesia (which had at one time been a Dutch colonial territory). In recent years there has been a good deal of debate about the status of English. Recommendations to use English in higher education have drawn much heat and evoked a great deal of strong feeling.

In all of these examples, ethnicity and the notion of community (e.g. Breton 1996) are key factors. In Canada, *Québecois* identity is a central issue and, in Belgium, French or Dutch identity is. In Luxembourg, on the other hand, the co-existing languages serve different functions from the national language, Luxemburger. Other important instances of the 'ethnic model' can be found in the former Soviet Union and in the Eastern bloc nations (see Comrie, 1981; see also Medgyes & Kaplan, 1992 for the effects in Hungary), where Russian was the official language or the first foreign language, but regional ethnic languages (e.g. Georgian in Georgia, etc.) were officially encouraged after the end of the Stalinist era. This is too complex an issue to be dealt with briefly at this point; we merely note the application of the Ethnic model in the former USSR and in eastern Europe. The realities of ethnic languages are playing themselves out now in a number of the newly independent states (see, e.g. recent events in Latvia, Lithuania and Estonia – Ozolins, 1994, Chechnia and Armenia; also see recent events in the former Yugoslavia – Tollefson 1993).

Yet another case can be examined in Nigeria where English, Igbo (15 million speakers in Nigeria), Hausa (25–30 million speakers in Northern Nigeria, the Niger Republic, and throughout West Africa), and Yoruba (16 million speakers in south-western Nigeria, Benin and Togo) co-exist. English constitutes a super-dialectal variety, but the country is geographically divided into regions where the several African languages are spoken. The use of Igbo as a second language in various parts of Nigeria was relatively limited up to the 1980s, but it is expanding fairly rapidly under the implementation of the National Policy on Education, which requires all secondary school students to learn a major Nigerian language other than their mother tongue (Fakuade, 1989; Oladejo, 1993). Hausa is also widely spoken as a second language. It is extensively used for governmental, educational, and commercial purposes and in the media. Clearly, language use is identified with ethnicity and geographic area; that is, languages are officially sanctioned in their 'home-lands' even when several home-lands are included within a single larger polity (also see Oladejo, 1991).

For individual bilinguals the various languages exist in complementary distribution, but for the multilingual societies in which these individuals exist, the languages are in competition for registers, social prestige and for territory (Laponce, 1987, 1993).

Majority vs. Minority Languages

Under the auspices of the European Union, the many western European languages seem to have fallen into a tri-partite structure as suggested in Figure 8.3.

In this diagram, TIER 1 represents the major European national languages (e.g. Danish, Dutch, French, German, Greek, Italian, Portuguese, Spanish, Norwegian and Swedish – which are not official EU languages). TIER 2 represents the lesser languages (e.g. Basque, Breton, Catalan, Irish, Luxemburger, Romansch, Welsh) while TIER 3 represents the smallest minority languages (e.g. Caló, Corsican, Faroese, Frisian, Gaelic, Galician, Ladino, Romani, Sami, Sardinian, Sicilian, Valencian). This is a fairly

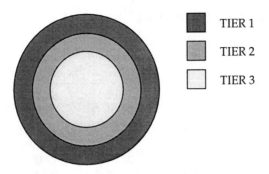

Figure 8.3 The tri-partite structure of languages in Europe

subjective list, based largely on numbers of speakers, and in all fairness some languages listed in TIER 3 might at present actually fall in TIER 2. A critical characteristic of TIER 3 languages, however, is that they are likely to become extinct in the not too distant future.

> There is now a considerable body of evidence suggesting that the diversity of human languages is decreasing at a rate many times faster than at most if not all previous periods of the history of human languages. (Of the 1200+ languages of the Pacific, Crocombe [1989: 47] estimates that about 20 will survive – Dixon [1989: 30] states that 'every Aboriginal language in Australia is currently at risk'. Worldwide, informed estimates suggest that 90% of all languages will disappear within a couple of generations). (Mühlhäusler, 1995c: 4, and note 4)

In the political reality of contemporary Europe, despite the best efforts of the European Union (so designated since 1993; formerly *European Community*), major resources (including educational resources) are likely to be devoted to TIER 1 languages. TIER 2 languages are likely to receive some attention – as much as economic policies permit (see Grin, 1993); but TIER 3 languages are likely to get relatively little attention. There just aren't adequate resources to spread around. If indeed these languages get little attention, the likelihood of their disappearance is substantially increased. This has been the case of minority languages worldwide.

A problem, however, is that the terms *majority* and *minority* are differently defined depending on the circumstances (e.g. the case of Taiwan, Chapter 7, pp. 202–3). If one bases the definitions solely on numbers of speakers, one finds a curiously anomalous situation in South Africa. Clearly, in numerical terms, Afrikaans (a variant of Dutch spoken in South Africa by only 15% of the population) is a *minority* language (see Table 8.1). But in a political sense, it has long been a *majority* language in that it was the language of that part of the total community which held virtually all of the political and economic power. Circumstances are changing since the

Table 8.1 Languages of South Africa

Language	Number	Total %	Urban population %	Rural %
Afrikaans	5,804,411	15.05	84.45	15.55
English	3,482,375	09.01	95.81	04.19
Zulu	8,483,720	21.96	37.16	62.84
Xhosa	6,580,380	17.03	37.97	62.03
Swazi	901,008	02.57	22.05	77.95
Ndebele	600,305	01.55	27.78	72.22
Northern Sotho	3,722,444	09.64	22.33	77.67
Southern Sotho	2,598,357	06.73	59.03	40.97
Tswana	3,319,951	08.59	34.45	65.55
Tsonga	1,681,575	04.35	21.66	78.34
Venda	858,704	02.22	12.56	87.44
Other languages	507,260	01.31	61.91	38.09
Total (11 +)	38,540,490	99.99		

collapse of apartheid. It will be interesting to see how, given economic and political constraints, the very liberal language policies espoused by the new government will play out in the future (Ridge, 1996). It seems fairly clear that Afrikaans will be replaced in the power structure, though whether it will be replaced by English or by an indigenous language is not entirely clear at the moment. The long-term security of Afrikaans is by no means assured.

Another interesting situation exists in the Scandinavian states. Sami (Lappish) – a Uralic language – is an indigenous minority language spoken across Finland (Aikio, 1991), Norway, Sweden and Russia. It exists as several (nine or more) local dialects (listed in Table 8.2 in alphabetical order). In total, the language is spoken by 25,000 to 30,000 people across a huge geographic area. Many Sami are, as noted, bilingual in Finnish, Norwegian, Swedish and/or Russian (Janhunen, 1975–80). Clearly, Sami is a minority language under serious threat (Magga, 1994).

> An initial finding concerning the Sami language is that its linguistic and social position is strongest and its chances for continued well-being are best where it has been given political support, and where it has been associated with development and economic progress, and where the language has been given legal status [i.e. in Norway under the Sami Language Act promulgated through the Sami Cultural Committee] . . . .

Table 8.2 Sami dialects, number of speakers and location

Inari Sami (400 speakers in Finland, all speakers thought to be bilingual in Finnish).
Kildin Sami (1000 speakers in the former USSR, most speakers thought to be bilingual in Russian).
Lule Sami (8500 speakers in Sweden).
Northern Sami (11,600 speakers in Norway + 1600 speakers in Finland).
Pite Sami (unknown number of speakers in Sweden and Norway).
Skolt Sami (1000 speakers roughly evenly spread between Finland and Russia, most speakers thought to be bilingual in either Finish or Russian).
Southern Sami (1000 speakers roughly evenly spread between Sweden and Norway).
Ter Sami (500 speakers in Russia, all thought to be bilingual in Russian).
Ume Sami (unknown number of speakers in Sweden).

> By comparison the fate of the Sami language in Sweden, Finland and Russia is much less well assured, suggesting that the 'laissez faire' assimilation policies of [those] countries continues to have an eroding effect on the Sami language. (Mühlhäusler, 1995c: 6)

Similarly, indigenous minority languages in Australia, Canada, New Zealand and the United States are also under serious threat, as are indigenous minority languages in other areas (e.g. Japan [Maher & Yashiro, 1995], Taiwan [Hsiau, 1997]). As suggested in Figure 8.3, many languages in TIER 3 around the world are likely to disappear within two or three generations. This is an instance in which languages are in competition. As the major languages capture greater numbers of registers, minority languages are subjected to greater threat. Evaluations like the following can be found in Alaska, Arctic Canada, and any number of other places (e.g. Tahiti).

> It is education on all levels and in all forms that is the chief instrument of the policy of gallization. From the most elementary level, all education is dispersed in French. At no stage in public education is Tahitian taught. Use of the vernacular is forbidden in the schools, not only to the teachers but to the pupils, who may not speak it in class or even during recreation. (Lavondès, 1971, cited in Mühlhäusler, 1994b: 125)

The 'Welsh Not' syndrome is alive and well.[7]

Religion and Language Planning

One of the most powerful forces acting on language change and language spread has been religion (Ferguson, 1982). Frederic Farrar (1899),

Archbishop of Canterbury, in a widely read book on language and language education, characterised 'primitive' people in the following way to demonstrate their need for Christianity (achieved through a knowledge of English) to rescue them from their sins:

> . . . the aborigines of Victoria [Australia], among whom new-born babies are killed and eaten by their parents and brothers, and who have no numerals beyond three . . . [and] the negros of New Guinea, who were seen springing from branch to branch of the trees, gesticulating, screaming and laughing. (cited in Mühlhäusler, 1994b: 124)

The first Vice-Chancellor of the University of Papua New Guinea said:

> There is no Education until people have a knowledge of English. Teach them English, English and more English; this is what they want . . . . Only Christianity can replace the original philosophies, legends, pagan practices and supernatural fears that 510 tongues have engendered. (cited in Mühlhäusler, 1994b: 124)

In sum, a widely held view during the height of colonial expansion was that subjugated people had fallen from grace (or never attained it) and, furthermore, that they spoke languages that were seriously deficient, should be obliterated as quickly as possible, and should be replaced by reverentially and systematically adequate languages – languages like French, Spanish or English. The institutionalised religions varied in their views of the best means for doing so – or rather they varied with respect to the sequence in which those means should be applied. Some Protestant denominations translated the Bible into these barbarous languages so that Christianity might be introduced, and then civilisation might be brought to the benighted people through a European language in church-regulated schools. The Roman Catholic Church sought to perform the two tasks simultaneously through the ritual of the Church (in Latin) (Liddicoat, 1993) and through church-regulated schools. Islam has made its contribution as well, using as its tools Classical Arabic and the Koran taught in Koranic schools. Both strategies worked wonderfully well. Equally important, however, was the fact that the only available education (the kind of education leading to the benefits of Western civilisation) was controlled entirely by the churches. Indeed, in many cases government subvented and supported church-controlled education.

Masagara (1991), in a carefully researched dissertation, showed how the introduction of Christianity in Rwanda (and to some extent across the border in Burundi) not only served to establish French but also served to modify the beliefs and values of the people as well as the language they spoke. Personal oaths, for example, were widely used in Rwandan society; if one's word were doubted, one would swear an oath to certify the truthfulness of the claim. Each individual had an 'ultimate oath' and, since the oath was known to everyone in the community, when that oath was invoked there was no question of the truthfulness of the claim. Indeed, anyone questioning the truthfulness of a claim supported by an ultimate oath might be killed for his impertinence. These oaths were based on such matters as familial relations (e.g. 'I would rather commit incest with my daughter than lie to you'.); others were based on the hierarchy implicit in the social structure (e.g. invoking the name of the king or of some other important leader in the community), while others were based on the economic structure of the community (e.g. 'I would rather that all my cattle died . . . .'). Once Christianity was introduced, all of these oaths were replaced by a very small number of Christian oaths (e.g. 'I swear by the Holy Mother . . . ,' or 'So help me God . . . '). The implications of this linguistic change are pervasive; Christianity not only changed the language structure but it also changed the nature of familial relationships, the social hierarchy, and the economic structure.

A most interesting condition is observable among the Maori people of New Zealand. In the period following the Treaty of Waitangi (1848 – which formally ended hostilities between the Maori and the British intruders, signed between tribal chieftains and the official representatives of the Crown in 1848), many Maori people converted to Christianity and learned English. Benton (1981) has demonstrated the rapid rate of attrition in the Maori language following the treaty. In recent times, there has been a significant effort to revive the Maori language – initially only among Maori people, but more recently taken up by the government – but the outcome has been that a large number of individuals of Maori ethnicity have learned Maori as a *second language*. Furthermore, as Christianity has pervaded the Maori community, Maori has come to be used extensively as a ritual language in Christian contexts; it has, otherwise, lost registers. Christianity is not entirely compatible with Maori phenomenology, so the phenomenology has changed to accommodate Christianity (Kaplan, 1993a). In general, then, the introduction of Christianity has, as in Rwanda, not only changed the language structure but it has also changed the nature of familial relationships, the social hierarchy, and the economic structure.

In summary, religion has played a key role in language policy and planning. In many instances, the events were not planned in an explicit way, but the end result has been massive change in language and society. As Mühlhäusler notes:

Linguistic imperialism . . . is the expansion of a small number of privileged languages at the cost of a large number of others. Linguistic imperialism is a promoter of one-way learning, the flow of knowledge and information from the powerful to the powerless . . . . [Ecology] is . . . the support system for [the] inhabitants and the structured diversity of [the] inhabitants . . . . Language [planning] involves the introduction of a new language into an existing language ecology. There may be good reasons for [introducing a new language], and there are also good reasons for devoting much energy to the question how newly introduced languages can be strengthened. However, it is equally important to pay attention to the affects of such an action on the wider linguistic ecology, and how this introduction affects the other languages, their speakers and their well-being. (1994b: 122–3)

What is true with respect to the introduction of a new language is certainly true with respect to the introduction of a new religion. It is reasonable to say that widespread missionary efforts have had the most insidious effects on language ecology, on languages, their speakers, and the well-being of those speakers.

Negative Language Planning

Certain types of language planning are intended not to increase the number of linguistic options, but rather to restrict severely the number of such options. An interesting case has been developing in the United States in the past decade. Gradually, there has been a widespread recognition that the United States is in fact a multilingual and multicultural society. Similar recognition in Australia led to the development of a policy which requires children to learn more than one language – that is, the number of linguistic options has been increased. In western Europe, as the European Union has taken cognisance of the linguistic diversity of Europe, the Treaty of Maastricht (1992) has lent considerable support to cultural diversity, which the Treaty considers to be one of Europe's major assets.

A general policy goal is to place the highest priority on educational mobility; the objective is to enhance the level of familiarity of as many European students as possible with other European cultures and languages as an element of quality in Education. Language learning remains a top priority, and to this end, member states are encouraged to promote trilingualism; they are advised to make language qualifi-cations desirable for entry into, and compulsory for exit from, higher education; and they are requested to give particular attention to the learning of minority languages [those we have, elsewhere in this chapter, labelled TIER 2 languages].[8] (Baetens Beardsmore, 1994: 94)

In any case, the point is that the number of linguistic options have been increased among the member states. In the United States, however, the movement has been in a quite different direction; the recognition of language diversity has raised widespread fears of national disunity (not a new issue in that nation or elsewhere), and that fear in turn has given rise to a powerful effort to have English made the sole official language of the United States by amending the federal Constitution. Historically, the governing documents of the nation have been silent on the question of language. There is evidence that the founding fathers, at the time of their determination of the contents of the federal Constitution (1787), debated the question of a national language, and – recognising that the fledgling nation was, even then, multilingual – consciously decided not to nominate a national language. But the several states, correctly perceiving the language question as being *ipso facto* a matter of States Rights, have subsequently pursued various paths in this context.[9] (Regrettably, many earlier liberal language policies have subsequently been amended or repealed as the English-speaking majority have increased in numbers and power.)

The political lobbying organisation known as *US English* came into existence in 1983; it has raised and spent millions of dollars ($28 million between 1983 and 1990) on the campaign to have English declared the official language of the United States (Crawford, 1989, 1992a, 1992b). As early as 1981, the late California Senator, S.I. Hayakawa, introduced a constitutional amendment to accomplish this objective. His amendment was never reported out of committee and thus failed. Similar legislation has, however, been introduced in every session of Congress since then (Ricento, 1996). At the time this chapter was written, there were, for example, four bills before the 104th Congress (First Session) – H. R. 123, H. R. 345, H. R. 739, H. R. 1005 – the intent of which, to varying degrees, was:

- to make English not only the official language of the US but also the *preferred* language of communication among citizens;
- to require all public ceremonies to be conducted in English (including citizenship ceremonies);
- to enforce assimilation;
- to encourage (unofficially) discrimination against those who do not speak English as a first language;
- to amend the Immigration and Nationality Act in such a way that it becomes ' . . . a duty of US citizens to read, write, and speak English to the extent of their physical and mental abilities . . . ' [H. R. 739] – though there is no definition of how these physical and mental abilities will be assessed;
- to repeal Title VII of the Elementary and Secondary Education Act (1965), and the Bilingual Education Act (which provided the legislative authority for Title VII), thereby eliminating bilingual education;
- to amend Section 203 of the Voting Rights Act (1965) to eliminate bilingual ballots; and
- to eliminate the Office of Bilingual Education and Minority Language Affairs (OBEMLA).

While, ostensibly, the intent involves cost-savings, and while the proposed legislation ostensibly ensures national unity, the actual objective is to restrict the number of linguistic options, to assuage the economic fears of the monolingual English-speaking population, and to foster ethnic homogeneity (see e.g. Thomas, 1996). This is an important example of negative language planning. There are, however, some serious problems that have not been addressed in these various efforts to limit the linguistic options to only English. Which English is it to be, and how will its purity be assured over time? In order to make the plan work, the United States would have to create, for the first time in its history – indeed, for the first time in the history of any English-speaking country – a language academy which would rule on disputed questions relating to English. No such academy has been envisioned as of the time this chapter was written, nor have the attendant costs been considered.

Another interesting example of negative language policy may be found in Mexico. The objective of Mexico's long-time ethnic language policy – as well as the implementation of that policy through the national educational system – was the integration of Mexico's native minorities into the national linguistic mainstream – that is, the Hispanization (*Castellanización*) of the entire population (Heath, 1972). Admittedly, Mexico is currently promoting something of a linguistic and ethnic revival. Language and education policies – initially intended to unify the nation through linguistic homogeneity – are currently being directed at cultivation of the 50 or so ethnic languages which have survived those efforts at unification (Patthey-Chavez, 1994).[10]

Similar examples can be found throughout Latin America (see, e.g. Hornberger, 1994; for Argentina and Chile, see Messineo & Wright, 1989). The spread of Spanish and Portuguese through the world was a function of Spanish and Portuguese colonial expansion in the fifteenth and sixteenth centuries. In Latin America, Spanish is the official language of nine of the 13 republics that make up the continent.[11] Throughout their collective histories these nine republics have practised policies of Hispanization, though in recent times the question 'Which Spanish?' has become increasingly important. It is no longer unchallenged *Castellanización*; though Hispanization imprecisely defined is alive and well. It has, in general, been the policy of these national states to limit linguistic variability in the interests of national unity.

Negative language planning, then, has been fairly widespread; its purpose has been to narrow language options, and indigenous languages and cultures have been the victims of this activity.

Code Borrowing/Switching

Code borrowing and *code switching* are processes that occur commonly along linguistic boundaries, when two languages come into contact. These terms implicate the mixing of two languages in a single utterance; e.g. along the US/Mexican border (a political boundary, but also to some extent an implied linguistic border), it is not unusual to hear such expressions as:

Vamos a mi casa watch the television.

Here, obviously, half of the sentence is Spanish, half English. In Chapter 3, under the heading Lexical Modernisation, we have already described how lexical borrowing occurs. That process occurs not only at linguistic borders but rather at any point at which two languages come into contact. An obvious cause of such borrowing is that the language doing the borrowing does not have a way of expressing simply some particular concept while the lending language has. We have previously mentioned the borrowing of technical terms which accompanies the transfer of technology from one language community to another. But code borrowing is much more pervasive. The academic variety of English has, for example, borrowed such terms as *Weltanschauung* and *Weltansicht* from German because these terms describe concepts that it would take many words to describe in English. Such terms, often retaining their original pronunciation (or as close an approximation of it as speakers of the borrowing language can manage), are simply dropped into an otherwise native sentence. The following two dozen or so expressions borrowed into English may serve as examples, simply to illustrate the point:

> *dhow, houri, jinn/genie* (Arabic);
> *aberglaube* (German);
> *amok, batek, kampong* (Malay);
> *jodhpurs* (Hindi);
> *kopeck, ruble* (Russian);
> *baksheesh* (Farsi);
> *impressario* (Italian);
> *hidalgo, lariat* (Spanish);
> *hibatchi, kimono* (Japanese);
> *wigwam* (Algonquin);
> *bateau, croissant, debonair, eau* [as in eau de Cologne], *e'clair, escargo,*
> *fabliau, fichu, gourmet, hauteur, laissez faire, lingerie, patisserie* (French).

More interestingly, in recent years, youth culture has been responsible for a great many borrowings, largely from English, into many other languages. Teenagers are inclined to wear T-shirts emblazoned with messages. These messages are often in English, often indecent, and rarely understood by the wearer. Such T-shirts are likely to be found on the streets of Buenos Aires, Manila, Moscow and Tokyo as readily as on the streets of New York, Sydney or San Francisco. Dr Nina Razinkina, Director of the English Division of the Foreign Languages Branch of the Russian Academy of Science, offers a remarkable testimonial of the effects of American (as

distinct from British) English code borrowing/switching on contemporary
Russian (2 October 1992, personal communication):

> The scope of the problem connected with the penetration of American
> English into the Russian language is really formidable. It demands the
> immediate attention of linguists, sociologists, psychologists, educa-
> tionist, and demographers. It is not by chance that I have used the
> adjective *formidable*; more and more people of various age and for
> various reasons use a lot of American words in their everyday
> speech. . . . Teenagers have for that a 'rich' source of T-shirts (with
> whole short stories on them), rock songs, chewing-gum labels, [etc.].
> While listening to the speech of teenagers, I have noticed a definite
> tendency; it is always one single word inserted in Russian speech and
> almost never a phrase . . . . Thus, 'a girl' is pronounced with American
> English accent and instead of 'smart' or some [other adjective] of that
> kind, a Russian word is [inserted]. The more American English words
> sprinkle the speech of a teenager, the more [sure] s/he feels of
> herself/himself, and the one who beats the record seems to become a
> leader of a small group. (My son argues [he is nearly 26], saying that
> the process goes in the opposite direction; that is, the leader, if he wants
> to preserve his status, has got to know many American words.)
>
> What troubles me is that it is very seldom when the desire to show 'the
> knowledge' of American English goes together with the desire to study
> it seriously and conscientiously. As to students, the picture here to my
> mind is a bit different. One can observe, in their speech, phrases and
> whole English sentences; their vocabulary includes words from their
> [academic] majors. The better an English textbook is written, the more
> English phrases they sprinkle their speech with.
>
> Another problem with students as well as with teenagers is that more
> often than not when they use Russian slang, it is invariably mixed with
> American slang . . . . Intellectual students are looking down on the
> practice of the unscrupulous mixture of Russian and American
> English, making a point of their disapproval of all kinds of showing
> off, and calling upon their friends to talk either entirely English or
> entirely Russian. I am afraid they [do not] receive a very positive
> response. With people beyond the student age, the situation is
> different. Here we rarely find a desire to show off or to profess a
> linguistic 'hipness'. The use of American English is fully justified by
> the lack of corresponding notions/ideas/concepts in Russian due to
> the country's rather isolated political and economic life in the last
> seventy years. The problem is sometimes (not infrequently) when there
> is a good adequate Russian word, an American one is used instead.

Mass media are usually blamed and are accused of bad linguistic taste. To my mind the problem has deeper roots.

The phenomenon might be corrected with inertia in spoken language when the American origin (it might be a name, a geographic indication, an event) of one word by mere chain reaction brings to one's mind another American word and pushes out the Russian equivalent . . . .For me, it is the [usage] (both written and oral) of scientists which is of the greatest importance. With our older branches of science such as, for instance, classical mechanics – with its very long and quite outstanding history – there are no problems at all. I have not seen a single borrowed word/term in articles dealing with this branch of science. As to the newer branches, the situation is quite different. At first glance, the problem is easy to solve – well, if the idea/notion/concept has made its first appearance in an English-speaking country, why should one invent something that is purely Russian? Unfortunately, it is not as simple as that. One example: There are frequent cases when the Russian term did exist earlier, but since a particular branch of science has developed [more quickly] in an English-speaking country (a flood of publications in special journals, conferences, symposia, etc. with English as the only working language, etc.) a Russian term has been pushed out. A friend of mine who is an editor of one of our biological journals says she is going to leave her job because she is losing patience with authors of papers. Most of them insist on borrowed terms and, when she makes a mild attempt to substitute some of them with Russian terms, there is a protest with a poorly concealed underlying [implication] that the author knows better which term to use and which not to [use] . . . .

This is evidence offered by a linguist and a teacher of English (largely to scientists studying at the Academy of Sciences) in Russia. Her observations are not only cogent, but demonstrate the way in which code borrowing/ switching both enriches language and frustrates more traditional scholars.

Similar illustrations may be drawn from Chinese, Japanese, Korean, Pilipino and other languages. The Japanese language academy controls the entry of foreign terms into Japanese, but in many other languages, it is a 'free market'. An English speaker can virtually read some pieces in the Pilipino newspapers in Manila because of the very large number of borrowed lexical items. Eggington (1987) has demonstrated the effects of English borrowing on written text in Korean, showing how some terms, literally, appear in triplicate – i.e. in English/Chinese characters/Hangul – in the same stretch of text.

As noted, popular music, slogans emblazoned on clothing, comic books and other facets of popular culture may contribute significantly to code borrowing/switching. Comic books, for example, are a major contributor to language change in South China. In Hong Kong, several million comic books are published weekly (collectively, about 5 million per month); they employ essentially three kinds of texts – the endless life of Bruce Lee, Chinese traditional and ghost stories, and the printed adaptations of the type of the English soap opera. The Hong Kong comic books are designed for a Hong Kong audience; that is, although there is a presumption that standard written Chinese can be read by any speaker of Chinese, the language of comic books is so salted with Cantonese expressions that speakers of other Chinese varieties have difficulty reading these texts (Snow, 1993a: 137, 1993b). As the PRC plays an increasing role in Hong Kong affairs in the countdown to the reversion of Hong Kong to China in 1997, it will be interesting to see what becomes of this language change-agent.

Thus, code borrowing/switching is a widespread process, serving to modify not only the lexical content of some languages, but modifying the visual appearance of written text, and, in more extreme cases, creating a 'pidgin' variety of the language for use in special registers (i.e. among teenagers). Certainly, code borrowing/switching plays a role in language development, but it is an uncontrolled variable which language planners rarely take account of in their development of policy. It is a variable that serves to blur the boundaries between languages. It would be inappropriate to limit by legislation code borrowing in any given language – it is rarely possible to legislate morality, including language purity; rather, it is a matter of understanding how the phenomenon works, what sorts of terms/structures are borrowed, where they are borrowed from, and what effect the borrowing has on the phonological and syntactic structure of the language.

Summary

This chapter has attempted to look at the question: Is it a matter of 'languages in competition' or can and do languages co-exist depending on their use, function, and status? For the individual bilingual, languages co-exist in his/her repertoire but, for the multilingual society, languages do in fact compete for registers, for power, for acceptability, for social status. Language ecology worldwide is changing. Except in their embodiment in the national state, languages are no longer absolutely bound up with land through geography and narrative as they were in Australian Aboriginal cultures (Russo & Baldauf, 1986), allowing for the co-existence of many small languages separated by cultural beliefs. Language has become a portable tool, a skill, an artefact to be used for particular purposes. In this environment the language that captures the largest number of registers is likely to push out other languages. Language revival, as we note in Chapter 10, cannot succeed unless an ecological niche can be found for the language being revived which normally means recapturing some significant number of registers. When a language serves only ritual functions, it is unlikly to enjoy a real revival, though it can certainly persist for quite a long time. In the multilingual community, the questions of languages in competition and language survival can be answered only in terms of the use, function and status of the various languages making up the language ecology of the community.

In order to examine issues related to bilingualism and ethnic status, five phenomena have been examined in some detail: The Ethnic Model, Majority vs. Minority Languages, Religion and Language Planning, Negative Language Planning, and Code Borrowing/Switching. Each of these has been noted to contribute in some way to language change, though often the contribution is an unconscious and unplanned one. These constitute phenomena which language planners have tended to ignore but to which they must pay greater attention.

Notes
1. The term mother-tongue is not used in this chapter. It is not a useful term because one's 'mother-tongue', taken literally to mean the language one learned from/spoke with one's mother, may not be one's first/dominant language (also see definitions in Chapter 1).
2. There are also a growing number of Australian Aboriginal, Native American and other indigenous languages where this is virtually the case, i.e. where there are only a very few remaining speakers.
3. It cannot be denied that an individual who knows Latin (or another classical language) may belong to a small elite coterie which uses Latin as an 'in' language, or such an individual may intersperse Latin expressions with his/her English, as some attorneys are wont to do, as a demonstration of membership of an exclusive group.
4. Robinson (1993) discusses the case of high linguistic diversity where no group of language speakers exceeds 50% of the population: 25 polities in Africa, nine in Asia, four in the Caribbean and Latin America and six in the Pacific are listed. Some of the polities with high linguistic diversity and a large numbers of living languages include: Papua New Guinea 867, Indonesia 701, Nigeria 427, India 405, Cameroon 275, Zaire 219, Philippines 168, Malaysia 141, Tanzania 131, Chad 126, Ethiopia 112 and Vanuatu 111.
5. Research has shown that a child growing up in a trilingual household, where individual languages are 'owned' by different persons, never uses the wrong language with a given individual. A child will understand that the Filipina maid speaks English, the grandfather speaks Chinese and mother, father, siblings and school friends speak Malay, and – although the child may not be able to name the languages involved – s/he will speak English with the maid, Chinese with the grandfather and Malay with mother, father, siblings and school friends.
6. Edwards (1995) provides a discussion of monolingualism, bilingualism and multiculturalism in the period between 1992 and 1994 and a review of recent developments in language planning and policy (Edwards, 1994) in Canada.
7. At least to the time of World War II, it is attested that Welsh pupils caught speaking Welsh at school were forced to wear a board on a thong around their

necks. The board carried the words 'Welsh Not.' Pupils continued to wear the board until another pupil was detected in this grievous crime. (See discussion of this humiliating punishment in Chapter 2.)

8. The European Union defines its working languages as Danish, Dutch, English, French, German, Greek, Italian, Portuguese and Spanish. These nine languages are legally allocated equal status. In reality English and French dominate as working languages. German, Italian and Spanish stand next in the rankings. Danish, Dutch, Greek and Portuguese are designated *de facto* 'minor' languages. All of those languages fall in what we have designated TIER 1 languages (see Ammon, 1994; Schlossmacher, 1995). When Baetens Beardsmore speaks of 'minority' languages, he may well mean the 'minor' languages of TIER 1 rather than 'minority' languages of TIERs 2 and 3.

9. The geographic sector that became the original 13 states of the United States was, at the point of initial union, made up of a number of different language enclaves – English in the former British colonies, French in the north, German in the middle (Commonwealth of Pennsylvania), and Spanish in the south – but also Russian, Swedish and Dutch, not to mention the Native American languages – perhaps as many as 1000 different languages in the period immediately prior to European contact, but whose language interests were ignored (Kloss, 1977). As various states gradually entered the union, some entered with bilingualism guaranteed as a matter of law – the Louisiana Treaty (1803), by which the United States acquired the Louisiana Territory (more than one million square miles, including the port of New Orleans) for example, contained in Article 3, language written by Napoleon:

> Let the Louisianans know that we separate ourselves from them with regret; that we stipulate in their favour every thing that they can desire, and let them hereafter, happy in their independence, recollect that they have been Frenchmen, and that France, in ceding them, has secured for them advantages which they could not have obtained from a European power, however paternal it might have been. Let them retain for us sentiments of affection; and may their common origin, descent, language, and customs perpetuate the friendship.

The French Commissioner, Laussat, officiating at the exchange of sovereign powers in New Orleans on 30 November 1803, issued a proclamation which read in part: 'The Treaty secures to you all the advantages and immunities of citizens of the United States. The particular government, which you will select will be adapted to your customs, usages, climate, and opinions.' As a result, when Louisiana entered the Union as a state in 1812, it had a large Francophone majority, and throughout most of the nineteenth century its laws and other public documents were printed in French, and the courts and the legislature operated bilingually. Bilingualism followed similar paths in Florida and California. Although the Treaty of Guadeloupe Hidalgo (1848) – which brought California into the United States – makes no specific reference to language, the Treaty itself is bilingual in English and Spanish. Written within a year of the Treaty, Article XI, Section 21, of the 1849 California Constitution gave Spanish and English equal status. New Mexico entered as a bilingual territory with Spanish and English granted equal status. The Constitutions of Alaska and Hawaii contain specific sections dealing with language rights.

10. According to a 1992 study by the Institute of Social Studies at the National Autonomous University of Mexico (UNAM), 48 more or less well-defined ethnic populations have been identified (approximately 5,300,000 individuals).

This represents a decrease from the mid–1980s when the officially recognised linguistic groups numbered 56 (more than 8 million individuals). At that time, 10 of the officially recognised languages were deemed to be extinct and 12 in danger of extinction within a generation.

11. Portuguese is the official language of Brazil (see, e.g. the work of the 25 *Centros de Estudos Brasileiros* around the world; Lopes, 1997). (The Falkland Islands use English, and French Guiana, Guyana, and Surinam use French and Dutch as well as their respective Creoles, Caribbean Hindi, and Javanese.)

9 Specific Purpose Language Planning

Introduction

In Chapter 3 we examined some of the macro goals targeted by language planners, and in the previous chapters we have seen some examples of how various groups have tried to reach those goals. However, much of what has gone on in recent years in the name of general language planning has in fact implicated planning for specific purposes. By this we mean language policy and planning which has had a limited focus, usually limited to one sector of a polity, or has a limited or specific set of objectives, or has been designed to meet the language needs of a specific group of individuals. Such planning has also been termed meso level planning (see the examples in Tables 2.3 and 3.1). While such language policy and planning may appear to have a more limited focus than macro language planning, it can also have a large wash-back effect on the social and economic situation in the society as a whole. In recent times much of such planning has been economically driven, at least in the first instance.

An example of such specific purpose or meso level language planning occurred when Algeria became an independent state and adopted a quasi-socialist governing system. One of the first non-political acts (that is, without an explicitly stated policy) undertaken was the development of a special school at Boumerdes designed to teach Algerian scientists English and Russian. Boumerdes was actually a planned city designed and built by the French prior to Algerian independence for a quite different purpose. Unfortunately, the Algerian economy of the time was not able to sustain the infrastructure of that city (e.g. water supply, trash removal, transportation), and the special school was, at least initially, not terribly successful, though at great expense (partially subsidised by the governments of the US and the USSR) native speaking English and Russian teachers were imported for the undertaking. Other governments (e.g. Malaysia, the Philippines, China, Vietnam, Jordan) also mounted efforts to provide English-language instruction for their technocrats, in some cases drawing on expatriate teachers provided under such plans as the United States Peace Corps or the New Zealand Volunteer Services Abroad.

It was quite natural that they should do so. The twentieth century has been a time of great technological development, and it was important to all these nations to encourage their scientists to participate in cutting edge research and to join the international scientific community, which at the time operated largely in English, French and Russian. Indeed, the four countries most clearly representing those languages – Britain, the United States, France, and the USSR – provided the means for young scientists from the developing world to study in their tertiary institutions, particularly at the post-graduate level. All four of these 'developed' nations engaged in technology transfer to less developed states, though history has shown that the technology transfer was not entirely altruistically driven nor always successful. In the US, for example, *technology transfer* was long defined as *village-level technology*.

The desire on the part of modernising nations (and their people) to become part of the 'modern' world underlies much of this effort. Indeed, a sort of 'cargo cult' has developed. A knowledge of one of these key languages is seen as the means leading inevitably to prosperity, better living conditions, opportunities to travel, and other clearly material benefits. In many developing countries, the 'modern' sector is too small to accommodate all those who wish to enter it. As a result, a kind of 'holding pattern', rather like that in the vicinity of most major airports, has developed. It is believed by those in this holding pattern that advanced education, and particularly the knowledge of one of the key world languages of science and technology, will enhance one's position in the 'holding pattern', thereby permitting earlier and more advanced entry into the 'modern sector'. Where entry into the local 'modern sector' seems unlikely, having a language like English can also be seen as a key to economic migration. It is useful to examine the causes of the conditions that drove this scientific outpouring and its correlative desire to learn one of the key languages, particularly in the scientific arena, because this serves as the motivation for a lot of specific purpose language planning.

Planning for Science and Technology

The background to this language problem extends proximately to the years immediately following World War II, though in fact it extends distally to the beginnings of the first industrial revolution in the eighteenth century and even earlier. Through most of human history (something on the order of 100,000 years), technological and scientific change proceeded at a slow and stately pace – so much so that an individual might live a long, full, and productive life without being much bothered by scientific change or technological innovation. Science (at least since the tenth century) was practised by more-or-less highly placed clerics and wealthy gentlemen possessed of an interest in advancing human knowledge and with a sufficient supply of money to allow them to indulge their fancy. Some were primarily interested in the occult and pursued alchemy; others followed the dominant scientific paradigms of their times and actually succeeded in some cases in making real contributions to knowledge. Invention – radical scientific change, and paradigmatic shift – were essentially accidents arising from these practices. There were no professional scientists; rather, the research was carried on by educated dilettantes and amateurs. Atkinson (1993), who examined the changing rhetoric of scientific discourse in Britain from the seventeenth to the twentieth centuries in the *Philosophical Transactions of the Royal Society of London*, writes:

> First, as described by Dear (1985), the Royal Society's early rhetoric was developed substantially in opposition to the prevailing philosophical rhetoric of the period – late scholasticism. What this view does not highlight, however – and what the work of Shapin (1988, 1991, 1994) has so clearly shown – is that the new scientific rhetoric was in fact allied with a critical pre-existing social resource – the genteel form of life. Pre-industrial British society constituted a social hierarchy in which power flowed from the landed aristocracy and gentry downward. The British gentleman, therefore, represented the moral and social ideal in this system, all other social categories being defined by reference to this one. The ideal gentleman had his own conventionalised set of ideal qualities: He was self-reliant and individualistic, being at the top of the social structure and independently wealthy; at the same time, he was modest and polite, due to a code of civility which strictly defined relations with other gentlemen; but above all else he was 'free' and independent – a disinterested social actor – and honest and honourable to a fault for this very reason. That is, he was incorruptible because he had nothing to gain by lying . . . . Early modern scientists . . . traded on this conventional social image of the gentleman for rhetorical purposes . . . . Thus, the enormously influential leading light of the early Royal Society, Robert Boyle [1627–1691], presented himself as a living symbol of both the quintessential 'experimental philosopher' and the quintessential gentleman, and in his writings strove constantly to unite the two concepts. (Atkinson, 1993,1995: 44–45)

The direct evidence for Boyle's view is most clearly presented by Boyle himself. In the *Proemial Essay* of 1660, which serves as a general preface to the body of his experimental work, Boyle writes:

> . . . in almost everyone of the following essays I . . . speak so doubtingly, and use so often, *perhaps, it seems, it is not improbable,* and other such expressions, as argue a diffidence of the truth of opinions I incline to, and that I should be so shy of laying down principles, and

sometimes of so much as venturing explications . . . . (cited in Shapin, 1984: 495)

Thus, in laying down the foundation for the contemporary scientific article, Boyle urged a modesty and caution which assured the use of the hedge as an integral part of the writing of scientists. Indeed, he essentially defined the rhetoric of scientific writing which has persisted into the end of the twentieth century and which has been disseminated along with the English language into every corner of the contemporary world. This rhetoric has influenced the reading and writing of scientific text in other languages as well (e.g. French, Liddicoat, 1992). In sum, English for specific purposes is as much involved in dispensing this rhetoric (and it preferred structural elements – e.g. the agentless passive) as it is with technical vocabulary.

With the coming of the first industrial revolution in the eighteenth century, things changed. Industrialists realised early on that the linking of science and technology made sense in terms of increasing the profit margin. They began to support scientific research because such research ultimately speeded technological innovation. Furthermore, government became interested in the contributions that scientific research might make. By 1875, the *Philosophical Transactions of the Royal Society of London* were reporting government sponsored research, though the tradition of government involvement goes back almost a century before that, when there was a government-funded research project which examined whether pointed or rounded lightning rods offered the greatest protection to powder magazines. The following opening section of an 1875 article attests to the government's role.

The investigations which form the subject of this memoir have occupied our attention for a considerable time . . . . They have been made collaterally with a series of experiments carried on by a Committee appointed by the Secretary of State for War, with the view . . . of determining the most suitable description of powder for use in heavy ordnance. (1875; cited in Atkinson, 1995: 25–26)

However, by this time, a tradition of contextualised research, conducted in 'research communities' working together on similar problems, is evident. During the nineteenth century, science departments began to emerge in tertiary institutions, and the class of professional scientists (individuals who made their living from the practice of science) was beginning to emerge. Both governmental and industrial involvement continued with increasing frequency through the nineteenth and early twentieth centuries, up to the years of the World War II, culminating, perhaps, in the 'Manhattan Project' – a government-funded research effort, involving large numbers of scientists, which produced the first atomic bomb.

The period immediately following the war saw the convergence of a number of fortuitous accidents (for English language speakers) in the pursuit of 'Big Science'. At the end of the war, the US was the only major industrialised power to emerge from the hostilities with its industrial and educational infrastructures completely intact. The Allies – China, England, France, the US, and the USSR – essentially dictated the post-war settlements. The United Nations was created, and these five major powers constituted the Security Council. Among them, they also determined the languages in which the United Nations would conduct its business – Chinese, English, French, and Russian. These developments coincided with the emergence of the computer and the development of the first great electronic international data banks. The earliest computers were 'English-speaking', and, indeed, they still are to a large extent. It was only natural that the major languages of the United Nations and its subsidiary bodies (e.g. UNESCO) defined the languages for computer use in these international information networks. As early computers could not deal with Chinese characters, or with the complex structure by which words are organised and classified in Chinese characters – based not on alphabetical order but rather in terms of the nature and number of strokes making up a character, Chinese was left out of those information storage and retrieval networks for purely practical reasons. The major languages became English, French, and Russian. However, scientists from the USSR did not contribute much to the international networks during the period of the 'Cold War'. Since a vast amount of scientific literature from the period preceding the war was written in German, and with the rapid re-emergence of Germany as an industrial power, a need was created for German in those networks.

There are certain 'laws' that function in regard to scientific and technical information. Scientific research (and its dependency – technological innovation) is cumulative; that is, it depends on extensive use of existing prior scientific information. The groups doing the largest amount of research draw most heavily on the information sources; consequently, the groups doing the largest amount of research also contribute the greatest amount of information to the networks. Since the United States was the only major industrialised nation essentially unscathed by the war, the greatest amount of research was conducted in English-speaking laboratories in the United States; thus, the greatest use of information and the greatest contributions to the fund of information occurred in English. It is an inevitable outcome that those who most use and most contribute to such networks come to 'own' them. The organisation of the networks takes on the organisation of the language most used. The access systems of these networks came to be based on an English sociology of knowledge.

Furthermore, the educational infrastructure of the US was also fully intact. Under the auspices of such programmes as the Marshall Plan and with the creation of the United States Agency for International Development (AID), the US opened its tertiary institutions to the youth of the rest of the world. In 1948, the first year for which records exist, there were some 2000 'foreign students' studying in some 20 United States tertiary institutions. The numbers grew at the rate of about 10% a year for the next 30 years, approaching a quarter of a million students studying in some 2000 institutions by 1980 (Jenkins, 1983). The great majority of these students were studying science and engineering. With time, the balance shifted to business administration, and the developing world sent its youth to learn how to organise business while the earlier cadre of returned students undertook the scientific research and technological innovation that resulted in products for business to sell. These students were studying science, engineering, and business administration in English, and as they began to contribute to the information networks, they did so in English. As a result, according to the International Federation on Documentation – a United Nations body that keeps track of all the information systems – something like 80% of all the scientific and technical information available in the world is either written in, or abstracted in, English. The proportion seems to be increasing (see, e.g. Baldauf & Jernudd, 1983, 1986).[1] Even in non-English speaking countries, internal publication increasingly occurs in English rather in the indigenous language (see Baldauf & Jernudd, 1986: Medgyes & Kaplan, 1992; Kaplan, 1993d).

The 'capture' of the networks by English-speaking scientists resulted in the development of a 'knowledge cartel' of enormous power – greater power than OPEC could conceive, since petrochemical resources diminish with use, but information expands with use. Probably as the result of another accident, the English-speaking nations did not understand the power of the information cartel they 'owned'. No attempt was made to limit the free flow of information in any way up to the time of the US Reagan administration. This is not to say that the flow of information was absolutely free; the flow was restricted by economic factors because it is expensive to develop systems to access the global information, and because it is even more expensive to train scientists not only to use it, but to use it in English – indeed, to develop a entirely new cadre of 'information managers' who can 'surf' the system and identify, select, and download the important research. Despite the fact that there was no formal inhibition on the free flow of scientific and technical information, the less-developed nations remained satellites of the developed nations in the sense that they were completely dependent on the developed nations for information and for technology transfer. The Reagan administration imposed the first political limits on the free flow of scientific and technical information. In the name of national security and the protection of patents and copyrights, the Reagan administration invented the term *technology haemorrhage*, and deliberately excluded scientists from 'enemy' states from access to such information. Thus, the scientists from what Reagan termed 'The Evil Empire' – the USSR – and from China, Vietnam, Cuba, Libya, the Warsaw Pact nations, and other states were actively excluded from access to scientific information. They were not permitted to study in tertiary institutions nor to attend international scientific conferences in the United States. The power of the information cartel was exercised for the first time. (For the effects of such policy, see, e.g. Grabe & Kaplan, 1986.)

A small number of nations were able to solve the problem of information access. At the end of the war, the Japanese government realised that, if it were ever to compete in the post-war world, it would need ready access to information. It created the Japanese Institute for Science and Technology (JIST). This Institute bought the first computers from the West. It sent bibliographic specialists to the West to learn how to access and use the information systems. It created a remarkable translation facility to make technical information rapidly available in Japanese. It developed university-industrial links, defining research projects and assuring the emergence of research communities to work on those projects the government deemed vital. This latter exercise culminated ultimately in the building of *Tsukuba* Science City. The Japanese government, at a time of great austerity in the 1950s, decided to commit a huge fraction of its gross national product to this effort. The success of the Japanese effort is readily apparent in the position that Japan occupies at the present time and in the fact that JIST has moved from a fully subsidised agency to an independent agency with a great deal of money to spend. It is necessary to remember, however, that Japan came at the project from a strong industrial tradition; after all, Japan had waged successful modern war against the major industrialised nations. (See Kaplan, 1983, 1994a; Grabe & Kaplan, 1986.)

Saudi Arabia took a different approach. It undertook to send a large fraction of its technocrats to the West to study in tertiary institutions in the US and Britain and to learn English. Saudi Arabia guaranteed those students would return home by providing not only generous scholarships but the means to live comfortably for the student and his family during the period of study. It guaranteed well-paying jobs on return, and it supplemented those jobs with substantial subsidies for the purchase of a home. In other words, instead of making scientific information available in Arabic, it undertook to guarantee that the technocratic segment of the population that needed access to scientific and technical information would have such access in English. When Saudi Arabia began this project, it had virtually no tertiary institutions of its own; at present, it has sufficient tertiary places to accommodate the needs of its population, and it has stopped supporting undergraduate study abroad, although it continues to support post-graduate education at a very high level. In particular, the Saudi government built the University of Petroleum and Minerals at Dhahran, immediately proximate to the ARAMCO oil fields. That university established close ties with the Massachusetts Institute of Technology (MIT), Harvard University and other major US universities, borrowing faculty, sending Saudi educators to those institutions for training, and involving those institutions in the accreditation (academic supervision) of the University of Petroleum and Minerals. The contemporary position of Saudi Arabia in the Arab world is testimony to the success of its efforts. It is important to note that only a nation with huge fiscal resources could undertake such an effort.

Taiwan (Tse, 1980) and Israel have pursued yet a third path. For complex political reasons, both of these states permit dual citizenship with the United States. In both cases, scientists are free to travel back and forth between the two countries and thus to access the English information networks in the United States, thereby avoiding the necessity of building an expensive infrastructure. With the advent of electronic communication (e.g. e-mail, World Wide Web, the Internet) access to information banks has become appreciably easier escaping even the necessity to travel. In fact, in more recent times, both have built such infrastructures. Again, both have been successful in their efforts as can readily be attested by examining their current economic status in the world.

More recently, Malaysia has followed a different path to access science, technology and business skills. Although Malaysia has had a small number of universities of international standing, it has never been able to provide the educational opportunities and range of studies needed to meet student demands for tertiary study, especially in recent years as the economy has rapidly developed. Not only were places limited, but ethnic quotas have been in place in universities for many years to ensure that students of all Malaysia's ethnic groups had equitable access to what tertiary study was available. For Malaysian-Chinese students, for whom secondary education was far better developed at independence, this meant that many were well qualified, but were denied university places and had to seek study opportunities overseas, often in English-speaking countries. The government also provided many *bumiputra* students (literally 'sons of the soil') with scholarships to study abroad, often in English.

While in the early years after independence these measures provided the science, technology and business skills required, they had several undesirable side-effects. First, there was a major outflow of capital to finance education, at a time when capital was needed in Malaysia for development. Second, overseas study provided an English (or foreign language) education at a time when Malaysia was developing a *Bahasa Malaysia* education language policy (i.e. was converting the medium of instruction in schools and universities to *Bahasa Malaysia*). Finally, it was culturally destabilising as young students were going overseas at a developmentally critical period for four or five years and returning as Westernised, English-speaking individuals. To counteract these problems, a programme of two-year colleges has been developed jointly between Malaysian companies and British, American or Australian universities, using local and overseas staff, where the first two years of degree work are done in Malaysia and the final years of the degree are completed overseas. Fully fledged branches of universities have also been allowed to be established (e.g. University of London) (Omar, 1995). This approach provides wider access to tertiary study, especially for *bumiputra* students, and to the English language, science, technology and business skills needed in a rapidly developing modern economy. These skills are developed more economically and in a more culturally appropriate environment than would otherwise be possible, and, as in Saudi Arabia, the seeds of an expanded externally accredited university system are being developed.

Many other countries in the 'South' remain in a dependent state. Indeed, as communication on the East-West axis has improved, especially since the end of the Cold War, communication along the North-South axis has suffered. Obviously, it is the poorest states (Albania, Ethiopia, Laos, Sudan, etc.) which, though they have the greatest need, have the least access. This situation is not likely to improve in the near future.

As this discussion suggests, an enormous amount of effort has gone into specific purpose language planning. The preceding discussion has focused on science and technology, but other areas are implicated as well. The language of air transportation is universally English, as is the language of sea transportation (Weeks *et al.*, 1988). The international language of business – or at least of banking – is substantially English. The problem is not limited to nations in which English is not a commonly used language; as Kachru (1982, 1983) has shown, English in some former colonies which are now English-speaking countries has 'nativised' away from the models of high status British and American English. It has, however, gradually become clear that the special registers of science and technology, business, and transportation are more complex than was initially believed. It is not enough to provide dictionaries of technical terms or to teach some sort of 'basic' grammar in the target language. More and more, it has become clear that whole discourse styles are involved, and much recent research has gone into trying to discover the differences in such matters as rhetorical structure, and in such functions as politeness, hedging, and the like (see, e.g. Ulijn & Strothers, 1995; Markkanen & Schröder, in press). As well, large new enterprises have come into existence to try to standardise the vocabulary of various technical areas, and these will be discussed in the following section.

Academies and Lexical Development

While language planning sometimes occurs at the macro level through legislation (e.g. the law in Québec that all government notices must be in

French), it often is developed through the work of language academies, which have taken on both macro and meso language planning functions. Since academies tend to concern themselves largely with written language and even more with academic language, and since such academies are often the bodies responsible for the production of official dictionaries, language academies are significantly responsible for lexical modernisation (see Chapter 3), particularly in the context of academic science and technology.

Since the sixteenth century, some nations have set up academies for corpus planning (see the discussion in Chapter 2; Domínguez & López, 1995; Lihani, 1988; Rubin, 1979). Prominent examples are the *Accademia della Crusca*, established in Florence in 1512, the *Académie Française*, established in Paris in 1635, and the *Real Academia de la Lengua*, established in 1714. Subsequently, several Latin American countries established their own academies, in part as a reaction against the hegemony of Castilian (e.g. the Argentinian Academy of Letters). Portugal has the *Instituto de Alta Cultura* (renamed in 1976 the *Instituto de Cultura e Lingua Portuguesa*). In 1989, the presidents of the seven nations where Portuguese is the official language (Brazil, Portugal, Cape Verde, Guinea-Bissau, Sao Tomé and Principe, Angola, and Mozambique) formally inaugurated the International Institute of the Portuguese Language with the aim of articulating a general policy of Portuguese language consolidation (see Silva & Gunnewiek, 1992).

Sweden is the only Scandinavian country to have a formal language academy (established in 1786). Since World War II, however, all the countries in Scandinavia have established language commissions; the first of these was founded in 1942 to protect Swedish in Finland. Norway established such a commission in 1951 and reorganised it in 1986; Denmark established a commission in 1955, and Iceland in 1964. In 1978 the *Nordisk spraksekretariat* [Nordic Language Secretariat] was established in Oslo to permit regular consultation among the several independent national commissions. New academies have been established in the last 50 years in a number of countries (e.g. Indonesia and Malaysia's *Dewan Bahasa dan Pustaka*). There are even academies for some small non-national languages (e.g. *Fryske Akademy* [Anonymous, 1991]). To the extent that these bodies are responsible for dictionary preparation, they provide inventories of acceptable words, appropriate meanings, and standard spellings and pronunciations. In some cases, the academies also provide volumes on 'correct usage' and even 'language advice bureaus'. In many cases language academies take the conservative view of language – holding the line against language change.[2]

There are also national and international committees on terminology and language standards (e.g. the Engineering Standards Committee in Britain, the International Electrotechnical Commission, The International

Union of Pure and Applied Chemistry, the International Association of Terminology, the TNC Swedish Centre for Technical Terminology (Anonymous, 1995), the International Commission on Zoological Nomenclature, and the International Standardization Organisation [ISO]). Technical Committee 37 of the ISO co-ordinates terminological work globally in co-operation with INFOTERM based in Vienna (Anonymous, 1990). Some pluricentric languages have co-ordinating organisations; e.g. *La Francophonie* (for French) and *De Taalunie* (for Dutch). In some cases, the 'cultural' branches of Ministries of Foreign Affairs (e.g. The British Council, The United States Information Agency, The *Instituto Cervantes* (Spain), The *Goethe Institut* (Germany), The *Instituto Dante Alighieri* (Italy)) assume some responsibility, if not for creating and standardising lexicon in dictionaries, at least for distributing such dictionaries. There are also private international bodies supported by language enthusiasts which serve a similar function (e.g. the *Alliance Française*, the English-Speaking Union – whose sponsor happens to be Prince Philip, the Duke of York). Some mass media organisations undertake (or support) specialised dictionaries (see, e.g. *The BBC English Dictionary*), and some multinational corporations produce documents which have a similar intent (e.g. the Canadian power company, Hydro Québec, publishes its own French/English dictionary of terms pertaining to power generating systems designed for the protection, control and monitoring of such power systems).

Lexical standardisation

Naming is, of course, a universal property of languages. Folk naming, as has been suggested in the literature (see, e.g. Berlin *et al.*, 1973, seems to contain five levels of classification for living things: universal beginner, life form, generic, specific, and varietal forms – to which must be added local usage (e.g. (1) animal, (2) canine, (3) dog, (4) terrier, (5) wire-haired fox terrier, and locally [6] my dog Spot). Scientific naming, which began in the seventeenth century on Aristotelian principles, culminated in the work of the Swedish botanist C. Linnaeus (1707–1778). He created an essentially binomial approach in which the first part of the name (one word or more) identifies family and genus, and a second part (also conceivably more than one word) which identifies species and/or sub species; e.g. [first part] Family *Cypraeidae*, Genus *Cypraea*, [second part] Species *Spadicea* is the technical term for the California Brown Cowry, a shell (actually a marine animal most easily identifiable by its shell) found along the coast of Southern California. It can be observed that the particular California Brown Cowry which rests in Kaplan's collection cannot, by this terminological process, be identified, any more than could 'my dog Spot'. That is, the desire for standardisation and uniformity in scientific terminology may suppress local knowledge and the practices of a particular language (i.e. 'my dog Spot' and 'the California Brown Cowry which rests in Kaplan's collection' reflect naming practices in English; naming practices in other languages would be different). Furthermore, 'my dog Spot' and 'the California Brown Cowry which rests in Kaplan's collection' reflect knowledge that is locally shared (i.e. among Kaplan's friends and family). This regrettable loss of specificity in the interests of uniformity may occur in any process of language standardisation.

The work of creating technical terminology belongs to the various national and international committees on terminology and language standards (see above, Jernudd, 1992); folk naming is often reflected in dictionaries devised for ordinary use. The name cowry will be found in any standard English desk dictionary, while the term *Cypraœidaœ Cyprœa Spadicea* will be found only in technical dictionaries of marine biology. An important function of national academies is to bridge the two kinds of naming – to provide intertranslatability – because the divergence between folk naming and scientific terminology causes division in society and therefore in knowledge. One can tell one's children that they have found a California Brown Cowry, but that does not mean that they will ever know that they have found a *Cypraœidaœ Cyprœa Spadicea* unless they happen to see one in a museum collection in which the technical terminology is supplied along with the common name. And, of course, they will need to see the name in a museum in which that common name is supplied in English, rather than, say, in the language of the Native Americans who lived along the Southern California coast before the coming of Europeans. Given that Latin and Greek sources are commonly employed in technical terminology, the division between folk naming and technical terminology is exacerbated, though the use of Latin and Greek sources in technical terminology facilitates universal agreement among scientists because it promotes a transparent morphological system. Professional experts will prefer technical terminology (which in part serves to legitimise their practices, and in part contributes to greater accuracy) while non-professionals will prefer vernacular naming systems which are said to be easier to remember and which preserve individual and locally shared knowledge.

A major problem lies in the development of vocabularies and terminologies in languages achieving some level of standardisation in more-or-less newly emerging polities. Not only is some standardisation necessary for internal communication within a speech community, but it is also needed for extra-territorial communications in such areas as the fishing industry (Jernudd & Thuan, 1984) to establish take-limits, calculate taxes and tariffs, gather statistics, and encourage cross-national trade. However, it is an enormous undertaking for a modernising language to develop hundreds of thousands of new lexical items and to put structures in place that encourage their use nationally. As an example, German is a language which has been modernising for more than 100 years, yet as Clyne (1988a, 1995) clearly demonstrates, it remains a pluricentric and dialectical language.

However, this linguistic levelling process also undermines linguistic diversity (Mühlhäusler, 1994c), i.e. dialects, local variation, minority languages and ways of knowing and identifying with the world. While it may produce better communication, it can also add to the feelings of alienation that exist within a society. Wertheim (1995) argues that the new cosmology created by science, which has replaced much of the folk and mythological knowledge of who we are, is generally not well understood, leaving individuals alienated and without an understanding of their place in the world.

Government Interpreting in Australia[3]

As has been suggested at several points in this volume, governments tend to act out of economic necessity, and rarely act out of pure altruism. They act in accord with some paradigm which they believe is consistent with the philosophy adopted by some particular political administration. While some outcomes of government may indeed be consistent with notions of social justice, government policy is not often driven exclusively by motivations based on social justice. The case of interpreting and translating (I/T) in Australia is an interesting case of meso language policy and planning as the development of I/T has occurred during a period when Australia was in the process of developing its multicultural identity. Occurring as it did during the transition from a 'White Australia' to a multicultural country, the development of I/T reflects these social changes and that environment has contributed to the creation of a unique I/T service based around community needs. While the service helps migrants to Australia to fit more easily into their new social, political and economic environment, thereby making them more cost-effective contributors to the nation, the I/T policy also ensures them access to a measure of social justice.

Although I/T has always played a part in international affairs, it is a rather recent invention as a profession, based largely on educated people who studied languages, travelled, conducted business and diplomacy. In Europe, at least, the universality of French in the eighteenth and nineteenth centuries made interpreting largely unnecessary, that is until the Versailles peace conference when the significant role played by the monolingual Americans made interpreting by bilingual French military officers necessary. Early interpreters were either drawn from the military, the diplomatic service or from a small group of people who came from similar social backgrounds. Whereas the World War II Nuremberg war trials and technology brought about the development of simultaneous interpreting, and this was extended to international conferences and organisations like the United Nations, these developments occurred in an elite context and had very little impact on the major I/T developments in Australia (Ozolins, 1991).

Post-World War II Australia saw large-scale immigration to provide labour to build up Australia's industrial base and to develop large-scale infrastructure projects like the Snowy Mountains hydro-electric and irrigation scheme. However, Australia's immigration programme encouraged permanent settlement (Australia has never had a guest worker programme, although in recent years workers with certain needed skills may get temporary work visas), and migrants were taught English from their arrival in Australia and were expected to assimilate quickly into Australian life.

> Assimilationist rhetoric and policies were very powerful, and the general presumption that the migrant would soon find his niche in Australia, and adopt English, was long clung to, even when large numbers of NESB [non-English speaking background] migrants in the 1950's were clearly maintaining their culture and languages. (Ozolins, 1991: 16)

Interpreters, or at least individuals who interpreted, were unheard of and initially were drawn from whoever happened to be available at the time, often a relative or a fellow worker. However, with the large NESB intakes in the 1940s and 1950s, it became obvious there was a need for interpreting at major institutions (e.g. hospitals, courts, immigration centres, housing agencies) to serve an otherwise unmanageable clientele. The use of multilingual individuals was a relatively cost-effective measure and individuals found their language ability was a way out of the menial labour in which most migrants were engaged. These people formed the basis of government interpreting services while some private agencies also developed in the major capital cities in the 1950s to take up medical, legal and social interpreting.

> To say that these practitioners 'invented' interpreting is to point to both the innovative nature of the undertaking, and its largely unplanned and ad hoc institutionalization. (Ozolins, 1991: 17)

As Ozolins (1991: 19–21) points out, the way that Australian interpreting developed was markedly different in a number of respects in terms of technique and social context of interpreting compared to interpreting done elsewhere as most work occurred in three-cornered liaison interpreting, where the interpreter was physically present with the other two parties, not as an 'invisible' voice as in conference interpreting. He notes that this social context brought about different relationships between interpreters, their clients and the institutions they served in four ways:

(1) Interpreters were identified with the migrant population. Generally, White Australian institutions avoided responding to migrants for as long as possible; if avoidance failed, then an interpreter was brought in.

(2) Interpreters came largely from minority groups, and largely reflected the social class background of the migrant population. Even trained professionals with qualifications found the qualifications went unrecognised.

(3) Little distinction was made between trained interpreting and that provided by family, friends or domestic staff in institutions.

(4) As there were few guidelines as to what an interpreter should do, some worked as a medium of communication between parties while others saw themselves there primarily to assist clients.

The situation described here resulted in concerns only rarely being expressed over issues such as adequacy of service provision and standards. The ideology of assimilation that prevailed from the 1950s to the 1960s meant these problems were regarded as being merely temporary: soon the migrants will assimilate and learn English. By the mid–1960s however, concern for structural discrimination and migrant disadvantage began to be expressed, and it was becoming clearer that the language issue was a permanent one. (Ozolins, 1991: 21)

In 1973 as part of Australia's gradual reorientation to multiculturalism, the Emergency Telephone Interpreter Service was established to deal with emergency situations (e.g. police, medical) for the cost of a local call. Initially it was established in Sydney and Melbourne in eight languages, but the service quickly expanded the number of Centres, languages and types of situations dealt with. In 1974 it was renamed the Telephone Interpreter Service (TIS) and made a national service providing a referral and information service as well as interpreting. The service, based in the Department of Immigration and Multicultural Affairs, is unique in the world today as it provides both interpreting and information services.

TIS provides an example of how unplanned language planning activity within one sector of society can eventually create a situation where the economic and social pressure for a specific purpose language policy is officially recognised. It took several decades for TIS to be implemented during a period when Australians began to face the reality that they had become a multilingual and multicultural society.

Business Translation in North America

As we saw in Chapter 6, the globalisation of business has meant that language skills are increasingly important to its conduct.[4] As an example of the meso level language planning that should be occurring to service the needs of business and industry, let us examine the case of the Canadian utility company, Hydro-Québec [H-Q] which in 1994 published a 'request for a proposal' (both technical and fiscal) for equipment to protect their power systems. H-Q wished to purchase some unspecified number of units over a two to three year period. The request for a proposal was in two parts: (1) a specification of how the product was to perform (issued in French and English); and (2) blanket specifications for equipment to go into H-Q's sub-stations (issued in French only).

A US company, Schweitzer Engineering Laboratories [SEL],[5] chose to make a bid. As a first step, one of SEL's sales representatives translated the 40 page French blanket specifications into ten pages of English, but the English design specifications proved to be inaccurate due to faulty translation. SEL then paid a Montreal-based engineering firm a very substantial sum to translate the specifications into English. Simultaneously, SEL paid an external consultant (a native French-speaking high school French teacher) to translate the instruction manual that accompanies the final product (already written in English by SEL engineers), but this external translator did not know engineering or its terminology.

In the design process, it was necessary to create instructional computer strings – used to communicate from the computer to the operator. These strings had to be translated from English (the language conventionally used for such purposes by SEL) into French (the operating language of H-Q). In this process, all computer strings were sent to H-Q with a request that H-Q undertake the translation. This translation process included not only the actual computer strings, but also the language on the face of the equipment components (e.g. switch labels). The translation of the language on the face of the components was a limited and relatively easy task, since there are equivalents in French for the English terms (though the French equivalents sometimes occupied more physical space than the English terms, thus implicating a small design problem).[6] The translation of the computer strings was lengthy and complex; the strings were produced in English and then translated into French, one at a time. As the translations became available from H-Q, they were introduced into the electronic components. The translation rate slowed as the project progressed because H-Q personnel were involved in other work which took them off the task.

As the project progressed, more work was required on the instruction manual and SEL hired a second translator, a French-speaking PhD-level graduate student in Physics from Washington State University (located in the same city). He was able to correct many of the first translator's errors. Even after all this effort, when H-Q personnel came to SEL to test the product, the French-speaking testers found many spelling errors (especially involving the omission of diacritical marks), and many abbreviations that didn't make sense in French. When SEL sent the finished components to H-Q for testing there, the components were found to be technically superior, but H-Q personnel found more translation errors SEL had to correct. Furthermore, SEL was required to send engineers to H-Q to train all the French-speaking operators with the new equipment.

This project was worth around $750,000, and something like 1000 man-hours were consumed in the language based processes alone. Although SEL is regularly engaged in international distribution of its products, its limited capacity to meet foreign language specifications substantially reduced the profit margin on this contract. It is an interesting irony that the People's Republic of China is willing to accept components which 'speak' English and are labelled in English on their faces, while a Québec company is not. For the French in Québec, where French is felt to be under threat, language loyalty is an important issue, as languages only survive and prosper if they are used in important domains, such as work; whereas in China, Chinese is not under threat and getting the best equipment at the best price is the major consideration. This example illustrates how language issues can affect profit and productivity and indicates the need for appropriate linguistic pre-planning for business projects.

Language Policies in Australian Universities

Most of the discussion in this book has focused on what language policy and planning has accomplished and the problems and issues associated with that work. However, language policy and planning is applicable to a wide variety of specific purpose situations where it is not currently applied, or where it is only applied in a haphazard manner. To begin to think about how and where language policy and planning might be applied, it may be appropriate to complete this section with an example of the failure to use language policy and planning for specific purposes and some of its consequences, using a case with which many readers would be familiar, the university setting. While the following material takes as its focus the academy in Australia, many of the issues being raised are more universal.

In Australia many university staff still implicitly believe that a high school/secondary school education provides, or at least should provide, students with the language and literacy skills necessary to gain a tertiary degree, although some would also acknowledge that these skills must be developed and learned as part of tertiary study. While some staff may still yearn for the 'good old days' – only 30 or so years ago – when tertiary literacy *may* have been less of a problem, but when only 4 out of 10 students completed a secondary education and where the secondary education system had as its prime focus tertiary study, most would acknowledge that the current more broadly based provision is more equitable and better suited to the needs of a modern society.

During this same period, Australian society has also changed, becoming more multicultural, with a higher audio and visual orientation which has partially displaced the use of the written word, and with the increased availability of electronic communication via the Internet or on CD ROM. Thus, in Australia of the 1990s, even well-prepared students may not be prepared for the oral, written and electronic discourse rigours of tertiary life. Nor in fairness should they be; tertiary study, like other social activities, has its own language domains, jargon and discourse, and its own way of being a student which neophytes must learn to be a success at university and in the discipline(s) that they have chosen to study.

However, it is not only students' backgrounds and societal communication which have changed in the last 30 years. Universities themselves have significantly diversified their intake of students, both in terms of sheer numbers[7] and in terms of student backgrounds.[8] They also offer a wider range of programmes of study and choices of subjects within those programmes. It would seem self-evident that modern tertiary institutions, like other modern institutions, are actually more diverse and demanding in their requirements than they previously were, and this includes the requirement for a wider range of literacy skills. While universities have increased their support for students to help them cope with the new language, literacy and communication rigours which they must face, many students still fail to complete their degree work or take longer than necessary to do so. A national survey has revealed that university staff rate content knowledge as more important than language, literacy and communication skills, while discipline based professional and employing bodies rated communication skills as their highest priority for graduates.

This analysis suggests that the principal language problem in tertiary education is not declining literacy standards but rather is about meeting changed social, cultural and informational requirements and circumstances (e.g. Luke, 1992; Green et al., 1994). Since language, literacy and communication demands have changed, universities must re-examine their language related strategies to see if they are meeting current demands, and in particular whether past policies of individual programatic solutions to language problems might now be better conceived of as part of an overall language, literacy and communication strategy or policy. If there were clear formal language, literacy and communication policies in place, universities could more systematically meet student needs and would have mechanisms to meet the changing nature of tertiary language and literacy provision. As a result there would be efficiency gains in terms of time and money, but most importantly some of the current waste of effort and human potential would be avoided.

Baldauf (1996) has argued that language problems in tertiary institutions can be viewed from two general perspectives: (1) from a student equity perspective, with a focus on the needs and skills that individual students bring to the university situation; and (2) from an institutional discourse perspective, with a focus on those things that the university requires or has carriage of as part of the academic certification process. For each of these two perspectives, there are six major issues which a university may confront. Although these 12 issues in reality overlap in a number of ways, they form the basis of what a university language and literacy policy might contain.

Student equity perspective

The issue of ensuring equity in higher education, although not specifically related to language, literacy and communication needs, has been an Australian government priority for some time (universities get much of their funding from the Commonwealth government). Although the six equity groups listed below are not mutually exclusive (i.e. there are mature age Aboriginal students, blind NESB students, English mother-tongue overseas students, etc.), they do broadly represent university clientele. Also, there are many individual equity programmes already in place in universities, there is a need to locate such language focused solutions in a holistic language, literacy and communication policy framework which would more comprehensively meet students' needs, and which would better prepare students for their studies and the world of work beyond the university.

However, it is easy in discussing tertiary literacy in general and equity groups in particular to get caught up in a language problem mentality or to frame the language, literacy and communication issues just in terms of accommodation to the new university or subject specific cultures that are to be learned, rather than acknowledging the positive language, literacy and cultural contributions that today's diverse groups of students bring to the university. Many current programmes seem to be set up on a 'fix the problem' model, although particular individuals working in these programmes may operate from quite different perspectives. The advantage of a university language, literacy and communication policy approach to tertiary literacy would be that it would bring together the current disparate programs to create a strategy that would be more than the sum of its parts. A university policy could stress that language problems are not just issues for students, but for staff, and that there are not only problems to be addressed, but cross-cultural understandings and information to be gained. Ultimately, universities will be most successful in dealing with language, literacy and communication issues if these matters are defined consultatively and supported at the top ('top-down'), provided for through expert assistance where necessary, but contextualised across the university's curriculum by individual university staff, in consultation with students ('bottom-up').

A university *Student Equity Perspective* suggests the need for a tertiary language, literacy and communication policy and the requisite language services to meet the needs of:

- *Most secondary graduates.* For most tertiary students, going to university is a cross-cultural experience and many students need assistance to make both the general transition to tertiary life and the skills to deal with a whole new set of literacy requirements for which they are often at best poorly prepared. Jernudd (1994a) argues that such tertiary literacy skills must be taught in meaningful contexts.

- *Aboriginal and Torres Strait Islander (indigenous) students.* 'Students entering university through equity programs are often inexperienced in understanding the language of the disciplines they have chosen', Draisma *et al.* (1994: 39). As one mature age Aboriginal woman put it: 'I'd never seen an essay so when we were told we had to write one, I didn't have a clue' (McDonald, 1993: 5). 'For marginalised minorities, becoming competent in the literacy practices of the dominant society involves more work than it does for those students who come from backgrounds that more closely reflect world views, norms and values of the dominant literacy practices of the university' (McDonald, 1993: 13).

- *Mature age students.* Many mature age students returning to studies have not had the opportunity to finish secondary school and do not have the educational, conceptual or writing skills for tertiary study. To succeed, they need to be able to do more than discuss in class; they need to understand the culture, context and conventions of knowledge and write so as to participate in the powerful discourses which shape modern society. Such discourses can be taught.

- *Deaf and blind students.* These students are under-represented in tertiary programmes and need access to facilities and a coherent programme of services so that they can fully participate in university life.

- *Students from culturally and linguistically different backgrounds.* Fiore and Elasser (1988: 287) argue that:

   . . . students found themselves strangers in a strange world. A wide gulf stretched between the classroom curriculum and their own knowledge gained in the barrios of Albuquerque and the rural towns and pueblos of New Mexico. Confronted by a course that negated their culture, many failed to master the skills they sought. Others succeeded by developing a second skin. Leaving their own customs, habits and skins behind, they participated in school and in the world by adapting themselves to fit the existing order. Their acquisition of literacy left them not in control of the social context, but controlled by it.

- *Overseas students.* Overseas students are big business in Australia. At the 10 universities attracting the largest numbers of overseas students, average enrolments amount to 10.1% and enrolments have been steadily increasing. Many of these students have cultural and language needs which need to be met, if they are to succeed in their studies; and universities need to meet these needs if they want to continue to attract overseas students.

The provision of 'Freshman English' courses along the lines found in American universities may only appear to be a solution to the problems these students face. However, such courses often focus on the wrong set of skills – a literary literacy, not an academic literacy – and they tend to ignore the specific social and skill needs of the categories of students just enumerated. Many universities take more students than they can educate, whether for political (e.g. all students with a B average or better in high school must be accepted) or economic (e.g. funding is based on a per capita intake) reasons. While the rhetoric is about equity of entry, the actual goal of *de facto* language policies in place may be the weeding out of students on some language-based quota system rather than providing a focus on retention. This creates a lot of 'failures' among a group of people who have the ability to succeed.

These six student equity groups face many of the same general literacy problems, but these manifest themselves in different ways and from different perspectives. These groups also bring with them linguistic and cultural skills which are often under-valued by universities. Commentators on these equity issues have noted the similarities of needs and have suggested the wisdom of sharing insights gained from working with one group with the others. One way of ensuring that this occurs would be through a university-wide language policy which could provide more effective and coherent language and literacy planning, thereby improving opportunities for all students to succeed.

Institutional discourse perspective

To be successful in any organisation or field, one must learn the specific domains of discourse relevant to that field. At the tertiary level, a number of different discourses must be mastered, depending on the situation. For example, a first-year education student (in a concurrent four-year BEd) may not only have to learn the epistemology and citation rules for education, but to keep them differentiated from those of English, History and Psychology. Thus, the discourse to be learned is not only new, but often conflicting with others to be learned. Furthermore, much of this discourse knowledge is what Martin (1990) has referred to in the Aboriginal context as 'secret knowledge'. In general, lecturers do not teach much of their disciplinary discourse explicitly, or even point it out. Rather they assume such things are taught elsewhere or that it will be part of university's rites of passage (i.e. if you aren't smart enough to figure it out, you shouldn't be in a university). In addition, some of the groups mentioned in the previous section, relating to student services, may bring their own epistemology of language, which frames their views of textual authority and discourse argumentation, to the university setting (see e.g. Table 5.3 for traditional Aboriginal people).

An *Institutional Discourse Perspective* suggests the need for a university language, literacy and communication policy which would address:

- *Discipline specific literacy skills.* Every discipline has its own discourse and set of presentation rules (see, e.g. Baldauf & Jernudd, 1986 for cross-cultural psychology). It is clear from this work, and from evidence of journal editors, that many university researchers themselves do not really consider or understand the language use decisions of their disciplines, and are therefore unprepared to teach these skills to their students. As students usually study several disciplines, a haphazard approach leaves them uncertain of what literacy skills to apply.
- *The use of non-sexist (non-discriminatory) language.* While all universities in Australia have policies related to equal opportunity provision, Pauwels (1993, in press) argues that non-sexist language issues have not found their way more generally into language policy and students are often unclear what standards they are expected to meet.
- *The acquisition of literacy skills in a LOTE.* To what extent does a tertiary institution promote the study of languages and the concept of bi-literacy or multiliteracies in a world where language skills are increasingly becoming more important for business and communication.
- *Recognition of prior learning.* To what extent are advanced placement, credit for prior learning or credit for advanced language skills credited to university programmes. A language policy should not only try to fill the gaps, but should reward those with advanced language or literacy skills.
- *Computer-related literacy skills.* There is a growing expectation that all students will graduate with computer literacy skills. Does the university provide this training? Is it available to all students? Are there policies related to the access of programmes required for courses? Can students use on-line dictionaries, reference grammars or translation programmes in language courses? A university language and literacy policy should address issues such as these.
- *Electronic literacy and collaboration.* Computers and the Internet are giving individuals and groups of students the ability to co-author, edit and comment on other students' work, which is affecting the nature of the work produced and the rules for citation and plagiarism. Winkelmann (1995) suggests universities should address the need for electronic criteria in their assessment of language and literacy based work.

In general, the six institutional discourse perspectives do not as yet seem to have become university issues, but by their very nature seem to be left mainly to Faculties, Departments or even individual lecturers to handle. A university wide language and literacy policy would make for a more equitable administration of these policies and would help students to obtain more quickly and accurately the skills necessary for their discipline studies and ultimately for their professions.

Developing a university language policy

The idea of developing a university language policy seems to be a relatively recent one in Australia. Dines (1994) proposed the idea in a paper to the Australian Linguistics Society in 1993 when 'thinking aloud' about all the issues related to linguistics which had recently come across her desk as Academic Registrar at the University of Adelaide. She noted that:

> [a]s a policy maker I think it is folly to try to deal with a smorgasbord of issues which clearly are interrelated. What universities need is a way of bringing these issues together so that they can be systematically addressed within a cohesive framework and linguists are the people professionally equipped to do this. (p. 14)

She went on to argue that there is a need

> . . . to lobby for the development of language policies in your institutions. Every university needs a language policy which addresses language issues across the whole university in a coordinated and systematic way. It should not be just a language centre policy or a section of the Faculty of Arts' strategic plan. It needs to be a university wide language policy, embracing all the diverse issues which university senior management need to address. (p. 15)

Mühlhäusler (1995a) has also argued cogently for the inclusion of low candidature languages in any university language policy. In Australia at least, some universities are already beginning to think about language and literacy policies and a few have even made important progress in developing a comprehensive approach to language or literacy issues. However, what has been done to date does not amount to a coherent broadly based language *and* literacy *and* communication policy.

While one can argue the case for a language, literacy and communication policy, this language problem is, of course, embedded in a much deeper set of issues. It is not 'merely' a question of dealing with literacy issues or even of cross-cultural issues, but with all the issues that implicate the whole cultural ambience of the university. Regardless of language background, people from cultures of poverty see the world differently (see, e.g. Gee, 1992; Heath, 1983). This problem implicates modes of dress, modes of social discourse, attitudes toward information, skills involved in identifying and locating material, personal hygiene, hair styles, etc. Just as a 'language-across-the curriculum course' or a 'foreign students centre' or an 'Aboriginal studies centre' does not deal with the problems universities face, a language policy, as desirable as it is, can be a snare and a delusion because, by itself, it does not address the fundamental issues and may even obscure them because it looks like a solution.

Thus, there is a need to see all of these issues as part of a world view which informs the university's whole outlook on students and which would then provide a general framework for the successful implementation of a language, literacy and communication policy.

Summary

In this chapter we have examined five instances of specific purpose language planning: planning for science and technology in the broadest sense, the role that academies and similar bodies play in terminological and lexical development, corporate language issues related to translation in one North American case, the development of the telephone interpreting and translating service in Australia, and the need to develop language policies in Australian universities. Much specific purpose language planning, with the exception of language academies, is meso level planning and as a consequence much of it has been left unplanned. There are opportunities for languages planners to work at this level to improve the effectiveness of language related solutions currently arrived at by trial and error methods.

Notes

1. On 27 July 1995 Kaplan received an invitation to attend the *Second International 'Transferre necesse est . . .' Conference on Current Trends in Studies of Translating and Interpreting*, in Budapest, organised by Kinga Klaudy, President of the Organising Committee, in association with the Training Centre for Translators and Interpreters, Faculty of Humanities, Eötvös Loránd University and the Translation Committee of the Hungarian Academy of Sciences. The invitation states specifically:

   > Plenary lectures will be in **English**, sectional lectures and posters can be presented in **English**, **German**, **French** and **Russian** (preferably with a résumé in **English**). Please take note that no interpreting services will be provided . . . .

   This example is offered as additional recent evidence of the extensive use of English in various academic activities, even in countries in which English is at best a foreign language.

2. The following editorial from 7 July 1995 *La Opinion*, the premier Spanish language newspaper in Los Angeles illustrates this point.

   La revolución del idioma en el suroeste de Estados Unidos

   Por José Armas

   Hoy, mi tema es acerca de . . . bueno . . . acerca de la revolución. Esta revolución ha venido ocurriendo en nuestras propias narices y oídos, aquí en el suroeste de Estados Unidos. Me di cuenta de ello cuando mi amigo, el doctor Bob Gish, administrador de una prestigiosa universidad de la costa occidental, termina una carta dirigida a mí, diciendo: 'Hasta *soon*'. Eso me hizo despertar sobre la insurrección que viene sucediendo con nuestro idioma, no sólo entre los latinos, sino en toda la cultura angloamericana y del otro lado de la frontera, en México. El cambio se está acelerando a velocidad alarmante. Esto va mucho más allá del *slang* (lenguaje callejero) y del idioma popular. Ahora esto es legítimo. La cultura fronteriza ha sido siempre algo híbrida en valores, costumbres, alimentos, idioma, música y arquitectura. El nuevo idioma está siendo legitimizado por muchos escritores contemporáneos y por las personalidades de la radio en español que han tomado el idioma diario de la gente y adoptado este singular formato bilingüe. Para el enfado de muchos académicos, maestros de español y nacionalistas culturales que sostienen que eso no es nada más que la bastardización de ambos idiomas que hará fracasar nuestra cultura, su uso y aceptación están extendiéndose a pasos agigantados. Atraviesan muchas fronteras geográficas, sociales y culturales. Ya no se trata más de un asunto de idioma adoptado por la gente. Está más allá de ser un dilema social. Jesse Quintana es mexicano; su esposa Ileana es latina nacida en Estados Unidos. Ellos tienen tres niños que son completamente bilingües. Ileana insiste que en su casa se hablen ambos idiomas correctamente. 'Cuando escucho las palabras *mapiar, cora, parkiar, lackiar, craquer* (equivalentes en español de trapear, moneda de 25 centavos, estacionarse, cerrar con llave, galletitas) eso rechina en mis oídos', dice ella. Puede ser que rechine en muchos oídos, pero no hay modo de poner un alto a la cultura que rueda como una aplanadora.

La estación de radio KABQ, de Albuquerque, ha sido precursora de esta transción que se legitima rápidamente. Han pasado cuatro años desde que su propietario, Ed Gómez, cambió a un formato completamente bilingüe. Los anunciadores, locutores de noticias y editoriales combinan palabras, frases y oraciones en español e inglés. En su discurso no traducen; al azar cambian del inglés al español. Gómes, que habla inglés y español perfectamente, precisa que este lenguaje ha sido usado siempre, especialmente a lo largo de la frontera. Su formato ha captado una audiencia más joven, cuyo lenguaje híbrido está más a tono con el español contemporáneo. El dice que 'aun algunos angloamericanos que problemente no son tan versados en español, escuchan porque pueden seguir la conversación'. Nuestro inglés, desde luego, guarda poca semejanza con el británico. Es un mestizaje de alemán, francés y español. Los británicos resoplan desdeñosamente por nuestra pronunciación de lo que ahora en Estados Unidos pasa por lenguaje apropiado. Y el modo de hablar de ellos nos divierte a nosotros. El inglés durante casi 200 años se ha apropiado de palabras españolas para su léxico. Algunas de las palabras más comunes incluyen el dialecto del *cowboy* (vaquero). Tan arraigadas se hallan estas palabras españolas en nuestra sociedad de cada día, que algunos angloamericanos argumentan que no son palabras españolas del todo; se refeiren a palabras tales como rodeo, hombre, coyote, corral, laso. El mestizaje del idioma ha estado efectuándose también en México durante varios años: '*okay*, gracias, es un refrán común de los dependientes y camareros. Ciertas palabras son versiones estropeadas de las originales de ambos lados de la forntera. Los fanáticos mecicanos del beisbol hablan con entusiasmo del *jonrón* que permitió ganar el juego. Aquí, la palabra inglesa *car* se convierte en carro y los frenos (*brakes*) se convierten en *brekas*. Ya se ha llegado mucho más allá de lo correcto o incorrecto. Se ha convertodo en realidad. Mi amigo Bob prometió, a su regreso a Albuquerque, invitarme a desayunar '*bagels* y huevos rancheros', pero eso queda para otro relato. Como dice el escritor Ed Chávez, de Nuevo México: 'Bueno, *bye*'.

3. The material in this section is based on the work of Ozolins (1991, 1993).
4. Language for business is often viewed as a customer communication skill, but Holden (1990) also notes its strategic importance. For example, Japanese businesses spend a lot of money on language learning, but it is not necessarily done to enhance customer communication, but rather to enhance the efficiency of their marketing intelligence.
5. SEL ' . . . exists to make power safer, more reliable, and more economical. SEL serves the electric power industry world wide through the design, manufacture, supply and support of products and services for systems protection, control, and monitoring.' [Corporate Brochure]
6. H-Q publishes its own French/English technical dictionary, which helped to some extent.
7. In 1939 there were about 14,000 students, and in 1995 there were around 600,000. The proportion of the 17–22-year-old age cohort in undergraduate university programmes rose from 3.75% in 1955 to 16% in 1975 to about 30% in 1995 (Postile, 1995: 1).
8. It has been estimated that students whose native language is not English now comprise up to 25% of the university population in some states. At least one-third of these are from overseas, largely from the Asian region. Most of them have considerable bilingual skills and bring rich linguistic potentialities to what they study. But not only do Australian universities often fail to draw creatively on those resources to enhance the scope for cultural exchanges across the whole learning community, they also often fail to provide adequate support – inside or outside the classroom – for students whose own first-language literacy practices differ significantly from those that are normative in Australian academic settings (Reid, 1995: 4).

Part 4: Towards a Theory of Language Planning

Having examined practice – how language planning is done, by whom, to whom and for what ends – both from a general perspective and in the context of specific examples, this section examines key elements and problems that are needed to underpin the development of a theory of language planning. Using this information an ecological model for language planning is then described that suggests the directions in which the discipline may be going.

In Chapter 10, eight key elements or variables are discussed which impact on the language situation and therefore language planning for a language ecology. These constructs include language death, language survival, language change, language revival, language shift and language spread, language amalgamation, language contact and pidgin and creole development and literacy development. These language change elements affect languages in different ways, leading to language problems which language planners may then need to address.

In Chapter 11, some key issues are discussed which affect language planning problems, and a description is given of the manner in which key elements and issues might work together in a linguistic eco-system, as a way of moving toward a theory of language planning.

10 Conceptualising Language Planning: Key Elements

Introduction

Language planning is often perceived as some sort of monolithic activity, designed specifically to manage one particular kind of linguistic modification in a community at a particular moment in time. It has tended to assume the modification of *one* language only and has largely ignored the interaction of multiple languages in a community and multiple non-linguistic factors – that is, the total *ecology* of the linguistic environment. This practice may be a direct outgrowth of the one nation/one language fallacy. Wherever its origins lie, it is not a productive way of looking at language planning. Rather, the language planning activity must be perceived as implicating a wide range of languages and of modifications occurring simultaneously over the mix of languages in the environment, some of which may constitute the motivation for an attempt at planned change while some may be dragged along willy-nilly as an outcome of an attempt at planned change in a given sector. Language planning must recognise as well that language modification may not be susceptible to containment within a particular nation-state or other entity that may be isolated for the purposes of discussion but which in truth always remains embedded in a larger context (e.g. an individual hospital may attempt a modification to its practices without realising that such a modification will impact on all agencies, organisations and individuals that serve that hospital as well as the community in which the hospital is embedded and the patients it serves). Rather, the language plan may cause a ripple effect in proximate communities, nation-states, across a region (or in other smaller or larger entities).

The 1994 French *'loi Toubon'*[1](see Anonymous, 1994b) is precisely a case in point, since neither M. Jacques Toubon, the Minister of Culture and *Francophonie* of the Balladur government (who proposed the initial bill), nor the legislature which ultimately enacted the law, understood what the prescriptive aspects of the *loi Toubon* would mean to the *Francophonie* movement outside of France, in Québec for example. Figure 10.1 is an attempt to illustrate the problem; in this illustration, there is one national/official language, one religious language which is different from the national language, and eight minority languages (one of which may be a non-standard variety of the official language). This is a rather limited example; as noted earlier, some polities contain hundreds of minority

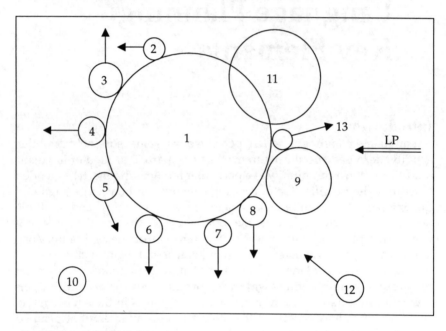

1. National/Official Language
2. minority language
3. minority language
4. minority language
5. minority language
6. minority language
7. minority language
8. minority language
9. Neighbouring language (another policy)
10. Classical/historial languages
11. Religious language
12. Language revival in progress
13. minority language

Language Planning
Effort

Figure 10.1 A schematic view of a national language planning situation

languages. In the figure, the size of the circle is intended to suggest the size of the language in terms of the number of its speakers. There is also a proximate language – i.e. a language spoken in a neighbouring polity – which may have some influence on the geographically nearest minority language(s). In addition, the illustration contains a set of classical languages (shown as an isolate, since dead languages are not much affected by the living languages). Finally, also shown as an isolate, is a representation of a language revival effort. The arrows deriving from each of the circles suggest the direction of change occurring in the minority language. In the illustration, all the minority languages are shown as diverging from the official language, though that is not necessarily the natural case. Language planning is shown as a double arrow entering from the right. The effect may be targeted at only one of the languages, but as the figure suggests, everything in the environment will be affected to some degree by the language planning effort.

Indeed if the language is a 'large' or *pluricentric* one, the ripple effect may be worldwide. Thus, the modification of French use of accents for certain words in France will not only have a ripple effect in Belgium, Britain, Germany, Spain and Switzerland, but in Francophone Africa, French Polynesia, and French speaking Canada, and eventually in all the polities in which French is taught as a foreign language as well. The fact is that language planning implicates not merely grammatical, lexical or phonological change (corpus planning) in one language, but also attitudinal change and values change as well – not to mention some potentially complex economic and political changes (status planning). Additionally – the point of the illustration – the planning activity *can not* be limited to one language; it will affect all the languages in the environment. Each language has its own ecology of support and relationships to other languages.

Variables in Language Planning

Therefore, more realistically, language planning may invoke any or all of the following constructs simultaneously (i.e. any given language in the environment may be undergoing several modifications at any given time, and all of the languages in a given environment may be undergoing modification at the same given time), each potentially impacting on a different language or variety present in the planning environment (which in turn may be very large):

- language death;
- language survival;
- language change;
- language revival;
- language shift and language spread;

- language amalgamation;
- language contact and pidgin and creole development;
- literacy development.

Because language planning implicates such a wide range of linguistic phenomena, any underlying theory that attempts to explain or predict events related to language planning must also be fairly broad. It is the intent of this chapter to suggest the key elements needed to underpin a theoretical model. In order to do that, it is necessary to examine each of the constructs previously listed to try to isolate from each what is common to all.

Language Death[2]

Languages die because they no longer have a viable function. The loss of function can be attributed to a number of causes, singly or in concert, including:

- the subtle introduction of another language which, for whatever reason, gradually takes over some (or all) societal functions (e.g. the introduction into a society of economic and social entities conducting important activities in another language – e.g. other-language speaking corporations setting up business in colonial areas or any religious body setting up missionary activities in a colonial area; see Masagara, 1991);
- the disappearance, for whatever reason, of the population speaking some particular language – e.g. the genocidal practices of some governments or groups which are intended literally to exterminate a community – the extermination of whole tribes of Aboriginal people in Australia (Dixon, 1989), the 'ethnic cleansing' in the 1990s in the component parts of Yugoslavia, the current activities of the Iraqi government with respect to the Kurdish population, the 'final solution' in Nazi occupied Europe during the 1930s and 1940s, or the massacre of all male Guamanians by the Spanish (Day, 1985). Also the less overt, but equally invasive efforts at linguacide in a variety of other places – e.g. the (sometimes implicit) policies implemented in the case of Native American people in North America, Aboriginal people in Australia, Aboriginal people in Taiwan and Japan, Maori people in New Zealand, Andean people in Latin America or Amazonian people in Brazil;
- the forceful imposition of a power language on a population such that certain functions *must* be conducted in the imposed language (e.g. the imposition of business, religious and governmental structures on indigenous peoples and immigrants in Australia, Canada, the United States (Tollefson, 1988), etc.; see, e.g. Touchstone *et al.*, (1995) for

effects on immigrants, recent work on Eskimo languages in Alaska for effects on indigenous people). (Often, all three of these forces may co-occur.)

In sum, language death occurs when at least the three following conditions pertain:

(1) Parents are reluctant or unable to pass on a language to their children.
(2) The language ceases to serve key communicative functions (registers) in the community.
(3) The community of speakers is not stable and/or expanding, but rather is unstable and/or contracting.

Parental roles
The inability of parents to pass on a language to their children may be the result of a variety of situations. Communities have been observed, for example, in which the adult population has decided that the young of the community have fallen so far away from the ways of the people that they do not deserve to learn the language (and heritage) of the people. Other communities hold the view that only 'full-blooded' members of the community are entitled to learn the language. Thus, as the maintenance of a viable gene pool in the potentially interbreeding population requires the entry of aliens into the community, no attempt is made to teach the language to the offspring of mixed partners. In situations in which the parents are first-language speakers of different languages, the parents may decide to pass on only one of the languages in the set (often the father's language) on the mistaken assumption that having to learn two (or more) languages will be confusing to the offspring. Thus, one of the languages ceases to function – a condition common in extremely multilingual situations (e.g. Cameroon – Robinson, 1993) or in some migrant situations. In other conditions accompanying migration, parents may decide that it is in the best interests of their offspring to learn only the language of the new community, and therefore they may actively prevent the learning of the language(s) of either or both migrant parents.[3] Conditions co-occurring with a military occupation or with the development of a colonial administration may inhibit the transmission of the indigenous language (on pain of death) and promote the language of the occupier (as has happened in the course of the Japanese occupation of Taiwan during World War II or within the Soviet Union in Belarussia and Ukraine under Communism, or as happened virtually all over Francophone Africa at the end of the nineteenth century). In sum, any activity that directly inhibits the transmission of parental language to the offspring contributes to the death of the parental language(s).

Language registers

Under some conditions of language contact, the language of the more powerful group gradually supersedes the language of the indigenous community in certain registers. An interesting illustration occurred in the gradual spread of Protestantism in the Celtic areas of Britain in the eighteenth and nineteenth centuries. As monolingual English-speaking clergy entered the communities and took control of religious practices in the 'established Church', English gradually replaced the Celtic languages of Scotland, Ireland, and Wales (Withers, 1988). But religious practice extends into a variety of societal functions – e.g. marriage, baptism, funeral rights, etc., as well as involving other more strictly ceremonial functions such as collective worship, prayer, etc. – and as these registers are taken over by the alien language, gradually the pertinent registers in the indigenous language are lost. Religion is not the only culprit in this context; employers at every level are major contributors, as has been demonstrated in French Canada with the expansion of English in the commercial sector (Daoust, 1991) prior to the passage of extensive language-protective legislation in the second half of the twentieth century. Once register replacement begins to occur, it tends to snowball, gradually subsuming greater and greater numbers of registers.

Speaker loss

Rapid decreases in the numbers of speakers of an indigenous language can, obviously, contribute to language death. In situations in Australia, Canada, Mexico and the United States, as colonising populations inadvertently – and sometimes deliberately – introduced into indigenous populations destructive diseases against which the indigenous population had no defences, and as colonising communities introduced alien social practices (e.g. use of alcohol), there were dramatic collapses in the indigenous populations. If, in addition, the indigenous population is inhibited from interbreeding with the newer power-holding population (or if interbreeding occurs but the offspring constitute a marginalised population acceptable on neither side), these decreases can be devastating to the community. Benton (1981) has, in his detailed study of the Maori of New Zealand, documented the factors involved in the decrease and general assimilation of the Maori population and the effects of that decrease/assimilation on the gradual demise of Maori as a viable language.

Language survival

The conditions for language survival are exactly the opposite of the conditions for language death, that is:

(1) Parents must be willing and able to transmit the language to their offspring and must actually do so.

(2) No condition may exist which will cause a more powerful language (H variety) to be imposed on a less powerful one (L variety), and functional registers must be retained.
(3) The community of speakers must be vibrant, stable, or increasing.

There are many examples of situations in which such a set of conditions exists; if one looks at the emergence of most of the nation-states of Europe, for example, one can observe an equation of the nation-state with a dominant monolingualism – i.e. one nation, one language. The condition requires support for the language from the highest levels of the social structure and of government – i.e. in oligarchies, for example, the ruling elite should be native speakers of the national language and so should the clergy. The condition also requires the emergence, under planned or unplanned circumstances, of a standard high prestige variety (H variety) – i.e. the language of the capital city becomes the language of the state (as was historically the case in Britain when London English became the standard, and as is now the case in France when Parisian French has become the world standard, or as is now the case in Japan where Tokyo Japanese is becoming the accepted standard). While parents may originate from any geographic or economic sector and may speak any variety, they must accept the recognised standard as having high prestige, and they must pass it along intergenerationally without questioning. The church, the business sector, the military, must contribute to the stability of the population and to the stability of the language (i.e. if the military constitutes a different language community, as in Angola in the 1980s, the standard is undermined and its survival cannot be assured). In the case of small languages, Winter (1993) has argued that motivation plays an all important role in their survival. If individuals are motivated to use the language, to pass it on to their children, to develop an active community of speakers within which the language is used, and the language is not unduly pressured by a high variety or a dominant external language, then small languages can and will survive.

As we saw in Chapter 7, the survival of minority languages depends, at least in part, on majority or high variety language group support. Skutnabb-Kangas & Phillipson (1994) argue very strongly that if there is to be a reversal of language shift (Fishman, 1991), and small languages are to survive, then support for them must be active, not merely *laissez-faire*. In the south-western part of the United States for example, Spanish is not an endangered language (cf. Hernández-Chávez, 1988, 1994). However, conservative groups, who are concerned about Spanish as a possible threat to English, are calling attention to the higher birth rate among the Hispanic population compared to the Anglo population. This growth in the Spanish-speaking population is seen as increasing the supposed threat to English language dominance. Rhetoric of this nature can undermine community support for minority languages and hamper their survival.

Language change

Language change may be said to be of two distinctly different types. One type of change is the sort codified, for the Indo-European languages, in Grimm's and Verner's laws, and for the Germanic sub-family in the Great Germanic Vowel Shift; linguistic processes begun in the distant past and continuing in the contemporary members of the Indo-European language family and the Germanic sub-family. Obviously, language planning activities must take account of this type of change, recognising the forces at work and incorporating such changes in the long-term planning programme. A second type of change, however, is the result of language contact. Indeed, it implicates a great deal more than language modification. Each time a new technology is brought into contact with a society and accepted by that society, this second type of language change occurs.

This second type can best be examined in a long historical context. For purposes of illustration, it can be assumed that, at some point, some early human societies had, perhaps, managed a hunting technology involving running up to the intended game and hitting it with a rock or a stick, or hitting it from a short distance with a thrown rock (as in a simple sling). When societies having such a technology came in contact with some society that had developed the technological innovation of the thrusting spear, they adopted it as more efficient, and along with the technology, they accepted a terminological system accompanying the new technological instrument as well as a new values configuration, a new social structure, and a number of other matters that came along with that technology (e.g. the individual skilled in running and hitting, or in stone throwing, was not necessarily the one skilled in thrusting, and so a new hierarchical social structure may have arisen). The case was repeated when the throwing spear and – later – the spear-thrower was introduced, when the throwing spear was replaced by the bow and arrow, when the bow and arrow was replaced by gun-powder technology. These weapons' technologies were applicable not only in hunting but in warfare as well, and as a consequence these technologies were shadowed by the parallel development of protective or defensive technologies – the adaptation of various types of body armour, for example, to defend against the stone axe, the chipped-flint spear, the bronze sword, the iron arrow (e.g. the Battle of Agincourt, 1415, is an illustration of the clash of two technologies), and the steel gun.

As each technology spread, by contact, from one community to another, the adopting community accepted not only the technological implement, but also the value system and the modified social structure accompanying that technological innovation. These new value systems changed the structure of the accepting society, nominated new sorts of leadership skills, and eventually changed the structure of time allocation in that society (that is, as hunting technologies became more efficient, hunting required a smaller portion of available time, and other activities could be introduced, or specialisation might develop). Technological change, of course, applies across all social functions and is not limited to hunting or warfare; e.g. fire, the wheel, written language. By the same token, technological change impacts language, at least in the sense of introducing new lexicon; but values change is likely to implicate much more than the lexicon.

As the spread of technology has increased in frequency and in scope over time, the number of cultural and linguistic innovations each community has had to accommodate has also increased.[4] Thus, for example, as Japanese speakers adopted the game technology of baseball, their society adopted as well the lexicon of baseball, the cultural phenomenon of competitive professional team sports, and the social phenomenon of the stadium, of the 'star' athlete, of the media broadcast, and of the 'big game' (see, e.g. the introduction of American style football in Europe in the 1990s, or the worldwide popularity of 'soccer', or the acceptance of 'cricket' across the former British Empire). The type of language change accompanying technological innovation is more rapid and more pervasive than the first kind of change, and modernising societies have undergone phenomenal technological and language change in the past 50 years in everything from science to popular music. (See Chapter 8, Code Borrowing/Switching (p. 232ff.) for a more extended discussion of these issues.)

To some extent, this second type of language change can be more readily controlled and planned. The various language academies across the world have been moderately successful in planning this sort of language change; the Japanese government – and therefore the Japanese language academy (*Kokugo Chosa Linkai* [National Language Research Council, established in 1902]) – for example, have consciously identified science areas in which they wished to pursue development and have intentionally encouraged the growth in borrowed or created lexicon in the chosen areas.[5] The negative version of this activity is commonly much less successful; that is, the attempts by various language academies to prevent the incursion of undesirable technological change and the accompanying lexical items into a language has generally been unsuccessful, as has been demonstrated most evidently by the French Academy but also and equally by the Mexican Academy, both trying to resist the incursions of English language and culture (e.g. see the current debates in France over the existence of EuroDisneyland).

The peculiar irony of the situation of the New Zealand Maori people will be discussed in greater detail below under the heading 'Language revival', but it is worth mentioning it here in passing; the Maori have adopted not only Christianity and the lexicon of Christianity but the accompanying value system, which is at odds with traditional Maori values. But there was, for most of modern Maori history, no Maori language academy, and the influx of this particular language modification was neither planned nor resisted. On the contrary, the wholesale adoption of Christianity, of its value system, and of its lexicon has contributed to the gradual weakening of Maori language and culture and the gradual increase of the power of English in the Maori community.

The situation in Samoa was similar to that of the New Zealand Maori with regard to early Christian contact, but different in the sustained nature of European contact and settlement. Faced with only limited missionary contact, and no European settlement, in the mid-1800s Samoans not only accepted Christianity, but took it over and effectively integrated it into their chiefly social system, developing *faife'au* (pastors') schools to teach Samoan and 'the word' using the Samoan language Bible as the authoratitive language source (Baldauf, 1990a). With Samoans in control of the social and linguistic change, the Samoan language and culture was modified, but not disrupted. It was only with the coming of educational television in 1961 that Samoans were firmly confronted by English and language change over which they had no control (Baldauf, 1981; Huebner, 1986, 1989; Schramm *et al.*, 1981).

Language revival

Successful language revival implies a reversal of all the forces discussed under the heading of *language death*. It is again instructive to look at the situation of the Maori people of New Zealand and their collective attempt to revive the Maori language. Under the present circumstances, given the fact that there are virtually no monolingual speakers of Maori language left, the intergenerational gap has increased; that is, a whole generation has been skipped in language transmission – the best that can now be hoped for is a third generation (or more than one subsequent generation) of more-or-less fluent *second-language* speakers of Maori. While such individuals may be able to use Maori in some limited or reduced number of registers, it is likely that the things to be discussed in Maori will be, at least in part, and perhaps to a significant degree, non-Maori. Even for these proficient second-language speakers of Maori, many important registers will function largely in English, not in Maori (or Maori will constitute a second, weaker, option for the discussion of some registers). Furthermore, there is a substantial danger that Maori is already becoming essentially a ritual language, used in that isolated and restricted segment of Maori life in which things Maori can be appropriately discussed. At the same time it must be noted that the inventory of things Maori has been substantially reduced by virtue of the fact that many registers have already been fully taken over by English and by virtue of gradual values shift resulting from the pressure of a large and powerful alien community.

Of course, Maori is already used by non-Maori New Zealanders in ceremonial public functions; most public meetings in New Zealand begin with a Maori greeting/prayer, even though a significant proportion of non-Maoris present at such a meeting do not understand what is being said. Maori is also quite widely used in official signage, and the identification of most government-bureaucracy structures occurs bilingually. There is even an attempt by the New Zealand Geographic Society to produce bilingual maps, showing both English and Maori place names; but this activity is at best problematic because Maori place names may have been lost over time, may be only proximate to the actual contemporary site where they exist, or may not be agreed upon by various *Iwi* (tribal groups) with overlapping territories (so that there may be several Maori names for the same place in the absence of a rational method for choosing among the options).

But Maori is not represented in some more salient functions: it is not available in New Zealand's postage, in its currency, in the codified law of the land, in official documents like passports; it may be used in the courts, but only if given ample prior notice, and the courts are not obliged to keep records in Maori nor are the presiding justices or the participating attorneys required to respond in Maori. It may generally not be used in university studies (except, obviously, in Maori studies); that is, in general, one may not submit tertiary examination papers in Maori (or for that matter in any other language, unless that language is the subject of instruction). It is not used in public transportation; it is not used by the police; it is not required for employment in the civil service, and it is not used in basic identificational functions – that is, in local street and road names, in building names, in addresses, etc. In sum, unless Maori finds a place in a variety of public registers, it is not likely to enjoy genuine revival.

There are also important economic issues to be considered. As the population of minority language speakers decreases, it becomes less economically viable to support the language, because textbooks, for example, must be produced for decreasing numbers of learners, because trained teachers of the language are harder to find, or because the minority population may represent such a small segment of the total population (as in the case of Tokelauan in New Zealand) that it becomes difficult to justify the expenditure of public funds on its maintenance. (See Chapter 6, New Zealand: The Economically Driven Plan (pp. 180ff.) for a more extended discussion of these issues.) While the economic issues are pertinent to the Maori situation, they are even more pertinent to some of the other Polynesian languages spoken in New Zealand – e.g. Tokelauan is spoken by only a few thousand people in the world, roughly half of them resident in New Zealand, half in the Tokelaus – and to some of the Aboriginal languages of Australia (few of which exceed 2000 speakers), to some of the Native American languages of North America, and to languages like Ainu in Japan or the Aboriginal languages of Taiwan and the Philippines.

Educational revival

While languages may be taught entirely through the educational system (as opposed to being transmitted through families/communities), there are a number of variables not accounted for through this mechanism. It is obvious that not everyone goes to school, and that not everyone goes to school at the same time. It is predictable that school learning is characterised by a bell-shaped curve of achievement; that is, not everyone acquires proficiency to the same degree or in the same amount of time of exposure. It is also the case that schooled proficiency may be essentially unrelated to any sort of real communicative proficiency; that is, languages learned in school tend to be too formal, too limited in practical registers (i.e. too 'literary'),[6] with relatively little accommodation to real communicative needs, often substantially ignoring pragmatic features entirely. In fact, it is probable that the education system is not, by itself, a very efficient means for language revival, since at best it takes a number of generations before the language can become pervasive – be disseminated through a potential community of speakers – since schools do not ordinarily reach adults, since the proficiency achievable in school is limited (because the time of exposure is severely curtailed), and since some portion of the school population is likely to be unmotivated to learn in any case.

Economic revival

In the economic sphere, however, the revival problem may be even more severe. Young adults are drawn away from the base community by both social and economic pressures. Intermarriage with dominant-language individuals inevitably draws away some number of young adults. But economic pressures may be even more extreme. To the extent that work availability draws individuals away from the base community as they seek economic opportunities outside of the geographic sphere and, to the extent that such withdrawal from the base community may become permanent (either through intermarriage or through the continuing lack of employment opportunity in the base community's geographic sphere), the next two generations of speakers may be depleted (that is, both the young adults who have left and their offspring will be missing from the language community's active population). Further, as dominant-language based business and industry permeates the minority community's geographic zone, employment even within that geographic zone becomes modified by the use of the language of the employer rather than that of the employee in the working environment.

In the migration situation, a similar phenomenon may be observed. In many instances, there is a primary migrant – an individual who has made the conscious decision to migrate. Such an individual often actively seeks to assimilate; that individual seeks employment, through employment is thrown into an environment in which the dominant language is spoken (or at least an environment so linguistically heterogeneous that the dominant language has to be used as the only available common language; see Clyne 1994), and is further drawn into social contexts beyond work where the dominant language is used. But behind each such primary migrant there may stand a comet's-tail full of other individuals holding very different attitudes toward the language and culture of the new community and having very different access opportunities. (1) A wife, for example, may stay at home, living in an ethnic community in which the first language is sufficient for all practical purposes; she may mix largely with other women living under similar linguistic constraints; (2) children born before migration will, through the educational system, be gradually assimilated; but (3) children born after migration will be assimilated by definition; (4) other adults (e.g. parents, aunts and uncles, in-laws or siblings) in the comet's-tail may become isolated or assimilated depending upon age, economic circumstances, or relative personal commitment to entry into the new community. Thus, a migrant population may not be perceived as homogeneous, because such a population represents a variety of orientations to the country of origin, to the new country, and to the question of language(s). It is likely that, over two or three generations, the first language of the parents will become attenuated and the dominant language of the matrix community will become the dominant language of the embedded community except in instances where radical difference in race or religion forces the minority community to cohere and consequently to remain collectively marginalised and isolated.

Ethnic revival

Thus, successful language revival depends not only on the availability of a large pool of speakers of the language being revived, not only on the willingness of those speakers to pass the language on intergenerationally, but on the availability of opportunities to use the language in a large number of registers and on the availability of economic opportunity in the language being revived. These conditions are not likely to coexist, particularly since the last may not be economically viable. Language revival is extremely difficult; various attempts at language revival have been unsuccessful, and only rare cases of successful revival can be drawn upon. The revival of the Navajo language is a case in point, but this revival was accomplished within a very tightly structured community which was stable (in fact, expanding), within which there was a high degree of intergenerational communication and co-operation, and the revival occurred in an environment in which ethnic pride was re-emerging, thus providing higher than normal motivation for language learning.

The attempt to revive Irish is, on the other hand, largely illustrative of failure. Although the Irish population is significantly united by religious preference and by ethnicity, the population is dispersed over a relatively large area, the number of first-language speakers has been depleted over more than a century (partly by out-migration), and many registers have been entirely captured by English. Even popular appeals to use Irish had to be promulgated in English. The fact that there is a readily recognisable dialect of Irish English as an alternative marker of identity is also a problem for Gaelic (Hindley, 1990). There are a number of other extremely interesting cases including those related to Hebrew in Israel, Basque in Spain, Catalan in Spain, French in Québec, Welsh in Wales, Scots Gaelic in Scotland and Mohawk in New York State and in Canada (see Appendix for relevant references by national situation).

Language transformation

However, a complex problem lies in the way in which language revival is conceived (Bentahila & Davies, 1993). The object of revival movements is past-oriented, that is the intent is to revive the language as it was, or to maintain the *status quo*. But successful modernising languages, like English, German, Swedish or Japanese, are in a constant state of change, so language revival is a highly unrealistic expectation because the language as it was is perhaps no longer viable. Moreover, that language has undoubtedly already undergone transformations in lexicon (i.e. has generated, or would need to generate, terminology to deal with new technologies like electronic media), in phonology (i.e. some bilingual speakers will bring to the language phonological characteristics from the other language partner in their repertoire), and perhaps in syntax (i.e. new technologies may require new syntactic structures). Furthermore, interlanguage contact may introduce new genres of discourse, new pragmatic structures – in sum, new ways of communicating. The language available for revitalisation is not the language as it was. To return to the case of Maori, the second-language Maori spoken by the new generations of Maori speakers is the only available Maori to be revived. Thus, modern Maori, if revival is successful, will be and must be a transformed Maori – one able to meet communication demands in a variety of new domains.

Language shift and language spread

The term *language shift* potentially implies a number of different situations. Fishman (1991b), for example, means by this term:

> . . . speech communities whose native languages are threatened because their intergenerational continuity is progressing negatively, with fewer and fewer users (speakers, readers, writers and even understanders) or uses every generation. (1991: 1)

In Fishman's sense, a language exposed to shift is threatened. The term is used here in a slightly different sense. All languages shift at various times in their histories, and a shift is not necessarily threatening to the continued existence of a language. There may be a great variety of causes for shift – it may, for example, result from proximity to a 'larger' language, or it may result from changes in social attitudes toward other language communities without reference to proximity. Fishman's view depends on the perception that the borders between languages are clearly identifiable. The reality may be that there are no borders, or that – if political borders do exist – they are extremely permeable.

Languages shift in the direction of a particular language-partner occurs either because that partner overwhelms a particular language – a condition that has already been discussed above, or because a particular language has resources to offer which are not available in the indigenous language. It is this latter shift condition which will be discussed here. Because English, for example, has become the international language of science, technology, and certain other discourse communities of scholars, it has linguistic resources which may not be available in one or another indigenous language; certainly, it will be richer in specialist vocabulary possibly not available in the indigenous language. For example, as the *Dewan Bahasa dan Pustaka* in Malaysia has worked to expand the technical vocabulary of Bahasa Malaysia, it has not only coined new terms from Malay resources but it has borrowed freely from English (and other languages) (see Omar, 1984 and for Indonesian, Alisjahbana, 1984; Vikør. 1993).

But in this process of borrowing, the *Dewan Bahasa dan Pustaka* has encountered problems in morphological and syntactic areas. For example, pluralisation in traditional Malay/Indonesian is accomplished by total reduplication; this is a strategy which can be seen to create some very clumsy items the existence of which would have a massive impact on printing costs, the size of manuscripts, and the storage of manuscripts. Compare the preceding 155-character text with the following representation of that text using total reduplication for plurals:

> this is a strategy which would create some very clumsy item-item the existence of which would have a massive impact on printing cost-cost, the size of manuscript-manuscript, and the storage of manuscript-manuscript,

– a 180 character text, an increase of 15%. In the 1970s the *Dewan Bahasa dan Pustaka* devised a strategy to deal with the problem of pluralisation, using a '2' as the marker of reduplication. However, this reform has had only limited success in practice. A check of newspapers from 1985 indicated that the reduplication '2' was sometimes used in newspaper headlines where space was critical (e.g. *Akhbar2 digesa supaya lebih bertanggungjawab*), but in the text full reduplication was still used (e.g. *Ahad: Akhbar-akhbar hendaklah lebih bertangungjawab dalam* . . .). A check of a sample of 1996 newspapers suggests the reform has disappeared altogether. In Indonesian this 'reform' was never adopted. While such shifts may be attempted by a language agency like the *Dewan Bahasa dan Pustaka*, language shift occurs in other ways as well. For example, as public interest in soccer has increased in Malaysia, and as Malay newspapers have undertaken to report international soccer activities, sports writers have had to devise a new English-like syntactic form of passivisation in Bahasa Malaysia which did not previously exist in traditional Malay. Similar shift toward English in certain domains can be detected in Tagalog (Pilipino) as well (where English is employed in the teaching of scientific subjects but not universally across the curriculum), and there are other examples of both lexical shift and syntactic shift in a variety of other languages.

Language shift is not only the result of the availability of greater resources in some registers in some external language; language shift may be the result of changing popular (or at least public) attitudes toward the external language. It is normally the case that, if a community of speakers does not like another community of speakers, the first community will actively resist learning the language of the second, or it may consciously try to purge its language of the influence of the second community. That was the case with respect to the influence of Dutch on Bahasa Indonesia in the 1960s. The purging process has already been referred to in the context of the activities of the French and Mexican language academies and their efforts to purge French and Mexican Spanish, respectively, of the invasive influence of English. But shift of this sort may occur in either direction, either purging or enhancing the influence of a particular language. When the culture (or some popular-culture phenomenon) of another community is widely admired, the indigenous language may, consciously or unconsciously, absorb lexical items and even syntactic structures from the admired community.

This is the case with the spread of certain aspects of American popular culture in Japan and even in parts of the former Soviet Union (now Russia). Certainly, American popular music has had an important linguistic impact, but so have T-shirts and sweatshirts emblazoned with slogans in American English (even if the slogans are incomprehensible to the wearers of the T-shirts and sweatshirts so emblazoned). Razinkina (personal communication – see pp. 234–235 in Chapter 8), for example, suggests that large numbers of English lexical items deriving from popular music (but also from T-shirt and sweat-shirt slogans) are entering certain registers (e.g. adolescent speech) of Russian and are displacing existing Russian items. As social/political circumstances change, so does the degree of shift in the direction toward, or away from, a particular external language. Thus, while Japanese continues to borrow English words, the registers from which such words are drawn and into which they enter have changed appreciably in the 50 years since the US occupation of Japan at the end of World War II. In the years immediately following the war, English was inclined toward French and Russian and away from German and Japanese for obvious political reasons; but as the political and social environments have shifted over time so has the inclination, and English now is more inclined toward Japanese and German and away from Russian.

Shift does not occur in an entirely unconstrained condition; as the influence of a particular external language increases, for whatever reason, the number of adaptations to that language increases. These shifts are hard to plan because they are dependent on such a large number of non-linguistic factors. Nor can they entirely be guarded against, since much shift activity occurs 'underground'; that is, the social sectors initially involved in shift may be marginal or proscribed sectors – e.g. adolescents, drug dealers or criminals. Such shift is an important factor in lexical expansion in any language and certainly in the 'underground' varieties.

A more active notion of language shift is encompassed in the term language spread. Cooper defines language spread as 'an increase over time, in the proportions of a communicative network that adopts a given language or language variety for a given communicative function' (1982a: 6). The notion of language spread serves as the basis for the development of his accounting scheme for the study of language (see Table 2.4) and for the argument that acquisition planning is a formal mechanism for language spread. As we have seen in the discussion of language academies in Chapter 9, many countries have formal language spread policies (e.g. Ammon & Kleineidam, 1992; Ammon, 1994a; Phillipson, 1992) which actively pursue the goal of maintaining and spreading a particular language.

Language amalgamation

Language amalgamation literally indicates the folding together of two independent language systems. Anglo-Saxon, at the time of the Norman invasion in 1066, was marked by an extremely complex syntactic system employing eight cases, three genders, and three numbers, and requiring agreement among a large number of word classes. The interpenetration of the two populations at a variety of levels and the resultant interpenetration of the two languages resulted in what may be called an amalgamation. Certainly, the amalgamation of Norman French with Anglo-Saxon did not occur over night; on the contrary, the process probably continued over some 400 years, but the end result was a new language, heavily indebted to its parent languages but significantly different from either of them (e.g. compare the language structure of *Beowulf* with that of Chaucer's *Canterbury Tales*). Whether such amalgamation inevitably implicated a pidginisation/creolisation process (see below) is a question that cannot be unambiguously answered from the perspective of a time 500 years later. Nor is it possible to show, except in retrospect, which sectors of the two languages were in fact interpenetrated. Certainly, by the time Chaucer was writing, the vernacular had lost a significant portion of its cases (only the genitive remains in Modern English), and numbers (the dual persists in Modern English only in a few vestigial instances) and had adopted prepositional structures to function in lieu of the explicit case-marking functions. The changes, of course, were not only syntactic; important phonological and morphological changes and great lexical changes also occurred. Some elements of the change continue to the present time; in the recent past, English seems to be in the process of surrendering much of its remaining gender and possessive marking.

Probably because amalgamations occur rather slowly, it is difficult to point to examples in the modern world (e.g. Pennsylvania Dutch). Furthermore, it is difficult to disambiguate pidginisation/creolisation from amalgamation (indeed, the pidginisation/creolisation process may well be a central stage in amalgamation). It is possible, however, that despite its name, *Hawaiian Pidgin*, a variety which is attested from the mid-eighteenth century and which is still in the process of change, may provide an example of amalgamation not merely from two sources (English and Hawaiian) but also involving a number of other languages (e.g. at least Cantonese, Japanese, Korean, Portuguese and Scandinavian languages).

Language contact and pidgin and creole development

When two communities speaking mutually unintelligible languages come into sustained contact with each other, a reduced form deriving from both of the contact languages may come into existence. Such a form – a *pidgin* – may remain viable over quite long periods of time, potentially as long as contact is maintained and as long as the economic need persists. There is a possibility that, when the contact is extended over several generations, some children may be born, most probably along the contact border, whose only language will be some form of the contact variety. When such a phenomenon occurs, the reduced system necessarily expands to accommodate the greater communicative demands of a population which has only this variety. This expansion process results in the development of a *creole* (see e.g. Arends *et al.*, 1995 for an introduction to these issues). Creoles tend to *decreolise* over time in the direction of the dominant language in the community. Thus, when slaves, speaking a variety of mutually unintelligible West African languages, were brought to the Americas from Africa, the contact required the development of a language for communication among the linguistically heterogeneous slaves, and between the slave population and their overseers (whatever the social status of the latter). The outcome was a *pidgin*. It is probable that African slave communities spoke their first languages among themselves to the extent that dispersion permitted them to do so, although it was a conscious policy of slave holders to create polyglot communities precisely to prevent slaves from organising against their masters. But the contact was long-term; slaves were not able to return to Africa but had over many generations to remain in North America.

Thus, children were born in the slave population who had no access to an African language but employed the pidgin for all their communication needs, creolising the variety into one or more systems (like *Gullah*, still spoken in the Georgia Sea Islands). But because the speakers of the creole were isolated in an English-speaking environment, many of the varieties gradually *decreolised* in the direction of English (there being no significant possibility of African-language contact, especially as the flow of slaves ceased after the US Civil War). The outcome of the decreolisation process is represented in the continuum now known as Black English – a complex continuum of varieties ranging from near-pidgin to near-English and varying in parallel with geographic dialects of English to some extent particularly in some phonological features.

A similar set of pidgins, developed in the Caribbean and north-eastern Latin America, pressed against French (in Haiti; St Lucia – Carrington, 1994), Portuguese (in Northern Brazil or the Cape Verde Islands), Dutch (in Curaçao or Surinam), and Spanish (in the Dominican Republic), decreolised in the direction of those H varieties. Mühlhäusler (1995), in his chapter on pidgins and creoles in the Pacific, provides an interesting discussion of these issues from a linguistic ecological perspective. He points out that while pidgins are symptomatic of a disturbance in the linguistic ecology as the result of linguistic imperialism, they developed to become important repositories of indigenous cultures, and finally

> that pidgins are more than by-products of change, they are promoters of change, from traditional to modern ways of communication. Having fulfilled that role they tend themselves to become victims of change and be replaced by more powerful and more highly regarded metropolitan languages. (1995b: 102–3)

It is, of course, possible that a pidgin may not develop in a sustained manner because contact is, for a variety of reasons, broken off, and the essential need for communication disappears. That was probably the case with respect to the pidgin that emerged during the US occupation of Japan in the late 1940s until the early 1950s. The need for a communication system in that situation was substantially economically driven, and some portion of the need was 'underground'; that is, some portion of the communication activity occurred between US military personnel and Japanese prostitutes, black-market dealers, professional gamblers, and a variety of other stigmatised economic sectors. As the nature of the military occupation changed – partly as the result of the gradual withdrawal of United States troops, partly as the result of recovery in the Japanese economy and in various sectors of Japanese society – the communicative need changed. The pidgin did not creolise; on the contrary, the pidgin gradually disappeared.

One should not be misled by the use of the generic term *Bamboo English*; that term is applied indiscriminately to a variety of similar but distinct pidgins that emerged in China during the Boxer Rebellion, in Korea during the Korean War, in Vietnam during the Vietnamese War, and so on. Each of these pidgins had in common the features of all pidgins – grammatical and lexical simplification – and in several of the cases the fact that US military personnel constituted one segment of the pidgin-speaking population (thus, English was one of the feeder languages). Since English was a component in each of these varieties, and since simplification generally appears to follow certain rules, some similar forms have been observed. But because the other partner in the pidginisation process was not the same, there were important syntactic and lexical differences deriving from the structure of that other partner; that is, some of the features of the emerging pidgins were specific to the places in which they emerged.

The examples cited above all involved military situations – the placement of large numbers of people in self-sufficient ghettoised environments within a contact cultural/linguistic system that was also entirely self-sufficient. In each case, the contact was broken off, and the need for the pidgin simply disappeared; in each such case the pidgin also disappeared. It is regrettable that these varieties were not better documented, because the process is an important one, because such environments continue to occur (e.g. the placement of a US military force in Saudi Arabia and Kuwait in 1991, in Somalia in 1992, the placement of United Nations forces in Rwanda in 1995 and in Bosnia in 1996), and because pidginisation may occur in non-military environments, and it would be important to discover whether the pidgins emerging from military environment are in any way different from the pidgins emerging in non-military contact situations. Undoubtedly, some military terminology would pervade all cases of US military presence as, a century ago it pervaded all cases of British military presence across the former British Empire.

Literacy development

All of the kinds of language modification described so far are considered primarily oral; modern societies, however, have not only invented writing but they have invented the need for writing. In many contemporary societies, social and economic mobility is dependent on literacy. Literacy is not a 'state' or a 'condition'; rather, it is a flexible continuum. The elite sub-communities in any society tend to define literacy; as pressure to enter the elite communities develops, those communities have the power to 'up the ante' so that the border between literacy and illiteracy keeps sliding – the requirements for literacy increase. It is not only elites that change the borderline, however; changes in technology may also impact on the local definition of literacy. The degree of literacy sufficient for survival in an agricultural community may not be sufficient for survival in an industrial or service-based community; the degree of literacy sufficient in a rural environment may not be sufficient in an urban environment. The situation may be complicated by the attitudes of a given community toward literacy; literacy may give access to information not considered vital in a given community, or literacy may be completely rejected by a community on the grounds that its introduction will change the uses of a language in ways that speakers cannot tolerate. Mühlhäusler (personal communication) reports this is the case for Allemanic, which is not written.

Another case in point is again that of the Maori language. Missionaries and other Europeans in contact with the Maori people over the past century devised a writing system for the Maori language some years ago, but many of the Maori people still feel that *te reo Maori* is essentially an oral language and should remain an oral language. There has been resistance in the Maori community to proposals to develop a standard Maori both because the emergence of a standard normally requires written forms and because various tribal groups speaking different varieties of Maori each believe that their variety is the only 'correct' one. Thus, although a written form of Maori exists, there is no tradition of writing in Maori, and literacy is not considered a significant issue by Maori speakers. English is readily available to Maori speakers, and literacy in English serves the literacy needs of the community. Obviously, considerations of literacy – to what degree, in what language(s) – are central to any language policy development effort.

An Example of Language Change Elements

All of the different kinds of language modification constructs described in the several sections of this chapter may occur simultaneously. If one takes the New Zealand language situation as an illustration, it is clear that language planning can involve not only English and/or Maori, but all of the other languages present there as well because all of the languages of New Zealand are simultaneously undergoing various modifications which must be taken into account. For example, at least the following circumstances must be considered:

- English is undergoing language *change* (as well as *shift, survival*);
- English in the global context, or at least in the other major English-speaking areas (i.e. Australia, Britain, Canada, the United States) is also simultaneously undergoing a number of changes;
- Maori is undergoing language *revival* (but also possibly *death, shift, amalgamation, contact*);
- Tokelauan, Cook Island Maori, Nuean and Tongan are undergoing language *death* (but also possibly *revival, shift, amalgamation,* and *contact*);

- Tokelauan, Cook Island Maori, Nuean and Tongan are simultaneously undergoing changes in their home-island environment;
- Samoan is undergoing language *shift* (but also *survival*, and *change*);
- Samoan is simultaneously undergoing changes to differing degrees in American and Western Samoa;
- all of the non-Maori languages other than English (Vietnamese, Laotian, Cambodian, Dutch, French, German, etc.) are undergoing language *amalgamation* (but also *shift*, *change*, and *contact*);
- all of these languages are simultaneously undergoing changes in their homelands;
- New Zealand sign language is undergoing *change* (but also *survival*, *revival* and *shift*)
- other sign languages (e.g. ASL (American Sign Language), Auslan) are also simultaneously undergoing changes in other polities in which they occur; and
- literacy constitutes an important issue in the context of all these languages.

The point is that these phenomena are occurring simultaneously in a single given polity and those changes are inevitably affected by other changes occurring outside the polity, and this is undoubtedly only a partial list of the modification constructs in progress since the linguistic situation in New Zealand subsumes 35 or 40 languages and dialects co-existing in a very dynamic environment. As one modifies the rate and direction of modification in any one language, the rate and direction of modification in all the other languages is inevitable affected. Any serious attempt at language planning must take account of the variety of activities occurring simultaneously and must recognise that attempts to modify rate or direction of movement in the context of any one language are likely to impact rate and direction of modification in all the others. Language planning does not occur in a vacuum, and it rarely occurs in absolutely monolingual environments (if any such exist)[7]; indeed, language planning is most often initiated specifically because the environment is multilingual and heterogeneous.

Language Change Elements and Language Systems

Thus, an important theoretical consideration for language planning lies in understanding the kinds of modification constructs already in progress in the society (see the discussion of the *loi Toubon* p. 269ff.) and the effect of modification in one language on the rate and direction of modification in all the other languages in the linguistic eco-system. For example, the choice of language 'A' as a 'national' language in a given polity implies that all the other languages are to some degree subordinate to 'A'. Resources in every domain will then be allocated in relation to that implicit hierarchy. While language 'A' may be enhanced, languages 'B', 'C', . . . 'N' may be disadvantaged. Other changes in relationships may also occur.

It is also important to recognise that the borders between the various types of modification discussed above are at best fuzzy; indeed, the difference between language *change* and language *shift*, for example, may be more political than linguistic. Finally, it is important to recognise that the various categories of modification are differently motivated; *revival*, for example, represents a conscious attempt on the part of a community of speakers, while *death* represents the failure of a community to act and depends on a causation essentially outside the community of speakers and possibly beyond their control.

Thus, one may speak of:

- static preservation of a variety, as opposed to
- dynamic survival of a variety by conscious modification in the context of speaker needs, as opposed to
- revival/renewal/reclamation of a variety through conscious language awareness.

Any of these views must take cognisance of the reality that language is:

- **not** simply *a set of rules* for generating all and only the possible structures of a language;
- **not** independent of the community of speakers, their values, beliefs, and conventional behaviours;
- **not** a clearly bounded system but rather one in active interchange with all those systems (linguistic and non-linguistic) tangential to it;
- **not** an *object* which can be 'handed down' to future generations.

As Mühlhäusler notes:

It is dangerous to generalise [on the basis of Western linguistic notions] on salient attributes of traditional . . . languages . . . :

a. Languages are not seen as objects which can be looked at in isolation from context, the event of speaking, or user . . . .
b. In many instances we are dealing with a chain of related modes of speaking rather than [with] separate linguistic systems . . . .
c. There is a marked difference between *knowing* and *owning* particular modes of speaking.
d. Particular modes of speaking may be linked to ownership of land, while others are related to religion and others to kinship relationships.
e. Multidialectism and multilingualism are necessary to communicate efficiently . . . .

The issue then is not just how to maintain a language, but how to maintain a complex network of inter-related factors which support . . . communication. When the term *language* is used, [one] needs to be aware of the many varying interpretations that this notion can have in different cultures. The fact that Westerners have become habituated to, and have been successful in speaking in, speaking about a particular culture-specific concept is no reason for its universal validity. Indeed, some linguists have begun to argue that a Western conception of *language* is at the root of many problems in the area of language planning . . . (Mühlhäusler, 1995c: 1–2)

Language Problems and Language Planning?

A key journal in the discipline is called *Language Problems & Language Planning*, and its title reflects the notion that the field has as its focus the identification of language problems and their solution through language correction, language treatment or language planning (e.g. Jernudd, 1981, 1982, 1992). In Chapter 3 a number of language problems, or language planning goals, were examined to help us better understand the kinds of problems that language planners have traditionally tried to solve. If we compare that list of eleven goals with the eight key variables discussed in this Chapter, it is clear that the notion of what constitutes a 'problem' rather than a solution to a problem is a recent one, stemming at least in part from the wider recognition of linguistic diversity. For example, the notion that the absence of literacy is a 'problem' simply cannot be maintained as the unequal distribution of literacy within a community often leads to a power disjunction which may be a greater 'problem' than the presence or absence of literacy itself. Language shift may not necessarily imply a 'problem' implicit in the loss of cultural identity. The notion that a variety should be statically preserved in its historically correct form may be a 'problem' causing speakers to change their perception of the variety from a natural thing to an awkward and difficult artefact. The notion that the inability of minority-language speakers to communicate adequately in the majority-language is a 'problem' while the inability of majority-language speakers to express themselves in a minority-language is not a 'problem' also reflects a recent nation-state conceptualisation.

Whether the loss of a language through language death is a 'problem' is an interesting question on which opinion differs. Some scholars hold that, in an environment in which governments have enacted legislation to protect 'endangered species', certainly those same governments should be equally concerned about the loss of human cultures, languages and alternative world views (see e.g. Breton, 1996, Grenoble & Whaley, 1996, Krauss, 1992). But there is no unequivocal evidence that the analogy has validity. Certainly if the objective of language planning is the static preservation of all varieties in a linguistic environment, then all of these areas in fact constitute 'problems'. But if the objective of language planning is to ensure the survival of languages as dynamic factors in a changing social context, the 'problem' is of a rather different sort.

> The situation of most small languages all over the world is very similar: They are experiencing structural and stylistic decline, social marginalization, and dramatic changes in patterns of transmission. Broadly speaking, this is caused by the fact that they are no longer isolated from mainstream culture and world languages . . . . [The real 'problem', then,] is to find solutions that do justice to both the wishes of the indigenous people and, at the same time, are compatible with the inevitable changes that will continue to affect languages world wide . . . . (Mühlhäusler, 1995b: 25–26)

While there has been an increasing discussion about the effects of language planning (see Chapter 7), much of the modification that has occurred in language communities has been unplanned. It has occurred as a result of accident or as the result of a *laissez faire* stance toward language in general. Having examined in this chapter some of the key elements which influence language change and therefore language planning, in the final chapter some key issues are discussed which affect language planning and a description is given of the manner in which elements and issues might work in a linguistic eco-system as a way of moving toward a theory of language planning.

Notes
1. The *loi Toubon* of 1993 was a bill which said that French must be used in documents intended for information of the public and that French was the language of teaching and of communication. The bill also sought to require the use of French terms listed in officially imposed glossaries instead of foreign, mainly English terms, which were creeping into the language (see Thody, 1995 for examples). This prescriptive aspect of the bill was eventually thrown out by the Constitutional Court which held that it infringed basic human rights and that usage (i.e. descriptive criteria) should determine whether a word had entered the French language (Anonymous, 1994b).
2. There is a growing literature on language death (e.g. Brenzinger, 1992, Dorian, 1989a). The topic is also closely related to language and power, discussed in Chapter 7 and the work of Mühlhäusler (1995a, 1995b, 1995c) on linguistic ecology.
3. Kaplan's wife constitutes a case in point. She grew up in South Dakota, in a home in which both Norwegian and Swedish were spoken, but her parents actively promoted the learning of English and – perhaps not actively, but effectively – inhibited the learning of the parental languages. She reached adulthood as a monolingual English speaker.
4. Through most of human history, the development of science and technology has proceeded at a slow and stately pace. An ordinary individual could normally live a full and happy life without ever encountering any sort of

threatening scientific and/or technological change. For the most part, scientists were, in the past, amateurs and dilettantes, working at science out of curiosity, and supporting that work either through personal wealth or through the generosity of patrons. It was not until well into the industrial revolution that industrialists and businessmen recognised the need to harness science to technology for profit, and it was not until quite recent times that the class of professional scientists emerged, working at science on a daily basis, largely in academic institutions but also in industry itself. Even more recent has been the emergence of 'Big Science' – the great 'research university' and the corporate 'think tank' which pursue particular directed (funded) scientific research and which have been driven largely by direct funding either from industry or from government. At present, a number of major industries (e.g. the aerospace industry, the automotive industry, the health industry, the so-called 'knowledge industry', the pharmaceutical industry, etc. – industries in which the turn-around time from scientific breakthrough to marketable technological innovation is very short) maintain large research and development ['R&D'] sections of professional scientists. These R&D sections are in turn supported by information scientists and information managers who funnel pertinent information to working scientists. The development of a class of professional scientists, of research venues for the pursuit of targeted science, and more recently of professional information scientists and information managers have had the most profound cultural and linguistic implications. (See Chapter 9, the section on Planning for Science and Technology (p. 241ff.) for a more extended discussion of these issues.)

5. Lexical growth of this sort can occur in at least three ways: the adaptation of unmodified lexical items directly from other languages, the adaptation and modification of such lexical items to the phonological and morphosyntactic rules of the accepting language, or the creation from some indigenous (or historical) source of parallel new lexical items. These changes are nicely illustrated in Japanese because of the presence of three syllabaries. Razinkina (personal communication – see in Chapter 8 pp. 234-235) reports the large intrusion (from popular music and even from the slogans emblazoned on T-shirts and sweat-shirts) of American English lexical items into standard Russian, in a good many instances replacing existing Russian lexicon.

6. Language education is, to some extent, still captured by an older paradigm; when language education was first introduced into the academy – in the medieval university – the languages at issue were the classical languages (essentially Classical Greek, Classical Hebrew, Latin and Sanskrit). These were dead languages, with fixed syntax and lexicon, and a limited, frozen inventory of texts. The objective of language study was not communicative proficiency (since there was no real community with which to communicate), but rather was access to the thought, culture and art of a dead civilisation. Under those circumstances, it was reasonable to select the most intellectually able students for instruction and to employ a grammar-translation methodology. When modern languages were introduced into the school curriculum in the late nineteenth century, the original instructional paradigm was retained; language instruction was reserved to the most intellectually able students, grammar-translation methodology was employed, and the object of instruction was access to the canonical literature of the language. Thus, communicative competence, because it was not an objective, was seldom achieved. (There is some evidence that, if children learn anything at all in school, they learn only what they are taught.) Though language curricula have gradually become more

concerned with communicative competence, the older literary bias remains, and the students coming out at the end of a period of instruction may still have largely a literary orientation. (Also see under Language-in-Education Planning, Chapter 5, p. 122ff.)

7. See, for example, Nance (1975) for an instance alleged to be accurate but which may have constituted a hoax.

11 Conceptualising Language Planning: Key Issues

Introduction

In Chapter 10 it was argued that while language planning is often perceived as some sort of monolithic activity, designed specifically to manage one particular kind of linguistic modification in a community at a particular moment in time, on the contrary, language planning activity must be perceived as implicating a wide range of languages and of modifications occurring simultaneously over the mix of languages in the environment – that is, implicating the total language eco-system. It was further argued that in the complex world in which we live, each language has its own ecology of support and relationships to other languages. Thus, an understanding of the linguistic ecology of language planning in any particular situation may invoke any or all of the following key language change elements simultaneously:

- language death;
- language survival;
- language change;
- language revival;
- language shift and language spread;
- language amalgamation;
- language contact and pidgin and creole development;
- literacy development.

However, it is not only these language change elements which impact on the language planning environment, as language planning issues also impact on outcomes. Many recent critics of the discipline of language planning have spent much time and energy condemning the outcomes of some (largely Western) imperialist language practices (e.g. Phillipson, 1992; Tollefson, 1991, 1995; cf. Davies, 1996; also see discussion under Critiques of Language Planning, Chapter 3, pp. 80–82 and Chapter 7), and no doubt the effects of much past language planning deserve to be condemned. While it is necessary to recognise the ill effects of much colonialist language policy, and to recognise the fact that much of it has produced inappropriate – even destructive – results, to dwell on these issues to the exclusion of reality is to freeze language planning and policy development in its current state. It may be that a moratorium on all language planning efforts should simply be declared, but the reality is that language planning is in progress – even if only informally – everywhere, at both the macro and micro levels, in many polities as well as in many other sub-national sectors. It is also the case that while one can see the ill effects of planning, one cannot know what the effects of 'non-planning' in these situations would have been. Would the results of 'non-planning' have produced a better result or merely another set of circumstances to condemn? Even with hindsight, the answer to this rhetorical question is not always clear.

The language planner's goal must be to take the linguistic ecology as s/he finds it. It is important for the language planner to understand the forces that have brought the language ecology to its present point, and to avoid the errors of the past in moving beyond the present point, but it appears unproductive to cease language planning activity because much of that activity was in the past ill conceived – especially in hindsight and with the benefit of current perspectives. Furthermore, we have consistently invoked the notion of language ecology as a guiding principle for language planners. It is important to remember, in thinking about language ecology, that more is invoked than language. Language is the carrier of the conventional goals and the conventional means of achieving them in any given society. Admittedly, the goals and means may change over time, and those changes will be reflected in the changing language and in a changing language ecology. The point is that the language planner must look beyond language itself to the societal values and practices underlying language itself. Therefore, before examining what a model for language planning might look like, a number of these key issues need to be discussed as these issues also raise 'problems' which the language planner must face.

Planned vs. Unplanned Language Change

While the focus of this book has been on language planning, i.e. planned language change, the previous chapter has demonstrated that modification that is unplanned in a formal sense also occurs to language in a community. Such language change may occur by accident or as the result of a *laissez-faire* stance toward language in general. Even when it involves planning, it is often not policy driven, but rather is part of a solution to an immediate problem, or it may arise out of a particular situation. Luke and Baldauf (1990: 349–350) in a critical rereading of language planning and education efforts in Australasia and the Pacific argue that whatever theoretical and practical reservations we might have about the courses and consequences of current efforts, language will indeed be planned. . . . the processes of language planning, whether official or unofficial, formal or informal, are already well underway. . . . [T]his situation can only partly be attributed to the evolution of 'language planning' as a formal, codified set of disciplinary assumptions and procedures to be used as an instrument of language change by international development agencies, national governments and others. . . . [S]everal contributions here have pointed to the tenacity of the ostensibly 'unplanned' in the face of a range of attempts to enforce technical order on language change, attempts variously consensual and authoritarian, centralized and localized.

Given the impact that 'unplanned' language planning may have on language change, Baldauf (1994) has suggested four reasons why there is a need to take more account of 'unplanned' language planning in language policy and planning situations.

(1) Planned and 'unplanned' language features often co-exist in the same situation and the unplanned can alter or pervert the planning process. For example, the States of Victoria and New South Wales (in Australia) have language-in-education policies and school programmes which prepare students for high school leaving exams in languages other than English (LOTE). However, some students from 'ethnic' backgrounds may also study that language at a 'Saturday School' or may speak the language at home (Janik, 1996). Do those students have an 'unfair' advantage in their studies, exams and entrance to university? Should they be penalised for their prior knowledge or excluded from such exams to be 'fair' to non-background learners?

(2) The absence of some activity (i.e. language planning) often provides information about that activity. For example, in diglossic situations where two languages are in use, typically for different purposes, the uses of those languages will often highlight important social and political information. Swan and Lewis (1990) note that in the Papua New Guinea situation where English has been the official language, and the language of schools and universities, for many decades, there has been a failure to do language planning work in Tok Pisin, the major lingua franca of the polity. Yet, the role of English in the language planning situation in Papua New Guinea cannot be fully understood without reference to Tok Pisin. In Malaysia, Ożóg (1993) suggests that the National Language Policy, which instituted Bahasa Melayu as the national language and ignored the role of English, may have hurt the Malays (the intended beneficiaries of the policy) as it left them with less access to English at a time when English was becoming an important language for economic advancement.

(3) Language policy and planning activities are power related and may be invoked to ensure social control rather than to implement desirable language change. For example, Souaiaia (1990) argues that the real obstacles to Arabisation in the Maghreb are the political interests of the ruling elites. Arabisation is used by the elites as a vehicle to legitimise political control without any intention of full implementation of Arabisation, which would jeopardise the basis of that control. The instances of negative language planning discussed in Chapter 8 (p. 230 ff.) are further examples of the political side of this phenomenon. However, Sommer (1991) and Cloonan and Strine (1991) demonstrate that power may also be exercised by bureaucracy, which can have a role in shaping or altering language plans to suit political needs.

(4) Much micro language planning is 'unplanned' and most people feel quite competent to become involved in such language activities. The notion that 'anyone who speaks both languages can translate' inherent in the Australian interpreting and translating and the Hydro-Québec examples in Chapter 9 (pp. 252ff. and 254ff. respectively) highlight the fact that little initial planning was found in those situations, as the difficulties of the tasks were underestimated. Rodriquez (1992) discusses the development of a state mandate for foreign language teaching in Arizona schools without there being any corresponding plans for school-based implementation. As many teachers would recognise, innovations in curriculum development are often simply decreed by systems and then left to the professionals (i.e. teachers) to work out how they will be implemented.

Thus, there is much in the way of unplanned language policy and planning occurring in societies, and this often goes unnoticed and therefore unrecorded by language planners. This has an impact on language change and the ability of language planners and bureaucrats to implement language change. Unplanned language change is a 'problem' for language planners because it alters the language eco-system making it more difficult to develop accurate and effective language planning strategies; yet as it occurs as a 'natural' part of the system, it needs somehow to be taken into account.

The Element of Time – Centuries vs. Decades

Historical evidence suggests that various language modifications occur within differing time frames. In Europe, for example, the identification of nation-state with particular languages occurred over a very long period of time – literally, centuries, while in Sub-Saharan Africa, as new states emerged out of the break-up of former colonial empires, national language selection, the creation of a unifying function for language, and the identity of extremely heterogeneous populations with the notion of *nation* was expected to occur over a very short period – two or three decades at most. The geographic borders of European states, while often a subject of controversy, eventually took some account of population dispersion; in Sub-Saharan Africa (or for that matter in most of the former colonial world) borders were drawn on quite different bases. Whereas in Europe, except in the lately reconfigured area of the Balkan states, the drawing of borders tended to place in one geographic zone populations that had some linguistic and cultural unity (though that was certainly not always the case, and more recent political settlements have tended to complicate the situation), in Sub-Saharan Africa, border definition had to do with geographic features and the locus of natural resources, not with human distribution; and borders – following a European pattern – tended to be drawn along rivers (which were not perceived by the occupants as separating populations but rather were seen as arteries for unifying populations), and other convenient geographic features which can readily be represented on maps.

As a consequence, extremely heterogeneous populations were allocated within one geographic polity. The newer nation-states of Sub-Sahara Africa are, for the most part, marked by extreme linguistic heterogeneity, some states subsuming populations speaking literally hundreds of different languages (e.g. Cameroon) and further divided by tribalism (see the recent tragic intertribal warfare in Burundi/Rwanda). This phenomenon is not restricted to Sub-Saharan Africa, as is exemplified by such Asian states as India, the Philippines, and Indonesia. Only a relatively small number of Sub-Saharan nation-states (e.g. Rwanda, Burundi) were genuinely more-or-less monolingual. Furthermore, the entire continent was divided by colonially based regions of influence deriving from the colonial language situation, so Luzophone, Francophone and Anglophone Africa have become quite distinct regional entities, unified by a set of imposed and often unrealistic linguistic conventions, without reference to the borders of created nation-states. Some such nation-states are divided by a regional border (Cameroon), and nation-states belonging to a set of linguistic isolates (e.g. Portuguese speaking [like Angola, Mozambique], Italian speaking [Somalia], Spanish speaking [Guinea-Bissau], Afrikaans speaking [South Africa]) may serve to break up an otherwise similar linguistic grouping (see Appendix).

Language planning activities need to consider the language situation not only in the polity for which planning is under way but also the language situation in proximate polities as well. Further, it is important to consider the relative permeability of the border between the planning polity and proximate polities. Modern electronic media make political borders even more permeable. Kaplan lives in the State of Washington, separated from Canada by only the Straits of Juan de Fuca; television is essentially indifferent to the political border. A similar situation exists in Kuwait and

Saudi Arabia, each able to pick up the other's television programming with ease. The rise of superstations makes it possible to receive broadcasting in virtually any European language in any European country. Satellite broadcasting makes it possible for people living in remote areas of Australia and Melanesia to receive Australian television services as well as those from hundreds of stations around the world. E-mail and the World Wide Web make almost instant distant communication in a variety of languages easy and inexpensive.

Political events in Sub-Saharan Africa over the past quarter-century have resulted in huge refugee flows across political borders, creating new linguistic problems for receiving polities. But perhaps most seriously the planning activity needs to consider the element of time. Rapid complementarity between nation-state and language is not likely to occur, even if it could be demonstrated that such an identity was highly desirable. On the contrary, attempts at nation-state and language complementarity are likely to lead to civil war, as such attempts have in the recent past. In sum, time is a 'problem' in language change of any sort – planned or unplanned – and the limitations of time to achieve linguistic goals that polities have imposed on themselves have often been highly unrealistic. Furthermore, even those time limitations have been disrupted by frequent major shifts in policy.

Description vs. Prescription: A Paradox or Just a Problem

Although language planners (and linguists in general) have carefully eschewed any contamination of prescriptivism and have repeatedly and consistently insisted that their function was primarily descriptive, it is impossible to escape the realisation that the development of a standard variety of a language and the putting in motion of rules for language use are prescriptive, at least to some degree. There is a long-standing division of views within the linguistic community concerning the extent to which linguists should prescribe language correctness. In the more traditional segment of the language and literature community, of course, there is a long tradition of prescriptivism. Indeed, Martin Joos' fictional Miss Fidditch — the quintessential English teacher (1961 *The Five Clocks*) exemplifies the essence of the prescriptivist tradition. Grammarians and dialectologists from Bishop Loth, Dr Johnson and Noah Webster to Edwin Newman, the *Oxford English Dictionary*, and Webster's unabridged dictionaries of the twentieth century have argued for 'standards' in English, and have been quick to prescribe 'correct' forms for the English language, entering into endless arguments about the appropriate uses of *shall* and *will*, whether *ain't* is really a word and whether split infinitives and sentence-final prepositions should be tolerated.

Newspapers and publishers have been embroiled in the correctness issue, many regularly publishing style sheets to ensure conformity to their prescriptions. Professional associations are regular participants in such debates, often publishing style sheets of their own (e.g. the Style Sheet of the American Psychological Association [APA] having become a guide for publication in the social sciences in North America; see, for example, Bazerman's [1988] study of the influence of the APA style sheet on the development of research writing and Atkinson's [1993, 1995] work on convention in the historical development of scientific text in English under the influence of the *Edinburgh Medical Journal* and the *Philosophical Transactions of the Royal Society of London*; see also Dear, 1985).

Modern linguists, on the other hand, during most of the twentieth century have taken the position that their task is to describe what speakers actually do rather than to try to prescribe what they ought to do. This movement has certainly been exemplified in the development of transformational generative theory in North America (the objective of which is to devise descriptions in precise, neutral, language accounting for all and only the possible sentences of any language) and to the current movement in lexicography to derive from massive computerised text corpuses the lexicon and meaning of actual users of the language (best exemplified in the CoBuild dictionaries of the University of Birmingham group and the other large corpuses of English being collected by Oxford University Press and other large publishing bodies) (see Murison-Bowie, 1996).

Language planners are caught in a dilemma between these two views. On the one hand, language planners tend to come out of linguistic (and educationalist) programmes and training and consequently are strong believers in the essentially descriptive functions of linguistics; on the other hand, language planning contains a kernel of prescriptivism by definition (Bruthiaux, 1992). Perhaps a distinction can be made in terms of the tasks that language planners perform; corpus planning is essentially descriptive – up to a point. That is, description is required, for example to determine what sort of orthography might be appropriate for a newly graphised language. But, once the appropriate orthography is determined, then it must, to a great extent be prescribed if the orthography is to 'take'.[1] By the same token status planning is essentially descriptive – up to a point. That is, determining who speaks what language to whom under what circumstances for what purpose is essentially a descriptive task; on the other hand, once the language planner sits down to write recommendations, s/he, by definition, becomes prescriptive because s/he has a data-based conviction that the recommendations are necessary to accomplish the objective.

To put the distinction in another way, language planning is essentially descriptive in its data gathering activities, but once the language planner (or government bureaucrat) moves beyond data gathering into recommendations, policy determination and policy implementation, s/he can no longer just describe. The activity becomes prescriptive. This distinction may create a 'problem' for language planners and explain their reluctance to involve themselves in the policy-determination/policy-implementation phases of the planning cycle. Once the descriptive tasks have been accomplished, language planners seem to be content to withdraw and leave articulation and implementation to bureaucrats, thereby avoiding soiling their hands in prescriptive activities. It is, consequently, necessary to temper the social scientists' predilection to consider themselves as disinterested and objective observers. At some point, the language planner becomes an involved participant. It is for this reason, perhaps, that the paradigmatic constraints of autonomous linguistics cannot apply in language policy and planning research – the ultimate *applied* linguistics.

In truth, however, even at his/her most objective and disinterested, the language planner is not a pure descriptivist. It is the language planner, after all, who defines the questions that will be asked and the means for answering those questions, and these acts by definition introduce into the objective research the researcher's bias – as indeed is the case in all research. The variety of research paradigms discussed in Chapter 4 illustrates this dilemma of research perspective. Thus, being a language planner and a social scientist can be a 'problem' which each individual must resolve for her/himself.

The Players – Who has the Right to do What to Whom?

Another way of approaching this dilemma is to look at language planning from a human resources point of view. In 1987 the Regional Language Centre in Singapore held a conference with an emphasis on human resource development, and the conference organisers defined human resource development as:

> activity undertaken to promote the intellectual, moral, aesthetic, cultural, social and economic development of the individual, so as to help him achieve his highest human potential as a resource for the community. The seminar will focus on the different ways in which language-related activity can help achieve these goals, particularly in the Southeast Asian context. (Das, 1987: v)

This definition alerts us to the fact that language planning is ultimately about human resource development, that is, who has the right to do what to whom for what purpose. In an eco-system approach to language planning, individual decisions about language use are the ultimate test for the language planner. Involving participants in the planning is therefore a critical 'problem' in wider situational contexts if language planning is to be meaningful and successful.

Trim (1987) suggests that human resource development can either be right branching (RB) or left branching (LB). LB is perhaps the model most closely associated with traditional aspects of language planning, the centralised development of the language resources of human beings to meet manpower and training requirements. LB represents the social planning side of human resource development. Here language planners are dealing with large-scale and often corporate issues. What language(s) should be planned? for whom? by whom? LB represents the 'top-down' approach to the problem.

On the other hand, there has been a growing recognition by those interested in language planning that the discipline has much to offer as well at the micro level. RB seems to view human resource development as persons developing their own language resources for their own purposes. Here the focus is on individuals striving for greater self-awareness, more developed skills and access to autonomous learning. RB reflects the 'bottom-up' approach to language planning. To use Trim's analogy:

> LB implies a view of society as a vast, intricate mechanism into which individuals are inserted like cogs – or perhaps rather silicon chips – or as an organism with its millions of specialized cells. We can specify what a machine part should do, how it should perform, how it must be formed in order to perform its specialized task efficiently.

[whereas:]

> RB takes not society but the individual as its unit. As autonomous entities, individuals build up resources which enable them to follow their own goals in varying, somewhat unpredictable circumstances adopting flexibly to change. In LB the common good is pursued through careful, centralised planning, in RB through innumerable individual decisions pursuing an enlightened self-interest. (Trim, 1987: 3–4)

This tension between society and its needs and individuals and their needs is one inherent in language planning. Those who are involved in language planning, particularly in the context of human resource development, need to keep this distinction in mind. However, what underlies both of these approaches is the increasingly urgent need for modern individuals to communicate. The 'problem' for the language planner is that, while language planning appears to be mainly LB, the information for and the ultimate success of a language plan depends on RB activities. Devising a plan for a particular language eco-system which creates an appropriate balance between these two approaches needs to be carefully considered.

Applied Linguistics vs. Linguistics Applied

In North America, at least, there have, historically, been two quite different ways of looking at the nature of language, and these divergent views have supported the independent development of applied linguistics.

On the one hand, in what has been called 'general' linguistics (or sometimes 'formal' linguistics, or 'autonomous' linguistics, or even 'theoretical' linguistics – though the latter is a misnomer since a variety of the alternative views are also concerned with theory) the object of inquiry has traditionally been seen as an independent language system composed of unique and invariant structural and semantic rules. In contemporary thinking, this system has been seen as innate to human beings – a species-specific phenomenon encoded into the human genetic structure. Given this biological explanation of its ontogeny, it has been, in this paradigm, perfectly reasonable to investigate language as a separate entity because it is said to have an independent existence unrelated to human production or use. The relationship in that system between the investigator and language is quite straightforward and unproblematic – *subject > object*. The objective of formal inquiry is systematic description in 'neutral' scientific language, quite isolated from the value-laden characteristics of everyday language. Such neutral description is seen to give rise to rational predictions about the internal operations of the system and about the directions of its future development. This perspective derives from the traditions of logical positivism and scientific realism, and is thought to provide parsimonious and invariant description. While there is no question that this approach to the study of language has produced useful information and has given rise to certain cognitive-linguistic structures that appear to be invariant, there are certain problems. As Sridhar (1990: 171) points out:

> . . . formal linguistics . . . identifies language with grammar and linguistic theory with grammatical theory, leading to an exclusive preoccupation with form and disregard of, or scepticism toward, language use and function. If linguistics is defined as the scientific study of language, why should it be limited to the study of . . . syntax, semantics, morphology, and phonology? . . . . Chomsky has stead-fastly asserted the autonomy of grammar and its independence from considerations of language use and function. He has even stated that 'language is not a task-oriented device' . . . (1990: 53)

There is no intent in this description to disparage that view; only to differentiate it from an alternative way of looking at language. Nevertheless, as Sridhar says:

> . . . the claim that grammar is independent of context is disingenuous, [and further], . . . while the successes of formal linguistics in discovering structural regularities are impressive, they have come at a price. It is arguable that linguistic theory may have become a science at the expense of its subject matter, namely language as an instrument of communication in real-life situations. (1990: 172)

There is a syndrome of alternative views, but that syndrome should not be conceived as a single powerful theoretical thrust, though various segments do hold in common certain basic assumptions. The syndrome represents elements of Applied Linguistics, Sociolinguistics, and Language Policy and Planning. From this perspective, language is seen not as an independent system, but rather as a human product and a social tool. The ontogenesis of this syndrome of views is influenced by hermeneutic philosophy – a position essentially antagonistic to scientific realism and logical positivism. The perception is that, while the physical sciences deal with inanimate objects outside the human sphere, language is the product of the human mind and is therefore inseparable from it and from the attendant subjectivity, value-orientation, and emotion.

In scientific realism, and thus in autonomous linguistics, the object of empirical research is to capture an invariant objective reality through repeated testing of hypothetical correspondences that occur between models and observed phenomena; that is, empirical research is a tool through which to test, repeatedly, the consistency, and thus to verify the validity, of any observed correspondences. In the alternative syndrome of views – in applied linguistics, and certainly in language policy and planning – deriving at least in part from the ideas of Husserl, that sort of empiricism was conceived as an error traceable to Galilean systematisation, because the notion *hypothesis > test > verification* is based on an assumption of the constancy of any given phenomenon. Such an assumption ignores even the practical problems inherent in setting up a consistent measurement system with respect to language. In the alternative views, the investigator is simultaneously both the subject and the object of inquiry; the study of language is the study of human beings, and the relationship between the researcher and the object of study, therefore, must be defined as *subject > subject*.

Such a perception challenges, on logical grounds, the notion of the independent existence and objectification of language as well as the possibility of devising an invariant abstract model. Given the complexity of language, given the fact that language changes over time, and given the fact that language exists within various cultural systems, it would be impossible to discover invariant laws as in the physical sciences. Thus, the study of language, at certain levels at least, should be descriptive rather than predictive and explanatory.

In addition, it would be impossible, from this perspective, to describe language in a context-free, 'neutral' scientific sense because there is constant movement between the parts and the whole and because there are no clearly identifiable beginning and ending points. Language, furthermore, cannot be perceived as ahistorical. As long as language is perceived as invariant and independent of human activity – as it is in autonomous linguistics – it cannot be examined in historical perspective; as long as language is perceived as genetically conditioned and independent of human agency, history is irrelevant. But, as soon as language is perceived as a product of the human mind and as a tool – as it is in applied linguistics – its continuing existence over time constitutes a theoretical problem (Grabe & Kaplan, 1992, Kaplan, 1993c).

We would want to argue that Language Planning is the ultimate form of Applied Linguistics. Unless one perceives of language as a social phenomenon, it is quite impossible to undertake language planning, except in the most restrictive sense of corpus planning. This is not to claim that insights from autonomous linguistics are irrelevant; on the contrary, some of the notions available in grammatical theory are central to corpus work. But status work requires a quite different approach to the definition of language and to the understanding of the inter-relationship between human populations and the language(s) they use in communicating with each other.

Given that, for example, literacy deals with a tool-function of language, and given that literacy is socially defined, autonomous linguistics has little to offer to the understanding of literacy as a societal phenomenon. Any given language is *the ideal means for a community of speakers to communicate with each other and to represent the phenomenological world in which they live.* That is a definition very much based in culture, behaviour, and belief systems, and obviously open to historical analysis, since phenomenologies change over time, but such a definition is not, in itself, sufficient. Such an 'ideal means' must be constrained by convention; that is, speakers of a language develop, over time, a set of common solutions to common communications problems, and these common solutions become institutionalised in the syntax, in the pronunciation, in the semantics, in the pragmatic functions, and in the discourse structures (see, Jesperson, 1933/1964: 16). Admittedly, those common solutions are, in turn, constrained by the capacity of the human mind and the human physiology, so all languages – invented by human beings, not sprung whole like Venus from the head of Zeus – have conventional means of naming, conventional means of arranging signs into meaningful strings, conventional means of selecting among the finite capabilities of the vocal mechanisms to articulate signs vocally, conventional means of selecting out of an infinite universe of arbitrary written marks to represent vocal signs in visual form, conventional means of solving discourse problems, etc. The biologist, V.C. Wynne-Edwards (1962), defines society in terms of convention: '*A society can be defined as a group of individuals competing for conventional prizes by conventional means.*' If that definition has any validity, then a language must implicate:

- the means of communicating about conventional prizes and means;
- the means of identifying and isolating those individuals who do not share those conventional prizes and means;

- the means of identifying the physical space in which those conventional prizes and means hold – the territorial border;
- the means of defending that border, preferably without involving a threat to life;
- the means of transmitting intergenerationally the values and symbols that underlie the conventional prizes and means.

It is important to recognise that, while individuals may be monolingual or bilingual (that is, able to participate in only one community of speakers, or able to participate in two or more such communities), the communities themselves are unlikely to be completely monolingual. (There is an old joke that a different language is something spoken ten miles down the road.) Language Policy and Planning, therefore, must invoke the conventional goals and means of each community of speakers subsumed within the planning space. It is for this reason that Applied Linguistics is central to Language Policy and Planning and that Autonomous Linguistics simply cannot be.

Summary of Key Elements and Issues

Chapter 10 looked at eight key language change elements in language planning including: (1) language death; (2) language survival; (3) language change; (4) language revival; (5) language shift and expansion; (6) language amalgamation; (7) language contact and pidgin and creole development; and (8) literacy development, each of which plays a unique role and which may be present in any combination in any given planning environment. In this chapter five key issues were also examined including: (1) planned vs. unplanned language change; (2) the element of time; (3) description vs. prescription; (4) human resource development; and (5) applied linguistics vs. linguistics applied. These key elements and issues all raise 'problems' for the language planner, and the discussion suggests that Western linguistic models of language may not be applicable to language planning and that certain conditions must exist in order for languages to survive:

(1) Parents must be willing and able to transmit the language to their offspring and must actually do so.
(2) No condition may exist which will cause a more powerful language (H variety) to be imposed on a less powerful one (L variety), and functional registers must be retained.
(3) The community of speakers must be vibrant, stable or expanding.

In the absence of these conditions, languages are likely to die. The discussion has explored the question of whether languages, once moribund, may be revived, suggesting that, if they may indeed be revived, the schooling environment is probably not the appropriate place to undertake revival (cf. Hornberger & King, 1996). The discussion also suggests that (the 'revival' ought not to seek to restore the past or the *status quo*, but build on the past to transform the language to meet real language use needs in important language domains) The discussion further suggests that certain phenomena perceived as 'problems' may not in fact be problems, and that the real problems may be quite different.

> [The real 'problem', then,] is to find solutions that do justice both to the wishes of indigenous people and, at the same time, are compatible with the inevitable changes that will continue to affect languages world wide . . . . (Mühlhäusler, 1995b: 26)

real prbm. real ans: diglossia

Language planning is not 'language engineering'; it must, ultimately, satisfy the speakers of all languages involved. While language planning solutions must be 'sold' to the public through conventional advertising techniques, the basic plan must be bottom-up, and must serve the interests of the community or it will not meet the conditions just enunciated for that language plan to survive.

Even under the best of circumstances, the language planner will be captured in the inevitable tension between political, linguistic and societal goals in the language planning environment. The political objectives generally invoke, to some extent, matters of control; the language planning agency or organisation undertakes language planning because it believes it has lost (or is losing) control over some sector of the environment, and the planning body believes that by planning language behaviour it can re-establish control. The linguistic objectives are generally to provide a neutral, scientific description of the language environment. As previously noted, linguists tend to become very nervous when they are asked to prescribe rather than only to describe, yet inevitably the planning environment requires some sort of prescription, and equally inevitably, the linguist is not entirely a dispassionate observer. S/he introduces her/his biases by defining the question to be addressed, by defining the means by which the question will be addressed and by sifting the data collected in order to provide a response to the question addressed. The social objectives are generally driven by some notion of social justice. In some segment of the ultimate plan, implementers will be driven by a desire to solve social problems through plan implementation. Early on in this volume we called attention to the reality that it is difficult at best to assess the outcomes of plan implementation because one simply does not know what would have happened if there had been no plan or if some other plan had been introduced.) More importantly, social problems tend to derive from complex causes. For example, while there may be some causal link between poverty and language, 'fixing' the language situation is unlikely to eliminate poverty. It is probably the case that 'stamping out illiteracy' will not solve complex social problems, though the spread of literacy may alleviate some problems; but the spread of literacy may cause equally

tension btw goals

control

prescribe/describe

social justice

same conclusion made by Cooper.

serious problems – it may contribute to the death of some language in the environment that is losing ground to dominant language literacy; it may reconfigure the social structure of the community; it may exacerbate the demise of cultural values (Mühlhäusler, 1995b).

It is likely that in any given environment, political, linguistic and social objectives may be flying off in quite different directions and with different degrees of intensity (Figure 11.1). It is part of the planner's task to try to achieve some coincidence among these disparate goals – to bring some order out of this chaos as part of the language planning process. This is an applied set of skills that involves the art of compromise and of developing a working consensus, which is often difficult for the linguist to handle as his/her training is often oriented to finding *the* correct solution, in some theoretical sense. However, a policy devised in an environment in which goals are not co-ordinated at least to some degree is doomed to failure.

All this does not mean that language policy development and language planning should not occur, because as we have seen, informally it will occur in any case. Rather, we contend that the present world environment mandates language planning. We tend to agree that language planning undertaken without an awareness of the eco-system in which one is intervening can be dangerous to the health of the community. But, in an environment in which the eco-system is understood – even only partially – in which pre-planning is undertaken, in which the objectives are clear, in which those whose language(s) will be tampered with are involved, in which ample time and resources are available, language planning can be undertaken. It may even produce surprisingly positive and useful results.

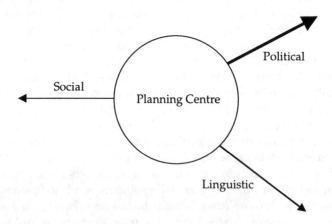

Figure 11.1 The pull of political, linguistic and social forces on language planning

Towards A Model for Language Planning

In this book we have attempted to review much of the accessible and internationally published literature on language planning. Based on this review, Figure 11.2 attempts to illustrate the various forces at work in a language planning activity. The largest circle represents the linguistic eco-system that is being planned for. Within the largest circle, the next largest circle represents the national/official language of this illustrative speech community. Smaller circles numbered 1 to 5 represent minority languages in the community. The smaller circle numbered 6 represents a language that is likely to die in the near future. The smaller circle numbered 7 represents a non-standard variety of the official language (e.g. in the US Black English or Mexican American Non-Standard English). The items down the left axis represent the various forces impacting on the language eco-system, previously discussed in Chapters 10 and 11; and the items across the bottom represent the agencies and organisations that impact on the system. These groups were discussed in Chapter 1 and are related in

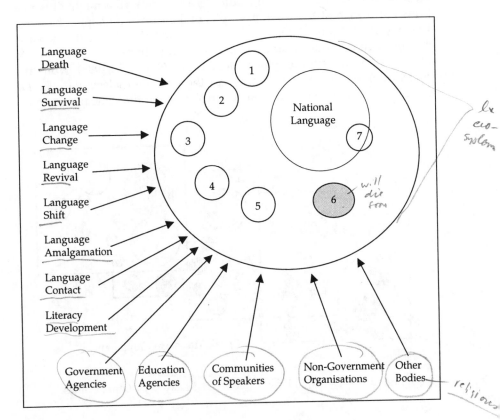

Figure 11.2 Forces at work in a linguistic eco-system

Chapter 2 to Haarmann's (1990) typology of organisational impact. As an illustration of what such an eco-system might contain, Table 11.1 lists these categories and provides a partial description of what some of them might contain for six polities: Australia, Malaysia, Mexico, South Africa, Sweden and the United States. A full description of such a system would be beyond the scope of this text.

Furthermore, although Figure 11.2 represents the various agencies and organisations as exerting equal influence, that is rarely the case; the several agencies and organisations would need to be weighted to represent the effects accurately. The figure is a simplified representation of the various matters that the language planner must take into consideration. Figure 4.2 in Chapter 4 suggests one means for gathering the data that would be required to make it possible to present the information in Figure 11.2.

Furthermore, because the figure is only two dimensional, it is not possible for it to represent historical time. One can imagine a series of such figures might exist illustrating the situation (e.g. Figure 11.3), say, at 10-year intervals over the past 100 years, much as a historical atlas might illustrate British or Jewish history.[2] For example, in the case of Singapore between 1960 and 1990 we might find the circle representing English on the increase, the circles representing Mandarin increasing, but from a later date due to the 'Speak Mandarin Campaign' (Kuo, 1984; Newman, 1988), while the circles representing Malay, Tamil and the Chinese dialects (i.e. Hakka, Cantonese, etc.) would be decreasing in size across the same time frame.

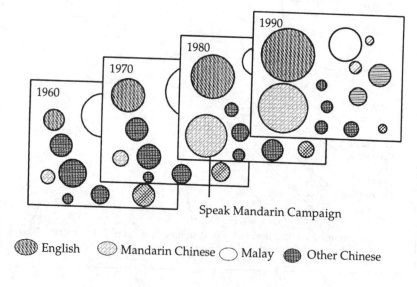

Figure 11.3 Effect of time on a linguistic eco-system

Table 11.1 Six illustrative partial cases of the eco-system model

Language eco-system	Australia
National Language	English (*de facto*).
Language of Wider Comm.	English.
Minority Languages	Perhaps 150 Aboriginal and Torres Strait Islander languages (e.g. Warlpiri, Kala Lagaw Ya, Aranda, Tiwi), Indigenous creoles (e.g. Kriol, Torres Strait Broken), and 150 immigrant languages (e.g. Italian, Greek, German, Chinese, Arabic, Vietnamese, Spanish).
Dying Language	As many as 120 Aboriginal languages have fewer than 10 speakers.
Non-Standard Variety	Aboriginal English, ethnolects of English, Australian sociolects, Torres Strait Broken.
Religious Language	Primarily English, but Church Greek, Classical Arabic, Hebrew, Old Church Slavonic, Coptic, and Latin. The spiritual use of indigenous languages.
Language Death	100 or more Aboriginal languages have ceased to be used.
Language Survival	Australian English, 10–15 Aboriginal and Torres Strait Islander languages and creoles (e.g. Kriol, Warlpiri, Tiwi, Kalaw Kawaw Ya); most immigrant languages survive through continuing immigration, but some learning and intergenerational maintenance occurs.
Language Change	Australian English has borrowed many Aboriginal words. Community languages (e.g. Italian) have borrowed from English as have Aboriginal languages. Grammatical simplification is occurring in community languages more quickly than in their national environment. Australian English is being influenced by other varieties of English (esp. American English).
Language Revival	There are a number of Aboriginal language projects aimed at language reclamation, renewal or revitalisation (e.g. Gumbaynggir, Numbulwar, Warra Kaurna, Djabugay, Jilkminggan).
Language Shift	There is a general shift from Aboriginal and Torres Strait Islander and immigrant languages to English with some languages (e.g. Dutch) shifting more rapidly than others (e.g. Greek and Italian).
Language Amalgamation	Kriol, Torres Strait Broken.
Language Contact	Mainly internally between English and Aboriginal and Torres Strait Islander languages or immigrant languages. Influences of American English (e.g. pop music, movies, television) and British English (e.g. residual status in judiciary, Anglican Church, media).
Literacy Development	ESL programmes such as the Australian Migrant Education Program (AMEP), national policies such as the 1987 National Policy on Languages started work in adult literacy on a federal level, Australian Language and Literacy Policy with adult and child emphases; National Literacy Policy being considered in 1996. Community and Aboriginal languages are being used for literacy development in some school curricula.

Government Agencies	Department of Immigration and Multicultural Affairs, Aboriginal and Torres Strait Islander Commission (Federation of Aboriginal and Torres Strait Islander Languages), SBS radio and television.
Education Agencies	Each of the eight States and Territories has its own Department of School Education setting language policies and programmes; the Department of Employment, Education, Training and Youth Affairs provides supplemental funding and funds demonstration programmes. Ethnic community organisations provide 'Saturday' school programmes in some States.
Non-Gov't Agencies	Language Australia (National Languages and Literacy Institute of Australia), Applied Linguistics Association of Australia, Australian Linguistics Society, ATESOL, Australian Federation of Modern Language Teachers Associations, Goethe Institute, Alliance Français.
Communities of Speakers	Some Aboriginal and immigrant groups live in communities where their languages can be spoken on a daily basis.
Other Bodies	Federation of Ethnic Community Councils of Australia, hundreds of ethnic specific organisations.

Malaysia (Conrad Ożóg, personal communication)

National Language	Bahasa Malaysia.
Language of Wider Comm.	English, Chinese, Indonesian/Malay (regionally).
Minority Languages	Chinese, Tamil, Iban, Murut, Kadazan/Dusan.
Dying Language	Orang Asli languages in Peninsula Malaysia; Kelabit and Penan in Sarawak.
Non-Standard Variety	Bazaar Malay, Kelantan Malay, Sarawak Coastal Malay, Sabah Malay.
Religious Language	Classical Arabic, Mandarin, Sanskrit.
Language Death	Many of the aboriginal languages of the Peninsula have died or are near death.
Language Survival	Chinese 'dialects' survive as do the Malay dialects of Kelantan, Sabah and Sarawak. Iban continues to survive and flourish in Sarawak despite attempts to downgrade the language to the status of a 'Malay dialect'.
Language Change	The indigenous languages and the Malay dialects now borrow extensively from Bahasa Malaysia.
Language Revival	Iban is enjoying a revival in Sarawak as an expression of Sarawakian identity (but it was not a language under threat).
Language Shift	The shift from indigenous languages and Malay dialects to Bahasa Malaysia (e.g. in Sarawak from Kelabit, Penan, Bidayuh).
Language Amalgamation	
Language Contact	All minority languages have extensive contact with Bahasa Malaysia leading to extensive borrowing from Bahasa Malaysia. Bahasa Malaysia borrows from English.
Literacy Development	
Government Agencies	Dewan Bahasa dan Pustaka; Radio Television Malaysia.
Education Agencies	Curriculum Development Agency.
Non-Gov't Agencies	Chinese clan associations eager to preserve Chinese 'dialects'.

Communities of Speakers	Many indigenous minority language speakers still live in homogeneous language communities.
Other Bodies	

Mexico (Patthey-Chavez, 1994)	
National Language	Spanish.
Language of Wider Comm.	Spanish, English.
Minority Languages	48 'well defined' ethnic groups with 5,282,347 indigenous speaking individuals.
Dying Language	12 languages are in danger of extinction.
Non-Standard Variety	
Religious Language	Spanish, Latin; Biblical literacy in indigenous languages.
Language Death	10 officially recognised languages are extinct.
Language Survival	Maya and Nahuatl with 500,000 and 800,000 speakers; Mazahua, Mazateco, Mixteco, Otomí, Totonaco, Tzeltal, Tzotzil and Zapoteco with over 100,000 speakers.
Language Change	
Language Revival	Nahuatl is being taught in secondary schools and at universities.
Language Shift	There has been a shift from indigenous languages to Spanish.
Language Amalgamation	There are a range of pidgins/creoles along both sides of the US/Mexico border with informal (and unflattering) names like Texmex.
Language Contact	Influence of English, especially along the border with the US; Indigenous language contact with Spanish.
Literacy Development	Summer Institute of Linguistics programmes until 1983 when they were thrown out; Government literacy programmes.
Government Agencies	Instituto Nacional Indigenista.
Education Agencies	Dirección General de Culturas Populares; Dirección General de Educacíon Indígena (DGEI); Instituto Nacionál para la Educacíon de los Adultos (INEA).
Non-Gov't Agencies	
Communities of Speakers	
Other Bodies	Council of Indigenous Peoples; Alianza National de Profesionistas Indígenas Bilingües, A. C.; Frente Independiente de Pueblos Indios; National Autonomous University of Mexico (UNAM).

South Africa (Webb, 1994, 1996)	
Official Languages	Zulu, Afrikaans, English, Xhosa, Northern Sotho, Tswana, Southern Sotho, Tsonga, Swazi, Venda, Ndebele.
Language of Wider Comm.	English.
Minority Languages	Hindi, Gujarati, Tamil, Urdu, Telugu; Portuguese, Greek, Italian, German, Dutch, French.
Dying Language	
Non-Standard Variety	Fanakalo, Tsotsitaal.
Religious Language	Classical Arabic.
Language Death	

Language Survival
Language Change
Language Revival
Language Shift
Language Amalgamation
Language Contact
Literacy Development
Government Agencies
Education Agencies
Non-Gov't Agencies
Communities of Speakers
Other Bodies

	Sweden (Birger Winsa, personal communication)
National Language	Swedish.
Language of Wider Comm.	English, German, French. Education in French is increasingly important. Finnish is an important language for communication in northern Sweden.
Minority Languages	Finnish, Tornedalen Finnish, Saami; Romani since the sixteenth century; many migrant languages (e.g. Danish, Norwegian, German, Polish, Hungarian).
Dying Language	Saami has good public support but few speakers. South Saami is spoken by a few hundred; North Saami by a few thousand. Overkalix Swedish, Alvdalen Swedish and Gotland Swedish are only spoken by older speakers and are close to extinction.
Non-Standard Variety	Tornedalan Finnish is not acknowledged by the government as a language, but as a variety of standard Finnish. South Saami and Luleo Saami are not accepted as Standard Saami, but as mutually incomprehensible varieties of North Saami. Gotland Swedish, Overkalix Swedish, Alvdalen Swedish are mutually incomprehensible varieties of Standard Swedish. There are also some immigrant varieties of Swedish.
Religious Language	Generally Swedish, although Finnish has been a religious language in the Laestadian movement in Northern Sweden and is actively used in the main cities with an active Finnish-speaking population. Saami used to a limited extent.
Language Death	Finnish was spoken in county Varmland from sixteenth Century to 1960s when it died. Besides Finnish, a number of other languages have ceased to exist (e.g. Lower German, Danish, Flemish, Yiddish).
Language Survival	Standard Swedish; Finnish, Saami and Romani (?) have survived due to replacement.
Language Change	Saami and Tornedalen Finnish have borrowed new terms and other features extensively from Swedish. Standard Finnish is now becoming more influential in the north. Standard Swedish terminological development through Swedish Centre for Technical Terminology (TNC).
Language Revival	Tornedalen Finnish has become more popular since the 1980s.

Language Shift	There is a general shift toward Standard Swedish, in particular from Finnish to Swedish (following the three generation rule), from Saami to Swedish in the north and until recently Tornedalen Finnish was losing ground every year. Swedish varieties are also shifting toward the standard.
Language Amalgamation	None.
Language Contact	All minority and immigrant languages have contact with Standard Swedish and some contact with Standard Finnish, and to a lessor extent Norwegian, Danish (regional languages) and other languages of wider communication. The lack of direct contact with Finnish since 1809 when Sweden lost the war against Russia has meant that Tornedalan Finnish has preserved features lost in other Finnish varieties. Saami is massively influenced by contact with Finnish varieties.
Literacy Development	Home language instruction exists for every migrant language as well as the minority languages of Sweden. Finnish immigrants have about 10 private schools with Finnish as the language of instruction.
Government Agencies	Sweden is the only Scandinavian country to have a formal language academy (established in 1786). *Invandrarverket* – Immigration Board.
Education Agencies	*Skolverket* – National Board of Education – provides a framework which every school must adapt, but responsibility for education now rests with local authorities – who may be more responsive, but try to save money by reducing home language instruction.
Non-Gov't Agencies	*Sverige Finska sproknamnden* – Swedish Finnish Language Board (works with Finnish immigrants); *Samiska sproknamnden* – The Saami Language Board; the Swedish Centre for Technical Terminology (TNC).
Communities of Speakers	Territorial communities – Saami & Tornedalian Finnish speakers; Gipsies (scattered); immigrants – Finns and perhaps another 150 language groups.
Other Bodies	The Saami community has the Saami Parliament (government financed) which tries to expand the use of Saami; Finns have an umbrella organisation named Svergefinska Riksforbundet; the Tornedalens have an organisation called Svenska Tornedalingars Riksforbund. The latter two are independent organisations working for language and culture. Corpus planning for Tornedalen Finnish has been done by individual volunteers including Matti Kentta, Bengt Pohjanen, Birger Winsa and Erling Wande. Other groups have their own organisations.

United States

National Language	English (*de facto*), Spanish (Puerto Rico), Samoan (American Samoa).
Language of Wider Comm.	English.
Minority Languages	Amerindian languages, Spanish.
Dying Language	Many Ameridian Languages.

Non-Standard Variety	Black English, MANSE, many Amerindian and immigrant languages have non-standard varieties.
Religious Language	English for most Christian demominations, but many other languages (e.g. Arabic, Church Greek, Hebrew, Hindi).
Language Death	Many Ameridian languages.
Language Survival	Despite the political rhetoric, English is not under threat. Many immigrant languages survive (e.g. Norwegian, Hungarian).
Language Change	
Language Revival	Navajo, partial revival of Mohawk.
Language Shift	There is a general shift to English from immigrant and Amerindian languages.
Language Amalgamation	Pennsylvania Dutch.
Language Contact	All languages with English, with Spanish in the Southwest and Florida, with French in the Northeast; contact through international business, through military occupation and UN Peace-Keeping efforts.
Literacy Development	
Government Agencies	Bureau of Indian Affairs, Department of Commerce, Postal Service, Federal Courts.
Education Agencies	OBEMLA
Non-Gov't Agencies	National Council for the Teaching of English, TESOL, ACTFL, E-SU, Goethe Institute, Alliance Français, Navajo Nation, Centre for Applied Linguistics.
Communities of Speakers	There are ethnic enclaves throughout the United States some local (e.g. in Los Angeles, Spanish in East Los Angeles, Portuguese/Italian in San Pedro, Samoan and Guamanian in Long Beach, Arab/Lebanese in Hollywood), but others more regionally (e.g. Swedes/Norwegians in Minnesota/South Dakota, Finns in Oregon/Washington, Russian Dukabors in Oregon or Spanish speakers throughout the Southwest and Florida and many large cities.
Other Bodies	

Thus it is apparent that, as any of the forces acting on the system are modified, the whole system is modified; that is, if the language plan for this eco-system requires an attempt to revive minority language 6 in Figure 11.2, all other languages in the system will be affected, or if the effort being made by the education agencies is increased or decreased, that change will affect all other forces at work in the eco-system. In addition, it must be remembered that the various interacting languages in this eco-system represent communities of speakers who use the several languages to communicate with each other and with other communities of speakers within this eco-system and in proximate eco-systems which may look quite different. This figure may illustrate the great difficulty of making language plans (necessarily preceding language policy) and the very great number of variables that must be kept in balance if the solutions are to ' ... do justice both to the wishes of indigenous people and, at the same time, are compatible with the inevitable changes that will continue to affect languages world wide . . . ' (Mühlhäusler, 1995b: 26).

While Figure 11.2 provides a global view of the total language eco-system, each of the individual languages should also be seen in its ecological perspective. It is the intent of Figure 11.4 to illustrate the fact that proximate language ecologies must be taken into account in any language planning activity. It will be noted that the principal language in *Ecology 2* occurs as a minority language in both of the proximate ecologies and that the principal language of *Ecology 3* occurs as a minority language in *Ecology 2*. It will also be noted that the arbitrary political borders do not coincide with the ecological borders. The heavy line indicates the principal target of the language planning activity, and the broken lines suggest that the language planning activity must give attention to the existence of some of the same languages in the proximate ecologies, without reference to the political borders. It must also be noted that there is a good deal of language overlap, a number of minority languages occurring in all three ecologies. Because the ecologies are shown as overlapping, some of the language duplication in this figure is hidden.

The figure suggests the presence of three major languages within the political boundaries: unfortunately, circumstances in the real world are rarely as neat as this. One might think of Malaysia (with four major

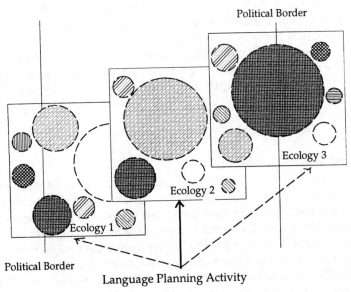

Figure 11.4 Effect of an ecological perspective on a language planning activity

languages and a number of minor languages) as a real-world model. In such a situation, each of the major languages has its satellite languages. If, for example, the major language in *Ecology* 2 is English, the major language in *Ecology* 3 is Bahasa Malaysia, and the major language in *Ecology* 1 is Mandarin, then at least some of the minority languages in *Ecology* 1 would be represented by other Chinese dialects (e.g. Hakka, Hokkien, Cantonese), some of the minority languages in *Ecology* 2 might be Malaysian English, Singaporean English and even more distantly languages like French and German (i.e. languages of overseas education, trade and tourism), and some of the minority languages in *Ecology* 3, might represent Bahasa Indonesia and other *bumiputra* minority languages in Malaysia (e.g. Bazaar Malay, Iban, Kadazan, Murit).[3] In the interests of space – and to keep the figure from getting too complex, the fourth major language – Tamil – has been omitted, as have the *bumiputra* languages of East Malaysia (e.g. Kadazan, Iban), but it would include among its satellites, other languages of South Asia.

One might also note that while the main focus of this hypothetical planning problem is English, perhaps as part of the government's 'Vision 2020' national development programme, English language planning will effect the ecology of the other languages in the system. The political boundary splits *Ecology* 3, that is, Bahasa Malaysia is a jointly shared and planned language concern with Bahasa Indonesia and with the Malay spoken in Brunei Darussalam and Singapore. Planning for Chinese also crosses political borders, with Singapore in the socio-political sense and with China and/or Taiwan linguistically. English language planning also raises the question of which English (see e.g. Zawiah Yahya, 1996). The intent of the figure is merely to suggest the complexity of the situation and the fact that political boundaries may be irrelevant to at least parts of the problem.[4]

Critical Issues Revisited

We have tried to argue throughout this volume that the underlying paradigm for language planning is in need of some significant revision. It seems no longer viable to think of corpus and status planning as clearly separate activities; and it seems no longer viable to think only in terms of general national language policy. Rather, as we have suggested early in this volume, language planning at the macro level is a function of what Trim (1987) has called Left Branching societal human resources development planning, and it must be treated as such. At the micro level, planning – what Trim has called Right Branching human resource development – is occurring more frequently and with increasingly greater impact. Unfortunately, the micro level has largely been ignored in the literature (but see Touchstone, 1996). Obviously, in the ideal situation, the two types are co-occurring, but it is not necessary that Left Branching development be in progress for Right Branching planning to occur; indeed, in the immediate future, it is far more likely that Right Branching planning will be practised widely, most commonly without benefit of Left Branching planning.

We have tried to argue that language planning doesn't necessarily follow the several stages suggested in Haugen's 2×2 model of the process (see Chapter 2); rather, we believe, language planning can begin at any point – it is not necessarily corpus driven, nor is it necessarily status driven. We have also tried to suggest that different polities (and different languages) may enter into the process at different points of development. We have tried to argue that language planning cannot any longer be conceived in terms of the one-language/one-nation myth, since – in any case – there are virtually no monolingual nations, and since any given language is likely to occur simultaneously in more than one polity. Most importantly, we have tried to show that every language constitutes part of an eco-system, and that any attempt to manage one language in the system inevitably has implications for all the other languages in the single system (and in proximate systems as well). And we have tried to show that eco-systems do not exist in isolation but of necessity implicate adjoining eco-systems, (without reference to the political boundaries) ? which separate any or all of the eco-systems – the more so in pluricentric languages.

In sum, language planning is a very large-scale activity, involving a reticulated structure of many languages – a genuinely multidimensional construct. To the extent that language planning is such a construct, it seems absurd to think of any one individual undertaking the activity of language planning. Rather, we believe, the process requires the attention of a wide range of academic specialists as well as of the communities of speakers of all the languages and varieties involved.

We have tried to suggest that the education sector – often the main, or at least a major, actor in language planning and in language policy implementation – may be precisely the wrong place to begin planning and policy implementation, simply because of the inherent scope of the activity. This is not to say that language planning and policy implementation ought never to occur in the education sector; on the contrary, such planning and policy development must include the education sector, but as a sub-structure of a larger more broadly conceived plan and implementation policy – the education sector occupies one niche in a larger plan. Admittedly, it is better for a plan and policy implementation to occur in the education sector than not to occur at all, but if the education sector constitutes the only actor, change is likely to be rather slow, limited in scope and in outcome.

While macro planning often devolves to the education sector, the increasingly frequent examples of micro planning show that the planning and policy development must originate from the highest levels of the structure, must implicate the entire structure, and must, centrally, derive its authority from the community(ies) of speakers; it need not involve the education sector centrally, but may do so peripherally. In other words, language planning and policy implementation ideally follows a bottom-up structure, rather than a top-down structure. We have attempted to illustrate the subordinate processes and objectives underlying language planning, to enumerate the actors, and to demonstrate potential interactions between the objectives and the actors. And we have tried to suggest that language planning is not a one-off activity, but that it is long term, spiral, and costly. We have also tried to suggest that the assessment of success is, at best, difficult.

In the end, what we have tried to do is to make language planning and policy development accessible to a wide range of potential actors – to practitioners and students, to applied linguists only tangentially involved in the process, and to government and corporate officials. (We hope that government and corporate officials will consult this volume before initiating a planning effort.) To achieve this objective, we have consulted a broad spectrum of the literature, and we have tried to encapsulate large quantities on information and of resources in easily accessible form.

The relative success of our efforts will, of course, be judged by those who read (and hopefully use) this volume. To those who succeed in reading to this final page, we express our gratitude, and we invite comments and criticisms, since we envision that this projection will soon be in need of revision as well.

Notes

1. However, even initial corpus planning often goes beyond pure description, as work with Aboriginal groups in Australia has shown. Even when a language is not written, in a world where literacy is all around us, the people whose language is being written often have some ideas about what their language should or shouldn't look like (i.e. not like a neighbouring language – 'we are a different people'). Linguists themselves may not agree about what is the best way to describe orthographically, a particular language (Russo & Baldauf, 1986). Redefining the orthography of a language to be easier and more descriptively accurate may divide a linguistic community between the adherents of the new and old systems (e.g. Guugu Yimithirr in North Queensland), and for small languages this may endanger the very survival of the language. Black (1990) argues against prescription for just these sorts of reasons.
2. See Martin Gilbert's Atlases of British History, of American History, of Russian History, of Jewish History (London: J.M. Dent)
3. The situation is also more complex than shown in the diagram in that some of these languages and dialects may overlap in terms of mutual intelligibility (e.g. Bahasa Melayu, Bahasa Indonesia, Bazaar Malay). For example, Djité (1988a) discusses the phenomenon of monolingual nuclei and multilingual satellites for the languages of the Côte d'Ivoire in Africa.

4. There is no simple research model which will deal with so many variables. Structural equation modelling analysis (Weasenforth, 1995) is a technique that may permit the tracking of such a large number of variables. We are not recommending the use of the technique; we merely suggest it as one possibility.

Appendix: Language Planning in National Contexts

This appendix is meant to serve as a brief introduction to language planning in national contexts. It is limited therefore to a brief description of the location, size and population of the country, as estimated in mid-1992, as well as brief information about its language(s).

As the language policy and planning literature is quite large and as the purpose of this appendix is to provide references to internationally accessible information, citations are generally limited to published sources; government documents and 'local' publications were avoided – as these are often hard to access. Where there are many references available, preferences is given to reviews or collections of papers. While information on all polities formed the starting point for our review of the literature, only those for which we could find at least one reference meeting these criteria are included.

In a book on language planning, the matter of language choice deserves some comment, not only as a topic in the text, but as an issue the authors must face when selecting work to present to readers. Baldauf and Jernudd (1983) and Jernudd and Baldauf (1987) have discussed these issues in detail, i.e. language choice in scientific communication and the fact that 'international' sources are for the most part available in a few modernised languages, predominantly English. While we have not deliberately excluded materials we have come across in languages other than English, English materials do make up the bulk of our references. We recognise that works in other languages certainly exist, e.g. there are important works in Hungarian on both Hungarian and Gypsy languages, but such works were not accessible to us, nor would they meet our general accessibility criteria set out in the previous paragraph. We must therefore leave it to those interested in language planning in those languages to locate those texts.

We hope this appendix will provide a starting point for those interested in language policy and planning in national contexts. Some useful general references to the language situation include Comrie's (1987) *The World's Major Languages* and Bright *et al.*'s (1992) *International Encyclopedia of Linguistics* which provide information on languages or language families, Horvath and Vaughan's (1991) profile of 58 community languages in English speaking countries, Katzner's (1986) overview of the languages of the world with sample texts, Fodor and Hegège's (1983a, 1983b, 1984, 1989, 1990) collected papers on language standardisation and reform, Laponce's (1987: 204 ff.) comparison of domains of language use in multilingual states, Adegbija's (1994a: 6–12) summary of sub-Saharan African languages, Robins and Uhlenbeck's (1991) overview of *Endangered Languages* and Wurm, Mühlhäusler and Tryon's (1996) *Atlas of Languages of International Communication in the Pacific, Asia and the Americas*. Rubin and Jernudd (1979) and Kennedy (1984), in a bibliography, provide references to early information on language planning.

domains [handwritten margin note]

Albania. Located in S central Europe with a total land area of 28,750 km² and a population of 3,285,224. Albanian, (Gheg is a major dialect, Tosk is official dialect), Greek spoken in the south, Romany. Kostallari (1989).

Algeria. Situated along the N coast of Africa with a total land area of 2,381,740 km² and a population of 26,000,000. Arabic (official), French, Berber dialects. El Aissati (1993), Souaiaia (1990).

Angola. Located along the W coast of Africa with a total land area of 1,246,700 km² and a population of 8,900,000: 24 languages, Portuguese (official), Kongo, Kimbundu, Umbundu, Bantu languages. Garcez (1995).

Argentina. Located on the SE coast of South America with a total land area of 2,780,092 km² and a population of 32,425,000. Spanish (official), English, French, German, Italian, Amerindian languages. Behares and Massone (1996), Kaplan (1990b), Messineo and Wright (1989).

Australia. Occupies whole of Island continent of Australia, lying between Indian and Pacific oceans, and its offshore islands, principally Tasmania to SE. A total land area of 7,682,300 km² and a population of 17,800,000. English, indigenous languages. ALLC (1994, 1995), Baldauf (1993, 1985, 1995b), Berthold (1995), Clyne (1982, 1985, 1988b, 1988c), Delbridge (1985), Djité (1994), East Asia Analytical Unit (1992), Eggington (1994), Herriman (1996), Horvath and Vaughan (1991), Ingram (1987, 1994), Janik (1996), Kaplan (1979, 1989), Kipp *et al.* (1995), Lo Bianco (1987a, 1987b, 1990, 1997), Lo Bianco and Monteil (1990), Mackerras (1995), Martin (1990), Moore (1991, 1996), Mühlhäusler (1995a, 1995c), Ozolins (1984, 1988, 1991, 1993), Pauwels (1985, 1993), Raby *et al.* (1992), Romaine (1991), Smolicz (1984a, 1994), Stanley *et al.* (1990), Stanton and Lee (1995), Stanton *et al.* (1992), Valverde (1992), Wierzbicka (1993). *Aboriginal Languages.* Austin (1991), Baldauf (1995a), Baldauf and Eggington (1989), Bell (1981), Black (1990), Devlin *et al.* (1995), Dixon (1989), Eggington (1992), Eggington and Baldauf (1990), Fesl (1982, 1987), Jernudd (1971), Johnson (1987), Kale

(1990), McKay (1996), Riley-Mundine and Roberts (1990), Russo (1983), Russo and Baldauf (1986), Sandefur (1977, 1985), Sommer (1991).

Austria. Situated in central W Europe with a total land area of 83,857 km² and a population of 7,900,000. German (Austrian dialect official) and minority languages. de Cillia (1996), Clyne (1988a, 1995), Rusch (1989).

Azerbaijan. Situated in the SE Caucasus bordering on Armenia, Georgia, Russia, Iran and Turkey with a total area of 86,600 km² and a population of 7,100,000. Azeri (official), Russian, Armenian and Other. Pool (1976).

Bangladesh. Situated in S Asia with a total land area of 143,998 km² and a population of 111,400,000. Bangla (official); Urdu, Bahari, Hindi, English widely used. Chaklader (1987), Moniruzzaman (1979), Musa (1984, 1985, 1989, 1996), Pachori (1990).

Belarus. A landlocked state in E Europe with a total area of 207,000 km² and a population of 10,300,000. Belorusian (official), Russian, Other. Maurais (1992), Wexler (1992).

Belgium. Situated in NW Europe with a total land area of 30,513 km² and a population of 10,000,000: 56% Flemish (Dutch), 32% French, 1% German; 11% legally bilingual; divided along ethnic lines. Baetens Beardsmore (1980), Beheydt (1994), Deprez and Wynants (1994b), Donaldson (1983), Falch (1973), Hermans, Vos and Wils (1992), Holvoet (1992), Nelde (1994), Sonntag (1989), Van de Craen and Willemyns (1988), Van der Plank (1988), Wardhaugh (1987: 203 ff), Willemyns (1984, 1993), Willemyns and van de Craen (1988).

Benin. Situated along the W coast of Africa with a total land area of 112,622 km² and a population of 5,000,000: 10 languages, French (official), Fon-Ewe, Yoruba, Bariba. Calvet *et al.* (1992), Tchitchi (1989).

Bolivia. A landlocked country in central S America with a total land area of 1,098,581 km² and a population of 7,800,000. Spanish, Quechua and Aymara (all official). von Gleich (1994), Hornberger and King (1996).

Brazil. Situated in central and NE S America with a total land area of 8,511,957 km² and a population of 156,275,397 (mid-1992). Portuguese (official), Spanish, English, French, German, Japanese, Amerindian. Gomez de Matos and Bortoni (1991), Garcez (1995), Silva and Gunnewiek (1992).

Brunei. Situated in SE Asia, on the NW coast of the island of Borneo with a total land area of 5,765 km² and a population of 300,000. Malay and English (official), Chinese, minority languages. Edwards (1993), Jones (1990), Jones *et al.* (1993), Pakir (1993a).

Bulgaria. Located in SE Europe, in the E Balkan Mountains with a total land area of 110,912 km² and a population of 8,900,000. Bulgarian (official), Turkish, Romany, Macedonian, minority languages. Cojnska (1992), Jernudd (1994b), Hill (1992).

Burundi. A landlocked country on the NE shore of Lake Tanganyika in central Africa with a total land area of 27,834 km² and a population of 5,800,000. Kirundi and French (both official), Swahili (along Lake Tanganyika and in Bujumbura area). Cembalo (1993), Eisemon *et al.* (1989), Masagara (1991).

Cambodia (Kampuchea). Occupies part of Indochinese Peninsula in SE Asia with a total land area of 181,035 km^2 and a population of 9,100,000. Khmer (official), Chinese, Vietnamese, French. Jacob (1986), Thong (1985).

Cameroon. Situated along the W coast of central Africa with a total land area of 475,442 km^2 and a population of 12,700,000: 200 languages, English and French (both official), Bamileke, Fang, Ewondo and Fulfulde, 24 major African language groups. Todd (1984), Calvet *et al.* (1992), Robinson (1993, 1994).

Canada. Located in the N part of N America with a total land area of 9,976,186 km^2 and a population of 27,400,000. English, French (both official); Amerindian and Inuit languages. Boulanger (1986, 1989), Bourhis (1984), Burnaby (1997), d'Anglejan (1984), Caldwell (1988), Cartwright (1988, 1993), Coulombe (1993), Cumming (1996), Daoust (1991), Dion and Lamy (1990), Edwards (1994, 1995), Fortier (1994), Hamers and Hummel (1994), Maurais (1996), McConnell (1977), Ridler and Pons-Ridler (1986), Robinson (1994), Wardhaugh (1987: 221 ff). *Inuit.* Collis (1990, 1992), Dorias (1990).

Cape Verde. An archipelago of 10 islands and five islets in the Atlantic Ocean, off the west coast of N Africa. A total land area of 4,033 km^2 and a population of 400,000. Portuguese and Criuolo (blend of Portuguese and West African). Garcez (1995).

China, People's Republic of. A country covering a vast area of E Asia with a total land area of 9,561,000 km^2 and a population of 1,165,800,000. Standard Chinese (Putonghua), or Mandarin (based on the Beijing dialect); also Yue (Cantonese), Wu (Shanghainese), Minbei (Fuzhou), Minnan (Hokkien-Taiwanese), Xiang, Gan, Hakka dialects and minority langs. Barnes (1982, 1983), Bo and Baldauf (1990), Cannon (1990), DeFrancis (1975), Harrell (1993), Lehmann (1975), Light (1980), Malischewshi (1987), Pride and Liu (1988), Snow (1993a, 1993b), Sun (1988/1989), Tse (1982), Yin (1987), Zhou and Feng (1987), Zhu and Chen (1991).

Côte d'Ivoire. Situated along the W coast of Africa with a total land area of 322,462 km^2 and a population of 13,000,000. French (official); 60 languages including Anyi-Baoule, Akan, Dyula and Senoufo. Calvet (1982), Calvet *et al.* (1992), Djité (1988a, 1988b, 1991).

Croatia. Located in S central Europe on the Adriatic Sea with a total land area of 56,537 km^2 and a population of 4,600,000. Croatian (official). Branko (1980), Hill (1992).

Czech Republic. Landlocked country in central Europe with a total land area of 78,865 km^2 and a population of 10,365,000. Czechs 81%, Slovaks 3%, Others 16%. Czech (official). Hübschmannová and Neustupný (1996), Neustupný (1989).

Denmark. Located in N Europe with a total land area of 43,075 km^2 and a population of 5,200,000. Danish (official), Faeroese, Greenlandic (Eskimo dialect); small German-speaking minority. Jarvad (1990), Loman (1988), Skyum-Nielson (1978).

Ecuador. Located on the NW coast of South America with a total land area of 276,840 km^2 and a population of 10,300,000. Spanish (official), Indian languages, especially Quéchua. Von Gleich (1994), Hornberger and King (1996).

Egypt. Situated on the NE coast of Africa, with an extension across the Gulf of Suez into Sinai peninsula, sometimes regarded as lying within Asia. Total land area of 1,002,000 km^2 and a population of 57,758,000. Arabic (official), English and French widely understood by educated classes. Mitchell (1985).

Estonia. Located on the E end of the Baltic Sea with a total land area of 47,549 km^2 and a population of 1,600,000. Estonian (official), Latvian, Lithuanian, Russian, Other. Grin (1991), Laitin (1996), Maurais (1992), Ozolins (1994), Rannut (1994).

Ethiopia. A country extending inland from the E coast of Africa with a total land area of 1,223,600 km^2 and a population of 54,300,000: 70 languages, Amharic (official), Tigrinya, Galla, Orominga, Arabic; English is a major foreign language taught in schools, Italian. Biber and Hared (1992), Cooper (1976), Fellman (1983), Ferguson (1971), Bloor and Tamrat (1996).

European Union. An emerging polity made up of the following countries: Belgium, Denmark, France, Germany, Greece, Ireland, Italy, Luxembourg, Netherlands, Portugal, Spain and the United Kingdom. The language of each country is an official language of the EU. Ammon (1994b), Baetens Beardsmore (1993a, 1993b, 1994), Corsetti and La Torre (1995), Coulmas (1991a), Deprez and Wynants (1994), Grin (1993), Leitner (1991), Mar-Molinero (1994), Schlossmacher (1995), Trim (1994), Truchot (1991), van Els and van Hest (1990), Wright (1995).

Faroe Islands. Eighteen islands in the N Atlantic 322 km NW of the Shetland Is. with a total land area of 1,399 km^2 and a population of 48,151 (July 1991). Faroese, Danish. Dorian (1989), Hagström (1989), Holm (1993).

Fiji. Consists of more than 300 islands of which 100 are inhabited, situated about 2,100 km N of Auckland, New Zealand, in the S Pacific Ocean. A total land area of 18,333 km^2 and a population of 800,000. English (official), Fijian, Hindustani. Geraghty (1989a, 1989b), Mangubhai (1987), Siegel (1989, 1992).

Finland. Situated in N Europe with a total land area of 337,009 km^2 and a population of 5,000,000. 93.5% Finnish, 6.3% Swedish (both official); small Sami and Russian speaking minorities. Aikio (1990, 1991), Haarmann (1974), Hansén (1991), Janhunen (1975–80), Paulston et al. (1993).

France. Located in W Europe with a total land area of 547,026 km^2 and a population of 56,900,000. French (official); declining regional dialects (Breton, Provençal, Alsacian, Corsican, Catalan, Basque, Flemish). Ager

(1990), Anonymous (1994b), Caldwell (1994), Djité (1992), Eastman (1983: 207ff), Grillo (1989), Joseph (1987), Schiffman (1995), Slone (1989), Tabouret-Keller (1981), Thody (1995), Varro (1992), Wardhaugh (1987: 97), Weinstein (1976, 1989). *Breton.* McDonald (1989), Trimm (1980, 1982). *Alsacian.* Veltman and Denis (1988). *Occitan.* Eckert (1983), Field (1981), Kremnitz (1974). *Francophonie.* Bélanger (1995), Bokamba (1991), Djité (1990), Kleineidam (1992), Weinstein (1989).

French Polynesia. Several scattered groups of 120 islands (25 uninhabited) in the S Pacific Ocean, about two-thirds of the way between the Panama Canal and New Zealand. A total land area of 4,000 km^2 and a population of 200,000. Lavondes (1971), Turcotte (1984).

Georgia. In the Caucasus on the Black Sea bordering on Armenia, Russia, Azerbaijan and Turkey with a total land area of 167,700 km^2 and a population of 5,500,000. Georgian (official) 71%, Russian 9%, Armenian 7%, Azeri 6%, Other 7%. Klarberg (1992), Weber (1990).

Germany. A central European country, with a total land area of 357,000 km^2 and a population of 80,600,000. German, Frisian, Sorbian. Ammon (1991, 1992), Augst and Ammon (1993), Barbour and Stevenson (1990), Besch (1988), Clyne (1995), Kirkness (1975), Takahashi (1995). **Sorbian.** Norberg (1994), Schuster-Šewe (1992), Walker (1980, 1984).

Ghana. Situated along the W coast of Africa with a total land area of 238,537 km^2 and a population of 16,000,000: 54 languages, Adangme, Nzema, Ga, Dagaari, English (all official); Akan, Hausa, Dagbani, Ewe. Amonoo (1994), Ansre (1975), Calvet (1982), Laitin and Mensah (1991).

Greece. Located in SE Europe with a total land area of 131,990 km^2 and a population of 10,300,000. Greek (official); English and French widely understood. Frangoudaki (1992), Jahr and Trudgill (1993), Kitis (1990), Sotiropoulos (1992).

Greenland. A large island in the N Atlantic with a total land area of 2,175,600 km^2 and a population of 57,407 (July 1992). Eskimo dialects, Danish. Moller (1988, 1990), Petersen (1990).

Guam. The southernmost and largest of the Mariana Islands in the western N Pacific Ocean with a total land area of 541 km^2 and a population of 133,152 (1991 census). English and Chamorro; most people are bilingual; Japanese also widely spoken. Combs and Jernudd (1981), Day (1985), Riley (1975, 1980), Underwood (1989a, 1989b).

Guatemala. Situated in the N part of the Central American isthmus with a total land area of 108,889 km^2 and a population of 9,700,000. Spanish, but over 40% population speaks an Indian language as primary tongue (18 dialects including Quiché, Cakchiquel, Kekchi). Morren (1988), Lewis (1993), Richards (1989), Stewart (1984).

Guinea-Bissau. Situated along NW coast of Africa with a total land area of 36,125 km^2 and a population of 1,000,000. Portuguese, Crioulo (both official), Balante, Fulani, numerous African languages. Garcez (1995).

Haiti. The W part of the island of Hispaniola and several small islands in northern Caribbean Sea with a total land area of 27,750 km^2 and a population of 6,400,000. French (spoken only by 10% of the population); all speak Creole (both official). Valdman (1986).

Honduras. Located in north central part of Central America on the Caribbean. A total land area of 112,088 km^2 and a population of 5,500,000. Spanish (official), Garifuna, some Indian dialects, English in the Bay of Islands Department. Reyburn (1975).

Hong Kong. Located in E Asia, off the S coast of China; consists of the island of Hong Kong, Stonecutters Island, Kowloon peninsula, and New Territories, which are on the mainland. A total land area of 1,031 km^2 and a population of 5,700,000. To revert from Britain to China in mid-1997. Chinese (Cantonese), English (both official). Bolton and Luke (1985), Boyle (1995), Cembalo (1993), Education Commission (1996), Gibbons (1982), Jernudd (1994b), Johnson (1994), Kwo and Bray (1987), Lee (1993), Yau (1989).

Hungary. A landlocked country in E Europe with a total land area of 93,033 km^2 and a population of 10,300,000. Magyar (official). Settlements of Romanians, Gypsies; German spoken. Benkő (1992), Medgyes and Kaplan (1992), Kaplan (1993), Radnai (1994), Szépe (1994).

Iceland. One large island and numerous smaller ones near Arctic Circle in North Atlantic Ocean with a total land area of 102,846 km^2 and a population of 300,000. Icelandic (official). Joseph (1987: 83–87), Kristinsson (1994).

India. Forms a natural subcontinent in Asia, with the Himalayan mountain range to the N. A total land area of 3,185,019 km^2 and a population of 882,600,000. Hindi, English and Bengali, Gujarati, Kashmiri, Malaylam, Marathi, Oriya, Punjabi, Tamil, Telugu, Urdu, Kannada, Assamese, Sanskrit, Sindhi (recognised by the constitution); 24 languages spoken by a million or more persons each; numerous other languages and dialects, for the most part mutually unintelligible; Hindi is the national language and primary tongue of 30% of the people; English enjoys associate status but is the most important language for national, political and commercial communication; Hindustani, a popular variant of Hindi/Urdu, is spoken widely throughout northern India. Aggarwal (1988, 1992), Bayer (1987), Chidambaram (1986), Das Gupta (1971), Dua (1991, 1994, 1996), Halemane (1992), Laitin (1993), James (1985), Kachru (1982), Kelkar (1986), Khubchandani (1975, 1983, 1994), Krishnamurthi (1985, 1986), Pattanayak (1986), Rahman (1996), Schiffman (1995), Singh (1987), Sreedhar et al. (1984), Sridhar (1988), Tickoo (1994), Verma (1991).

Indonesia. An archipelago of about 13,700 islands lying between the mainland of SE Asia and Australia, stretching from the Malay peninsula to New Guinea. A total land area of 1,904,344 km^2 and a population of 184,500,000. Indonesian (modified form of Malay; official); English and

Dutch, leading foreign languages; more than 583 languages and dialects, most widely spoken of which is Javanese. Alisjahbana (1976, 1984), Anderson (1987), Anwar (1979), De Vries (1988), Kentjono (1986), Lowenberg (1992), Moeliono (1994), Rubin (1977a, 1977b), Walker (1993).

Iran. Located in W Asia with a total land area of 1,648,000 km^2 and a population of 59,700,000. Farsi (official), Turkish, Kurdish, Arabic, English, French. Karimi-Hakkak (1989), Modarresi (1990).

Ireland. Twenty-six out of 32 counties comprising the Island of Ireland, an island in the Atlantic Ocean; remaining six counties, in NE, form Northern Ireland, which is part of the United Kingdom. A total land area of 70,282 km^2 and a population of 3,500,000. Irish (Gaelic) and English (official); English widely spoken. Ahlqvist (1993), Commins (1988), Hindley (1990), Kallen (1988), Ó Buachalla (1984), Ó Baoill (1988), Ó Ciosáin (1988), O'Donoghue (1995), Ó Gadhra (1988), Ó Gliasáin (1988), Ó hAilin (1969), Ó Laoire, 1995, Ó Murchú (1990), Ó Riagain (1988), Ó Riagain et al. (1989), Tovey (1988), Ureland (1993), Williams (1988).

Israel. Located in W Asia, occupying a narrow strip of territory on the eastern shore of the Mediterranean Sea; also having a narrow outlet to the Red Sea at the northern tip of the Gulf of Aqaba. A total land area of 20,772 km^2 with a population of 5,200,000. Hebrew (official), Arabic (official for Arab minority); Yiddish, English, Russian, Romanian. Alloni-Fainberg 1974), Dagut (1985), Eastman (1983: 215 ff), Fellman (1976, 1993), Fisherman (1990), Glinert (1991, 1995), Gold (1989), Hallel and Spolsky (1993), Nahir (1988), Rabin (1971, 1976), Shohamy (1994), Spolsky (1995).

Italy. A peninsula, extending from S Europe into the Mediterranean Sea with a number of adjacent islands, principally Sicily to SW, and Sardinia to W. A total land area of 301,278 km^2 and a population of 58,000,000. Italian; parts of Trentino-Alto Adige region (e.g. Bolzano) are predominantly German-speaking; significant French-speaking minority in Valle d'Aosta region; Slovene-speaking minority in Trieste-Gorizia area. De Mauro and Vedovelli (1994).

Japan. A chain of more than 3,000 islands extending some 2,200 km NE to SW between the Sea of Japan and the Pacific Ocean in eastern Asia; southern Japan is about 150 km E of S. Korea; four large islands – (from N to S) Hokkaido, Honshu, Shikoku, and Kyushu – account for more than 98% of the land area; plus Okinawa. A total land area of 377,815 km^2 and a population of 124,400,000. Japanese (official); Ainu, Korean. Carroll (1995), Coulmas (1989), DeChicchis (1995), Jernudd (1994b), Kay (1986), Hirataka (1992), Holden (1990), Maher and Yashiro (1995), Morrow (1987), Neustupný (1976, 1978, 1984, 1986), Ogino et al. (1985), Stanlaw (1987), Takashi (1992), Twine (1991).

Jordan. Situated in W Asia with a total land area of 89,544 km^2 and a population of 3,600,000. Arabic (official); English widely understood among upper and middle classes. Harrison et al. (1975), Ibrahim (1979).

Kazakhstan. Located in central Asia with a total land area of 2,717,300 km^2 and a population of 16,900,000. Kazakh (Qazaq) (official), Russian. Maurais (1992).

✳ **Kenya.** An equatorial country on the E coast of Africa with a total land area of 582,646 km^2 and a population of 26,200,000. 50 languages, English, Swahili, Kikuyu, Luhya, Luo, Kamba (all official). Crampton (1986), Eastman (1990a, 1983: 225ff), Scotton (1982), Whiteley (1971, 1974).

Korea, North. Located in the N part of the Korean peninsula in eastern Asia with a total land area of 121,129 km^2 and a population of 22,200,000. Korean (official), Chinese. **South.** Situated in the S part of the Korean peninsula in eastern Asia with a total land area of 98,500 km^2 and a population of 44,300,000. Korean (official); English widely taught in high school. Baik (1992), Eggington (1987), Hannas (1995), Park (1989), Rhee (1992), Soh (1985).

Kyrgyzstan. Located in central Asia with a total land area of 198,500 km^2 and a population of 4,500,000. Kirghiz (Kyrgyz). Maurais (1992).

Latvia. Situated between Estonia and Lithuania on the Baltic Sea with a total land area of 65,786 km^2 and a population of 2,700,000. Latvian (official), Russian, Ukrainian, Belorussian. Druviete (1992, 1995), Maurais (1992), Ozolins (1994).

Lithuania. Located on the E shore of the Baltic bordering Latvia, Belarus and Poland with a total land area of 64,445 km^2 and a population of 3,700,000. Lithuanian (official), Russian. Maurais (1992), Ozolins (1994).

Luxembourg. A landlocked country in W Europe with a total land area of 2,586 km^2 and a population of 400,000. German, French (official), Letzeburgesch, many also speak English. Baetens Beardsmore (1993b), Clyne (1995), Davis (1990, 1994), Newton (1996), Pou (1993), Schiffman (1993).

Macedonia. A landlocked country in SE Europe bordered by Serbia, Bulgaria and Greece with a total land area of 25,713 km^2 and a population of 1,900,000. Macedonian (official). Branko (1980), Hill (1992).

Madagascar. One large island and several smaller ones in the W Indian Ocean with a total land area of 587,050 km^2 and a population of 11,900,000. French and Malagasy (both official). Boulanger (1989), Cembalo (1993), Dahl (1993), Rambelo (1991a, 1991b).

✳ **Malaysia.** Thirteen states in SE Asia; 11 are in Peninsular Malaysia and two, Sabah and Sarawak, lie about 640 km across the South China Sea on the N and W coast of the island of Borneo. A total land area of 332,337 km^2 and a population of 18,700,000. Malaya – Malay (official); English, Chinese dialects, Tamil; Sabah – Malay (official), English, Kadazan and other tribal dialects, Mandarin and Hakka dialects predominate among Chinese; Sarawak – Malay (official), English, Mandarin, numerous tribal languages. Comber (1983), Gaudart (1992), Gupta (1985), Hawes and Thomas (1995), Heah Lee Hsia (1989), Khong and Khong (1984), Lee (1995), LePage (1984),

Nik Safiah (1987), Omar (1975, 1982, 1983, 1984, 1985, 1992, 1995), Ożóg (1990, 1993), Pakir (1993a), Stedman (1986), Vikør (1993), Watson (1980), Williams (1966, 1969), Zawiah Yahya (1996). *English.* Anonymous (1994a), Lowenberg (1986).

Mali. A landlocked country in NW Africa with a total land area of 1,240,142 km^2 and a population of 8,500,000: 10 languages, French (official); Bambara spoken as a lingua franca, Fulfulde, Arabic. Calvet (1982), Calvet *et al.* (1992).

Marshall Islands. Two groups of islands, the Ratak and Ralik chains, comprising 31 atolls in the western Pacific Ocean with Guam about 2,100 km to NW, Hawaii about 3,200 km to NE, Kiribati to S, Federated States of Micronesia to W. A total land area of 181.3 km^2 with a population of 48,000. English and Marshalese (official); two major dialects from Malayo-Polynesian family, Japanese. Pine and Savage (1989).

Mauritania. Situated on the NW coast of Africa with a total land area of 1,030,700 km^2 and a population of 2,100,000. French (official), Hasaniya Arabic (national), Fulfulde, Wolof. Mahmud (1986), Sounkolo (1994).

Mauritius. One large and seven small islands about 800 km E of Madagascar in the SW Indian Ocean with a total land area of 2,040 km^2 and a population of 1,100,000. English, French (both official), Creole, Hindi, Urdu, Hakka, Bojpoori. Hookoomsing (1986).

Mexico. The largest state in central America with a total land area of 1,972,547 km^2 and a population of 87,700,000. Spanish, many Indian languages. Heath (1972), Hidalgo (1994), Patthey (1989), Patthey-Chavez (1994).

Morocco. Situated along the NW coast of Africa with a total land area of 446,550 km^2 and a population of 26,200,000. Arabic (official), several Berber dialects; French is the language of business, government, diplomacy and post-primary education. El Assati (1993), Ennaji (1988), Souaiaia (1990).

Mozambique. Located along the E coast of Africa with a total land area of 783,073 km^2 and a population of 16,000,000: 20 languages, Portuguese (official), Makua, Tsonga, Bantu languages. Garcez (1995), Lopes (1997).

Myanmar. Formerly known as Burma and situated on the NW portion of the Indochinese peninsula with total land area of 676,560 km^2 and a population of 42,500,000. Burmese (official), minority languages. Allott (1985).

Namibia. Situated in SW Africa with a total land area of 824,296 km^2 and a population of 1,500,000. English (official), Afrikaans, German, several indigenous languages. Cluver (1991), Haacke (1994), Harlec-Jones (1993), Phillipson, Skutnabb-Kangas and Africa (1986), Pütz (1992, 1995).

Nepal. A landlocked Asian country in the Himalayan mountain range with a total land area of 141,059 km^2 and a population of 19,900,000. Nepali (official); Newari, Bhutia, Maithali and 17 langs. Divided into numerous dialects. Dahal and Subba (1986), Sonntag (1980).

Netherlands. Situated in W Europe with a total land area of 41,548 km^2 and a population of 15,300,000. Dutch (official). Anonymous (1991), Deprez and Wynants (1994b), De Rooji and Verhoeven (1988), Extra and Vallen (1988), Kroon and Vallen (1994), Nelde (1988), Van der Plank (1988), van Els (1994), Willemyns (1984). *Frisian*. Feitsma (1989), van Langevelde (1993).

New Zealand. Located in the S Pacific Ocean about 1,750 km SE of Australia with a total land area of 269,062 km^2 and a population of 3,400,000. English; Maori (official). Bell and Holmes (1990), Benton (1996), Holmes (1997), Kaplan (1980, 1981, 1993a, 1994b), Kennedy (1982, 1989), Levett and Adams (1987), McGregor and Williams (1991), Peddie (1996) *Maori*. N. Benton (1989), R.A. Benton (1975, 1980, 1981, 1986, 1989, 1991a, 1991b), Fishman (1991: 230ff), Government of New Zealand (1987), Hirsh (1987), Hohepa (1984), Karetu (1991, 1994), Peddie (1991a, 1991b, 1996), Spolsky (1989, 1995), Waite (1992).

Nigeria. Situated along the W coast of Africa with a total land area of 923,770 km^2 and a population of 88,500,000 (1991): 350 languages, English, Ibo, Edo, Ijo, Efik, Idoma (all official); Hausa, Yoruba, Fulfulde, Pidgin English and Kanuri also widely used. Adegbija (1994), Akinnaso (1989, 1991), Akinnaso and Ogunbiyi (1990), Brann (1994), Fakuade (1989, 1994), Goke-Pariola (1987), Oladejo (1991, 1992, 1993).

Norway. Located in the NW part of the Scandinavian peninsula in N Europe with a total land area of 323,878 km^2 and a population of 4,300,000. Norwegian (official), small Lapp- and Finnish-speaking minorities. Bull (1991, 1993), Bjorge (1989), Collis (1990), Haugen (1966), Jahr (1989), Jahr and Trudgill (1993), Jernsletten (1993), Loman (1988), Magga (1990), Venås (1993), Vikør (1989), Wiggen (1995).

Pakistan. Located in S Asia with a total land area of 803,936 km^2 and a population of 121,700,000. Urdu (national) and English (official); total spoken languages 64% Punjabi, 12% Sindhi, 8% Pashtu, 7% Urdu (official), 9% Baluchi and other; English is lingua franca of Pakistani elite and most government ministries; however, official policies are promoting its gradual replacement by Urdu. Baumgardner (1993), Das Gupta (1971), Huizinga (1994), Hussain (1990), Rahman (1995).

Papua New Guinea. The E section of the island of New Guinea and about 600 smaller islands, including the Bismarck Archipelago and the northern part of the Solomon Islands. A total land area of 462,840 km^2 and a population of 3,900,000: 717 indigenous languages; English spoken by 1–2%, Melanesian pidgin (Tok Pisin) widespread, Hari Motu spoken in Papua region. Brennan (1983), Kale (1990b), Nekitel (1989), Romaine (1989), Smith (1990), Swan and Lewis (1990), Taylor (1981), Wurm (1978).

Paraguay. A landlocked country in central S America with a total land area of 406,752 km² and a population of 4,500,000. Spanish (official), Guarani. Corvalan (1981), Englebrecht and Ortiz (1983), Rubin (1968a, 1968b).

Peru. Located along the W coast of S America with a total land area of 1,285,216 km² and a population of· 22,500,000. Spanish and Quéchua (official), Aymara. Cerrón-Palomino (1989), Hornberger (1987, 1988, 1992, 1994, 1995), von Gleich (1994).

Philippines. An archipelago of some 7100 islands and islets lying about 2000 km off the SE coast of Asia; spans about 2800 km from N to S at longest extent and about 1684 km from W to E at widest point; main islands are Luzon in N and Mindanao in S, accounting for 66% of country's land area. A total land area of 300,000 km² and a population of 63,700,000. Filipino (based on Tagalog) and English (both official), Tagalog, Ilocano, Cebuano, others. Cruz (1986), Gonzalez (1980, 1982, 1985, 1988a, 1988b, 1989, 1990), Gupta (1985), Kaplan (1982), Luzares (1982), McFarland (1981), Nance (1975), Sibayan (1984), Sibayan and Gonzalez (1977), Smolicz (1984), Tucker (1988).

Poland. Situated in E Europe with a total land area of 312,683 km² and a population of 38,400,000. Polish (official). Chciuk-Celt (1990).

Portugal. Located in W Europe, on the Atlantic side of the Iberian Peninsula; also includes two archipelagos in the Atlantic Ocean. A total land area of 92,075 km² and a population of 10,500,000. Portuguese (official). Cristovao (1989), Garcez (1995), Silva and Gunnewiek (1992).

Puerto Rico. A US Territory. The large island of Puerto Rico, together with Vieques, Culebra and many smaller islands, in the NE Caribbean Sea. A total land area of 8959 km² and a population of 3,522,037 (1990 census). Spanish and English (both official). Laguerre (1989), Morris (1996), Resnick (1993), Schweers and Vélez (1993).

Romania. Situated in SE Europe with a total land area of 237,500 km² and a population of 22,760,449 (1992). Romanian (official), Magyar, German, Romany. Bochmann (1992), Petyt (1975), Schmitt (1988).

Russia. (Includes references to the former Soviet Union.) Located in E Europe and central Asia with a total land area of 17,075,400 km² and a population of 149,527,479 (June 1992). Russian (official); more than 200 languages and dialects (at least 18 with more than one million speakers). Bugarski (1987), Collis (1990), Comrie (1981), Haarmann (1992a, 1992b), Isaev (1979), Kirkwood (1989), Kreindler (1982), Leontiev (1994), Lewis (1982, 1983), Marshall (1996), Ozolins (1996), Panzer (1992), Pool (1976), Rannut (1991a, 1991b, 1994), Shorish (1984), Silver (1985), Taksami (1990), Tollefson (1981a).

Rwanda. A landlocked country in central Africa surrounded by Zaire, Uganda, Tanzania and Burundi with a total land area of 10,169 km² and a population of 7,700,000. Kinyarwanda and French (both official), Swahili. Jouannet (1991), Nkusi (1991).

Saint Lucia. An island in the SE Caribbean Sea, lying between French overseas department of Martinique to N and St Vincent to SW. A total land area of 616 km^2 and a population of 200,000. English (official), French patois. Carrington (1990, 1994).

Samoa, American. Seven islands (Tutuila, Tau, Olosega, Ofu, Aunuu, Rose, Swain's) in the S central Pacific Ocean with a land area of 194.8 km^2 and a population of 39,254 (1988). English, Samoan. Baldauf (1981, 1982, 1990), Huebner (1986, 1989), Schramm *et al.* (1981), Thomas (1981).

Samoa, Western. Two large and seven small islands, five of which are inhabited, in the S central Pacific Ocean with a land area of 2,831 km^2 and a population of 200,000. Samoan and English. Baldauf (1990), Duranti and Ochs (1986), Huebner (1986, 1989).

São Tomé and Príncipe. Two main islands, São Tomé and Príncipe, and the rocky islets of Caroco, Pedras, Tinhosas (off Principe) and Rolas (off São Tomé), off the W coast of Africa. A total land area of 958 km^2 and a population of 100,000. Portuguese (official). Garcez (1995).

Senegal. Located on the NW coast of Africa with a total land area of 192,722 km^2 and a population of 7,900,000: 10 languages, French, Serer, Diola, Soninke (all official), Arabic, Wolof, Fula, Malinke. Mansour (1980), Calvet (1982).

Sierra Leone. Located on the Alantic Ocean in West Africa with a total land area of 71,740 km^2 and a population of 4,400,000. English (official), Mende, Temne, Krio. Pemagbi (1989).

Singapore. Singapore Island and some 57 islets situated off S extremity of Malay peninsula to which Singapore Island is linked by a causeway; on passageway between Indian and Pacific oceans about 124 km N of equator. A total land area of 639 km^2 and a population of 2,800,000. Chinese (Mandarin), Malay, Tamil, and English (official); Malay (national). Alte-henger-Smith (1990), Anderson (1985), Gupta (1985), Harrison (1980), Jernudd (1994b), Koh Tai Ann (1996), Kuo (1980, 1984), Kuo and Jernudd (1993), LePage (1984), Newman (1988), Pakir (1993a, 1993b), Platt (1985), Platt and Weber (1980), Talib (1994).

Slovak Republic. Landlocked country in central Europe with a total land area of 49,035 km^2 and a population of 5,310,000. Slovaks 85.6%, Hungarians 10.8%, Czechs 1%, Others 2.6%. Slovak (official), Hungarian, Romany, Ruthenian, Czech, other minority languages. Hübschmannová and Neustupný (1996), Kontra (1996), Lanstyák and Szabómihály (1996), Neustupný (1989), Skutnab-Kangas and Phillipson (1994).

Slovenia. Located in S central Europe bordering on Austria, Hungary and Croatia with an area of 20,251 km^2 and a population of 1,962,000. Slovenian (official). Most can speak Serbian, Croatian; Italian. Tollefson (1981b).

Solomon Islands. A scattered archipelago in the S Pacific Ocean E of Papua New Guinea and about 1,600 km NE of Australia. A total land area of 29,785 km^2 and a population of 400,000: 120 indigenous languages;

Melanesian pidgin in much of the country is lingua franca; English spoken by 1–2% of population. Keesing (1990), Jourdan (1989, 1990), Watson-Gegeo (1987), Watson-Gegeo and Gegeo (1995).

Somalia. Located along the E coast of Africa with a total land area of 637,655 km^2 and a population of 8,300,000. Somali, Arabic, Italian, English (all official), Italian. Andrzejewski (1980), Biber and Hared (1992), Fellman (1983), Mezei (1989).

South Africa. Situated at the S extremity of the African mainland with a total land area of 1,221,030 km^2 and a population of 41,700,000. Afrikaans, English, isiZulu, isiXhosa, North and South Sotho, TsiVenda, XiTsonga, siNdebele, siSwati, Pedi (all official). Cluver (1992), Coetzee (1993), Eastman (1990b), Penn and Reagan (1990), Reagan (1986), Reagan and Ntshoe (1987), Ridge (1996), Webb (1994, 1996).

Soviet Union. See Russia.

Spain. Consists of more than four-fifths of the Iberian Peninsula in SW Europe with a total land area of 504,750 km^2 and a population of 39,301,000 (1990). Castilian Spanish; second langs. include 17% Catalan, 7% Galician, 2% Basque. Hoffmann (1995), Mar-Molinero and Stevenson (1991), Sánchez (1992), Vila i Moreno (1990), Wardhaugh (1987:119). *Basque.* Hualde, Lakarra and Trask (1996), Rotaetxe (1994). *Catalan.* Barrera i Vidal (1994), Leprêtre i Alemany (1992), Mar-Molinero (1989), Neugaard (1995), Petherbridge-Hernández (1990), Tabouret-Keller (1981), Woolard (1989), Woolard and Gahng (1990).

Sri Lanka. One large island and several smaller islands in the Indian Ocean about 80 km SE of peninsular India with a total land area of 65,616 km^2 and a population of 17,600,000. Sinhala (official); Sinhala and Tamil listed as national languages.; Sinhala spoken by about 74% of population, Tamil spoken by about 18%; English commonly used in government and spoken by about 10% of population. Dharmadasa (1977), Gair (1983), James (1985), Schiffman (1993), Sivasegaram (1991).

Sudan. Situated in NE Africa with a total land area of 2,505,802 km^2 and a population of 26,500,000: 100 languages, Arabic, Shilluk, Bari, Latuka, Zande, Kreish, Ndogo, Moru, French (all official), English; programme of Arabisation in progress. Abakar (1989), Cembalo (1993), Hurreiz (1975), Mahmud (1982).

Suriname. Located along the NE coast of S America with a total land area of 163,820 km^2 and a population of 400,000. Dutch (official), English widely spoken, Sranan Tongo (sometimes called Taki-Taki, the native language of Creoles and much of younger population and lingua franca among others), Hindi, Suriname Hindustani, Javanese. Glock (1983).

Sweden. Consists of about two-thirds of the Scandinavian peninsula in NW Europe with a total land area of 449,964 km^2 and a population of 8,700,000 (1988). Swedish, small Saami- and Finnish-speaking minorities; immigrants speak native languages. Anonymous (1995), Bucher (1981),

Clausen (1986), Collis (1990), Eastman (1983: 232ff), Helander (1990), Jaakkola (1976), Jernudd (1986, 1994b), Loman (1988), Molde (1975), Skutnabb-Kangas (1996).

Switzerland. A landlocked country in central Europe with a total land area of 41,288 km² and a population of 6,900,000. German, French, Italian (all official) Romanish. Andres (1990), Clyne (1995) Darms (1994), Mar-Molinero and Stevenson (1991), Pap (1990), Schiffman (1993), Stotz and Andres (1990), Wardhaugh (1987: 211), Watts (1988).

Taiwan (Formosa). One large island and several smaller islands about 160 km off the SE coast of mainland China with a total land area of 35,988 km² and a population of 20,800,000. Mandarin Chinese (official); Tai-yü and Hakka dialects also used. Kaplan and Tse (1982), Snow (1993b), Tse (1982, 1986), Young (1988), Hsiau (1997).

Tajikistan. Located in central Asia bounded by China, Afghanistan, Uzbekistan and Kyrgyzstan with a total land area of 143,100 km² and a population of 5,680,242 (July 1992). Tajik (official). Maurais (1992).

 Tanzania. Tanganyika, on the E coast of Africa, and the islands of Zanzibar and Pemba, about 40 km off Tanganyika coast in the Indian Ocean. A total land area of 945,037 km² and a population of 27,400,000: 120 languages, Kiswahili (official); Sukuma, English primary language of commerce, administration, and higher education; Swahili widely understood and generally used for communication between ethnic groups; first language of most people is one of the local languages; primary education generally in Swahili. Barrett (1994), Dunn (1985), Eastman (1983: 225ff), Khamisi (1986), Maina (1987), Mekacha (1993), Rumbagumya (1986, 1989), Scotton (1982), Whiteley (1971), Woods (1985b).

Thailand. Extends S along the Isthmus of Kra, to Malay peninsula, in SE Asia with a total land area of 514,000 km² and a population of 56,300,000. Thai (official); Chinese; English is secondary language of elite; ethnic and regional dialects. Aksornkool (1983), Bradley (1985b), Brudhiprabha (1986), Gupta (1985).

Togo. Situated along the W coast of Africa with a total land area of 56,785 km² and a population of 3,800,000: 15 languages, French (both official language and language of commerce); Hausa; Ewé and Mina in south, Cotocoli and Kabiye in north. Calvet *et al.* (1992).

Tonga. Consists of 172 islands in the S Pacific Ocean with a total land area of 751 km² and a population of 96,800. Tongan, English. Spolsky *et al.* (1983).

Trinidad and Tobago. Two islands in the SW Caribbean Sea, just off the N coast of S America with a total land area of 5128 km² and a population of 1,300,000. English (official), Hindi, French, Spanish. Winer (1990).

Tunisia. Located along the N coast of Africa with a total land area of 16,152 km² and a population of 8,400,000. Arabic (official), Arabic and

French (commerce). Cembalo (1993), Payne (1983), Souaiaia (1990), Stevens (1983).

Turkey. Situated partly in SE Europe and partly in W Asia with a total land area of 779,452 km² and a population of 59,200,000. Turkish (official), Arabic, Kurdish. Doğançay-Aktuna (1995), Eastman (1983:221ff), Gallagher (1971), Skutnabb-Kangas and Bucak (1994).

Turkmenistan. Located in central Asia with the Caspian Sea to the W with a total land area of 488,100 and a population of 3,900,000. Turkmen 72%, Russian 12%, Uzbek 9%, Other 7%. Pool (1976).

Tuvalu. A scattered group of nine small atolls, extending about 560 km from N to S, in the S Pacific Ocean with a total land area of 26 km² and a population of 9300. Tuvaluan, English. Vetter (1991).

Uganda. A landlocked equatorial country in E Africa with a total land area of 236,880 km² and a population of 17,500,000: 30 languages, English, Luo, Runyankore, Lugbara (all official), Luganda, Ateso/Akarimo-jong, Swahili. Ladefoged, Glick and Criper (1972), Scotton (1982).

Ukraine. Located in E Europe with a total land area of 603,700 km² and a population of 52,100,000. Ukrainian, Russian, Romanian, Polish. Maurais (1992), Shamshur (1994).

United Kingdom. Located in NW Europe, occupying a major portion of the British Isles with a total land area of 244,100 km² and a population of 57,533,000. English, Welsh (about 26% of population of Wales), Scottish form of Gaelic (about 60,000 in Scotland). Baugh and Cable (1993), Bourne (1997), Grillo (1989), Hagen (1988, 1992, 1994), Hawes and Thomas (1995), Phillipson (1994), Pointon (1988), Thompson (1994), Thompson *et al.* (1996), Trudgill (1984), Wardhaugh (1987: 64 ff.). *Welsh.* Ball (1988), Edwards (1984, 1993), Lewis (1982), Pryce and Williams (1988), Thomas (1987), Williams (1991, 1994). *Scots Gaelic.* Dorian (1981), Withers (1988), Wood (1977). *Irish.* Northover and Donnelly (1996), Pritchard (1990).

United States. Occupies a large central portion of the N American continent and includes Alaska to the NW and Hawaii 2100 mi. SW in the Pacific Ocean Basin and Puerto Rico in the Carribean. A total land area of 9,159,123 km² with a population of 255,600,000. English, Spanish and other languages. Adams and Brink (1990), Amorose (1989), Arjona (1983), Baugh and Cable (1993), Bikales (1986), Cloonan and Strine (1991), Crawford (1989, 1992a, 1992b), Cummins (1994), Daniels (1990), Dillard (1992), Ferguson and Heath (1981), Fishman (1988a, 1989), Hernández-Chávez (1988, 1994), Huss (1990), Jernudd and Jo (1986), Judd (1987), Kloss (1977), Marshall (1986), McGroarty (1997), McKay *et al.* (1993), Peña (1991), Ricento (1996), Rodriquez (1992), Rubin (1978/1979), Schiffman (1995), Sonntag (1990), Tatalovich (1995), Thomas (1996), Tollefson (1988, 1993). *Black English.* Dillard (1977). *Amerindian.* Boseker (1994), Grenoble and Whaley (1996), Leap (1975, 1983), Shonerd (1990), St Clair and Leap (1982). *Hawaiian.* Day (1985), Sato (1985).

Uruguay. Located on the E coast of S America, S of Brazil and NE of Argentina, with a total land area of 176,224 km^2 and a population of 3,100,000. Spanish. Behares and Massone (1996).

Uzbekistan. Located in central Asia with a total land area of 447,400 km^2 and a population of 21,700,000. Uzbek 85%, Russian 5%, Other 10%. Fierman (1991), Turkic. Maurais (1992).

Vanuatu. A chain of 12 principal and some 60 smaller islands in the S Pacific Ocean, about 800 km W of Fiji and 2800 km E of Australia. A total land area of 14,763 km^2 and a population of 200,000. English and French (official); Bislama (national). Crowley (1989a, 1989b, 1994), Thomas (1990), Topping (1982), Tryon and Charpentier (1989).

Vietnam. Situated on the E coast of SE Asia with a total land area of 329,566 km^2 and a population of 69,200,000. Vietnamese (official); French, Chinese, English, Khmer, ethnic langs. (Mon-Khmer and Malayo-Polynesian.) DeFrancis (1977), Nguyen (1985), Lo Bianco (forthcoming).

Wallis and Futuna. Twenty-three islands and islets located two-thirds of the way between Honolulu and New Zealand in the S Pacific with a total land area of 274 km^2 and a population of 17,095 (June 1992). French, Wallisian. Rensch (1990).

Yugoslavia. (Also see the successor states of Slovenia, Croatia, Bosnia-Hercigovina, Macedonia). Located in S central Europe consisting of the States of Serbia and Montenegro with a total land area of 69,775 km^2 and a population of 10,000,000. Serbian, Slovene, Macedonian (all official), Albanian, Hungarian. Branko (1980), Bugarski (1987), Novak-Lukanivic (1988), Tollefson (1980, 1981a).

Zaire. An equatorial country in central Africa with a total land area of 2,344,885 km^2 and a population of 37,900,000: 300 languages, French (official), Lingala, Swahili, Luba, Kikongo. Calvet *et al.* (1992), Goyvaerts *et al.* (1983), Kamwangamalu (1997), Ndoma (1984), Nyembwe *et al.* (1992), Polomé (1968).

Planned Languages. The are many hundreds of planned/artificial languages the best known of which is Esperanto. Corsetti and La Torre (1995), Dasgupta (1987), Harry (1989), Large (1988), Sakaguchi (1996), Tonkin (1987).

Romani. The Roma/Romanies/Gypsy population, which is estimated at 9 million — about 50% of whom speak Romani, is located mainly in Europe. There are some 50 dialects. The language is related to ancient Sanskrit. Hübschmannová and Neustupný (1996), Kenrick (1996).

References

This list of references includes a variety of specialised citations which are not cited in the text of the volume but are included only in the Appendix. It was our intent that this volume provide an extensive post-1980 bibliography in order to make available to students and researchers in one place a moderately inclusive survey of the extant literature. Further materials on the earlier literature can be found in the annotated references by Rubin and Jernudd (1979) and in the bibliography in Kennedy (1984).

Abakar, M.A. (1989) Pour une autre politique des langues au Soudan. *Language Problems & Language Planning* 13, 291-7.

Abbott, G. (1988) Mascaraed and muumuu-ed: the spelling of imported words. *English Today* 4 (2), 43-6.

Adams, K.L. and Brink, D.T. (eds) (1990) *Perspectives on Official English. The Campaign for English as the Official Language of the USA.* Berlin/New York: Mouton de Gruyter.

Adegibija, E. (1994a) *Language Attitudes in Sub-Saharan Africa.* Clevedon: Multilingual Matters.

Adegibija, E. (1994b) The context of language planning in Africa: an illustration with Nigeria. In M. Pütz (ed.) (1994) (pp. 139-63).

Ager, D. (1990) *Sociolinguistics and Contemporary French.* Cambridge: Cambridge University Press.

Aggarwal, K.S. (1988) English and India's three-language formula: an empirical perspective. *World Englishes* 7, 289-98.

Aggarwal, K.S. (1992) To include or not to include: an attempt to study the language conflict in Manipur. *Language Problems & Language Planning* 16, 21-37.

Ahlqvist, A. (1993) Language conflict and language planning in Ireland. In E.H. Jahr (ed.) (1993) (pp. 7-20).

Aikio, M. (1990) The Finnish perspective: language and ethnicity. In D.R.F. Collis (ed.) (1990) (pp. 366-400).

Aikio, M. (1991) The Sámi language: pressure of change and reification. *Journal of Multilingual and Multicultural Development* 12, 93-103.

Akinnaso, F.N. (1989) One nation, four hundred languages: unity and diversity in Nigeria's language policy. *Language Problems & Language Planning* 13, 133-46.

Akinnaso, F.N. (1991) Toward the development of a multilingual language policy in Nigeria. *Applied Linguistics* 12, 29-61.

Akinnaso, F.N. and Ogunbiyi, I.A. (1990) The place of Arabic in language education and language planning in Nigeria. *Language Problems & Language Planning* 14, 1-19.

Aksornkool, N. (1983) *An Historical Study of Language Planning.* Singapore: Singapore University Press. [RELC Monograph]

Alderson, J.C. and Beretta, A. (eds) (1992) *Evaluating Second Language Education.* Cambridge: Cambridge University Press.

Alisjahbana, S.T. (1976) *Language Planning for Modernization: The Case of Indonesia and Malaysia.* The Hague: Mouton.

Alisjahbana, S.T. (1984) The concept of language standardization and its application to the Indonesian language. In F. Coulmas (ed.) *Linguistic Minorities and Literacy: Language Policy Issues in Developing Countries* (pp. 77–98). Berlin: Walter de Gruyter.

Alloni-Fainberg, Y. (1974) Official Hebrew terms for parts of the car: a study of knowledge, usage and attitudes. In J.A. Fishman (ed.) (1974) (pp. 493–517).

Allott, A.J. (1985) Language policy and planning in Burma. In D. Bradley (ed.) (1985a) (pp. 131–154).

Altehenger-Smith, S. (1990) *Language Change via Language Planning.* Hamburg: Helmut Buske.

Ammon, U. (1991) *Die internationale Stellung der deutschen Sprache.* Berlin/New York: de Gruyter.

Ammon, U. (1992) The Federal Republic of Germany's policy of spreading German. *International Journal of the Sociology of Language* 95, 33–50.

Ammon, U. (1994a) Language-spread policy. Vol. 2: languages of former colonial powers and former colonies. *International Journal of the Sociology of Language* 107.

Ammon, U. (1994b) The present dominance of English in Europe. With an outlook on possible solutions to the European language problems. *Sociolinguistica* 8, 1–14.

Ammon, U. and Kleineidam, H. (1992) Language-spread policy. Vol. 1: languages of former colonial powers. *International Journal of the Sociology of Language* 95.

Ammon, U., Mattheier, K.J. and Nelde, P.H. (1988) Standardisation of European National Languages: Romania, Germania. *Sociolinguistica* 2.

Amonoo, R.F. (1994) La situation linguistique au Ghana et les problèmes de standardisation. In G. Lüdi (ed.) (1994) (pp. 23–32).

Amorose, T. (1989) The official-language movement in the United States: contexts, issues and activities. *Language Problems & Language Planning* 13, 264–79.

Anderson, E.A. (1985) Sociolinguistic surveys in Singapore. *International Journal of the Sociology of Language* 55, 89–114.

Anderson, E.A. (1987) Indonesian language month 1986: tempest at the forum. *New Language Planning Newsletter* 1 (3), 1–3.

Andres, F. (ed.) (1990) Bilingual education in a multilingual society. *Multilingua* 9 (1). [Special issue]

Andrzejewski, B.W. (1980) The implementation of language planning in Somalia: a record of achievement. *Language Planning Newsletter* 6 (1), 1, 4–5.

Annamalai, E. (1986) Language rights and language planning. *New Language Planning Newsletter* 1 (2), 1–3.

Annamalai, E., Jernudd, B.H. and Rubin, J. (eds) (1986) *Language Planning: Proceedings of an Institute.* Mysore: Central Institute of Indian Languages.

Annamalai, E. and Rubin, J. (1980) Planning for language code and language use: some considerations in policy–formation and implementation. *Language Planning Newsletter* 6 (3), 1–4.

Anonymous. (1990) New era for Infoterm. *Language International* 2 (4), 30–2.

Anonymous. (1991) The Fryske Akademy. *New Language Planning Newsletter* 6 (2), 5.

Anonymous. (1994a) English comeback. *Language International* 6 (3), 33.

Anonymous. (1994b) Toubon bill watered down. *Language International* 6 (5), 38–9.

Anonymous. (1995) TNC Swedish Centre for technical terminology. *New Language Planning Newsletter* 9 (4), 2–4.

Ansre, G. (1975) Madina: Three polyglots and some implications for Ghana. In S. Ohannessian, C.A. Ferguson and E.C. Polomé (eds) (1975) (pp. 159–77).

Anwar, K. (1979) *Indonesian: The Development and Use of a National Language.* Yogyakarta: Gadjah Mada.

Arends, J., Muysken, P. and Smith, N. (1995) *Pidgins and Creoles: An Introduction.* Amsterdam: John Benjamins.

Arjona, E. (1983) Language planning in the judicial system: a look at the implementation of the US court interpreters act. *Language Planning Newsletter* 9 (1), 1–6.

Ashby, W. (1985) The need for an international auxiliary language. *Language Planning Newsletter* 11 (1), 8.

Atkinson, D. (1993) A historical discourse analysis of scientific research writing from 1675 to 1975: the case of the *Philosophical Transactions* of the Royal Society of London. Los Angeles, CA: University of Southern California. [PhD Dissertation]

Atkinson, D. (1995) The *Philosophical Transactions* of the Royal Society of London, 1675–1975: a sociohistorical discourse analysis (unpublished paper). Auburn, AL: Auburn University.

Augst, G. and Ammon, U. (1993) A new attempt at orthographic reform in the German-speaking countries. *New Language Planning Newsletter* 8 (2), 2–4.

Austin, P. (1991) Australian Aboriginal languages. In M. Clyne (ed.) *Linguistics in Australia: Trends in Research* (pp. 55–74). Canberra: Academy of the Social Sciences in Australia.

Australian Language and Literacy Council (ALLC) (1994) *Speaking of Business: The Needs of Business and Industry for Language Skills.* Canberra: Australian Government Publishing Service.

Australian Language and Literacy Council (ALLC) (1995) *Teacher Education in English Language and Literacy.* Canberra: Australian Government Publishing Service.

Bachman, L. (1990) *Fundamental Considerations in Language Testing.* Oxford: Oxford University Press.

Bachman, L. and Palmer, A.S. (1996) *Language Testing in Practice: Designing and Developing Useful Language Tests.* Oxford: Oxford University Press.

Baetens Beardsmore, H. (1980) Bilingualism in Belgium. *Journal of Multilingual and Multicultural Development* 1, 145–54.

Baetens Beardsmore, H. (1993a) *European Models of Bilingual Education.* Clevedon: Multilingual Matters.

Baetens Beardsmore, H. (1993b) European models of bilingual education: practice, theory and development. *Journal of Multilingual and Multicultural Development* 6, 103–20.

Baetens Beardsmore, H. (1994) Language policy and planning in Western European countries. In W. Grabe *et al.* (eds) *Annual Review of Applied Linguistics, 14* (pp. 93–110). New York: Cambridge University Press.

Baik, M.J. (1992) Language shift and identity in Korea. *Journal of Asian Pacific Communication* 3, 15–31.

Baker, P. and Mühlhäusler, P. (1990) From business to pidgin. *Journal of Asian Pacific Communication* 1, 87–115.

Baldauf, R.B., Jr (1981) Educational television, enculturation and acculturation: a study of change in American Samoa. *International Review of Education* 27, 227–45.

Baldauf, R.B., Jr (1982) The language situation in American Samoa: planners, plans, and planning. *Language Planning Newsletter* 8 (1), 1–6.

Baldauf, R.B., Jr (1985) Linguistic minorities and bilingual communities in Australia. In R.B. Kaplan *et al.* (eds) *Annual Review of Applied Linguistics, 6* (pp. 100–12). New York: Cambridge University Press.

Baldauf, R.B., Jr (1990a) Education and language planning in the Samoas. In R.B. Baldauf, Jr and A. Luke (eds) (1990) (pp. 259-76).

Baldauf, R.B., Jr (1990b) Language planning: corpus planning. In R.B. Kaplan *et al.* (eds) *Annual Review of Applied Linguistics*, 10 (pp. 3-12). New York: Cambridge University Press.

Baldauf, R.B., Jr (1993) Fostering bilingualism and national development through school second language study. *Journal of Multilingual and Multicultural Development* 14, 121-34.

Baldauf, R.B., Jr (1994) 'Unplanned' language planning. In W. Grabe *et al.* (eds) *Annual Review of Applied Linguistics, 14* (pp. 82-9). New York: Cambridge University Press.

Baldauf, R.B., Jr (1995a) Back from the brink? Revival, restoration and maintenance of Aboriginal and Torres Strait Islander languages. Paper presented at Symposium on Language Loss and Public Policy, Albuquerque, NM.

Baldauf, R.B., Jr (ed.) (1995b) *Viability of Low Candidature LOTE Courses in Universities.* Canberra: DEET Higher Education Division. [DEET Evaluations and Investigations Program 95/9]

Baldauf, R.B., Jr (1997) Tertiary language, literacy and communication policies: Needs and practice. In Z. Gołebiowski (ed.) *Policy and Practice of Tertiary Literacy.* Melbourne: Victoria Institute of Technology.

Baldauf, R.B., Jr and Eggington, W. (1989) Language reform in Australian languages. In I. Fodor and C. Hegégé (eds) (1989) (pp. 29-43).

Baldauf, R.B., Jr and Jernudd, B.H. (1983) Language of publication as a variable in scientific communication. *Australian Review of Applied Linguistics* 6 (1), 97-108.

Baldauf, R.B., Jr and Jernudd, B.H. (1986) Aspects of language use in cross-cultural psychology. *Australian Journal of Psychology* 32, 381-92.

Baldauf, R.B., Jr and Jernudd, B.H. (1987) Academic communication in a foreign language: the example of Scandinavian psychology. *Australian Review of Applied Linguistics* 10 (1), 98-117.

Baldauf, R.B., Jr and Lawrence, H. (1990) Individual characteristics and affective domain effects on LOTE retention rates. *Language and Education* 4, 225-48.

Baldauf, R.B., Jr and Luke, A. (eds) (1990) *Language Planning and Education in Australasia and the South Pacific.* Clevedon: Multilingual Matters.

Ball, M. J. (1988) *The Use of Welsh.* Clevedon: Multilingual Matters.

Bamgboṣe, A. (1989) Issues for a model of language planning. *Language Problems & Language Planning* 13, 24-34.

Barbour, S. and Stevenson, P. (1990) *Variation in German.* Cambridge: Cambridge University Press.

Barnes, D. (1982) Nationalism and the Mandarin movement: the first half-century. In R.L. Cooper (1982b) (ed.) (pp. 260-90).

Barnes, D. (1983) The implementation of language planning in China. In J. Cobarrubias and J. Fishman (eds) (1983b) (pp. 291-308).

Baron, D.E. (1982) *Grammar and Good Taste: Reforming the American Language.* New Haven and London: Yale University Press.

Barrera i Vidal, A. (1994) La politique de diffusion du catalan. *International Journal of the Sociology of Language* 107, 41-65.

Barrett, J. (1994) Why is English still the medium of education in Tanzanian secondary schools? *Language, Culture and Curriculum* 7, 3-16.

Bartsch, R. (1987) *Norms of Language.* London/New York: Longman.

Battison, R. (1980) Document design: language planning for paperwork. *Language Planning Newsletter* 6 (4), 1-5.

Baugh, A.C. and Cable, T. (1993) *A History of the English Language* (4th edn). London: Routledge.

Bauman, R. and Sherzer, J. (eds) (1974) *Explorations in the Ethnography of Speaking*. New York: Cambridge University Press.

Baumgardner, R.J. (1993) *The English Language in Pakistan*. Karachi: Oxford University Press.

Bayer, J. (1987) Language planning in India: a perspective on the three language formula. *New Language Planning Newsletter* 1 (3), 4–5.

Bazerman, C. (1988) *Shaping Written Knowledge*. Madison, WI: University of Wisconsin Press.

Behares, L.E. and Massone, M.I. (1996) The sociolinguistics of Uruguayan and Argentinian deaf communities as a language conflict situation. *International Journal of the Sociology of Language* 117, 99–113.

Beheydt, L. (1994) The linguistic situation in the new Belgium. *Current Issues in Language and Society* 1, 147–63.

Bélanger, C.H. (1995) La mondialisation et l'apprentissage d'une langue de spécialité. *La Revue Canadienne des Langues Vivantes* 52, 101–14.

Bell, A. and Holmes, J. (eds) (1990) *New Zealand Ways of Speaking English*. Clevedon: Multilingual Matters.

Bell, J. (ed.) (1981) *Language Planning for Australian Aboriginal Languages*. Alice Springs: Institute for Aboriginal Development.

Benkő, L. (1992) Sprachliche Standardisierungsprozesse im Ungarischen. *Sociolinguistica* 6, 84–99.

Bentahila, A. and Davies, E.E. (1993) Language revival: restoration or transformation. *Journal of Multilingual and Multicultural Development* 14, 355–74.

Benton, N. (1989) Education, language decline and language revitalization: the case of Maori in New Zealand. *Language and Education* 3 (2), 65–82.

Benton, R.A. (1975) Sociolinguistic survey of Maori language use. *Language Planning Newsletter* 1 (2), 3–4.

Benton, R.A. (1980) Changes in language use in a rural Maori community 1963–1978. *Journal of the Polynesian Society* 89, 455–78.

Benton, R.A. (1981) *The Flight of the Amokura: Oceanic Languages and Formal Education in the South Pacific*. Wellington: New Zealand Council for Educational Research.

Benton, R.A. (1986) Schools as agents for language revival in Ireland and New Zealand. In B. Spolsky (ed.) (1986) (pp. 53–76).

Benton, R.A. (1989) Maori and Pacific Island languages in New Zealand Education. *Ethnies: Droits de l'homme et peuples autochtones* 8/9/10, 7–12.

Benton, R.A. (1991a) Notes on the case for Maori language television. *New Language Planning Newsletter* 5 (4), 1–4.

Benton, R.A. (1991b) 'Tomorrow's schools' and the revitalization of Maori: stimulus or tranquilliser? In O. García (ed.) *Bilingual Education: Focusschrift in Honor of Joshua A Fishman on the Occasion of his 65th Birthday Vol. 1.* (pp. 136–47). Amsterdam: John Benjamins.

Benton, R.A. (1996) Language policy in New Zealand: defining the ineffable. In M. Herriman and B. Burnaby (eds) (pp. 62–98).

Beretta, A. (1992) Evaluation in language education: an overview. In J.C. Alderson and A. Beretta (eds) (1992) (pp. 5–24).

Berlin, B. *et al.* (1973) General principles of classification and nomenclature in folk biology. *American Anthropologist* 75, 214–42.

Berthold, M. (ed.) (1995) *Rising to the Bilingual Challenge*. Canberra: NLLIA.

Besch, W. (1988) Standardisierungsprozesse im deutschen Sprachraum. *Sociolinguistica* 2, 186–208.

Biber, D. (1993) The multi-dimensional approach to linguistic analysis of genre variation: an overview of methodology and findings. *Computers and the Humanities* 26, 331–45.

Biber, D. and Hared, M. (1992) Literacy in Somalia: linguistic consequences. In W. Grabe *et al.* (eds) *Annual Review of Applied Linguistics, 12* (pp. 260–82). New York: Cambridge University Press.

Bikales, G. (1986) Comment: the other side. *International Journal of the Sociology of Language* 60, 77–85.

Bjorge, A.K. (1989) Norwegian. *Language International* 1 (4), 33–4.

Black, P. (1990) Some competing goals in Aboriginal language planning. In R.B. Baldauf, Jr and A. Luke (eds) (1990) (pp. 80–8).

Bloor, T. and Tamrat, W. (1996) Issues in Ethiopian language policy and education. *Journal of Multilingual and Multicultural Development* 17, 321–38.

Bo Yin and Baldauf, R.B., Jr (1990) Language reform of spoken Chinese. *Journal of Multilingual and Multicultural Development* 11, 279–89.

Bochmann, K. (1992) La formation du roumain standard: conditions sociolinguistiques. *Sociolinguistica* 6, 100–7.

Bokamba, E.G. (1991) French colonial language policies in Africa and their legacies. In D.F. Marshall (ed.) (1991) (pp. 175–215).

Bolton, K, and Luke, K.-k. (1985) The sociolinguistic survey of language in Hong Kong: the background to research and methodological considerations. *International Journal of the Sociology of Language* 55, 41–56.

Boseker, B.J. (1994) The disappearance of American Indian languages. *Journal of Multilingual and Multicultural Development* 15, 147–60.

Boulanger, J.-C. (1986) La néologie et l'aménagement linguistique du Québec. *Language Problems & Language Planning* 10, 14–29.

Boulanger, J.-C. (1989) Développement, aménagement linguistique et terminologie: un mythe? L'exemple de la malgachisation. *Language Problems & Language Planning* 13, 243–63.

Bourdieu, P. (1991) *Language and Symbolic Power*. Cambridge: Harvard University Press.

Bourhis, R.Y. (1984) *Conflict and Language Planning in Quebec*. Clevedon, Avon: Multilingual Matters.

Bourne, J. (1997) The grown-ups know best: language policy making in Britain in the 1990s. In W. Eggington and H. Wren (eds) (1997) (pp. 49–65).

Boyle, J. (1995) Hong Kong's educational system: English or Chinese? *Language, Culture and Curriculum* 8, 291–304.

Bradley, D. (ed.) (1985a) (ed.) *Papers in South-East Asian Linguistics No. 9: Language Policy, Language Planning and Sociolinguistics in South-East Asia* (pp. 87–102). Canberra: Australian National University. [Pacific Linguistics Series A No. 67].

Bradley, D. (1985b) Traditional minorities and language education in Thailand. In D. Bradley (ed.) (1985a) (pp. 87–102).

Branko, F. (1980) Language policy and language planning in Yugoslavia with special reference to Croatian and Macedonian. *Lingua* 51, 55–72.

Brann, C. (1994) A prognosis for language management in the third republic. In M. Pütz (ed.) (1994) (pp. 165–80).

Brennan, P.W. (1983) Issues of language and law in Papua New Guinea. *Language Planning Newsletter* 9 (2), 1–7.

Brenzinger, M. (ed.) (1992) *Language Death: Factual and Theoretical Explorations with Special Reference to East Africa*. Berlin: Mouton de Gruyter.

Breton, R. (1991) The handicaps of language planning in Africa. In D.F. Marshall (ed.) (1991) (pp. 153–74).

malaysia

Breton, R. (1996) The dynamics of ethnolinguistic communities as the central factor in language policy and planning. *International Journal of the Sociology of Language* 118, 163–79.

Bright, W. *et al.* (eds) (1992) *International Encyclopedia of Linguistics*: New York: Oxford University Press.

Brown, J.D. (1988) *Understanding Research in Second Language Learning: A Teacher's Guide to Statistics and Research Design*. Cambridge: Cambridge University Press.

Brown, J.D. (1995) Language program evaluation: decisions, problems and solutions. In W. Grabe *et al.* (eds) *Annual Review of Applied Linguistics, 15* (pp. 227–48). New York: Cambridge University Press.

Brudhiprabha, P. (1986) Towards language planning in Thailand: with special reference to regional dialects languages and minority languages. In E. Annamalai, B.H. Jernudd and J. Rubin (1986) (pp. 220–37).

Bruthiaux, P. (1992) Language description, language prescription and language planning. *Language Problems & Language Planning* 16, 221–34.

Bruthiaux, P. (1993) Literacy and development: evidence from the Pacific rim and beyond. *Journal of Asian Pacific Communication* 4, 49–65.

Bruthiaux, P. (1996) *The Discourse of Classified Advertising: Exploring the Nature of Linguistic Simplicity*. New York: Oxford University Press.

Bucher, A.L. (1981) The Swedish Centre for Technical Terminology – 40 years old. *Language Planning Newsletter* 7 (2): 1–2.

Bugarski, R. (1987) Unity in diversity: aspects of language policy in the Soviet Union and Yugoslavia. *Sociolinguistica* 1, 1–12.

Bühler, H. (1987) Language and translation: translating and interpreting as a profession. In R. B. Kaplan *et al.* (eds) *Annual Review of Applied Linguistics, 7* (pp. 105–19). New York: Cambridge University Press.

Bull, T. (1991) Current issues in official Norwegian language planning. *New Language Planning Newsletter* 6 (2), 1–3.

Bull, T. (1993) Conflicting ideologies in contemporary Norwegian language planning. In E.H. Jahr (ed.) (1993) (pp. 21–37).

Burnaby, B. (1996) Language policy in Canada. In M. Herriman and B. Burnaby (eds) (pp. 159–219).

Caldwell, G. (1988) Being English in French Québec: on the denial of culture and history in a neo-liberal state. *Language, Culture and Curriculum* 1, 187–96.

Caldwell, J.A.W. (1994) Provision for minority languages in France. *Journal of Multilingual and Multicultural Development* 15, 293–310.

Calvet, L.-J. (1982) The spread of Mandingo: military, commercial and colonial influence on a linguistic datum. In R.L. Cooper (1982b) (ed.) (pp. 184–97).

Calvet, L.-J. *et al.* (1992) *Les langues des marchés en Afrique*. Paris: Didier Érudition.

Cannon, G. (1990) Sociolinguistic implications of Chinese-language borrowings in English. *International Journal of the Sociology of Language* 86, 41–55.

Carrington, L.D. (1990) The instrumentalization of St Lucian. *International Journal of the Sociology of Language* 85, 71–80.

Carrington, L.D. (1994) Writing and the survival of minor languages: the case of Antillean French-Lexicon Creole. In G. Lüdi (ed.) (1994) (pp. 33–40).

Carroll, T. (1995) NHK and Japanese Language policy. *Language Problems & Language Planning* 19, 271–93.

Cartwright, D. (1988) Language policy and internal geopolitics: the Canadian situation. In C.H. Williams (ed.) (1988) (pp. 238–66).

Cartwright, D. (1993) Sociolinguistic events in an intranational borderland: a nudge to a diverging nation. In E.H. Jahr (ed.) (1993) (p. 39–58).

Cassidy, F.G. (1987) The fallible computer and DARE. *English Today* 9, 27–30.

Cembalo, S.M. (1993) Langage et formation supérieure. *Mélanges CRAPEL* 21, 59–69.

Cerrón-Palomino, R. (1989) Language policy in Peru: a historical overview. *International Journal of the Sociology of language* 77, 11–33.

Chaklader, S. (1987) Panshimbanga Bangala Akademy. *New Language Planning Newsletter* 2 (1), 4–5.

Charrow, V.R. (1982) Language in bureaucracy. In R. DiPietro (ed.) *Linguistics and the Professions: Proceedings of the Second Annual Delaware Symposium on Language Studies* (pp. 173–88). Norwood, NJ: Ablex.

Chaudenson, R. (1989) Langue et économie: l'état des recherches interdisciplinaires. In R. Chaudenson and D. de Robillard (eds) (1989/1991) *Tome 1.* (pp. 23–38).

Chaudenson, R. and Robillard, D. de (eds) (1989/1991) *Langues, Économie et Développement, Tome 1 et 2.* Provence: Diffusion Didier Érudition.

Chciuk-Celt, A. (1990) Polish language and writing. *Language International* 2 (2), 13–14.

Chidambaram, M. (1986) The politics of language planning in Tamil Nadu. In E. Annamalai, B.H. Jernudd and J. Rubin (1986) (pp. 338–59).

Chomsky, N. (1980) *Rules and Representations.* New York: Columbia University Press.

Clausen, U. (1986) Principles in Swedish language cultivation. *Språbruk.* 2. 9–14.

Cloonan, J.D. and Strine, J.M. (1991) Federalism and the development of language policy: preliminary investigations. *Language Problems & Language Planning* 15, 268–81.

Cluver, A.D. de V. (1991) A systems approach to language planning: the case of Namibia. *Language Problems & Language Planning* 15, 43–64.

Cluver, A.D. de V. (1992) Language planning models for a post-apartheid South Africa. *Language Problems & Language Planning* 16, 105–36.

Clyne, M. (1981) Foreigner talk. *International Journal of the Sociology of Language* 28. [Special issue]

Clyne, M. (1982) *Multilingual Australia.* 1st edn. Melbourne: River Seine.

Clyne, M. (ed.) (1985) *Australia, Meeting Place of Languages.* Canberra: Australian National University. [Pacific Linguistics, C–92]

Clyne, M. (1988a) A *Tendenzwende* in the codification of Austrian German. *Multilingua* 7, 335–41.

Clyne, M. (1988b) Community languages in the home: a first progress report. *Vox* 1, 22–7. [Journal of AACLAME]

Clyne, M. (1988c) Language planning in multilingual Australia. *New Language Planning Newsletter* 2 (4), 1–5.

Clyne, M. (1994) *Intercultural Communication at Work: Cultural Values in Discourse.* Cambridge: Cambridge University Press.

Clyne, M. (1995) *The German Language in a Changing Europe.* Cambridge: Cambridge University Press.

Clyne, M., Ball, M. and Neil, D. (1991) Inter-cultural communication at work in Australia: complaints and apologies in turns. *Multilingua* 10, 251–73.

Clyne, M., Jenkins, C., Chen, I.Y., Tsokalidou, R., Wallner, T. (1994) *Developing Second Language from Primary School: Models and Outcomes.* Canberra: National Languages and Literacy Institute of Australia.

Cobarrubias, J. (1983a) Ethical issues in status planning. In J. Cobarrubias and J.A. Fishman (eds) (1983b) (pp. 41–85).

Cobarrubias, J. and Fishman, J.A. (eds) (1983b) *Progress in Language Planning.* Berlin: Mouton.

Coetzee, A.E. (1993) The maintenance of Afrikaans in a new South Africa. *AILA Review* 10, 37–51.

Cojnska, R. (1992) Zur Charakteristik der bulgarischen Schriftsprache in der vornationalen Epoche. *Sociolinguistica* 6, 151–62.

Collins, C. (1996) *Authority Figures: Metaphors of Mastery from the Illiad to the Apocalypse.* Lanham, MD: Rowman and Littlefield.

Collis, D.R.F. (1990) *Arctic Languages: An Awakening.* Paris: UNESCO.

Collis, D.R.F. (1992) The use of distributed language translation in language management. *Language Problems & Language Planning* 16, 53–71.

Comber, L. (1983) *13 May 1969: A Historical Survey of Sino-Malay Relations.* Kuala Lumpur: Heinemann Asia.

Combs, M. and Jernudd, B.H. (1981) Kumision I Fino' Chamorro (Guam). *Language Planning Newsletter* 7 (3/4), 1–2.

Commins, P. (1988) Socioeconomic development and language maintenance in the Gaeltacht. *International Journal of the Sociology of Language* 70, 11–28.

Communities for Accountable Reinvestment (CAR) (1993) Communities for Accountable Reinvestment.

Comrie, B. (1981) *The Languages of the Soviet Union.* Cambridge: Cambridge University Press.

Comrie, B. (ed.) (1987) *The World's Major Languages.* New York: Oxford University Press.

Cooper, R.L. (1976) The spread of Amharic. In M.L. Bender, J.D. Bowen, R.L. Cooper and C.A. Ferguson (eds) *Language in Ethiopia* (pp. 287–301). London: Oxford University Press.

Cooper, R.L. (1982a) A framework for the study of language spread. In R.L. Cooper (ed.) (1982b) (pp. 5–36).

Cooper, R.L. (1982b) (ed.) *Language Spread: Studies in Diffusion and Social Change.* Bloomington: Indiana University Press and Washington, DC: Center for Applied Linguistics.

Cooper, R.L. (1988) Planning language acquisition. In P.H. Lowenberg (ed.) (1988) (pp. 140–51).

Cooper, R.L. (1989) *Language Planning and Social Change.* Cambridge: Cambridge University Press.

Corsetti, R. and La Torre, M. (1995) Quale lingua prima? Per un experimento CEE che utilizzi l'esperanto. *Language Problems and Language Planning* 19, 26–46.

Corson, D. (1993) *Language, Minority Education and Gender: Linking Social Justice and Power.* Clevedon: Multilingual Matters.

Corvalan, G. (1981) Bilingualism in education in Paraguay: is it creative or oppressive? *Revista Paraguaya de Sociologia* 18 (52), 179–200.

Coulmas, F. (1989a) The surge of Japanese. *International Journal of the Sociology of Language* 80, 115–31.

Coulmas, F. (1989b) *The Writing Systems of the World.* Oxford: Blackwell.

Coulmas, F. (1991a) *A Language Policy for the European Community: Prospects and Quandaries.* Berlin: Mouton de Gruyter.

Coulmas, F. (ed.) (1991b) The economics of language in the Asian Pacific. *Journal of Asian Pacific Communication* 2. [Special Issue]

Coulmas, F. (1991c) The language trade in the Asian Pacific. *Journal of Asian Pacific Communication* 2, 1–27.

Coulombe, P.A. (1993) Language rights, individual and communal. *Language Problems & Language Planning* 17, 140–52.

Cowie, A.P. (1990) Pedagogical descriptions of language: lexis. In R.B. Kaplan *et al.*

(eds) *Annual Review of Applied Linguistics, 10* (pp. 196–209). Cambridge: Cambridge University Press.

Crampton, D. (1986) Language policy in Kenya. *Rassegna Italiana di Linguistica* 18 (3), 109–22.

Crawford, J. (1989) *Bilingual Education: History, Politics, Theory and Practice*. Trenton, NJ: Crane Publishing Co.

Crawford, J. (1992a) *Hold your Tongue: Bilingualism and the Politics of 'English Only'*. Reading, MA: Addison-Wesley.

Crawford, J. (1992b) *Language Loyalties: A Source Book on the Official English Controversy*. Chicago: University of Chicago Press.

Cressy, D. (1980) *Literacy and the Social Order: Reading and Writing in Tudor and Stuart England*. Cambridge: Cambridge University Press.

Cristovao, F. (1989) The Portuguese language in the world. *Language International* 1 (5), 10–11.

Crocombe, R.G. (1989) *The South Pacific: An Introduction*. Christchurch: Institute of Pacific Studies.

Crooks, T. and Crewes, G. (eds) (1995) *Language and Development*. Jakarta: Indonesian Australian Language Foundation.

Crowley, T. (1989a) English in Vanuatu. *World Englishes* 8, 37–46.

Crowley, T. (1989b) Language issues and national development in Vanuatu. In I. Fodor and C. Hagège (eds) (1989) (pp. 111–39).

Crowley, T. (1994) Linguistic demography: interpreting the 1989 census results in Vanuatu. *Journal of Multilingual and Multicultural Development* 15, 1–16.

Cruz, I.R. (1986) English and Tagalog in Philippine literature: a study of literary bilingualism. *World Englishes* 5 (2/3), 163–76.

Crystal, D. (1987) *The Cambridge Encyclopedia of Language*. Cambridge: Cambridge University Press.

Crystal, D. (1996) Swimming with the tide in a sea of language change. *Australian Language Matters* 4 (2), 19–20.

Cumming, A. (1997) English language-in-education policies in Canada. In W. Eggington and H. Wren (eds) (1997) (pp. 91–105).

Cummins, J. (1989) Language and literacy acquisition in bilingual contexts. *Journal of Multilingual and Multicultural Development* 10, 17–31.

Cummins, J. (1994) The discourse of disinformation: the debate on bilingual education and language rights in the United States. In T. Skutnabb-Kangas *et al.* (eds) (1994) (pp. 159–77).

Dagut, M. (1985) The revival of Hebrew and language planning. In J.D. Woods (ed.) (1985) (pp. 65–75).

Dahal, B.M. and Subba, S. (1986) Language policies and indigenous languages of Nepal. In E. Annamalai, B.H. Jernudd and J. Rubin (1986) (pp. 238–51).

Dahl, O.C. (1993) Language conflict in Madagascar around AD 700. In E.H. Jahr (ed.) (1993) (p. 59–68).

d'Anglejan, A. (1984) Language planning in Quebec: an historical overview and future trends. In R.Y. Bourhis (ed.) (1984) (pp. 29–52).

Daniels, H.A. (ed.) (1990) *Not Only English: Affirming America's Multilingual Heritage*. Urbana, Illinois: National Council of the Teachers of English.

Daoust, D. (1991) Terminological change within a language planning framework. In D.F. Marshall (ed.) (1991) (pp. 281–309).

Darms, G. (1994) Zur Schaffung und Entwicklung der Standardschriftsprache Rumantsch grischun. In G. Lüdi (ed.) (1994) (pp. 3–21).

Das, B.K. (ed.) (1987) *Language Education in Human Resource Development*. Singapore: RELC.

Dasgupta, P. (1987) Toward a dialogue between sociolinguistic sciences and Esperanto culture. *Language Problems & Language Planning* 11, 305–34.

Das Gupta, J. (1971) Religion, language, and political mobilization. In J. Rubin and B.H. Jernudd (eds) (1971a) (pp. 53–62).

Davies, A. (1990) *Principles of Language Testing*. Oxford: Blackwell.

Davies, A. (1996) Review article: ironising the myth of linguicism. *Journal of Multilingual and Multicultural Development* 17, 485–496.

Davis, K.A. (1990) Language legislation, class and schooling in multilingual contexts: the case of Luxembourg. *Language, Culture and Education* 3, 125–40.

Davis, K.A. (1994) *Language Planning in Multilingual Contexts: Policies, Communities, and Schools in Luxembourg*. Amsterdam: John Benjamins.

Davis, K.A. (1995) Qualitative theory and methods in applied linguistics research. *TESOL Quarterly* 29, 427–53.

Day, R.R. (1985) The ultimate inequality: linguistic genocide. In N. Wolfson and J. Manes (eds) (1985) (pp. 165–81).

Dear, P. (1985) Totius in verba: rhetoric and authority in the early Royal Society. *Isis* 76, 144–61.

DeChicchis, J. (1995) The current state of the Ainu language. In J.C. Maher and K. Yashiro (1995) (pp. 103–24).

de Cillia, R. (1996) Linguistic policy aspects of Austria's accession to the European Union. *New Language Planning Newsletter* 10 (3), 1–3.

DeFrancis, J. (1975) Language planning in China. *Language Planning Newsletter* 1 (2), 1, 5.

DeFrancis, J. (1977) *Colonialism and Language Policy in Viet Nam*. The Hague. Mouton.

Delbridge, A. (1985) Australian English. In J.D. Woods (ed.) (1985) (pp. 58–64).

De Mauro, T. and Vedovelli, M. (1994) La diffusione dell'italiano nel mondo: problemi istituzionali e sociolinguistici. *International Journal of the Sociology of Language* 107, 25–39.

Department of Finance. (1992) *Introduction to Cost-benefit Analysis for Program Managers*. Canberra: Australian Government Publishing Service.

Deprez, K. and Wynants, A. (1994a) La Flandre nationaliste face à l'Europe. *Language Problems & Language Planning* 18, 113–27.

Deprez, K. and Wynants, A. (1994b) Les Flamands et leur(s) langue(s). In G. Lüdi (ed.) (1994) (pp. 41–63).

de Rooij, J. and Verhoeven, G. (1988) Orthography reform and language planning for Dutch. *International Journal of the Sociology of Language* 73, 65–84.

Devlin, B., Harris, S., Black, P. and Enemburu, I.G. (eds) (1995) Australian Aborigines and Torres Strait Islanders: sociolinguistic and educational perspectives. *International Journal of the Sociology of Language* 113.

De Vries, J.W. (1988) Dutch loanwords in Indonesian. *International Journal of the Sociology of Language* 73, 121–36.

Dharmadasa, K. (1977) Nativism, diglossia and the Singhalese identity in the language problem in Sri Lanka. *International Journal of the Sociology of Language* 13, 21–31.

Dillard, J.L. (1977) *Black English*. Englewood Cliffs, NJ: Prentice Hall.

Dillard, J.L. (1992) *A History of American English*. London: Longman

Dines, E. (1994) The public face of linguistics. In P. Mühlhäusler (ed.) *The Public Face of Linguistics* (pp. 12–15). Adelaide: Centre for Language teaching and Research.

Dion, de S. and Lamy, G. (1990) La francisation de la langue de travail au Québec: constraintes et réalisations. *Language Problems & Language Planning* 14, 119–41.

Dixon, R.M.W. (1989) The original languages of Australia *Vox* 3, 26–33.

Djité, P.G. (1988a) Correcting errors in language classification: monolingual nuclei and multilingual satellites. *Language Problems & Language Planning* 12, 1–14.

Djité, P.G. (1988b) The spread of Dyula and popular French in Côte d'Ivoire: implications for language policy. *Language Problems & Language Planning* 12, 213–25.

Djité, P.G. (1990) Les langues africaines dans la nouvelle francophonie. *Language Problems & Language Planning* 14, 20–32.

Djité, P.G. (1991) Langues et développement en Afrique. *Language Problems & Language Planning* 15, 121–38.

Djité, P.G. (1992) The French revolution and the French language: a paradox? *Language Problems & Language Planning* 16, 163–77.

Djité, P.G. (1994) *From Language Policy to Language Planning: An Overview of Languages Other than English in Australian Education.* Canberra: NLLIA.

Doğançay-Aktuna, S. (1995) An evaluation of the Turkish language reform after 60 years. *Language Problems & Language Planning* 19, 221–49.

Domínguez, F. and López, N. (1995) *Language International World Directory of Sociolinguistic and Language Planning Organisations.* Philadelphia, PA: John Benjamins.

Donaldson, B. (1983) *Dutch: A Linguistic History of Holland and Belgium.* Leiden: Martinus Nijhoff.

Dorais, L.-J. (1990) The Canadian Inuit and their language. In D.R.F. Collis (ed.) (1990) (pp. 185–289).

Dorian, N.C. (1981) The evaluation of Gaelic by different mother-tongue groups resident in the Highlands. *Scottish Gaelic Studies* 13 (2), 169–82.

Dorian, N.C. (1989a) *Investigating Obsolescence: Studies in Language Contraction and Death.* New York: Cambridge University Press.

Dorian, N.C. (1989b) Small languages and small language communities: news, notes, and comments 3. *International Journal of the Sociology of Language* 80, 139–41.

Draisma, K., Gluck, R., Hancock, J., Kanitz, R., Knell, W., Price, G. and Squires, J. (1994) Tutorials in chemistry for Aboriginal nursing students. In *Best Practice in Aboriginal and Torres Strait Islander Education.* Canberra: NLLIA.

Druviete, I. (1992) Language policy in the Baltic States: a Latvian Case. In K. Sagatavojis (ed.) *Language Policy in the Baltic States Valodas Politika Baltijas Valstis.* Riga: Official Language Bureau of Latvia.

Druviete, I. (1995) *The Language Situation in Latvia. Sociolinguistic Survey. Part 1. Language Use and Attitudes among Minorities in Latvia.* Riga: Latvian Language Institute.

Dua, H.R. (1991) Language planning in India: problems, approaches and prospects. In D.F. Marshall (ed.) (1991) (pp. 105–33).

Dua, H.R. (1994) Hindi language spread policy and its implementation: achievements and prospects. *International Journal of the Sociology of Language* 107, 115–43.

Dua, H.R. (1996) The politics of language conflict: implications for language planning and political theory. *Language Problems & Language Planning* 20, 1–17.

Dunn, A.S. (1985) Swahili policy implementation in Tanzania: the role of the National Swahili Council (BAKITA). *Studies in Linguistic Sciences* 15 (1), 31–47.

Duranti, A. and Ochs, E. (1996) Literary instruction in a Samoan village. In B.B. Schieffelin and P. Gilmore (eds) *The Acquisition of Literacy: Ethnographic Perspectives.* Norwood, NJ: Ablex.

East Asia Analytical Unit (1992) *Australia's Business Challenge: South-East Asia in the 1990's.* Canberra: Australian Government Publishing Service.

Eastman, C. (1983) *Language Planning: An Introduction.* San Francisco: Chandler and Sharp.

Eastman, C. (1990a) Disassociation: a unified language policy outcome for Kenya. *International Journal of the Sociology of Language* 86, 67–85.

Eastman, C. (1990b) What is the role of language planning in post-apartheid South Africa? *TESOL Quarterly* 24, 9–21.

Eckert, P. (1983) The paradox of national language movements. *Journal of Multilingual and Multicultural Development* 4, 289–300.

Education Commission. (1996) Enhancing language proficiency: a comparative strategy. *New Language Planning Newsletter* 10 (3), 3–6.

Edwards, D.G. (1984) Welsh-medium education. *Journal of Multilingual and Multicultural Development* 5, 25–44.

Edwards, D.G. (1993) Education and Welsh language planning. *Language, Culture and Curriculum* 6, 257–73.

Edwards, J. (1985) *Language, Society and Identity.* Oxford: Basil Blackwell.

Edwards, J. (1993) Implementing bilingualism: Brunei in perspective. *Journal of Multilingual and Multicultural Development* 14, 25–38.

Edwards, J. (1994) Language policy and planning in Canada. In W. Grabe *et al.* (eds) *Annual Review of Applied Linguistics, 14* (pp. 126–36). New York: Cambridge University Press.

Edwards, J. (1995) Monolingualism, bilingualism, multiculturalism and identity: lessons and insights from recent Canadian experience. *Current Issues in Language and Society* 2, 5–37.

Eggington, W. (1987) Written academic discourse in Korean: implications for effective communication. In U. Connor and R.B. Kaplan (eds) *Writing Across Languages: Analysis of L2 Text* (pp. 153–68). Reading, MA: Addison-Wesley.

Eggington, W. (1992) From oral to literate culture: an Australian Aboriginal experience. In F. Dubin and N. Kuhlman (eds) *Cross-Cultural Literacy: Global Perspectives on Reading and Writing* (pp. 81–98). Englewood Cliffs, NJ: Prentice Hall.

Eggington, W. (1994) Language policy and planning in Australia. In W. Grabe *et al.* (eds) *Annual Review of Applied Linguistics, 14* (pp. 137–55). New York: Cambridge University Press.

Eggington, W. and Baldauf, R.B., Jr (1990) Towards evaluating the Aboriginal bilingual education program in the Northern Territory. In R.B. Baldauf, Jr and A. Luke (1990) (pp. 89–105).

Eggington, W. and Wren, H. (1997) *Language Policy: Dominant English, Pluralist Challenges.* Amsterdam/Canberra: Benjamins/NLLIA.

Eisemon, T.O., Prouty, R. and Schwille, J. (1989) What language should be used for teaching? Language policy and school reform in Burundi. *Journal of Multilingual and Multicultural Development* 10, 473–97.

El Aissati, A. (1993) Berber in Morocco and Algeria: revival or decay? *AILA Review* 10, 88–109.

Englebrecht, G. and Ortiz, L. (1983) Guarani literacy in Paraguay. *International Journal of the Sociology of Language* 42, 53–67.

Ennaji, M. (1988) Language planning in Morocco and changes in Arabic. *International Journal of the Sociology of Language* 74, 9–39.

Extra, G. and Vallen, T. (1988) Language and ethnic minorities in the Netherlands. *International Journal of the Sociology of Language* 73, 85–110.

Fairclough, N. (1989) *Language and Power.* London: Longman.

Fakuade, G. (1989) A three language formula for Nigeria: problems of implementation. *Language Problems & Language Planning* 13, 54–9.

Fakuade, G. (1994) Lingua franca from African sources in Nigeria: the journey so far. *Language Problems & Language Planning* 18, 38–46.

Falch, J. (1973) *Contribution à l'etude du statut des langues en Europe.* Québec: Presses de l'Université Laval.

Farrar, F.W. (1899) *Language and Languages.* London: Longman, Green.

Fasold, R. (1984) *The Sociolinguistics of Society.* Oxford: Basil Blackwell.

Fasold, R. (1988) Language policy and change: sexist language in the periodical news media. In P.H. Lowenberg (ed.) (1988) (pp. 187–206).

Federal Reserve Bank of San Francisco (1991) *Community Reinvestment Act Performance Evaluation, California Central Bank.* San Francisco: Federal Reserve Bank.

Fédération Internationale des Professeurs de Langues Vivantes. (1992) Human language rights. *FIPLV World News* 58, 1–2.

Feitsma, A. (1989) The history of the Frisian linguistic norm. In I. Fodor and C. Hagège (eds) (1989) (pp. 247–72)

Fellman, J. (1976) Language planning in Israel: the Academy of the Hebrew Language. *Language Planning Newsletter* 2 (2), 1, 6.

Fellman, J. (1983) The Academy of Ethiopian Languages. *Language Planning Newsletter* 9 (3), 1.

Fellman, J. (1993) Some thoughts on the Hebrew revival. *Language Problems & Language Planning* 17, 62–5.

Ferguson, C.A. (1971) The role of Arabic in Ethiopia: a sociolinguistic perspective. In A.S. Dil (ed.) *Language Structure and Language Use* (pp. 293–312). Stanford: Stanford University Press.

Ferguson, C.A. (1982) Religious factors in language spread. In R.L. Cooper (ed.) (1982b) (pp. 95–106).

Ferguson, C.A. (1988) Standardization as a form of language spread. In P.H. Lowenberg (ed.) (1988) (pp. 119–32).

Ferguson, C.A. (1992/1981) Foreword to the First Edition. In B.B. Kachru (ed.) (1992) (pp. xiii–xvii).

Ferguson, C.A. and Heath, S.B. (eds) (1981) *Language in the USA.* Cambridge: Cambridge University Press.

Fesl, E. (1982) Australian Aboriginal languages. *Australian Review of Applied Linguistics* 5 (2), 100–15.

Fesl, E. (1987) Language death among Australian languages. *Australian Review of Applied Linguistics* 10 (2), 12–22.

Field, T.T. (1981) Language survival in a European context: the future of Occitan. *Language Problems & Language Planning* 5, 251–63.

Fierman, W. (1991) *Language Planning and National Development: The Uzbek Experience.* Berlin/New York: Mouton de Gruyter.

Fiore, K. and Elasser, N. (1988) Strangers no more. In E.R. Kintgen, B.M. Kroll and M. Rose (eds) *Perspectives on Literacy.* Carbondale: Southern Illinois University Press.

Fisherman, H. (1990) Attitudes toward foreign words in contemporary Hebrew. *International Journal of the Sociology of Language* 86, 5–40.

Fishman, J.A. (1972) *Language and Nationalism.* Rowley, MA: Newbury House.

Fishman, J.A. (ed.) (1974) *Advances in Language Planning.* The Hague: Mouton.

Fishman, J.A. (1981) Theoretical issues and problems in the sociolinguistic enterprise. In R.B. Kaplan *et al.* (eds) *Annual Review of Applied Linguistics, 1* (pp. 161–67). Rowley, MA: Newbury House.

Fishman, J.A. (1983) Modeling rationales in corpus planning: modernity and tradition in images of the good corpus. In J. Cobarrubias and J.A. Fishman (eds) (1983b) (pp. 107–18).

Fishman, J.A. (1988a) 'English only': its ghosts, myths, and dangers. *International Journal of the Sociology of Language* 74, 125–40.

Fishman, J.A. (1988b) Language spread and language policy for endangered languages. In P.H. Lowenberg (ed.) (1988) (pp. 1–15).

Fishman, J.A. (1989) Language policy in the USA past, present, and future. In J.A. Fishman (ed.) *Language and Ethnicity in Minority Sociolinguistic Perspective.* Clevedon: Multilingual Matters. pp. 403–17.

Fishman, J.A. (1991) *Reversing Language Shift: The Theoretical and Empirical Foundations of Assistance to Threatened Languages.* Clevedon: Multilingual Matters.

Fishman, J.A. (1994) Critiques of language planning: a minority languages perspective. *Journal of Multilingual and Multicultural Development* 15, 91–9.

Fishman, J.A., Ferguson, C. and Das Gupta, J. (eds) (1968) *Language Problems of Developing Nations.* New York: John Wiley & Sons.

Fodor, I. and Hagège, C. (eds) (1983a) *Language Reform: History and Future.* Vol. I. Hamburg: Helmut Buske.

Fodor, I. and Hagège, C. (eds) (1983b) *Language Reform: History and Future.* Vol. II. Hamburg: Helmut Buske.

Fodor, I. and Hagège, C. (eds) (1984) *Language Reform: History and Future.* Vol. III. Hamburg: Helmut Buske.

Fodor, I. and Hagège, C. (eds) (1989) *Language Reform: History and Future.* Vol. IV. Hamburg: Helmut Buske.

Fodor, I. and Hagège, C. (eds) (1990) *Language Reform: History and Future.* Vol. V. Hamburg: Helmut Buske.

Follett, W. (1966) *Modern American Usage: A Guide* (ed. and completed by J. Barzun). New York: Hill and Wang.

Fortier, D. (1994) Official languages policies in Canada: a quiet revolution. *International Journal of the Sociology of Language* 105/106, 69–97.

Fowler, H.W. (1965) *A Dictionary of Modern English Usage* (2nd edn rev. by E. Gowers). London: Oxford University Press.

Frangoudaki, A. (1992) Diglossia and the present language situation in Greece: a sociolinguistic approach to the interpretation of diglossia and some hypotheses on today's linguistic reality. *Language in Society* 21, 365–81.

French, P. and Coulthard, M. (1994–) (eds) *Forensic Linguistics: The International Journal of Speech, Language, and the Law.* London: Routledge.

Friere, P. (1970) *Pedagogy of the Oppressed.* New York: Seabury.

Friere, P. (1985) *The Politics of Education.* South Hadley, MA: Bergin and Garvey.

Friere, P. and Macedo, D. (1987) *Literacy: Reading the Word and the World.* South Hadley, MA: Bergin and Garvey.

Gair, J. (1983) Sinhala and English: the effects of a language act. *Language Problems & Language Planning* 7, 43–59.

Gallagher, C.F. (1971) Language reform and social modernization in Turkey. In J. Rubin and B.H. Jernudd (eds) (1971) (pp. 159–78).

Garcez, P.M. (1995) The debatable 1990 Luso-Brazilian orthographic accord. *Language Problems & Language Planning* 19, 151–78.

Gaudart, H. (1992) *Bilingual Education in Malaysia.* Townsville: Centre for South-East Asian Studies.

Gee, J. (1990) *Social Linguistics and Literacies: Ideologies in Discourse.* London: Falmer.

Gee, J. (1992) Socio-cultural approaches to literacy (literacies). In W. Grabe *et al.* (eds) *Annual Review of Applied Linguistics, 12* (pp. 31–48). New York: Cambridge University Press.

Genesee, F. (1994) *Integrating Language and Content: Lessons from Immersion.* University of California at Santa Cruz: National Centre for Research on Cultural Diversity and Second Language Learning. [Educational Practice Report: 11, 1–15]

Geraghty, P. (1989a) Language reform: history and future of Fijian. In I. Fodor and C. Hagège (eds) (1989) (pp. 377–95).

Geraghty, P. (1989b) The reawakening of the Fijian language. *Ethnies: Droits de l'homme et peuples autochtones* 8/9/10, 91–95.

Gibbons, J. (1982) The issue of the language of instruction in the lower forms of Hong Kong secondary schools. *Journal of Multilingual and Multicultural Development* 3, 117–28.

Gibbons, J. (1994) Depth or breadth? Some issues in LOTE teaching. *Australian Review of Applied Linguistics* 17 (1), 1–22.

Glinert, L.G. (1991) The 'Back to the Future' syndrome in language planning: the case of modern Hebrew. In D.F. Marshall (ed.) (1991) (pp. 215–43).

Glinert, L.G. (1995) Inside the language planner's head: tactical responses to a mass immigration. *Journal of Multilingual and Multicultural Development* 16, 351–71.

Glock, N. (1983) Extending the use of Saramaccan in Suriname. *Journal of Multilingual and Multicultural Development* 4, 349–60.

Goke-Pariola, B. (1987) Language transfer and the Nigerian writer of English. *World Englishes* 6, 127–36.

Gold, D.L. (1989) A sketch of the linguistic situation in Israel today. *Language in Society* 18, 361–88.

Gomes de Matos, F. (1985) The linguistic rights of language learners. *Language Planning Newsletter* 11 (3), 1–2.

Gomes de Matos, F. and Bortoni, S.M. (1991) Sociolinguistics in Brazil. *International Journal of the Sociology of Language* 89. [Special issue]

Gomes de Matos, F. (1994) A plea for language planning plus: using languages positively. *New Language Planning Newsletter* 9 (1); 3–4.

Gonzalez, A. FSC (1980) *Language and Nationalism: The Philippine Experience Thus Far.* Manila: Ateneo de Manila University Press.

Gonzalez, A. FSC (1982) Language policy and language-in-education policy in the Philippines. In R.B. Kaplan *et al.* (eds) *Annual Review of Applied Linguistics,* 2 (pp. 48–59). Rowley, MA: Newbury House.

Gonzalez, A. FSC (ed.) (1984) *Panagani: Essays in Honor of Bonifacio P. Sibayan on his Sixty-Seventh Birthday.* Manila: Linguistic Society of the Philippines.

Gonzalez, A. FSC (1985) Language use surveys in the Philippines (1968–1983). *International Journal of the Sociology of Language* 55, 57–77.

Gonzalez, A. FSC (1988a) The 1987 policy on bilingual education. *New Language Planning Newsletter* 2 (3), 3–5.

Gonzalez, A. FSC (1988b) Philippine language policy today. *New Language Planning Newsletter* 2 (3), 1–3.

Gonzalez, A. FSC (1989) Language and nationalism in the Philippines: an update. *New Language Planning Newsletter* 4 (2), 1–3.

Gonzalez, A. FSC (1990) Evaluating bilingual education in the Philippines: towards a multidimensional model of evaluation in language planning. In R.B. Baldauf, Jr and A. Luke (eds) (pp. 319–334).

Görlich, M. (1988) 'Sprachliche Standardisierungsprozesse im englishsprachigen Bereich'. *Sociolinguistica* 2, 131–85.

Government of New Zealand (1987) *The Maori Language Act.* Wellington: Government Printer.

Goyvaerts, D., Semikenke, M. and Naeyaert, D. (1983) Language and education policy in the multilingual city of Bukavu. *Journal of Multilingual and Multicultural Development* 4, 47–62.

Grabe, W. (1992) Applied linguistics and linguistics. In W. Grabe and R.B. Kaplan (eds) (1992) (pp. 33–58).

Grabe, W. and Kaplan, R.B. (1986) Science, technology, language and information: implications for language- and language-in-education planning. *International Journal of the Sociology of Language* 59, 47–71.

Grabe, W. and Kaplan, R.B. (eds) (1992) *Introduction to Applied Linguistics*. Reading, MA: Addison-Wesley.

Green, B., Hodgens, J. and Luke, A. (1994) *Debating Literacy in Australia: A Documentary History, 1945–1994*. Melbourne. Australian Literacy Foundation. [Published on diskette in computer readable format]

Greenbaum, S. (1986) English and a grammarian's responsibility: the present and the future. *World Englishes* 5, 189–95.

Greenbaum, S. (1988) Language spread and the writing of grammars. In P.H. Lowenberg (ed.) (1988) (pp. 133–39).

Greenberg, J.H. (1963) The languages of Africa. *International Journal of American Linguistics* 29 (1). [Special supplementary issue]

Grenoble, L.A. and Whaley, L.J. (1996) Endangered languages: current issues and future prospects. *International Journal of the Sociology of Language* 118, 209–23.

Grillo, R. D. (1989) *Dominant Languages: Language and Heirarchy in Britain and France*. Cambridge: Cambridge University Press.

Grin, F. (1991) The Estonian language law: presentation with comments. *Language Problems & Language Planning* 15, 191–201.

Grin, F. (1993) European economic integration and the fate of lesser-used languages. *Language Problems & Language Planning* 17, 101–16.

Grin, F. (1994a) Combining immigrant and autochthonous language rights: a territorial approach to multilingualism. In T. Skutnabb-Kangas *et al.* (eds) (1994) (pp. 31–48).

Grin, F. (1994b) The bilingual advertising decision. *Journal of Multilingual and Multicultural Development* 15, 269–92.

Grin, F. (1994c) The economics of language: match or mismatch? *International Political Science Review* 15, 27–44.

Grin, F. (1995) The economics of foreign language competence: a research project of the Swiss national science foundation. *Journal of Multilingual and Multicultural Development* 16, 227–31.

Grin, F. (1996) Economic approaches to language and language planning. *International Journal of the Sociology of Language* 121.

Grin, F. and Vaillancourt, F. (1997) The economics of multilingualism: Overview and analytical framework. In W. Grabe *et al.* (eds) *Annual Review of Applied Linguistics*, 17 (pp. 1–23). New York: Cambridge University Press.

Gumperz, J.J. and Hymes, D. (eds) (1964) The ethnography of communication. *American Anthropologist* 66 (6), Part 2. [Special issue]

Gumperz, J.J. and Hymes, D. (eds) (1972) *Directions in Sociolinguistics: The Ethnography of Communication*. New York: Holt, Rinehart & Winston.

Gupta, A.F. (1985) Language status planning in the ASEAN countries. In D. Bradley (ed.) (1985a) (pp. 1–14).

Haacke, W. (1994) Language policy and planning in independent Namibia. In W. Grabe *et al.* (eds), *Annual Review of Applied Linguistics*, 14 (pp. 240–53). New York: Cambridge University Press.

Haarmann, H. (1974) *Die finnisch-ugrischen Sprachen – Soziale und politische Aspekte ihrer Entwicklung* (in Kooperation mit A.-L. Värri Haarmann). Hamburg: Buske.

Haarmann, H. (1990) Language planning in the light of a general theory of language: a methodological framework. *International Journal of the Sociology* 86, 103–26.

Haarmann, H. (1992a) Historical trends of cultural evolution among the non-Russian languages in the European part of the former Soviet Union. *Sociolinguistica* 6, 11–41.

Haarmann, H. (1992b) Measures to increase the importance of Russian within and outside the Soviet Union – a case study of covert language-spread policy (A historical outline). *International Journal of the Sociology of Language* 95, 109–29.

Haas, W. (ed.) (1982) *Standard Languages: Spoken and Written*. Manchester: Manchester University Press. [Mont Follick Series 5.]

Hagen, S. (ed.) (1988) *Languages in British Business – An Analysis of Current Needs*. Newcastle on Tyne: Centre for English Language Teaching and Research.

Hagen, S. (1992) Foreign language needs in the European workplace. *Australian Review of Applied Linguistics* 15 (1), 107–24.

Hagen, S. (1994) Language policy and planning for business in Great Britain. In R.D. Lambert (ed.) (1994) (pp. 111–29).

Hagström, B. (1989) Language reforms in the Faroe Islands. In I. Fodor and C. Hagège (eds) (1989) (pp. 431–57).

Hakuta, K., Ferdman, B.M. and Diaz, R.M. (1987) Bilingualism and cognitive development: three perspectives. In S. Rosenberg (ed.) *Advances in Applied Linguistics* Vol. 2 (pp. 284–319). Cambridge: Cambridge University Press.

Halemane, L. (1992) Language policy of the national literacy mission in India. *New Language Planning Newsletter* 6 (4), 2–3.

Hallel, M. and Spolsky, B. (1993) The teaching of additional languages in Israel. In W. Grabe *et al.* (eds) *Annual Review of Applied Linguistics*, 13 (pp. 37–49). New York: Cambridge University Press.

Halliday, M.A.K. (1978) *Language as a Social Semiotic*. London: Edward Arnold.

Hamel, R.E. (1994) Linguistic rights for Ameridian peoples in Latin America. In T. Skutnabb-Kangas *et al.* (1994) (pp. 289–303).

Hamers, J.F. and Hummel, K.M. (1994) The francophones of Quebec: language policies and language use. *International Journal of the Sociology of Language* 105/106, 127–52.

Hannas, W.C. (1995) Korea's attempts to eliminate Chinese characters and the implications for romanizing Chinese. *Language Problems & Language Planning* 19, 250–70.

Hansén, S.-E. (1991) Word and world in mother tongue teaching in Finland: curriculum policy in a bilingual society. *Language, Culture and Curriculum* 4, 107–17.

Harlec-Jones, B. (1993) Conflict or resolution? Aspects of language politics in Namibia. *New Language Planning Newsletter* 7 (3), 1–6.

Harrell, S. (1993) Linguistics and hegemony in China. *International Journal of the Sociology of Language* 103, 97–114.

Harrison, G. (1980) Mandarin and the mandarins: language policy and the media in Singapore. *Journal of Multilingual and Multicultural Development* 1, 175–180.

Harrison, W., Prator, C.H. and Tucker, R.G. (1975) *English Language Policy Survey of Jordan: A Case Study of Language Planning*. Arlington, VA: Center for Applied Linguistics.

Harry, R.L. (1989) Development of a language for international law: the experience of Esperanto. *Language Problems & Language Planning* 13, 35–44.

Hasan, R. (1996) On teaching literature across cultural distances. In J.E. James (ed.) (1996) (pp. 34–63).

Hatch, E. and Lazaraton, A. (1991) *The Research Manual: Design and Statistics for Applied Linguistics.* New York: Newbury House.

Haugen, E. (1966) *Language Planning and Language Conflict. The Case of Modern Norwegian.* Cambridge, MA: Harvard University Press.

Haugen, E. (1983) The implementation of corpus planning: theory and practice. In J. Cobarrubias and J.A. Fishman (eds) (1983b) (pp. 269–89).

Havelock, E. (1976) *Origins of Western Literacy.* Toronto: Ontario Institute for Studies In Education.

Hawes, T. and Thomas, S. (1995) Language bias against women in British and Malaysian newspapers. *Australian Review of Applied Linguistics* 18 (2), 1–18.

Heah Lee Hsia, C. (1989) *The Influence of English on Lexical Expansion of Bahasa Malaysia.* Kuala Lumpur: Dewan Bahasa dan Pustaka.

Healey, A. (ed.) (1975) *Language Learner's Field Guide.* Ukarumpa, PNG: Summer Institute of Linguistics.

Heath, S.B. (1972) *Telling Tongues – Language Policy in Mexico: Colony to Nation.* New York: Teachers College Press.

Heath, S.B. (1983) *Ways with Words: Language, Life, and Work in Communities and Classrooms.* New York: Cambridge University Press.

Heather, M.A. and Rossiter, B.N. (1988) Specialist dictionaries in electronic form. *Literary and Linguistic Computing* 3, 109–21.

Heidelberger Forschungsprojekt 'Pidgin-Deutsch' (Heidelberg Research Project) (1975) *Sprache und Kommunikation ausländisher Arbeiter.* Kronberg/Ts.: Scriptor.

Heidelberger Forschungsprojekt 'Pidgin-Deutsch' (Heidelberg Research Project) (1976) *Untersuchengen zur Erlernung des Deutschen durch ausländische Arbieter.* (Arbeitsbrecht III), Germanistches Seminar der Universität Heidelberg.

Heidelberger Forschungsprojekt 'Pidgin-Deutsch' (Heidelberg Research Project) (1977) *Die ungesteuerte Erlernung des Deutschen durch spanische und italienische Arbeiter.* Osnsbrücker Beiträge zur Sprachtheorie, Beiheft 2.

Heidelberger Forschungsprojekt 'Pidgin-Deutsch' (Heidelberg Research Project) (1979) *Studien zum Spracherwerb ausländischer Arbieter.* (Arbeitsbericht V), Germanistisches Seminar der Universität Heidelberg.

Helander, E. (1990) Situation of the Sámi language in Sweden. In D.R.F. Collis (ed.) (1990) (pp. 401–17).

Henning, G. (1987) *A Guide to Language Testing: Development, Evaluation, Research.* Cambridge, MA: Newbury House.

Hermans, T., Vos, L. and Wils, L. (eds) (1992) *The Flemish Movement: A Documentary History 1780–1990.* London/Atlantic Highlands, NJ: Althone Press.

Hernández-Chávez, E. (1988) Language policy and language rights in the United States: issues in bilingualism. In T. Skutnabb-Kangas and J. Cummins (eds) (1988) (pp. 45–56).

Hernández-Chávez, E. (1994) Language policy in the United States: a history of cultural genocide. In T. Skutnabb-Kangas *et al.* (eds) (1994) (pp. 141–58).

Herriman, M. (1996) Language policy in Australia. In M. Herriman and B. Burnaby (eds) (1996) (pp. 35–61).

Herriman, M. and Burnaby, B. (eds) (1996) *Language Policy in English-Dominant Countries: Six Case Studies.* Clevedon: Multilingual Matters.

Hidalgo, M. (ed.) (1994) Mexico's language policy and diversity. *Language Problems & Language Planning* 18 (3). [Special issue]

Hill, J.H. (1992) Anthropological linguistics: an overview. In W. Bright *et al.* (eds) (1992) (pp. 65–9).

Hill, P. (1992) Language standardization in the South Slavonic area. *Sociolinguistica* 6, 108–50.

Hindley, R. (1990) *The Death of the Irish Language*. London: Routledge.

Hirataka, F. (1992) Language-spread policy of Japan. *International Journal of the Sociology of Language* 95, 93–108.

Hirsh, W. (ed.) (1987) *Living Languages: Bilingualism and Community Languages in New Zealand*. Auckland: Heinemann.

Hoffmann, C. (1995) Monolingualism, bilingualism, cultural pluralism and national identity: twenty years of language planning in contemporary Spain. *Current Issues in Language and Society* 2, 59–90.

Hohepa, P. (1984) Current issues in promoting Maori language use. *Language Planning Newsletter* 10 (3), 1–4.

Holden, N.J. (1990) Language learning in Japanese corporations: the wider sociolinguistic context. *Multilingua* 9, 257–69.

Holgate, A. (1991) Survey of demand for engineers with foreign language skills: summary responses and initial analyses. Melbourne: Monash University. [Mimeograph]

Holm, E. (1993) Language values and practices of students in the Faroe Islands: a survey report. *AILA Review* 10, 23–36.

Holmes, J. (1997) Keeping tabs on language shift in New Zealand: some methodological considerations. *Journal of Multilingual and Multicultural Development* 18, 17–39.

Holvoet, A. (1992) Language policies in Belgium. In K. Sagatavojis (ed.) *Language Policy in the Baltic States Valodas Politika Baltijas Valstis*. Riga: Official Language Bureau of Latvia.

Hookoomsing, V.Y. (1986) Creole and the language situation in Mauritius. In E. Annamalai, B.H. Jernudd and J. Rubin (1986) (pp. 309–37).

Hornberger, N.H. (1987) Bilingual education success, but policy failure. *Language in Society* 16, 205–26.

Hornberger, N.H. (1988) Language planning orientations and bilingual education in Peru. *Language Problems & Language Planning* 12, 14–29.

Hornberger, N.H. (1992) Literacy in South America. In W. Grabe *et al.* (eds) *Annual Review of Applied Linguistics, 12* (pp. 190–215). New York: Cambridge University Press.

Hornberger, N.H. (1993) The first workshop on Quechua and Aymara writing. In J.A. Fishman (ed.) *The Earliest Stage of Language Planning: The 'First Congress' Phenomenon* (pp. 233–56). New York: Mouton de Gruyter.

Hornberger, N.H. (1994) Language policy and planning in South America. In W. Grabe *et al.* (eds) *Annual Review of Applied Linguistics, 14* (pp. 220–39). New York: Cambridge University Press.

Hornberger, N.H. (1995a) Ethnography in linguistic perspective: understanding school processes. *Language and Education* 9, 233–48.

Hornberger, N.H. (1995b) Five vowels or three? Linguistics and politics in Quechua language planning in Peru. In J.W. Tollefson (1995) (pp. 187–205).

Hornberger, N.H. and King, K. (1996) Language revitalization in the Andes: can the schools reverse language shift? *Journal of Multilingual and Multicultural Development* 17(6), 427–41.

Horvath, B.M. and Vaughan, P. (1991) *Community Languages: A Handbook*. Clevedon: Multilingual Matters.

Hsiau, A-Chin (1997) Language ideology in Taiwan: the KMT's language policy, the Tai-yü language movement and ethnic politics. Unpublished manuscript submitted to *Journal of Multilingual and Multicultural Development*.

Hualde, J.I., Lakarra, J.A. and Trask, R.L. (1996) *Towards a History of the Basque Language*. Philadelphia, PA: John Benjamins.

Hübschamannová, M. and Neustupný, J. (1996) The Slovak-and-Czech dialect of Romani and its standardisation. *International Journal of the Sociology of Language* 120, 85–109.

Huebner, T. (1986) Vernacular literacy, English as a language of wider communication and language shift in American Samoa. *Journal of Multilingual and Multicultural Development* 7, 393–411.

Huebner, T. (1989) Language and schooling in Western and American Samoa. *World Englishes* 8, 59–72.

Huizinga, M.W.M. (1994) Multilanguage policy and education in Balochistan (Pakistan). *Language Problems & Language Planning* 18, 47–57.

Hurreiz, S.H. (1975) Arabic in the Sudan. *Language Planning Newsletter* 1 (4), 1, 3–4.

Huss, S. (1990) The education requirement of the US Immigration Reform and Control Act of 1986: a case study of ineffective language planning. *Language Problems & Language Planning* 14, 142–61.

Hussain, S. (1990) Language planning in Pakistan (1947–1960). Townsville: James Cook University. [Unpublished MEd dissertation.]

Hymes, D. (1974) *Foundations in Sociolinguistics: An Ethnographic Approach*. Philadelphia: University of Pennsylvania Press.

Ibrahim, M.H. (1979) The Arabic language academy of Jordan. *Language Planning Newsletter* 5 (4), 1–3.

Ingram, D.E. (1987). Language policy and economic and social development. In B.K. Das (ed.) (1987) (pp. 23–57).

Ingram, D.E. (1990) Language-in-education planning. In R.B. Kaplan *et al.* (eds) *Annual Review of Applied Linguistics, 10* (pp. 53–78). New York: Cambridge University Press.

Ingram, D.E. (1994) Language policy in Australia in the 1990s. In R.D. Lambert, (ed.) (1994) (pp. 69–105).

Isaev, M.I. (1979) Jazykovoe stroitel'stvo v SSSR (Processy sozdanija pis'mennostej narodov SSSR). Moscow: Nauka.

Jacob, J.M. (1986) The deliberate use of foreign vocabulary by the Khmer: changing fashions, methods and sources. In M. Hobart and R.H. Taylor (eds) *Context Meaning and Power in Southeast Asia* (pp. 115–29). Ithaca, NY: Cornell Southeast Asian Program.

Jahr, E.H. (1989) Limits of Language planning? Norwegian language planning revisited. *International Journal of the Sociology of Language* 80, 33–9.

Jahr, E.H. (ed.) (1993) *Language Conflict and Language Planning*. Berlin: Mouton de Gruyter.

Jahr, E.H. and Trudgill, P. (1993) Parallels and differences in linguistic development of modern Greece and modern Norway. In E.H. Jahr (ed.) (1993) (p. 83–98).

James, G.C.A. (1985) The Tamil script reform: a case study in folk linguistic standardization. In J.D. Woods (ed.) (1985) (pp. 102–39).

James, J.E. (ed.) (1996) *The Language-Culture Connection*. Singapore: SEAMEO Regional Language Centre.

Janhunen, J. *et al.* (eds) (1975–80) *Ndytteiï uralilaisista kielisť. The Uralic Languages: Examples of Contemporary Usage*. 5 Vols. Helsinki: Suomalaisen Kirjallisuuden Seura.

Janik, J. (1996) Polish language maintenance of the Polish students at Princes Hill Saturday school in Melbourne. *Journal of Multilingual and Multicultural Development* 17, 3–15.

Jarvad, P. (1990) Danish words of the 1980s. *Language International* 2 (4), 27–8.

Jenkins, H.M. (ed.) (1983) *Educating Students from Other Countries*, San Francisco: Jossey Bass.

Jernsletten, N. (1993) Sami language communities and the conflict between Sami and Norwegian. In E.H. Jahr (ed.) (1993) (p. 115–32).

Jernudd, B.H. (1971) Social change and Aboriginal speech variation in Australia. *Anthropological Linguistics* 13, 16–32.

Jernudd, B.H. (1977) Linguistic sources for terminological innovation: policy and opinion. In J. Rubin, B.H. Jernudd, J. Das Gupta, J.A. Fishman, and C.A. Ferguson (eds) (1977) (pp. 215–36).

Jernudd, B.H. (1981) Planning language treatment: linguistics for the third world. *Language in Society* 10, 43–52.

Jernudd, B.H. (1982) Language planning as a focus for language correction. *Language Planning Newsletter* 8 (4), 1–3.

Jernudd, B.H. (1986) Language heterogeneity also in Sweden. In E. Annamalai, B.H. Jernudd and J. Rubin (1986) (pp. 252–58).

Jernudd, B.H. (1988) Essai sur les problèmes linguistique. In J. Maurais (ed.) *Politique et Aménagement Linguistique* (pp. 495–552). Paris: Le Robert.

Jernudd, B.H. (1992) Scientific nomenclature. In W. Bright *et al.* (eds) (1992) (Vol. 3, pp. 383–384).

Jernudd, B.H. (1993) Language planning from a management perspective: an interpretation of findings. In E.H. Jahr (ed.) (1993) (p. 133–42).

Jernudd, B.H. (1994a) Improving tertiary learners' professional writing skills. *Journal of English and Foreign Languages* 12, 34–9.

Jernudd, B.H. (1994b) Personal names and human rights. In T. Skutnabb-Kangas *et al.* (eds) (1994) (pp. 121–32).

Jernudd, B.H. and Baldauf, R.B., Jr (1987) Planning science communication for human resource development. In B.K. Das (ed.) (1987) (pp. 144–89).

Jernudd, B.H. and Jo, S.-H. (1985) Bilingualism as a resource in the United States. In R.B. Kaplan *et al.* (eds) *Annual Review of Applied Linguistics, 6* (pp. 10–18). New York: Cambridge University Press.

Jernudd, B.H. and Neustupný, J.V. (1987) Language planning: for whom? In L. Laforge (ed.) *Proceedings of the International Colloquium on Language Planning* (pp. 71–84). Québec: Les Presses de l'Université Laval.

Jernudd, B.H. and Shapiro, M.J. (eds) (1989) *The Politics of Language Purism*. Berlin: Mouton de Gruyter.

Jernudd, B.H. and Thuan, E. (1984) Naming fish: a problem exploration. *Language in Society* 13, 235–44.

Jesperson, O. (1933/1964) *Essentials of English Grammar*. University, AL: University of Alabama Press. [Alabama Linguistic and Philological Series, 1]

Johansson, S. (1995) ICAME – Quo vadis? Reflections on the use of computer corpora in linguistics. *Computers and the Humanities* 28, 243–52.

Johnson, E. (1994) Policespeak. *New Language Planning Newsletter* 8 (3), 1–5.

Johnson, R.K. (1994) Language policy and planning in Hong Kong. In W. Grabe *et al.* (eds) *Annual Review of Applied Linguistics, 14* (pp. 177–99). New York: Cambridge University Press.

Johnson, S. (1987) The philosophy and politics of Aboriginal language maintenance. *Australian Aboriginal Studies* 2, 54–8.

Jones, G. (1990) How bilingualism is being integrated in Negara Brunei Darussalam. In R.B. Baldauf, Jr and A. Luke (eds) (1990) (pp. 295–304).

Jones, G., Martin, P.W. and Ożóg, A.C.K. (1993) Multilingualism and bilingual education in Brunei Darussalam. *Journal of Multilingual and Multicultural Development* 14, 39–58.

Joseph, J.E. (1987) *Eloquence and Power: The Rise of Language Standards and Standard Languages*. London: Frances Pinter.

Jouannet, F. (1991) Préalables à l'aménagement linguistique: le cas du Rwanda. In R. Chaudenson and D. de Robillard (eds) (1989/1991) *Tome 2*. (pp. 201–45)

Jourdan, C. (1989) Nativization and anglization in Solomons Islands Pijin. *World Englishes* 8, 25–35.

Jourdan, C. (1990) Solomons Pijin: an unrecognized national language. In R.B. Baldauf, Jr and A. Luke (eds) (1990) (pp. 166–81).

Judd, E.L. (1987) The English language amendment: a case study on language and politics. *TESOL Quarterly* 21, 113–35.

Kachru, B.B. (1982) *The Indianization of English*. New Delhi: Oxford University Press.

Kachru, B.B. (1983) The bilingual's creativity: discoursal and stylistic strategies in contact literatures in English. *Studies in the Linguistic Sciences* 13 (2), 37–56.

Kachru, B.B. (1988) The spread of English and sacred linguistic cows. In P. H. Lowenberg (ed.) (1988) (pp. 207–28).

Kachru, B.B. (ed.) (1992) *The Other Tongue: English Across Cultures* (2nd edn). Urbana: University of Illinois Press.

Kachru, B.B. (1996) World Englishes: agony and ecstasy. *Journal of Aesthetic Education* 30, 135–55.

Kahane, H. and Kahane, R. (1988) Language spread and language policy: the prototype of Greek and Latin. In P.H. Lowenberg (ed.) (1988) (pp. 16–24).

Kale, J. (1990a) Controllers or victims: language and education in the Torres Strait. In R.B. Baldauf, Jr and Allan Luke (eds) (1990) (pp. 106–26).

Kale, J. (1990b) Language planning and the language of education in Papua New Guinea. In R.B. Baldauf, Jr and Allan Luke (eds) (1990) (pp. 182–96).

Kallen, J.L. (1988) The English language in Ireland. *International Journal of the Sociology of Language* 70, 127–42.

Kamwangamalu, N.M. (1997) The colonial legacy and language planning in sub-Saharan Africa: the case of Zaire. *Applied Linguistics* 18, 69–85.

Kane, K. (1991) *A Banker's Guide to the Community Reinvestment Act: Case Studies of 33 Institutions*. Washington, DC: The Bureau of National Affairs.

Kaplan, R.B. (1979) The language situation in Australia. *The Linguistic Reporter* 22 (5), 2–3.

Kaplan, R.B. (1980) *The Language Needs of Migrant Workers*. Wellington: New Zealand Council for Educational Research.

Kaplan, R.B. (1981) The language situation in New Zealand. *Linguistic Reporter* 23 (9), 1–3.

Kaplan, R.B. (1982) The language situation in the Philippines. *Linguistic Reporter* 24, 5.

Kaplan, R.B. (1983) Language and science policies in new nations. *Science* 221, 4614. [Guest editorial]

Kaplan, R.B. (1987) English in the language policy of the Pacific rim. *World Englishes* 6, 137–48.

Kaplan, R.B. (1989) Language planning vs. planning language. In C.H. Candlin and T.F. McNamara (eds) *Language, Learning and Community* (pp. 193–203). Sydney: NCELTR.

Kaplan, R.B. (1990a) Foreword: language planning in theory and practice. In R.B. Baldauf, Jr and A. Luke (eds) (1990) (pp. 3–12).

Kaplan, R.B. (1990b) Literacy and language planning. *Lenguas Modernas* 17, 81–91.

Kaplan, R.B. (1991) Literacy, language planning and pedagogy. In M. Travis (ed.) *Equity: Report of the 17th Annual Bilingual Multicultural Education Equity Conference*. Fairbanks: Alaska State Department of Education. [Also in ERIC ED 338 451]

Kaplan, R.B. (1993a) Conquest of paradise – Language planning in New Zealand. In M. Hoey and G. Fox (eds) *Data, Description, Discourse: Papers on the English Language in Honour of John McH Sinclair on his 60th Birthday* (pp. 151–75). London: HarperCollins.

Kaplan, R.B. (1993b) Review of 'A Matter of Language: Where English Fails'. *Journal of Language and Social Psychology* 12, 369–72.

Kaplan, R.B. (1993c) TESOL and applied linguistics in North America. In S. Silberstein (ed.) *State of the Art TESOL Essays: Celebrating 25 Years of the Discipline* (pp. 373–81). Alexandria, VA: TESOL, Inc.

Kaplan, R.B. (1993d) The hegemony of English in science and technology. *Journal of Multilingual and Multicultural Development* 14, 151–72.

Kaplan, R.B. (1994a) Language-in-education policy: relevance for developing nations. *Lenguas Modernas* 21, 39–58.

Kaplan, R.B. (1994b) Language policy and planning in New Zealand. In W. Grabe *et al.* (eds) *Annual Review of Applied Linguistics, 14* (pp. 156–76). New York: Cambridge University Press.

Kaplan, R.B. (1995a) Applied linguistics, AAAL, and the political scene. *AAALetter* 17 (2): 2–3. [Editorial]

Kaplan, R.B., Touchstone, E.E. and Hagstrom, C.L. (1995) Image and reality: banking in Los Angeles (pp. 427–56). In J.M. Ulijn and D.E. Murray (eds) *Intercultural Discourse in Business and Technology.* [Special issue of *TEXT* 15 (4)]

Kaplan, R.B. (ed.) (1995b) The teaching of writing in the Pacific basin. *Journal of Asian and Pacific Communication* 6 (1/2). [Special issue]

Kaplan, R.B. and Tse, J.K.-P. (1982) The language situation in Taiwan. *Linguistic Reporter* 25 (2), 1–5.

Karam, F.X. (1974) Toward a definition of language planning. In J.A. Fishman (ed.) (1974) (pp. 103–24).

Karetu, T.S. (1991) Te Ngahurutanga: a decade of protest, 1980–1990. In G. McGregor and M. Williams (eds) *Dirty Silence: Aspects of Language and Literature in New Zealand.* Auckland: Oxford University Press.

Karetu, T.S. (1994) Maori language rights in New Zealand. In T. Skutnabb-Kangas *et al.* (eds) (1994) (pp. 209–18).

Karimi-Hakkak, A. (1989) Language reform movement and its language: the case of Persian. In B.H. Jernudd and M.J. Shapiro (1989) (pp. 81–104).

Katzner, K. (1986) *The Languages of the World.* London/New York: Routledge & Kegan Paul.

Kay, G.S. (1986) The English in Japan. *English Today* 6, 25–7.

Keesing, R.M. (1990) Solomons Pijin: colonial ideologies. In R.B. Baldauf, Jr and A. Luke (eds) (1990) (pp. 149–65).

Kelkar, A.R. (1986) Language planning in Maharashtra. In E. Annamalai, B. H. Jernudd and J. Rubin (1986) (pp. 360–84).

Kennedy, C. (ed.) (1984) *Language Planning and Language Education.* London: George Allen & Unwin.

Kennedy, C. (ed.) (1989) *Language Planning and English Language Teaching.* New York: Prentice Hall.

Kennedy, G.D. (1982) Language teaching in New Zealand. In R.B. Kaplan *et al.* (eds) *Annual Review of Applied Linguistics, 2* (pp. 189–202). Rowley, MA: Newbury House.

Kennedy, G.D. (1989) The learning of English in New Zealand by speakers of other languages. *New Language Planning Newsletter* 4 (1), 1–5.

Kenny, B. and Savage, W. (1997) *Language and Development: Teachers in a Changing World.* London: Longman.

Kenrick, D. (1996) Romani literacy at the crossroads. *International Journal of the Sociology of Language* 119, 109–23.

Kentjono, D. (1986) Indonesian experiences in language development. In E. Annamalai, B.H. Jernudd and J. Rubin (1986) (pp. 279–308).

Khamisi, A.M. (1986) Language planning processes in Tanzania. In E. Annamalai, B.H. Jernudd and J. Rubin (1986) (pp. 259–78).

Khong C.P. and Khong K.H. (1984) Language planning and national unity: 1956–67. *Negara* VII (2), 28–35.

Khubchandani, L.M. (1975) Language planning in modern India. *Language Planning Newsletter* 1 (1), 1, 3–4.

Khubchandani, L.M. (1983) *Plural Languages, Plural Cultures*. Honolulu: University of Hawaii Press.

Khubchandani, L.M. (1994) 'Minority' cultures and their communication rights. In T. Skutnabb-Kangas *et al.* (eds) (1994) (pp. 305–15).

Kinnaird, B. (1992) *Tourism 2000: Key Directions for Human Resource Development.* Sydney: Tourism Training Authority.

Kipp, S., Clyne, M. and Pauwels, A. (1995) *Immigration and Australia's Language Resources*. Canberra: Australian Government Publishing Service. [Bureau of Immigration, Multicultural and Population Research]

Kirkness, A. (1975) *Zur Sprachreinigung im Deutschen 1789–1871 – Eine historische Dokumentation*, 2 Vols. Tübingen: Narr. [Tübinger Beiträge zur Linguistik 26.1 and 26.2]

Kirkwood, M. (ed.) (1989) *Language Planning in the Soviet Union*. London: Macmillan.

Kitis, E. (1990) Hellas: dialect and school. *Language International* 2 (1), 15–17.

Klarberg, M. (1992) Georgia in transition. *New Language Planning Newsletter* 6 (4), 3–4.

Kleineidam, H. (1992) Politique de diffusion linguistique et francophonie: l'action linguistique menée par la France. *International Journal of the Sociology of Language* 95, 11–31.

Klersey, G.F., Jr (1989) Representing auditors' propositions about the collectibility of trade accounts receivable with evidence acquired from discourse. Los Angeles, CA: University of Southern California. [PhD dissertation]

Kloss, H. (1977) *The American Bilingual Tradition*. Rowley, MA: Newbury House.

Kontra, M. (1996) The wars over names in Slovakia. *Language Problems & Language Planning* 20, 160–67.

Koh Tai Ann (1996) Literature, the beloved of language. In J.E. James (ed.) (1996) (pp. 17–33).

Koslow, S., Shandansani, P.N. and Touchstone, E.E. (1994) Exploring language effects in ethnic advertising: a sociolinguistic perspective. *Journal of Consumer Research* 20, 575–85.

Kostallari, A. (1989) La base populaire de la langue littéraire albanaise et la diaspora albanaise contemporaine. *International Journal of the Sociology of Language* 80, 61–7.

Krauss, M. (1992) The world's languages in crisis. *Language* 68, 4–10.

Kreindler, I. (1982) The changing status of Russian in the Soviet Union. *International Journal of the Sociology of Language* 33, 7–39.

Kremnitz, G. (1974) *Versuche zur Kodifizierung des Okzitanischen seit dem 19. Jahrhundert und ihre Annahme durch die Sprecher*. Tübingen: Narr. [Tübinger Beiträge zur Linguistik 48]

Krishnamurti, B. (1985) A survey of Telugu dialect vocabulary used in native occupations. *International Journal of the Sociology of Language* 55, 7–21.

Krishnamurti, B. (1986) A fresh look at language in school education in India. *International Journal of the Sociology of Language* 62, 105–18.

Kristinsson, A.P. (1994) Language planning in Iceland. *New Language Planning Newsletter* 9 (2), 1–3.

Kroon, S. and Vallen, T. (1994) Multilingualism and education: an overview of language and education policies for ethnic minorities in the Netherlands. *Current Issues in Language and Society* 1, 103–29.

Kuo, E.C.Y. (1980) Language planning in Singapore. *Language Planning Newsletter* 6 (2), 1–5.

Kuo, E.C.Y. (1984) Mass media and language planning: Singapore's 'Speak Mandarin' campaign. *Journal of Communication* 34 (2), 24–35.

Kuo, E.C.Y. and Jernudd, B.H. (1993) Balancing macro- and micro-sociolinguistic perspectives in language management: the case of Singapore. *Language Problems & Language Planning* 17, 1–21.

Kwo, O. and Bray, M. (1987) Language and education in Hong Kong: new policies but unresolved problems. *RELC Journal* 18 (1), 98–108.

Ladefoged, P. (1964) *A Phonetic Study of West African Languages*. Cambridge: Cambridge University Press.

Ladefoged, P., Glick, R. and Criper, C. (1972) *Language in Uganda*. London: Oxford University Press.

Laguerre, M.L. (1989) *Bilingüismo en Puerto Rico*. Río Piedras, Puerto Rico: the author.

Laitin, D.D. (1993) Migration and language shift in urban India. *International Journal of the Sociology of Language* 103, 57–72.

Laitin, D.D. (1996) Language planning in the former Soviet Union: the case of Estonia. *International Journal of the Sociology of Language* 118, 43–61.

Laitin, D.D. and Mensah, E. (1991) Language choice among Ghanaians. *Language Problems & Language Planning* 15, 139–61.

Lambert, R.D. (ed.) (1994) *Language Planning Around the World: Contexts and Systemic Change*. Washington, DC: National Foreign Language Center.

Lang, K. (1993) Language and economists' theories of discrimination. *International Journal of the Sociology of Language* 103, 165–83.

Lanstyák, I. and Szabómihály, J. (1996) Contact varieties of Hungarian in Slovakia: a contribution to their description. *International Journal of the Sociology of Language* 120, 111–30.

Laponce, J.A. (1987) *Languages and Their Territories*. Toronto: University of Toronto Press.

Laponce, J.A. (1993) Do languages behave like animals? *International Journal of the Sociology of Language* 103, 19–30.

Large, A. (1988) *The Artificial Language Movement*. Oxford: Basil Blackwell.

Lavondès, H. (1974) Language policy, language engineering and literacy in French Polynesia. In J.A. Fishman (ed.) (1974) (pp. 255–76).

Lazaraton, A. (1995) Qualitative research in applied linguistics: a progress report. *TESOL Quarterly* 29, 455–72.

Leap, W.L. (1975) Stories from Iseta: an Indian language reading project. In G. Harvey and F.M. Heiser (eds) *Southwest Languages and Linguistics in Educational Perspective* (pp. 295–311). San Diego: Institute for Cultural Pluralism.

Leap, W.L. (1983) Linguistics and written discourse in particular languages: contrastive studies: English and American Indian languages. In R. Kaplan *et al.* (eds) *Annual Review of Applied Linguistics, 3* (pp. 24–37). Rowley, MA: Newbury House.

Lee, P.W. (1995) The inception, development and prospects for independent

Chinese secondary schools in Malaysia. *Journal of Asian Pacific Communication* 6, 167–82.

Lee, W.O. (1993) Social reactions towards education proposals: opting against the mother tongue as the medium of instruction in Hong Kong. *Journal of Multilingual and Multicultural Development* 14, 203–16.

Leech, G. and Fligelstone, S. (1992) Computers and corpus analysis. In C.S. Butler (ed.) *Computers and Written Texts*. Oxford: Blackwell.

Lehmann, W. (1975) *Language and Linguistics in the People's Republic of China*. Austin: University of Texas.

Leitner, G. (1991) Europe 1992: a language perspective. *Language Problems & Language Planning* 15, 282–96.

Leontiev, A.A. (1994) Linguistic human rights and educational policy in Russia. In T. Skutnabb-Kangas *et al.* (eds) (1994) (pp. 63–70).

LePage, R.B. (1984) Retrospect and prognosis in Malaysia and Singapore. *International Journal of the Sociology of Language* 45, 113–26.

LePage, R.B. (1988) Some premises concerning the standardization of languages, with special reference to Caribbean Creole English. *International Journal of the Sociology of Language* 71, 25–36.

Leprêtre i Alemany, M.J. (1992) Language planning in Catalonia: theoretical survey, aims and achievements. *New Language Planning Newsletter* 6 (3), 1–6.

Levett, A. and Adams, A. (1987) *Catching Up with Our Future: The Demand for Japanese Skills in New Zealand*. Wellington: New Zealand Japan Foundation.

Lewis, E.G. (1982) Movements and agencies of language spread: Wales and the Soviet Union compared. In R.L. Cooper (1982b) (ed.) (pp. 214–59).

Lewis, E.G. (1983) Implementation of language planning in the Soviet Union. In J. Cobarrubias and J. Fishman (eds) (1983b) (pp. 309–26).

Lewis, M.P. (1993) Real men don't speak Quiché: Quiché ethnicity, Ki-che ethnic movement, K'iche' nationalism. *Language Problems & Language Planning* 17, 37–54.

Liddicoat, A. (1991) *Language Planning in Australia*. Canberra: Applied Linguistics Association of Australia. [*ARAL* S/11]

Liddicoat, A. (1992) The use of the active and passive in French scientific prose: some examples from the biological sciences. *Rassegna Italiana di Linguistica Applicata* 24, 105–21.

Liddicoat, A. (1993) Choosing a liturgical language: language policy and the Catholic mass. *Australian Review of Applied Linguistics* 16 (2), 123–41.

Light, T. (1980) Bilingualism and standard language in the People's Republic of China. In J. Alatis (ed.) *Current Issues in Bilingual Education*. Washington, DC: Georgetown University Press.

Lihani, J. (ed.) (1988) *Global Demands on Language and the Mission of the Language Academies*. Lexington: University of Kentucky Press.

Lo Bianco, J. (1987a) *National Policy on Languages*. Canberra: Australian Government Publishing Service.

Lo Bianco, J. (1987b) The national policy on languages. *Australian Review of Applied Linguistics* 10 (2), 23–32.

Lo Bianco, J. (1990) Making language policy: Australia's experience. In R.B. Baldauf, Jr and A. Luke (eds) (1990) (pp. 47–79).

Lo Bianco, J. (1995) Playing with languages: the Sydney Olympic Games. *Australian Language Matters* 3 (2), 1.

Lo Bianco, J. (1997) English and pluralistic policies: the case of Australia. In W. Eggington and H. Wren (eds) (1997) (pp. 107–119).

Lo Bianco, J. (forthcoming) Viet Nam: *Quoc Ngu*, colonialism and language policy.

In N.R. Gottlieb and P. Chen (eds) *Language Policy in East Asia: A Reader.* Honolulu: University of Hawaii Press.

Lo Bianco, J. and Monteil, A. (1990) *French in Australia: New Prospects.* Canberra: Centre d'Etudes et d'Echanges Francophones en Australie and Australian Federation of Modern Language Teachers' Associations.

Logan, H.M. (1991) Electronic lexicography. *Computers and the Humanities* 25, 351–61.

Loman, B. (1988) Sprachliche Standardisierungsprozesse in Skandinavien. *Sociolinguistica* 2, 209–31.

Lopes, A.J. (1997) *Language Policy: Principles and Problems.* Maputo: Livraria Universitària, Universidade Eduardo Mondlane.

Lowenberg, P.H. (1986) Sociolinguistic context and second language acquisition: acculturation and creativity in Malaysian English. *World Englishes* 5, 71–83.

Lowenberg, P.H. (ed.) (1988) *Language Spread and Language Policy: Issues, Implications and Case Studies.* Washington, DC: Georgetown University Press.

Lowenberg, P.H. (1992) Language policy and language identity in Indonesia. *Journal of Asian Pacific Communication* 3, 59–77.

Lüdi, G. (ed.) (1994) *Sprachstandardisierung.* Schweiz: Universitätsverlag Freiburg.

Luke, A. (1992) Literacy and work in 'new times'. *Open Letter* 3 (1), 3–15.

Luke, A. and Baldauf, R.B., Jr (1990) Language planning and education: a critical rereading. In R.B. Baldauf, Jr and A. Luke (eds) (1990) (pp. 349–56).

Luke, A., McHoul, A. and Mey, J.L. (1990) On the limits of language planning: class, state and power. In R.B. Baldauf, Jr and A. Luke (eds) (1990) (pp. 25–44).

Lundin, R. and Sandery, P. (1993) Open learning for teachers' professional development: consultancy report. Canberra: National Open Learning Policy Unit, Department of Employment, Education and Training. [Unpublished report]

Luzares, C. (1982) Languages-in-education in the Philippines. In R.B. Kaplan *et al.* (eds) *Annual Review of Applied Linguistics, 2* (pp. 122–28). Rowley, MA: Newbury House.

Mackerras, C. (1995) A policy initiative in Asian languages. *Australian Review of Applied Linguistics* S/12, 1–16.

Magga, O.H. (1990) The Sámi language in Norway. In D.R.F. Collis (ed.) (1990) (pp. 418–36).

Magga, O.H. (1994) The Sami Language Act. In T. Skutnabb-Kangas *et al.* (eds) (1994) (pp. 219–33).

Maher, J.C. and Yashiro, K. (eds) (1995) Multilingual Japan. *Journal of Multilingual and Multicultural Development* 16 (1&2). [Special issue]

Mahmud, U.A. (1982) Language spread as a wavelike diffusion process: Arabic in the southern Sudan. In R.L. Cooper (1982b) (ed.) (pp. 158–83).

Mahmud, U.A. (1986) Sociolinguistic determinants in terminology planning: the case of Mauritania. In C. Rondeau and J.C. Sager (eds) *TERMIA 84. Terminology and International Cooperation* (pp. 66–75). Canada: GIRSTERM.

Maina, S.J. (1987) Principles adopted for the enrichment of Kiswahili language. *New Language Planning Newsletter* 2 (2), 1–3.

Malischewshi, E.-A. (1987) Kai Fàng: loan words to the middle kingdom. *English Today* 12, 40–1.

Mangubhai, F. (1987) Literacy in Fiji: its origins and its development. *Interchange* 18, 124–35.

Mann, C. (1992) Universities and LOTE proficiency. In C. Mann and R.B. Baldauf, Jr (eds) *Language Teaching and Learning in Australia* (pp. 49–68). Canberra: Applied Linguistics Association of Australia. [*ARAL* S/9]

Mansour, G. (1980) The dynamics of multilingualism: the case of Senegal. *Journal of Multilingual and Multicultural Development* 1, 273–93.

Mar-Molinero, C. (1989) The teaching of Catalan in Catalonia. *Journal of Multilingual & Multicultural Development* 10, 307–26.

Mar-Molinero, C. (1994) Linguistic nationalism and minority language groups in the 'new' Europe. *Journal of Multilingual and Multicultural Development* 15, 319–28.

Mar-Molinero, C. and Stevenson, P. (1991) Language, geography and politics: the 'territorial imperative' debate in the European context. *Language Problems & Language Planning* 15, 162–76.

Markkanen, R. and Schröder, H.I. (eds) (In press) *Hedging and Discourse: Approaches to the Analysis of a Pragmatic Phenomenon*. Munich: Iudicium Verlag.

Marriott, H.E. (1990) Intercultural business negotiations: the problem of norm discrepancy. *Australian Review of Applied Linguistics* Series S/7, 33–65.

Marshall, D.F. (1986) The question of an official language: language rights and the English language amendment. *International Journal of the Sociology of Language* 60, 7–75.

Marshall, D.F. (ed.) (1991) *Language Planning: Focusschrift in Honour of Joshua A. Fishman on the Occasion of his 65th Birthday. Vol. 3*. Amsterdam/ Philadelphia: John Benjamins.

Marshall, D.F. (1996) A politics of language: language as a sympol in the dissolution of the Soviet Union and its aftermath. *International Journal of the Sociology of Language* 118, 7–41.

Martin, J. (1990) Language and control: fighting with words. In C. Walton and W. Eggington (eds) *Language: Maintenance, Power and Education in Australian Aboriginal Contexts* (pp. 12–43). Darwin: NTU Press.

Masagara, N. (1991) Oath-taking in Kirundi: the impact of religion on language change. Los Angeles, CA: University of Southern California. [PhD Dissertation]

Mattheier, K.J. and Panzer, B. (eds) (1992) The rise of national languages in Eastern Europe. *Sociolinguistica* 6.

Maurais, de J. (1992) Redéfinition du statut des langues en Union Soviétique. *Language Problems & Language Planning* 16, 1–20. *p. 332 Kazakhstan*

Maurais, J. (ed.) (1996) *Quebec's Aboriginal Languages: History, Planning and Development*. Clevedon: Multilingual Matters.

Mauranen, A. (1993) *Cultural Differences in Academic Rhetoric*. Frankfurt am Main: Peter Lang. [Scandinavian University Studies in the Humanities and Social Sciences, Vol. 4]

Mazrui, A.A. (1996a) Language planning and gender planning: some African perspectives. *International Journal of the Sociology Language* 118, 125–38.

Mazrui, A.M. (1996b) Language policy and the foundations of democracy: an African perspective. *International Journal of the Sociology of Language* 118, 107–24.

McConnell, G.D. (1977) Language treatment and language planning in Canada. *Language Planning Newsletter* 3 (3), 1, 3–6; 3 (4), 1–6.

McCrum, R., Cran, W. and MacNeil, R. (1986) *The Story of English*. New York: Viking.

McDonald, H. (1993) Identity and the acquisition of academic literacy: a case study. *Open Letter* 4 (1), 3–14.

McDonald, M. (1989) *We are not French: Language, Culture and Identity in Brittany*. London: Routledge.

McFarland, C.D. (1981) *A Linguistic Atlas of the Philippines*. Manila: Linguistic Society of the Philippines.

McGregor, G. and Williams, M. (eds) (1991) *Dirty Silence: Aspects of Language and Literature in New Zealand*. Auckland, New Zealand: Oxford University Press.

McGroarty, M. (1997) Language policy in the USA: national values, local loyalties, pragmatic pressures. In W. Eggington and H. Wren (eds) (1997) (pp. 67–90).

McKay, G. (1996) *The Land Still Speaks: Review of Aboriginal and Torres Strait Islander Maintenance and Development Needs and Activities.* Canberra: Australian Government Printing Service. [NBEET Report No. 44]

McKay, S.L. and Weinstein-Shr, G. (1993) English literacy in the US: national policies, personal consequences. *TESOL Quarterly 27,* 399–419.

McNamara, T.F. (1996) *Second Language Performance Assessment: Theory and Research.* London: Longman.

Medgyes, P. and Kaplan, R.B. (1992) Discourse in a foreign language: the example of Hungarian scholars. *International Journal of the Sociology of Language 98,* 67–100.

Mehrotra, R.R. (1985) Sociolinguistic surveys in South Asia: an overview. *International Journal of the Sociology of Language 55,* 115–24.

Meijs, W. (1992) Computers and dictionaries. In C.S. Butler (ed.) *Computers and Written Texts.* Oxford: Blackwell.

Meijs, W. (1996) Linguistic corpora and lexicography. In W. Grabe *et al.* (eds) *Annual Review of Applied Linguistics, 16* (pp. 99–114). New York: Cambridge University Press.

Mekacha, R.D.K. (1993) Is Tanzania diglossic? The status and role of ethnic community languages. *Journal of Multilingual and Multicultural Development 14,* 307–20.

Messineo, C. and Wright, P. (1989) De la oralidad a la ecritura: el caso Toba. *Lenguas modernas 16,* 115–26.

Mey, J.L. (1985) *Whose Language? A Study in Linguistic Pragmatics.* Amsterdam: John Benjamins.

Mey, J.L. (1989) 'Saying it don't make it so': 'Una Grande Libre' of language politics. *Multilingua 8,* 333–55.

Mezei, R. (1989) Somali language and literacy. *Language Problems & Language Planning 13,* 211–23.

Milroy, J. and Milroy, L. (1991) *Authority in Language: Investigating Language Prescription and Standardisation* (2nd edn). London: Routledge.

Mitchell, T.F. (1985) Sociolinguistic and stylistic dimensions of the educated spoken Arabic of Egypt and the Levant. In J.D. Woods (ed.) (1985) (pp. 42–57).

Modarresi, Y. (1990) Language problems and language planning in Iran. *New Language Planning Newsletter 5* (1), 1–6.

Moeliono, A.M. (1994) Standardisation and modernisation in Indonesian language planning. In G. Lüdi (ed.) (1994) (pp. 117–30).

Molde, B. (1975) Language planning in Sweden. *Language Planning Newsletter 1* (3), 1, 3–4.

Møller, A. (1988) Language policy and language planning after the establishment of the home rule in Greenland. *Journal of Multilingual and Multicultural Development 9,* 177–9.

Møller, A. (1990) Language policy and planning under the home rule administration. In D.R.F. Collis (ed.) (1990) (pp. 361–4).

Moniruzzaman, M. (1979) Language planning in Bangladesh. *Language Planning Newsletter 5* (3), 1, 3–4.

Moore, H. (1991) Enchantment and displacements: multiculturalism, language policy and Dawkins-speak. *Melbourne Studies of Education* (pp. 45–85). Melbourne: University of Melbourne.

Moore, H. (1996) Language policies as virtual realities: two Australian examples. *TESOL Quarterly 30,* 473–97.

Morren, R.C. (1988) Bilingual education curriculum development in Guatemala. *Journal of Multilingual and Multicultural Development* 9, 353–70.

Morris, N. (1996) Language and identity in twentieth century Puerto Rico. *Journal of Multilingual and Multicultural Development* 17, 17–32.

Morrow, P.R. (1987) The users and uses of English in Japan. *World Englishes* 6, 49–62.

Mühlhäusler, P. (1994a) Language planning and small languages – the case of the Pacific area. In G. Lüdi (ed.) (1994) (pp. 131–53).

Mühlhäusler, P. (1994b) Language teaching = linguistic imperialism? *Australian Review of Applied Linguistics* 17 (2), 121–30.

Mühlhäusler, P. (1994c) What is the use of language diversity? In P. Mühlhäusler (ed.) *The Public Face of Linguistics*. Adelaide: Centre for Language teaching and Research, University of Adelaide.

Mühlhäusler, P. (1995a) Ecological perspectives on low candidature languages. In R.B. Baldauf, Jr (ed.) (1995b) (pp. 39–50).

Mühlhäusler, P. (1995b) *Linguistic Ecology: Language Change and Linguistic Imperialism in the Pacific Region*. London: Routledge.

Mühlhäusler, P. (1995c) The ecology of small languages (pp. 1–14). In R.B. Baldauf, Jr (ed.) *Backing Australian Languages: Review of the Aboriginal and Torres Strait Islander Languages Initiatives Program*. Canberra: National Languages and Literacy Institute of Australia.

Murison-Bowie, S. (1996) Linguistic corpora and language teaching. In W. Grabe *et al.* (eds) *Annual Review of Applied Linguistics, 16* (pp. 182–99). New York: Cambridge University Press.

Musa, M. (1984) Issues of term planning for Bengali. *Language Planning Newsletter* 10 (2), 1–5.

Musa, M. (1985) The ekuske: a ritual of language and liberty. *Language Problems & Language Planning* 9, 200–14.

Musa, M. (1989) Purism and correctness in the Bengali speech community. In B.H. Jernudd and M.J. Shapiro (eds) (1989) (pp. 105–12).

Musa, M. (1996) Politics of language planning in Pakistan and the birth of a new state. *International Journal of the Sociology of Language* 118, 63–80.

Nahir, M. (1984) Language planning goals: a classification. *Language Problems & Language Planning* 8, 294–327.

Nahir, M. (1988) Language planning and language acquisition: the 'great leap' in the Hebrew revival. In C.B. Paulston (ed.) *International Handbook of Bilingualism and Bilingual Education* (pp. 273–95). New York: Greenwood Press.

Nance, J. (1975) *The Gentle Tasaday: A Stone Age People in the Philippine Rain Forest*. New York: Harcourt Brace Jovanovich.

Ndoma, U. (1984) National language policy in education in Zaire. *Language Problems & Language Planning* 8, 172–84.

Nekitel, O. (1989) What is happening to vernaculars in Papua New Guinea? *Ethnies: Droits de l'homme et peuples autochtones* 8/9/10, 18–23.

Nelde, P.H. (1988) Dutch as a language in contact. *International Journal of the Sociology of Language* 73, 111–19.

Nelde, P.H. (1994) Languages in contact and conflict: the Belgian experience and the European Union. *Current Issues in Language and Society* 1, 165–82.

Neugaard, E.J. (1995) The continuing Valencian language controversy. *Language Problems & Language Planning* 19, 60–6.

Neustupný, J.V. (1976) Language correction in contemporary Japan. *Language Planning Newsletter* 2 (3), 1, 3–5.

Neustupný, J.V. (1978) *Post-structural Approaches to Language: Language Theory in a Japanese Context*. Tokyo: University of Tokyo Press.

Neustupný, J.V. (1984) Language planning and human rights. In A. Gonzalez (ed.) (1984) (pp. 66–74).

Neustupný, J.V. (1986) A review of Japanese kana spelling. *New Language Planning Newsletter* 1 (1), 2–3.

Neustupný, J.V. (1987) Towards a paradigm in language planning. In U.N. Singh and R.N. Srivastava (eds) (1987) (pp. 1–10).

Neustupný, J.V. (1989) Czech diglossia and language management. *New Language Planning Newsletter* 3 (4), 1–2.

Newman, J. (1988) Singapore's speak Mandarin campaign. *Journal of Multilingual and Multicultural Development* 9, 437–48.

Newton, G. (ed.) (1996) *Luxembourg and Lëtzebuergesch*. Oxford: Oxford University Press.

Nguyen D.-H. (1985) Terminology work in Vietnam. In D. Bradley (ed.) (1985a) (pp. 119–30).

Nichols, P.C. (1988) Language policy and social power: gender and ethnic issues. In P.H. Lowenberg (ed.) (1988) (pp. 175–86).

Nik Safiah, K. (1987) Language cultivation, the school system and national development: the case of Bahasa Malaysia. In B.K. Das (ed.) (1987) (pp. 58–69).

Nkusi, L. (1991) Situations sociolinguistiques des payes faisant usage de la langue française: la cas du Rwanda. In R. Chaudenson and D. de Robillard (eds) (1989/1991) Tome 2 (pp. 247–62).

Norberg, M. (1994) The Sorbs between support and suppression. *International Journal of the Sociology of Language* 107, 149–58.

Northover, M. and Donnelly, S. (1996) A future for English/Irish bilingualism in Northern Ireland. *Journal of Multilingual and Multicultural Development* 17, 33–48.

Noss, R.B. (1985) The evaluation of language planning in education. *South East Asian Journal of Social Science* 13, 82–105.

Novak-Lukanivič, S. (1988) Bilingual education in Yugoslavia: some experiences in the field of education for national minorities/nationalities in Yugoslavia. *Journal of Multilingual and Multicultural Development* 9, 169–76.

Nunan, D. (1992) *Research Methods in Language Learning*. Cambridge: Cambridge University Press.

Nyembwe, N., Makokila, N. and Mundeke, O. (1992) Enquête sur les marchés: la cas de Kinshasa. In L.-J. Calvet *et al.* (eds) (1992) (pp. 291–341).

Ó Baoill, D.P. (1988) Language planning in Ireland: the standardization of Irish. *International Journal of the Sociology of Language* 70, 109–26.

Ó Buachalla, S. (1984) Educational policy and the role of the Irish language from 1831 to 1981. *European Journal of Education* 19, 75–90.

Ó Ciosáin, S. (1988) Language planning and Irish: 1965–74. *Language, Culture and Curriculum* 1, 263–79.

O'Donoghue, T.A. (1995) Bilingual education at the beginning of the twentieth century: the bilingual programme of instruction in Ireland 1904–1922. *Journal of Multilingual and Multicultural Development* 15, 491–505.

Ó Gadhra, M. (1988) Irish government policy and political development of the Gaeltacht. *Language, Culture and Curriculum* 1, 251–61.

Ogino, T., Misono, Y. and Fukushima, C. (1985) Diversity of honorific usage in Tokyo: a sociolinguistic approach based on a field survey. *International Journal of the Sociology of Language* 55, 23–39.

Ó Gliasáin, M. (1988) Bilingual secondary schools in Dublin 1960–1980. *International Journal of the Sociology of Language* 70, 89–108.

Ó hAilin, T. (1969) Irish revival movements. In B.Ó Cuiv (ed.) *A View of the Irish Language* (pp. 91–100). Dublin: Stationery Office.

Ohannessian, S., Ferguson, C.A. and Polomé, E.C. (eds) (1975) *Language Survey in Developing Nations: Papers and Reports on Sociolinguistic Surveys.* Arlington, VA: Centre for Applied Linguistics.

Ohannessian, S. and Ansre, G. (1975) Some reflections on the educational use of sociolinguistic surveys. In S. Ohannessian, C.A. Ferguson and E.C. Polomé (eds) (1975) (pp. 51–69).

Oladejo, J. (1991) The national language question in Nigeria: is there an answer? *Language Problems & Language Planning* 15, 255–67.

Oladejo, J. (1992) The national language question in Nigeria: a place for pidgin? *New Language Planning Newsletter* 7 (1), 1–4.

Oladejo, J. (1993) How not to embark on a bilingual education policy in a developing nation: the case of Nigeria. *Journal of Multilingual and Multicultural Development* 14, 91–102.

O Laoire, M. (1995) an historical perspective on the revival of Irish outside the Gaeltacht, 1880–1930, with reference to the revitalization of Hebrew. *Current Issues in Language and Society* 2, 223–235.

Omar, A.H. (1975) Supranational standardization of spelling system: the case of Malaysia and Indonesia. *International Journal of the Sociology of Language* 5, 77–92.

Omar, A.H. (1982) Language spread and recession in Malaysia and the Malay archipelago. In R.L. Cooper (ed.) (1982b) (pp. 198–213).

Omar, A.H. (1983) *The Malay Peoples of Malaysia and Their Languages.* Kuala Lumpur: Dewan Bahasa dan Pustaka, Kementerian Pelajaran Malaysia.

Omar, A.H. (1984) The development of the national language of Malaysia. In A. Gonzalez (ed.) (1984) (pp. 7–23).

Omar, A.H. (1985) The language policy of Malaysia: a formula for balanced pluralism. In D. Bradley (ed.) (1985a) (pp. 39–49).

Omar, A.H. (1992) *The Linguistic Scenery in Malaysia.* Kuala Lumpur: Dewan Bahasa dan Pustaka.

Omar, A.H. (1995) Language policy and management in Malaysia. *Journal of Asian Pacific Communication* 6, 157–65.

Ó Murchú, H. (1990) A language policy for Irish schools. *Teangeolas* 27, 15–20.

Onions, C.T. (ed.) (1966) *The Oxford Dictionary of English Etymology.* New York: Oxford University Press.

Ó Riagáin, P. (1988) Bilingualism in Ireland 1973–1983: an overview of national sociolinguistic surveys. *International Journal of the Sociology of Language* 70, 29–51.

Ó Riagáin, P., Paulston, C.B., Peillon, M., Verdoodt, A. and Fréine, S. de (1989) Review symposium of *The Irish Language in a Changing Society: Shaping the Future. Language, Culture and Curriculum* 2, 135–52.

Ożóg, C.K. (1990) English language in Malaysia and its relationship with the national language. In R.B. Baldauf, Jr and A. Luke (eds) (1990) (pp. 305–18).

Ożóg, C.K. (1993) Bilingualism and national development in Malaysia. *Journal of Multilingual and Multicultural Development* 14 (1&2), 59–72.

Ozolins, U. (1984) Language planning in Australia: the Senate inquiry into language policy. *Language Planning Newsletter* 10 (1), 1–7.

Ozolins, U. (1988) Government language policy initiatives and the future of ethnic languages in Australia. *International Journal of the Sociology of Language* 72, 113–29.

Ozolins, U. (1991) *Interpreting, Translating and Language Policy.* Melbourne: National Languages and Literacy Institute of Australia.

Ozolins, U. (1993) *The Politics of Language in Australia.* Melbourne: Cambridge University Press.

Ozolins, U. (1994) Upwardly mobile languages: the politics of languages in the Baltic states. *Journal of Multilingual and Multicultural Development* 15, 161–69.

Ozolins, U. (1996) Language policy and political reality. *International Journal of the Sociology of Language* 118, 181–200.

Pachori, S.S. (1990) The language policy of the East India Company and the Asiatic Society of Bengal. *Language Problems & Language Planning* 14, 104–18.

Pakir, A. (1993a) Making bilingualism work: developments in Bilingual Education in ASEAN. *Language, Culture and Curriculum* 6, 209–23.

Pakir, A. (1993b) Two tongue tied: bilingualism in Singapore. *Journal of Multilingual and Multicultural Development* 14, 73–90.

Panzer, B. (1992) Zur Geschichte der russischen Standardsprache. Identität, Kontinuität, Entwicklung. *Sociolinguistica* 6, 1–10.

Pap, L. (1990) The language situation in Switzerland: an updated survey. *Lingua* 80 (2/3), 109–48.

Park, N.-S. (1989) Language purism in Korea today. In B.H. Jernudd and M.J. Shapiro (eds) (1989) (pp. 113–40).

Pattanayak, D.P. (1986) Language and the new education policy of India. *New Language Planning Newsletter* 1 (1), 1–2.

Patthey, G.G. (1989) Mexican language policy. *New Language Planning Newsletter* 3 (3), 1–6.

Patthey-Chavez, G.G. (1994) Language policy and planning in Mexico: indigenous language policy. In W. Grabe *et al.* (eds) *Annual Review of Applied Linguistics, 14* (pp. 200–19). New York: Cambridge University Press.

Paulston, C.B., Pow C.C., and Connerty, M.C. (1993) Language regenesis: a conceptual overview of language revival, revitalisation and reversal. *Journal of Multilingual and Multicultural Development* 14, 275–86.

Paulston, C.B. and McLaughlin, S. (1994) Language-in-education policy and planning. In W. Grabe *et al.* (eds) *Annual Review of Applied Linguistics, 14.* New York: Cambridge University Press.

Pauwels, A. (1985) Australia as a multilingual nation. In R.B. Kaplan *et al.* (eds) *Annual Review of Applied Linguistics, 6* (pp. 78–99). New York: Cambridge University Press.

Pauwels, A. (1991) *Cross-cultural Communication in Medical Encounters.* Clayton, Victoria, Australia: Monash University. National Centre for Community Language in the Professions.

Pauwels, A. (1992) *Cross-cultural Communication in Legal Encounters.* Clayton, Victoria, Australia: Monash University. National Centre for Community Language in the Professions.

Pauwels, A. (1993) Language planning, language reform and the sexes in Australia. In J. Winter and G. Wigglesworth (eds) *Language and Gender in the Australian Context* (pp. 13–34). Canberra: Applied Linguistics Association of Australia. [ARAL S/10]

Pauwels, A. (in press) *Language Planning and the Sexes.* London/New York: Longman.

Payne, R.M. (1983) *Language in Tunisia.* Tunis: Bourguiba Institute of Modern Languages.

Peddie, R.A. (1991a) Coming – ready or not? Language policy development in New Zealand. *Language Problems & Language Planning* 15, 25–42.

Peddie, R.A. (1991b) *One, Two, or Many? The Development and Implementation of Languages Policy in New Zealand.* Auckland: University of Auckland.

Peddie, R.A. (1997) Why are we waiting? Languages policy development in New Zealand. In W. Eggington and H. Wren (eds) (1997) (pp. 121–146)

Pemagbi, J. (1989) Still a deficient language? *English Today* 5 (1), 20–4.

Peña, F. de la (1991) *Democracy or Babel? The Case for Official English in the United States.* Washington, DC: US English.

Penn, C. and Reagan, T. (1990) How do you sign 'apartheid'? The politics of South African sign language. *Language Problems & Language Planning* 14, 91–103.

Petersen, R. (1990) The Greenlandic language: its nature and situation. In D.R.F. Collis (ed.) (1990) (pp. 293–308).

Petherbridge-Hernández, P. (1990) The recatalanisation of Catalonia's schools. *Language, Culture and Curriculum* 3, 97–108.

Petyt, K. (1975) Romania, a multilingual nation. *International Journal of the Sociology of Language* 4, 75–101.

Phillipson, R. (1988) Linguicism: structures and ideologies in linguistic imperialism. In T. Skutnabb-Kangas and J. Cummins (eds) (1988) (pp. 339–58).

Phillipson, R. (1992) *Linguistic Imperialism*. Oxford. Oxford University Press.

Phillipson, R. (1994) English language spread policy. *International Journal of the Sociology of Language* 107, 7–24.

Phillipson, R. and Skutnabb-Kangas, T. (1994) Language rights in post-colonial Africa. In T. Skutnabb-Kangas *et al.* (eds) (1994) (pp. 335–45).

Phillipson, R., Skutnabb-Kangas, T. and Africa, H. (1986) Namibian educational language planning: English for liberation or neo-colonialism? In B. Spolsky (ed.) (1986) (pp. 77–95).

Pine, P. and Savage, W. (1989) Marshallese and English: evidence for an immersion model of education in the Republic of the Marshall Islands. *World Englishes* 8, 83–94.

Platt, J.T. (1985) Bilingual policies in a multilingual society: reflections of the Singaporian Mandarin campaign in the English language press. In D. Bradley (ed.) (1985a) (pp. 15–30).

Platt, J.T. and Weber, H. (1980) *English in Singapore and Malaysia: Status, Features, Functions.* Kuala Lumpur: Oxford University Press.

Pointon, G. (1988) The BBC and English pronunciation. *English Today* 4 (3), 8–12.

Pool, J. (1976) Some observations on language planning in Azerbaijan and Turkmenistan. *Language Planning Newsletter* 2 (2), 3–4, 6.

Poole, D. (1991) Discourse analysis in ethnographic research. In W. Grabe *et al.* (eds) *Annual Review of Applied Linguistics, 11* (pp. 42–56). New York: Cambridge University Press.

Postile, G. (1995) *Equity, Diversity and Excellence: Advancing the National Equity Framework.* Canberra: NBEET. [Higher Education Council Discussion Paper]

Pou, J. C. (1993) Le trilingualism au Luxembourg. *Language Problems & Language Planning* 17, 55–61.

Pride, J.B. and Liu R.-S. (1988) Some aspects of the spread of English in China since 1949. *International Journal of the Sociology of Language* 74, 41–70.

Pritchard, R.M.O. (1990) Language policy in Northern Ireland. *Teangolas* 27, 26–35.

Pryce, W.T.R. and Williams, C.H. (1988) Sources and methods in the study of language areas: a case study of Wales. In C.H. Williams (ed.) (1988) (pp. 167–237).

Pütz, M. (1992) The present and future maintenance of German in the context of Namibia's official language policy. *Multilingua* 11, 293–323.

Pütz, M. (1994) (ed.) *Language Contact and Language Conflict.* Amsterdam/ Philadelphia: John Benjamins.

Pütz, M. (ed.) (1995) *Discrimination Through Language in Africa: Perspectives on the Namibian Experience.* Berlin: de Gruyter.

Quirk, R., Greenbaum, S., Leech, G. and Svartvik, J. (1985) *A Comprehensive Grammar of English.* New York: Longman.

Raban-Bisby, B. (1995) Early childhood years — problem or resource? Inaugural Professorial Lecture, 27 July, University of Melbourne, Australia.

Rabin, C. (1971) Spelling reform – Israel 1968. In J. Rubin and B.H. Jernudd (eds) (1971) (pp. 95–121).

Rabin, C. (1976) Language treatment in Israel: especially the development and spread of Hebrew. *Language Planning Newsletter* 2 (4), 1, 3–4, 6.

Raby, G. *et al.* (1992) *Australia and North-east Asia in the 1990s: Accelerating Change.* Canberra: Australian Government Publishing Service.

Radnai, A. (1994) The educational effects of language policy. *Current Issues in Language and Society* 1, 65–87.

Rahman, T. (1995) The Siraiki movement in Pakistan. *Language Problems & Language Planning* 19, 1–25.

Rahman, T. (1996) British language policies and imperialsim in India. *Language Problems & Language Planning* 20, 91–115.

Rambelo, M. (1991a) Langue nationale, français et développement. Éléments pour une politique d'aménagement linguistique à Madagascar. In R. Chaudenson and D. de Robillard (eds) (1989/1991) *Tome 2* (pp. 5–73).

Rambelo, M. (1991b) Madagascar: la politique de relance du français et ses effets sur la situation linguistique. In R. Chaudenson and D. de Robillard (eds) (1989/1991) *Tome 2* (pp. 75–121).

Rannut, M. (1991a) Influence of ideology in the linguistic policy of the Soviet Union. *Journal of Multilingual and Multicultural Development* 12, 105–110.

Rannut, M. (1991b) Linguistic policy in the Soviet Union. *Multilingua* 10, 241–50.

Rannut, M. (1994) Beyond linguistic policy: the Soviet Union vs Estonia. In T. Skutnabb-Kangas *et al.* (eds) (1994) (pp. 179–208).

Reagan, T. (1986) The role of language policy in South African education. *Language Problems & Language Planning* 10, 1–13.

Reagan, T. (1995) Neither easy to understand nor pleasing to see: the development of manual sign codes as language planning activity. *Language Problems & Language Planning* 19, 133–50.

Reagan, T. and Ntshoe, I. (1987) Language policy and black education in South Africa. *Journal of Research and Development in Education* 20 (2), 1–8.

Reid, I. (1995) Student literacy in a cross-cultural perspective. *Australian Language Matters* 3 (2), 4.

Rensch, K.H. (1990) The delayed impact: post colonial language problems in the French overseas territory of Wallis and Futuna (Central Polynesia). *Language Problems & Language Planning* 14, 224–36.

Resnick, M.C. (1993) ESL and language planning in Puerto Rican education. *TESOL Quarterly* 27, 259–75.

Reyburn, W.D. (1975) Assessing multilingualism: an abridgment of 'Problems and Procedures in Ethnolinguistic Surveys'. In S. Ohannessian, C.A. Ferguson and E.C. Polomé (eds) (1971) (pp. 87–114).

Rhee, M.J. (1992) Language planning in Korea under the Japanese colonial administration, 1910–1945. *Language, Culture and Curriculum* 5, 87–97.

Ricento, T. (1996) Language policy in the United States: an overview. In M. Herriman and B. Burnaby (eds) (1996) (pp. 122–58).

Richards, J.B. (1989) Mayan language planning for bilingual education in Guatemala. *International Journal of the Sociology of Language* 77, 93–115.

Ridge, S.M.G. (1996) Language policy in a democratic South Africa. In M. Herriman and B. Burnaby (eds) (1996) (pp. 15–34).

Ridler, N. B. and Pons-Ridler, S. (1986) An economic analysis of Canadian language policies: a model and its implications. *Language Problems & Language Planning* 10, 42–58.

Riley, G. (1975) Language loyalty and ethnocentrism in the Guamanian speech community. *Anthropological Linguistics* 17, 286–92.

Riley, G. (1980) Language loyalty and ethnocentrism in the Guamanian speech community: seven years later. *Anthropological Linguistics* 22, 329–33.

Riley-Mundine, L. and Roberts, B. (1990) *Review of National Aboriginal Languages Program.* Perth: Pitman Roberts and Partners. (AACLAME Occasional Paper No. 5)

Roberts, R.P. (1992) Translation and interpretation. In W. Bright *et al.* (eds) (1992) (Vol. 4, pp. 177–80)

Robins, R.H. and Uhlenbeck, E.M. (eds) (1991) *Endangered Languages.* Oxford/New York: Berg.

Robinson, C.D.W. (1993) Where linguistic minorities are in the majority: language dynamics amidst high linguistic diversity. *AILA Review* 10, 52–70.

Robinson, C.D.W. (1994) Is sauce for the goose sauce for the gander? Some comparative reflections on minority language planning in North and South. *Journal of Multilingual and Multicultural Development* 15, 129–45.

Rodriquez, C. (1992) Informal language planning for elementary school language development: the case of Arizona. In C. Mann and R.B. Baldauf, Jr (eds) *Language Teaching and Learning in Australia* (pp. 6–18). Canberra: Applied Linguistics Association of Australia. [ARAL S/9]

Romaine, S. (1989) English and Tok Pisin (New Guinea Pidgin English) in Papua New Guinea. *World Englishes* 8, 5–23.

Romaine, S. (1991) *Language in Australia.* Cambridge: Cambridge University Press.

Rotaetxe, K. (1994) Normativisation et normalisation d'une langue: l'expérence basque. In G. Lüdi (ed.) (1994) (pp. 77–99).

Rubagumya, C.M. (1986) Language planning in the Tanzanian educational system: problems and prospects. *Journal of Multilingual and Multicultural Development* 7, 283–300.

Rubagumya, C.M. (1989) *Language in Education in Africa: A Tanzanian Perspective.* Clevedon: Multilingual Matters.

Rubin, J. (1968a) Language education in Paraguay. In J. Fishman, C. Ferguson, and J. Das Gupta (eds) *Language Problems of Developing Nations* (pp. 477–88). New York: Wiley.

Rubin, J. (1968b) *National Bilingualism in Paraguay.* The Hague: Mouton.

Rubin, J. (1971) Evaluation and language planning. In J. Rubin and B.H. Jernudd (eds) (1971) (pp. 217–52).

Rubin, J. (1977a) Language problems and educational systems in Indonesia. In B.P. Sabayan and A.B. Gonzalez FSC (eds) *Language Planning and the Building of a National Language* (pp. 155–69). Manila: Philippine Normal College.

Rubin, J. (1977b) Language standardization in Indonesia. In J. Rubin, B.H. Jernudd, J. Das Gupta, J.A. Fishman, and C.A. Ferguson (eds) (1977) (pp. 157–79).

Rubin, J. (1978/1979) The approach to language planning within the United States. *Language Planning Newsletter* 4 (4), 1, 3–6; 5 (1), 1, 3–6.

Rubin, J. (1979) *Directory of Language Planning Organizations.* Honolulu: East-West Center.

Rubin, J. (1983) Evaluating status planning: what has the past decade accomplished? In J. Cobarrubias and J.A. Fishman (eds) (1983b) (pp. 329–43).

Rubin, J. and Jernudd, B.H. (1979) *References for Students of Language Planning.* Honululu: East-West Center.

Rubin, J. and Jernudd, B.H. (1971a) (eds) *Can Language be Planned?* Honolulu: East West Center and University of Hawaii Press.

Rubin, J. and Jernudd, B.H. (1971b) Introduction: language planning as an element in modernization. In J. Rubin and B.H. Jernudd (eds) (1971a) (pp. xii–xxiv).

Rubin, J., Jernudd, B.H., Das Gupta, J., Fishman, J.A. and Ferguson, C.A. (eds) (1977) *Language Planning Processes*. The Hague: Mouton.

Rusch, P. (1989) National vs. regional models of language variation: the case of Austrian German. *Language, Culture and Curriculum* 2, 1–16.

Russo, C.P. (1983) Developing educational policies for traditionally oriented Aborigines. *Interchange* 14, 1–13.

Russo, C.P. and Baldauf, R.B. Jr (1986) Language development without planning: a case study of tribal Aborigines in the northern territory, Australia. *Journal of Multilingual and Multicultural Development* 7, 301-17.

Safire, W. (1984) *I Stand Corrected: More on Language*. New York: New York Times Books.

Sager, J.C. (ed.) (1975) Standardization of nomenclature. *International Journal of the Sociology of Language* 23.

Sager, J.C. (1990) *A Practical Course in Terminology Processing*. Amsterdam: John Benjamins.

Sakaguchi, A. (1996) Die Dichotomie 'künstlich' vs. 'natürlich' und das historische Phänomen einer funktionieren den Plansprache. *Language Problems & Language Planning* 20, 18–38.

Sánchez, A. (1992) Politica de difusión del español. *International Journal of the Sociology of Language* 95, 51–69.

Sandefur, J.R. (1977) Bilingual education for Aboriginal Australians. *Language Planning Newsletter* 3 (2), 1, 6.

Sandefur, J.R. (1985) Language planning and the development of an Australian Aboriginal creole. *Language Planning Newsletter* 11 (1), 1–4.

Sato, C.J. (1985) Linguistic inequality in Hawaii: the post-creole dilemma. In N. Wolfson and J. Manes (eds) (1985) (pp. 255–72).

Saussure, F. de (1916/1959) *Cours de Linguistique Générale*. New York: McGraw-Hill. [C. Bailey *et al.* (eds); trs. Wade Baskin]

Scaglione, A. (ed.) (1984) *The Emergence of National Languages*. Ravenna: Longo Editore.

Schiffman, H.F. (1992) 'Resisting arrest' in status planning: structural and covert impediments to status change. *Language and Communication* 12, 1–15.

Schiffman, H.F. (1993) The balance of power in multiglossic languages: implications for language shift. *International Journal of the Sociology of Language* 103, 115–48.

Schiffman, H.F. (1995) *Linguistic Culture and Language Policy*. London: Routledge.

Schlossmacher, M. (1995) Official languages and working languages in the political bodies of the European Union. *New Language Planning Newsletter* 9 (4), 1–2.

Schmitt, C. (1988) Typen der Ausbildung und Durchsetzung von Nationalsprachen in der Romania. *Sociolinguistica* 2, 73–116.

Scholfield, P. (1994) *Quantifying Language: A Researcher's and Teacher's Guide to Gathering Language Data and Reducing it to Figures*. Clevedon: Multilingual Matters.

Schramm, W., Nelson, L.M. and Betham, M.T. (1981) *Bold Experiment: The Story of Educational Television in American Samoa*. Stanford: Stanford University Press.

Schuster-Šewe, H. (1992) Zur schriftsprachlichen Entwicklung im Bereich des Sorbischen. *Sociolinguistica* 6, 65–83.

Scollon, R. and Scollon, S.B.K. (1979) *Linguistic Convergence: An Ethnography of Speaking at Fort Chipewyan, Alberta*. New York: Academic Press.

Scotton, C.M. (1982) The linguistic situation and language policy in eastern Africa. R.B. Kaplan *et al.* (eds) *Annual Review of Applied Linguistics*, 2 (pp. 8–20). Rowley, MA: Newbury House.

Scotton, C.M. (1993) Elite closure as a powerful language strategy: the African case. *International Journal of the Sociology of Language* 103, 149–63.

Seliger, H.W. and Shohamy, E. (1989) *Second Language Research Methods*. Oxford: Oxford University Press.

Senate Standing Committee on Foreign Affairs, Defence and Trade (SSCFADT) (1992). *Australia and Latin America*. Canberra: Senate Printing Unit.

Shamshur, O. (1994) Multilingual education as a factor of inter-ethnic relations: the case of the Ukraine. *Current Issues in Language and Society* 1, 29–39.

Shapin, S. (1984) Pump and circumstances: Robert Boyle's literary technology. *Social Studies of Science* 14, 481–520.

Shapin, S. (1991) 'A scholar and a gentleman': the problematic identity of the scientific practitioner in early modern England. *History of Science* 29, 279–327.

Shapin, S. (1994) *A Social History of Truth: Civility and Science in Seventeenth Century England*. Chicago: University of Chicago Press.

Shohamy, E. (1994) Issues in language planning in Israel: language and ideology. In R.D. Lambert (ed.) (1994) (pp. 131–42).

Shonerd, H.G. (1990) Domesticating the barbarous tongue: language policy for the Navajo in historical perspective. *Language Problems & Language Planning* 14, 193–208.

Shorish, M.M. (1984) Planning by decree: the Soviet language policy in central Asia. *Language Problems & Language Planning* 8, 35–49.

Short, D. and Gómez, E.L. (1996) TESOL develops ESL standards for pre-K–12 students. *ERIC/CLL News Bulletin* 19 (2), 4–5.

Shuy, R. (1993) *Language Crimes*. Cambridge, MA: Blackwell.

Sibayan, B. (1984) Some Philippine sociolinguistic concerns: 1967–1992. *International Journal of the Sociology of Language* 45, 127–37.

Sibayan, B. and Gonzalez, A. (eds) (1977) *Language Planning and the Building of a National Language*. Manila: Linguistic Society of the Philippines.

Siegel, J. (1989) English in Fiji. *World Englishes* 8, 47–58.

Siegel, J. (1992) Indian languages and identity in Fiji. *Journal of Asian Pacific Communication* 3, 115–32.

Silva, J.F. da and Gunnewiek, L.K. (1992) Portuguese and Brazilian efforts to spread Portuguese. *International Journal of the Sociology of Language* 95, 71–92.

Silver, B.D. (1985) Language policy and practice in the Soviet Union. *Social Education* 49, 107–10.

Sinclair, J. McH. (ed.) (1987) *Looking Up: An Account of the COBUILD Project in Lexical Computing*. London: Collins ELT.

Sinclair, J. McH., Hanks, P., Fox, G., Moon, R. and Stock, P. (eds) (1987) *Collins COBUILD English Language Dictionary*. London: Collins.

Sinclair, J. McH. *et al.* (eds) (1992) *BBC English Dictionary*. London: HarperCollins.

Singh, F.B. (1987) Power and politics in the content of grammar books: the example of India. *World Englishes* 6, 253–61.

Singh, U.N. and Srivastava, R.N. (eds) (1987) *Perspectives in Language Planning*. Calcutta: Mithila Darshan.

Sivasegaram, S. (1991) Language and the politics of nationalism in Sri Lanka. *New Language Planning Newsletter* 6 (1), 1–3.

Skutnabb-Kangas, T. (1996) The colonial legacy in educational language planning in Scandinavia: from migrant labor to a national ethnic minority. *International Journal of the Sociology of Language* 118, 81–106.

Skutnabb-Kangas, T. and Bucak, S. (1994) Killing a mother tongue – how the Kurds are deprived of linguistic human rights. In T. Skutnabb-Kangas *et al.* (eds) (1994) (pp. 347–370).

Skutnabb-Kangas, T. and Cummins, J. (1988) *Minority Education: From Shame to Struggle*. Clevedon: Multilingual Matters.

Skutnabb-Kangas, T. and Phillipson, R. (1994) Linguistic human rights, past and present. In T. Skutnabb-Kangas *et al.* (eds) (1994) (pp. 71–110).

Skutnabb-Kangas, T. and Phillipson, R. with Rannut, M. (eds) (1994) *Linguistic Human Rights: Overcoming Linguistic Discrimination*. New York/Berlin: Mouton de Gruyter.

Skyum-Nielsen, P. (1978) Language problems and language treatment in the Danish speech community. *Language Planning Newsletter* 4 (1), 1, 3–5.

Sless, D. (1995) The plain English problem. *Australian Language Matters* 3 (4), 3.

Slone, G.T. (1989) Language revival in France: the regional idioms. *Language Problems & Language Planning* 13, 224–42.

Smith, L.E. (1987) *Discourse Across Cultures: Strategies in World Englishes*. London: Prentice Hall.

Smolicz, J.J. (1984) National language policy in the Philippines: a comparative study of the educational status of colonial and indigenous languages with special reference to minority tongues. *South East Asian Journal of Social Science* 12, 51–67. Reprinted in Spolsky (ed.) (1986) (pp. 96–116).

Smolicz, J.J. (1994) Australia's language policies and minority rights: a core value perspective. In T. Skutnabb-Kangas *et al.* (eds) (1994) (pp. 235–52).

Snow, D.B. (1993a) A short history of published Cantonese: what is a dialect literature? *Journal of Asian Pacific Communication* 4 (3), 127–48.

Snow, D.B. (1993b) Chinese dialect as written language: the cases of Taiwanese and Cantonese. *Journal of Asian Pacific Communication* 4 (1), 15–30.

Soh, J.-C. (1985) Social changes and their impact on speech levels in Korean. In J.D. Woods (ed.) (1985) (pp. 29–41).

Sommer, B. (1991) Yesterday's experts: the bureaucratic impact on language planning for Aboriginal bilingual education. In A. Liddicoat (ed.) (1991) (pp. 109–34).

Sonntag, S. (1980) Language planning and policy in Nepal. *ITL: Review of Applied Linguistics* 48, 71–92.

Sonntag, S.K. (1989) The school as a bargaining point in language politics: the Belgian Language Law of 1932. *Language, Culture and Curriculum* 2, 17–29.

Sonntag, S.K. (1990) The US National Defense Education Act: failure of supply-side language legislation. *Language, Culture and Curriculum* 3, 153–71.

Sotiropoulos, D. (1992) The standardization of modern Greek. *Sociolinguistica* 6, 163–83.

Souaiaia, M. (1990) Language, education and politics in the Maghreb. *Language, Culture and Curriculum* 3, 109–23.

Sounkalo, J. (1995) Code-switching as indexical of native language lexical deficiency in Mauritania. *Journal of Multilingual and Multicultural Development* 16, 403–21.

Spolsky, B. (ed.) (1986) *Language and Education in Multilingual Settings*. Clevedon: Multilingual Matters.

Spolsky, B. (1989) Maori bilingual education and language revitalisation. *Journal of Multilingual and Multicultural Development* 10, 89–106.

Spolsky, B., Englebrecht, G, and Ortiz, L. (1983) Religious, political and educational factors in the development of biliteracy in the Kingdom of Tonga. *Journal Multilingual and Multicultural Development* 4, 459–69.

Spolsky, B. (1995) Conditions for language revitalization: A comparison of the cases of Hebrew and Maori. *Current Issues in Language and Society* 2, 177–201.

Språk i Norden (1986) *Årsskrift for Nordisk språksekretariat og språknemndene i Norden.* Gyldendal.

Sreedhar, M.V., Dua, H.R. and Rajyashree, K.S. (eds) (1984) *Questionnaire Bank for Sociolinguistic Surveys in India.* Mysore: Central Institute for Indian Languages.

Sridhar, S.N. (1988) Language variation, attitudes and rivalry: the spread of Hindi in India. In P.H. Lowenberg (ed.) (1988) (pp. 300–19).

Sridhar, S.N. (1990) What are applied linguistics? *Studies in the Linguistic Sciences.* 20 (2), 165–76.

St. Clair, R. and Leap, W. (1982) *American Indian Language Renewal.* Rosslyn, VA: National Clearinghouse for Bilingual Education.

Stanlaw, J. (1987) Japanese and English: borrowing and contact. *World Englishes* 6, 93–109.

Stanley, J., Ingram, D.E., and Chittick, G. (1990) *The Relationship Between International Trade and Linguistic Competence.* Canberra: Australian Government Publishing Service.

Stanton, P.J., Aislabie, C.J. and Lee, J. (1992) The economics of a multicultural Australia: a literature review. *Journal of Multilingual and Multicultural Development* 13, 407–21.

Stanton, P.J. and Lee, J. (1995) Australian cultural diversity and export growth. *Journal of Multilingual and Multicultural Development* 16, 497–511.

Stedman, J.B. (1986) *Malaysia.* Washington, DC: American Association of Collegiate Registrars and Admission Officers. [World Education Series]

Stevens, P. (1983) Ambivalence, modernisation and language attitudes: French and Arabic in Tunisia. *Journal of Multilingual and Multicultural Development* 4, 101–14.

Stewart, S.O. (1984) Language planning and education in Guatemala. *International Education Journal* 1, 21–37.

Stoberski, Z. (1990) Terminology: Warsaw agreements. *Language International* 2 (2), 26.

Stotz, D. and Andres, F. (1990) Problems in developing bilingual education programs in Switzerland. *Multilingua* 9, 113–36.

Strevens, P. and Weeks, F. (1985) The creation of a regularized subset of English for mandatory use in maritime communications: SEASPEAK. *Language Planning Newsletter* 11 (2), 1–6.

Sun H.-K. (1988/1989) Minorities and language planning in China: an outline. *New Language Planning Newsletter* 3 (1), 1–5; 3 (2), 1–6; 3 (4), 2–6.

Swales, J. (1985) ESP – the heart of the matter or the end of an affair? In R. Quirk and H.G. Widdowson (eds) *English in the World: Teaching and Learning the Language and Literature* (pp. 212–23). Cambridge: Cambridge University Press.

Swan, J. and Lewis, D.L. (1990) Tok Pisin at university: an educational and language planning dilemma in Papua New Guinea. In R.B. Baldauf, Jr and A. Luke (eds) (1990) (pp. 210–33).

Szépe, G. (1994) Central and Eastern European language policies in transition (with special reference to Hungary). *Current Issues in Language and Society* 1, 41–64.

Tabouret-Keller, A. (1981) Introduction: regional languages in France. *International Journal of the Sociology of Language* 29, 5–14.

Takahashi, H. (1995) Pluricentric codification of the German standard pronunciation. *New Language Planning Newsletter* 9 (3), 1–2.

Takashi, K. (1992) Language and desired identity in contemporary Japan. *Journal of Asian Pacific Communication* 3, 133–44.

Taksami, C. (1990) Ethnic groups of the Soviet North: a general historical and ethnographical description. In D.R.F. Collis (ed.) (1990) (pp. 22–38).

Talib, I.S. (1994) The development of Singaporean Literature in English. *Journal of Multilingual and Multicultural Development* 15, 419–29.

Tatalovich, R. (1995) Voting on official English language referenda in five states: what kind of backlash against Spanish-speakers? *Languages Problems & Language Planning* 19, 47–59.

Tauli, V. (1984) The failure of language planning research. In A. Gonzalez (ed.) (1984) (pp. 85–92).

Taylor, A. (1981) Language policy in Papua New Guinea. *Linguistic Reporter* 24, 1.

Tchitchi, T.Y. (1989) Littérature en langues Africaines ou littérature de minorité? La situation en République Populaire du Bénin. *International Journal of the Sociology* 80, 69–81.

The New London Group (1996) A pedagogy of multiliteracies: designing social futures. *Harvard Educational Review* 66, 60–92.

Thody, P. (1995) *Le Franglais: Forbidden English, Forbidden American.* New York: Athlone Press.

Thomas, A. (1990) Language planning in Vanautu. In R. B. Baldauf, Jr. and A. Luke (eds) (1990) (pp. 234–58).

Thomas, A.R. (1987) A spoken standard for Welsh: description and pedagogy. *International Journal of the Sociology of Language* 66, 99–113.

Thomas, L. (1996) Language as power: a linguistic critique of US English. *The Modern Language Journal* 80, 129–40.

Thomas, R.M. (1981) Evaluation consequences of unreasonable goals – the plight of education in American Samoa. *Educational Evaluation and Policy Analysis* 3 (2), 41–99.

Thompson, L. (1994) A response to Kroon and Vallen: a parallel overview of the education policy for bilingual children in Britain. *Current Issues in Language and Society* 1, 131–42.

Thompson, L., Fleming, M. and Byram, M. (1996) Languages and language policy in Britain. In M. Herriman and B. Burnaby (eds) (1996) (pp. 99–121)

Thong, T. (1985) Language planning and language policy of Cambodia. In D. Bradley (ed.) (1985a) (pp. 103–17).

Thorburn, T. (1971) Cost-benefit analysis in language planning. In J. Rubin and B.H. Jernudd (eds) (1991) (pp. 253–62).

Thumboo, E. (1986) Language as power: Gabriel Okara's *The Voice* as a paradigm. *World Englishes* 5 (2/3), 249–64.

Tickoo, M.L. (1994) Kashmiri, a majority-minority language: an exploratory essay. In T. Skutnabb-Kangas *et al.* (eds) (1994) (pp. 317–33).

Tinio, R. (1990) *A Matter of Language: Where English Fails.* Quezon City: University of the Philippines Press.

Todd, L. (1984) *Modern Englishes: Pidgins & Creoles.* Oxford: Blackwell.

Tollefson, J.W. (1980) The language planning process and language rights in Yugoslavia. *Language Problems & Language Planning* 4, 141–56.

Tollefson, J.W. (1981a) Centralized and decentralized language planning. *Language Problems & Language Planning* 5, 175–88.

Tollefson, J.W. (1981b) *The Language Situation and Language Policy in Slovenia.* Washington, DC: University Press of America.

Tollefson, J.W. (1988) Covert policy in the United States refugee program in Southeast Asia. *Language Problems & Language Planning* 12, 30–43.

Tollefson, J.W. (1991) *Planning Language, Planning Inequality.* London: Longman.

Tollefson, J.W. (1993) Language policy and power: Yugoslavia, the Philippines and southeast Asian refugees in the United States. *International Journal of the Sociology of Language* 103, 73–95.

Tollefson, J.W. (ed.) (1995) *Power and Inequality in Language Education.* Cambridge: Cambridge University Press.

Tonkin, H. (1987) One hundred years of Esperanto: a survey. *Language Problems & Language Planning* 11, 264–82.

Topping, D.M. (1982) Language planning issues in Vanuatu. *Language Planning Newsletter* 8 (2), 1–3, 6.

Touchstone, E.E. (1996) Language services planning in the banking industry: an example of unplanned language policy. Los Angeles: University of Southern California. [PhD Dissertation]

Touchstone, E.E., Kaplan, R.B., and Hagstrom, C.L. (1996) Home, sweet casa: access to home loans in Los Angeles (A critique of English and Spanish home loan brochures). *Multilingua* 15, 329–48.

Tovey, H. (1988) The state and the Irish language: the role of Bord na Gaeilge. *International Journal of the Sociology of Language* 70, 53–68.

Tribble, C. and Jones, G. (1990) *Concordances in the Classroom: A Resource Book for Teachers*. Essex: Longman.

Trim, J.L.M. (1987) Planning the development of multilingualism as a human resource. In B.K. Das (ed.) (1987) (pp. 1–22).

Trim, J.L.M. (1994) Some factors influencing national foreign language policy making in Europe. In R.D. Lambert (ed.) (1994) (pp. 1–15)

Trimm, L.A. (1980) Bilingualism, diglossia and language shift in Brittany. *International Journal of the Sociology of Language* 25, 29–41.

Trimm, L.A. (1982) Language treatment in Brittany. *Language Planning Newsletter* 8 (3), 1–6.

Truchot, C. (1991) Towards a language planning policy for the European Community. In D.F. Marshall (ed.) (1991) (pp. 87–104).

Trudgill, P. (1984) *Language in the British Isles*. Cambridge: Cambridge University Press.

Tryon, D.T. and Charpentier, J-M. (1989) Linguistic problems in Vanuatu. *Ethnies: Droits de l'homme et peuples autochtones* 8/9/10, 13–17.

Tse, J.K. (1980) Language planning and English as a foreign language in middle-school education in the Republic of China [Taiwan]. Los Angeles, CA: University of Southern California. [PhD Dissertation]

Tse, J.K. (1982) Language policy in the Republic of China. In R.B. Kaplan *et al.* (eds) *Annual Review of Applied Linguistics, 2* (pp. 33–47). Rowley, MA: Newbury House.

Tse, J.K. (1986) Standardization of Chinese in Taiwan. *International Journal of the Sociology of Language* 59, 25–32.

Tucker, A.N. and Bryan, M.A. (1966) *Linguistic Analysis: The Non-Bantu Languages of North-Eastern Africa*. London: Oxford University Press.

Tucker, G.R. (1988) Educational language policy in the Philippines: a case study. In P.H. Lowenberg (ed.) (1988) (pp. 331–41).

Turcotte, D. (1984) *Politique linguistique et modalitiés d'application en polynésie française*. B–109. Quebec: Centre International de Recherche Sur Le Bilingualisme.

Twine, N. (1991) *Language and the Modern State: The Reform of Written Japanese*. London: Routledge.

Ulijn, J.M. and Strother, J.B. (1995) *Communicating in Business and Technology: From Psycholinguistic Theory to International Practice*. Frankfurt am Main: Peter Lang.

Underwood, R.A. (1989a) Education and Chamorro identity in Guam. *Ethnies: Droits de l'homme et peuples autochtones* 8/9/10, 36–40.

Underwood, R.A. (1989b) English and Chamorro on Guam. *World Englishes* 8, 73–82.

Ureland, P.S. (1993) Conflict between Irish and English in the secondary schools of the Connemara Gaeltacht 1986–1988. In E.H. Jahr (ed.) (1993) (pp. 193–261).

Vaillancourt, F. (1983) The economics of language and language planning. *Language Problems & Language Planning* 7, 162–78.

Vaillancourt, F. (1991) The economics of language: theory, empiricism and application to the Asian Pacific. *Journal of Asian Pacific Communication* 2, 29–44.

Valdman, A. (1986) Emploi du créole comme langue d'enseignement et décréolisation en Haïti. *Language Problems & Language Planning* 10, 116–39.

Valverde, E. (1992) *Language for Export: A Study of the Use of Language and Language Related Skills in Australian Export Companies*. Canberra: Office of the Prime Minister and Cabinet.

Van de Craen, P. and Willemyns, R. (1988) The standardization of Dutch in Flanders. *International Journal of the Sociology of Language* 73, 45–64.

Van der Plank, P.H. (1988) Growth and decline of the Dutch standard language across the state borders. *International Journal of the Sociology of Language* 73, 9–28.

van Els, T.J.M. (1994) Foreign language planning in the Netherlands. In R.D. Lambert (ed.) (1994) (pp. 47–68).

van Els, T.J.M. and van Hest, E.W.C.M. (1990) Foreign language teaching policies and European unity: the Dutch national action programme. *Language, Culture and Curriculum* 3, 199–211.

van Langevelde, A. (1993) Migration and language in Friesland. *Journal of Multilingual and Multicultural Development* 14, 393–409.

Varennes, F. de (1996) *Language, Minorities and Human Rights*. Leiden: Martinus Nijhoff.

Varro, G. (1992) Les 'langues immigrées' face à l'école française. *Language Problems & Language Planning* 16, 137–62.

Vélez, J.A. and Schweers, C.W. (1993) A US colony at a linguistic crossroads: the decision to make Spanish the official language of Puerto Rico. *Language Problems & Language Planning* 17, 117–39.

Veltman, C. and Denis, M.N. (1988) Usages linguistique en Alsace: présentation d'un enquête et premiers résultats. *International Journal of the Sociology of Language* 74, 71–89.

Venås, K. (1993) On the choice between two written standards in Norway. In E.H. Jahr (ed.) (1993) (p. 263–78).

Verma, S.K. (1991) The three language formula: its sociopolitical and pedagogical implications. *ITL* 91/2, 49–60.

Vetter, R. (1991) Discourses across literacies: personal letter writing in a Tuvaluan context. *Language and Education* 5, 125–45.

Vikør, L.S. (1988) *Språkplanlegging. Prinsipp og Praksis*. Oslo: Novus. [Language Planning: Principles and Practice]

Vikør, L.S. (1989) The position of standardized vs. dialectal speech in Norway. *International Journal of the Sociology of Language* 80, 41–59.

Vikør, L.S. (1993) Principles of corpus planning – as applied to the spelling reforms of Indonesia and Malaysia. In E.H. Jahr (ed.) (1993) (p. 279–98).

Vila i Moreno, F.X. (1990) Language planning in Spain. *New Language Planning Newsletter* 5 (2), 1–6.

Vilfan, S. in conjunction with Sandvik, G. and Wils, L. (1993) *Ethnic Groups and Language Rights (Comparative Studies on Governments and Non-dominant Ethnic Groups in Europe, 1850–1940, Vol. 3.* Aldershot: Dartmouth Publishing Company.

von Gleich, U. (1994) Language spread policy: the case of Quechua in the Andean republics of Bolivia, Ecuador, and Peru. *International Journal of the Sociology of Language* 107, 77–113.

Wabenhorst, H. (1989) The potential and the importance of the German language for Australian Business. (Mimeograph).

Waite, J. (1992) *Aoteareo: Speaking for Ourselves: Issues for the Development of a New Zealand Languages Policy*, 2 Vols. Wellington: New Zealand Ministry of Education.

Wales (Prince of) (1990) The importance of foreign languages to business success in the 1990s. *Europe 2000* II (5), 1–4.

Walker, R. (1993) Language shift in Europe and Irian Jaya, Indonesia: toward the heart of the matter. *AILA Review* 10, 71–87.

Wardhaugh, R. (1987) *Languages in Competition: Dominance, Diversity and Decline.* Oxford: Basil Blackwell.

Watanabe, O. (1989) Internationalisierung und die zweite Fremdsprache. In H.L. Bauer (ed.) *Deutsch al zweite Fremdsprache in der gegenwärtigen japanischen Gesellschaft* (pp. 44–55). München: Iudicium Verlag.

Watson, J.K.P. (1980) Cultural pluralism nation-building and educational policies in peninsular Malaysia. *Journal of Multilingual and Multicultural Development* 1, 155–74.

Watson-Gegeo, K.A. (1987) English in the Solomon Islands. *World Englishes* 6, 21–32.

Watson-Gegeo, K.A. and Gegeo, D.W. (1995) Understanding language and power in the Solomon Islands: methodological lessons for educational intervention. In J.W. Tollefson (ed.) (pp. 59–72).

Watts, R.J. (1988) Language, dialect and national identity in Switzerland. *Multilingua* 7, 313–34.

Weasenforth, D. (1995) *A Rhetorical Abstraction as a Facet of Expected Response: A Structurural Equation Modeling Analysis.* Los Angeles: University of Southern California. [PhD dissertation]

Webb, V. (1994a) Language policy and planning in South Africa. In W. Grabe *et al.* (eds.) *Annual Review of Applied Linguistics, 14* (pp. 254–73). New York: Cambridge University Press.

Webb, V. (1994b) Revalorizing the autochthonous languages of Africa. In M. Pütz (ed.) (1994) (pp. 181–203).

Webb, V. (1996) Language planning and politics in South Africa. *International Journal of the Sociology of Language* 118, 139–62.

Weber, G. (1990) Kartulis Ena – the Georgian language. *Language International* 2 (4), 5–9.

Weeks, F., Glover, A., Johnson, E. and Strevens, P. (1988) *Seaspeak Training Manual.* Oxford: Pergamon Press.

Weiner, E. (1987) The new *OED* and world English. *English Today* 11, 31–4.

Weinstein, B. (1989) Francophonie: purism at the international level. In B.H. Jernudd and M.J. Shapiro (eds.) (1989) (pp. 53–80).

Wertheim, M. (1995) *Pythagoras' Trousers: God, Physics and the Gender Wars.* New York: Times Books, Random House.

Wexler, P. (1991) Yiddish: The fifteenth Slavic language. *International Journal of the Sociology of Language* 91, 9–150

Wexler, P. (1992) '*Diglossia et schizoglosia perpetua* – the fate of the Belorussian language'. *Sociolinguistica* 6, 42–51.

Whiteley, W.H. (1971) Some factors influencing language policies in eastern Africa. In J. Rubin and B.H. Jernudd (eds) (1971) (pp. 141–58).

Whiteley, W.H. (ed.) (1974) *Language in Kenya.* Nairobi: Oxford University Press.

Widdowson, H.G. 1988. Language spread in modes of use. In P.H. Lowenberg (ed.) (1988) (pp. 342–60).

Wierzbicka, A. (1993) Intercultural communication in Australia. In G. Shulz (ed.) *The Languages of Australia* (pp. 83–103). Canberra: Australian Academy of the Humanities.

Wiggen, G (1995) Norway in the 1990s: a sociolinguistic profile. *International Journal of the Sociology of Language* 115, 47–83.

Wijst, van der, P. and Ulijn, J.M. (1991) Netherlanders en Fransen in zakelijke onderhandelingen: Beïnvloedt beleefdheid het resultaat? *Negotiation Magazine* 4 (1), 31–43.

Willemyns, R. (1984) The treaty of linguistic union in the Dutch language area. *Language Planning Newsletter* 10 (3), 5–7.

Willemyns, R. (1993) The 'Nederlandse Taaluneie' as an innovating instance of official language planning. *New Language Planning Newsletter* 8 (2), 1–2.

Willemyns, R. and van de Craen, P. (1988) Growth and development of standard Dutch in Belgium. *Sociolinguistica* 2, 117–30.

Williams, C.H. (ed.) (1988a) *Language in Geographic Context*. Clevedon: Multilingual Matters.

Williams, C.H. (1988b) Language planning and regional development. Lessons from the Irish Gaeltacht. In C.H. Williams (ed.) (1990) (pp. 267–301).

Williams, C.H. (1991) Language planning and social change: ecological speculations. In D.F. Marshall (ed.) (1991) (pp. 53–74).

Williams, C.H. (1994) Development, dependency and the democratic deficit. *Journal of Multilingual and Multicultural Development* 15, 101–27.

Williams, T.R. (1966) *The Dusan: A North Borneo Society*. New York: Holt, Rinehart and Winston.

Williams, T.R. (1967) *Field Methods in the Study of Culture*. New York: Holt, Rinehart and Winston.

Williams, T.R. (1969) *A Borneo Childhood: Enculturation in Dusan Society*. New York: Holt, Rinehart and Winston.

Willis, D. (1990) *The Lexical Syllabus: A New Approach to Language Teaching*. London and Glasgow: Collins ELT.

Willis, J.R. and Willis, J.D. (1988) *Collins COBUILD English Course*. London and Glasgow: Collins ELT.

Winer, L. (1990) Orthographic standardization for Trinidad and Tobago: linguistic and sociopolitical considerations in an English creole community. *Language Problems & Language Planning* 14, 237–68.

Winkelmann, C.L. (1995) Electronic literacy, critical pedagogy, and collaboration: a case for cyborg writing. *Computers and the Humanities* 29, 431–48.

Winter, W. (1993) Some conditions for the survival of small languages. In E.H. Jahr (ed.) (1993) (p. 299–314).

Withers, C.W.J. (1988) The geographical history of Gaelic in Scotland. In C.H. Williams (ed.) (1988) (pp. 136–166).

Wolfson, N. and Manes, J. (eds) (1985) *Language of Inequality*. Berlin: Mouton.

Wood, R.E. (1977) Potential issues for language planning in Scotland. *Language Planning Newsletter* 3 (1), 1–4, 6.

Woods, J.D. (ed.) (1985a) *Language Standards and their Codification: Process and Application*. Exeter: University of Exeter.

Woods, J.D. (1985b) Swahili as a lingua franca. In J.D. Woods (ed.) (1985a) (pp. 76–101).

Woolard, K.A. (1989) *Double Talk: Bilingualism and the Politics of Ethnicity in Catalonia*. Stanford: Stanford University Press.

Woolard, K.A. and Gahng, T.-J. (1990) Changing language policies and attitudes in autonomous Catalonia. *Language in Society* 19, 311–30.

Wright, S. (1995) Language planning and policy making in Europe. *Language Teaching* 28, 148–59.

Wurm, S.A. (1978) Towards language planning in Papua New Guinea. *Language Planning Newsletter* 4 (3), 1, 4–6.

Wurm, S.A. (1994a) Graphisation and standardisation of languages. In G. Lüdi (ed.) (1994) (pp. 255–72).

Wurm, S.A. (1994b) The red book of languages in danger of disappearing. *New Language Planning Newsletter* 8 (4), 1–4; 9 (1), 1–3.

Wurm, S.A., Mühlhäusler, P. and Tryon, D.T. (1996) *Atlas of Languages of Intercultural Communication in the Pacific, Asia and the Americas*. Berlin/New York: Mouton de Gruyter.

Wynne-Edwards, V.C. (1962) *Animal Dispersion in Relation to Social Behavior*. London: Oliver and Boyd.

Yau, M.-S. (1989) The controversy over teaching medium in Hong Kong – An analysis of language policy. *Journal of Multilingual and Multicultural Development* 10, 279–95.

Yin, B. (1987) The language planning of Chinese minor-nationalities. *New Language Planning Newsletter* 2 (1), 2–4.

Youmans, M.N. (1995) Communicative rights and responsibilities in an East Los Angeles barrio: an analysis of epistemic modal use. Los Angeles: University of Southern California. [PhD Dissertation]

Young, R.L. (1988) Language maintenance and shift in Taiwan. *Journal of Multilingual and Multicultural Development* 9, 323–38.

Yule, V. (1988) English spelling and pidgin. *English Today* 4 (3), 29–35.

Zawiah Yahya. (1996) Literature in English and nation building. In J.E. James (ed.) (1996) (pp. 9–16).

Zhou Z.P. and Feng W.C. (1987) The two faces of English in China: Englishization of Chinese and nativization of English. *World Englishes* 6, 111–25.

Zhu W. and Chen J. (1991) Some economic aspects of the language situation in China. *Journal of Asian Pacific Communication* 2, 91–101.

Authors

Richard B. Baldauf, Jr is Research Manager at the National Languages and Literacy Institute of Australia and Associate Professor of Education at James Cook University (on leave), where he has served as Head of Department. He has also served as President of the Applied Linguistics Association of Australia. He has published more than 70 articles in refereed journals and chapters in books as well as contributing reviews and more informal work. He co-edited *Language Planning and Education in Australasia and the South Pacific* (Multilingual Matters, 1990) and was principal researcher for the *Viability of Low Candidature LOTE Courses in Universities* (DEET, 1995). His research interests include sociolinguistics, scientometrics, measurement and evaluation, culture and language learning, and language policy, language planning and language-in-education planning with a particular interest in the Pacific region.

Robert B. Kaplan is Emeritus Professor of Applied Linguistics in the Department of Linguistics at the University of Southern California, where he has been a member of the faculty for over 30 years – and has served as President of the Faculty Senate. He has published some two dozen books, about 125 articles in refereed journals and as chapters in books, and some 80 more ephemeral pieces including newsletter contributions and book reviews. He is the founding Editor-in-Chief of the *Annual Review of Applied Linguistics* and is a member of the editorial board of the *Oxford International Encyclopedia of Linguistics* and of a number of professional journals. He has served as President of the National Association for Foreign Student Affairs, of TESOL, and of the American Association for Applied Linguistics. His work has been primarily concerned with the definition of applied linguistics, with discourse analysis and contrastive rhetoric, and with language policy, language planning, and language-in-education planning.

Index

389